MW00756733

Taming the Sun

Taming the Sun

Innovations to Harness Solar Energy and Power the Planet

Varun Sivaram

A Council on Foreign Relations Book
The MIT Press
Cambridge, Massachusetts
London, England

This book was set in Stone Serif by Westchester Publishing Services. Printed and bound in the United States of America.

Library of Congress Cataloging-in-Publication Data

Names: Sivaram, Varun, author.
Title: Taming the sun : innovations to harness solar energy and power the planet / Varun Sivaram.
Description: Cambridge, MA : The MIT Press, [2018] | Includes bibliographical references and index.
Identifiers: LCCN 2017032337 | ISBN 9780262037686 (hardcover : alk. paper)
Subjects: LCSH: Solar energy.
Classification: LCC TJ810 .S48534 2018 | DDC 333.792/3--dc23 LC record available at https://lccn.loc.gov/2017032337 ISBN: 978-0-262-03768-6

10 9 8 7 6 5 4 3 2 1

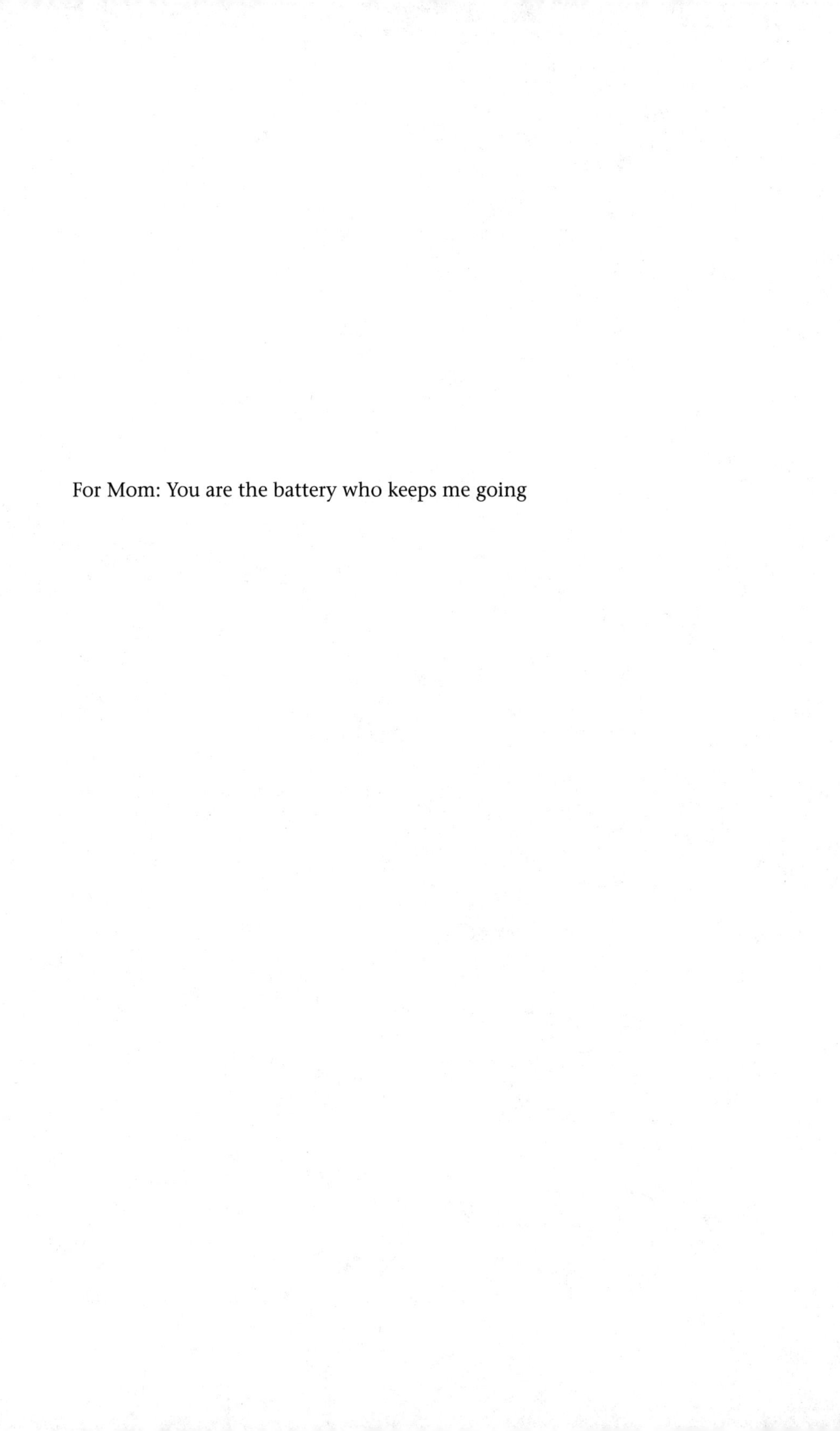

For Mom: You are the battery who keeps me going

Contents

List of Figures and Boxes

Preface

Chapter 1

Chapter 2

Chapter 3

Chapter 10

Boxes

Preface

In 2012, I met the mayor of Los Angeles, Antonio Villaraigosa, at a reception in Washington, D.C. At the time, I was a PhD student at the University of Oxford, where I was developing new materials to generate more electricity at lower cost than existing solar panels. When I shared my research with the mayor, he wrote his cell-phone number on a card and told me to call him. I assumed that he was just being polite, so I returned to Oxford and got busy finishing my thesis. A few days later, the deputy mayor emailed asking if I'd like to serve as the mayor's senior advisor and, if so, could I speak with the mayor tomorrow about the role. Within a week, I'd moved to Los Angeles.

I arrived underprepared but overconfident. I had never installed a single solar panel, yet Mayor Villaraigosa envisioned deploying more solar power than any other city in the country. Nevertheless, I was well versed in the latest advances made in scientific labs around the world, so I believed I could fulfill the mayor's vision by using brand new solar technologies far superior to the off-the-shelf solar panels that every other city was deploying.

I would soon discover this was naïve. Shortly after starting at the mayor's office, I had the bright idea to hitch a ride on a city helicopter. A few times a week, the Department of Water and Power would send one to survey the precious aqueduct that makes Los Angeles an improbable oasis in the middle of a desert. Roughly along the patrol route, on the western tip of the Mojave Desert, was a recently installed solar power project that used conventional solar panels. A helicopter would be a great way to get a look at it.

As we approached the solar farm, two thousand football fields' worth of solar panels stretched out as far as I could see in every direction, all of them tilting south to bask in the rays of summer. To my delight, the pilot obliged my request to fly closer to the ground. As we swooped in, I could see the details on each panel, down to the individual cells of silicon—mottled blue-black wafers about as big as your hand—that convert nearly 20 percent of the sunlight striking them to electricity. Connecting these repeating units together—by first wiring cells together into panels and then panels together into a massive solar farm—makes it possible to generate ever more energy, limited only by the amount of available land.

That helicopter ride introduced me to the massive scale of solar power. I had built only fingernail-sized solar cells in my ivory tower (actually, in a laboratory in a limestone basement) at Oxford. Witnessing solar "in the wild" disabused me of the fiction that the city could immediately deploy newly invented cells on the scale required to realize the mayor's vision; billions would be needed to carpet a square mile of desert.

Under Mayor Villaraigosa, Los Angeles would ultimately lead the country in its deployment of solar power.[1] And we did so with tried-and-true technology. Silicon solar panels have been used for decades, and today the Chinese can mass-produce them reliably. By using those panels, we minimized the risk that deploying them would cost more than expected or that they would stop working. The mayor's quest to use more solar power—an erratic source of electricity that only works when the sun is shining—was hard enough, given the city's mandate to keep the lights on for 4 million Angelenos. So we strove to avoid taking any further risks on unproven solar technologies.

From that experience, I learned that no single perspective will suffice to realize the enormous potential of solar energy (the sun beams down more energy to the Earth's surface in an hour than the world uses in a year). For instance, Ron Nichols—the practical-minded head of the city's electricity utility—remarked to me that adding renewable energy to the electricity grid is like "repairing the engine of a 747 midflight"; the last thing you want to do is add another moving part by trying out a new technology. But my colleagues in academia had shown me that solar technologies far superior to today's already exist in the lab. If they could be refined and mass-produced, they could one day make it possible to harness the sun's energy much more efficiently and cheaply.

Indeed, where you stand depends on where you sit when it comes to assessing the progress of solar technology. Observers within the energy sector regard the declining cost of conventional solar panels as astounding, even revolutionary. The top panel in figure 0.1 illustrates this descent, displaying the plunging cost of solar power in the United States compared with the average cost of electricity, which has held steady for decades.

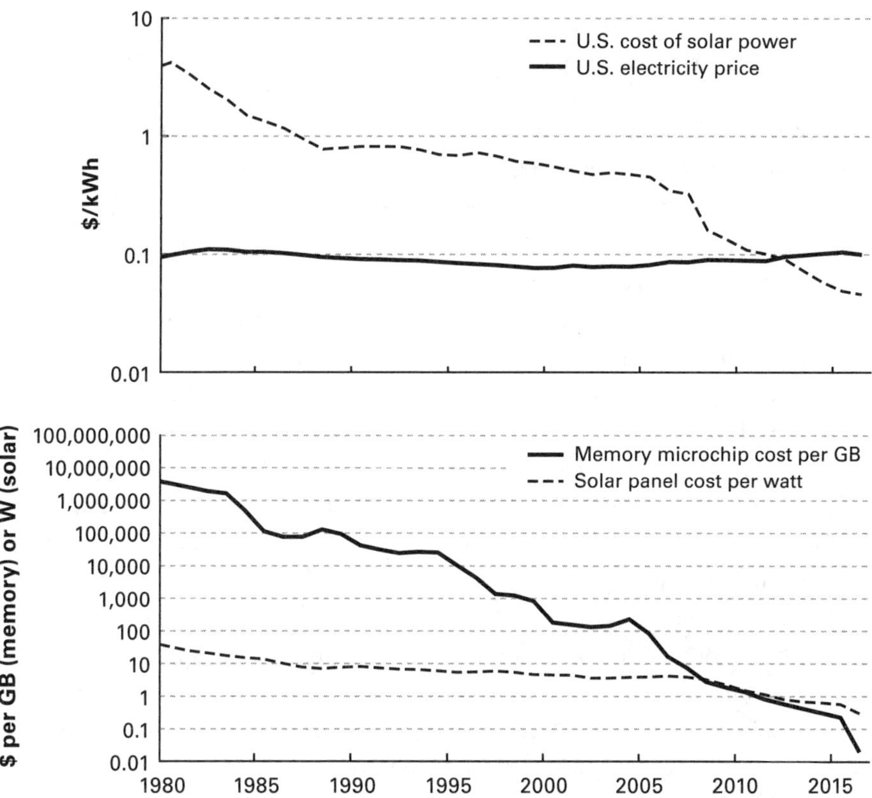

Figure 0.1

The falling cost of solar power, in different contexts. The top chart compares the cost of a kilowatt-hour of electricity from solar panels installed in the United States with the average cost of electricity for U.S. homes. (The calculation of the cost of solar power takes into account the cost of solar panels, as well as other costs, like those of associated equipment, land, labor, and financing.) The bottom chart compares the cost of solar panels, per watt of power-generating capacity, with the cost of memory microchips, per gigabyte of data-storage capacity.

Sources: U.S. Energy Information Administration, IC Knowledge.

But technology experts consider solar's cost declines to be unremarkable. Instead of comparing the cost of electricity from solar with that from fossil fuels, they might compare the cost of 1 watt of power generated from solar with the cost to achieve an analogous performance metric in a microchip, like a gigabyte of memory storage. That comparison, in the bottom panel of figure 0.1, is unflattering. Microchip costs have fallen *a million times faster* than those of solar panels. That rapid decline is a corollary of Moore's Law.

(Moore's Law, by some reports, is dying for computer chips known as microprocessors. But it is alive and well for memory chips, as I've learned from my father—the technology chief at a major chipmaker—who recently unveiled a new flash memory chip design that is actually beating Moore's Law and is already in your iPhone.)[2]

Recognizing the value of different perspectives, I've eagerly sought out more over the last decade. In addition to my time in academia and in Los Angeles, I've worked at two Silicon Valley start-ups, consulted for large energy companies, advised U.S. federal and state officials, and visited burgeoning markets for solar power all over the world.

There, too, I've found contradictions. Scientists despair that commercial solar technology is stagnating, whereas the industry trumpets its progress. Some scholars predict that solar panels and wind turbines could keep multiplying until the world runs off of 100% clean energy; others reject this idea as folly. Many policymakers on the left fiercely support incentives and mandates to install more solar power, whereas many on the right dismiss those policies as wasteful.

This minefield of contradictions can be disorienting. But careful consideration of what each perspective gets right and wrong has helped me make some sense of it all. I've written this book to pass on an evenhanded take on the future of solar energy that considers a kaleidoscope of valuable perspectives spanning the realms of business, science, and public policy.

I have a broad audience in mind. That includes anyone interested in the future of solar energy, students exploring energy and sustainability, scientists who want to grasp the financial aspects of commercializing their new technologies, executives and investors looking to understand the next big technology trend, and policymakers around the world who need to understand which interventions make the most sense.

In the chapters that follow, I contend that today's red-hot solar market could cool down tomorrow unless countries around the world urgently invest in innovation. (The book is divided into four parts, and each part starts off with a bulleted summary of the two to three chapters it comprises; if you're interested in a particular topic, those summaries can help you find the right chapter.) Even though existing solar panels are cost-competitive as a niche energy source, their economics could look far less attractive as more of them are deployed (part I). Fueling solar's continued rise will take three kinds of innovation: financial innovation to recruit massive levels of investment in deploying solar energy (part II); technological innovation to harness the sun's energy more cheaply and store it to use around the clock (part III); and systemic innovation to redesign systems like the power grid to handle the surges and slumps of solar energy (part IV).

The sun is the Earth's most abundant energy source. And the planet's best hope for confronting climate change, I argue, is for humanity to use solar energy to meet a majority of its energy needs sometime this century. Still, only by deploying insights from multiple vantage points can we ensure that solar lives up to its extraordinary promise.

PART I PLAYING THE LONG GAME

Highlights

- The year 2050 could see cities around the globe choked by pollution and the planet reeling from catastrophic climate change; or it might see a world equipped to address a range of global challenges. Chapter 1, "Two Futures," argues that the main determinant of which future materializes will be how well humanity can harness solar energy. The first future, in which solar's rise sputters to a halt, would not be unprecedented. In fact, we've seen this movie before: nuclear energy was once the great hope for cheap, clean, and abundant energy for all—yet its share of global energy peaked in the 1990s and has steadily declined ever since. The world can't afford for this to happen again with solar. Unfortunately, countries aren't proactively investing in the innovation solar will need to realize the second future.
- Instead, they are celebrating the arrival of cheap solar panels today. Chapter 2, "Coming of Age," documents solar's coming of age over the last decade, capping off three millennia of humanity's efforts to harness the sun's energy. After intense competition among countries and solar technologies, China has emerged as the solar industry's largest producer and consumer. And the silicon solar photovoltaic technology that it churns out has become the cheapest, fastest-growing power source on Earth.
- The recent momentum does not guarantee success, however. The most plausible way to limit catastrophic climate change is for solar power to provide at least a third of global electricity by mid-century, up from 2 percent today, and grow even faster from there. For that to happen, solar will

have to sidestep major pitfalls as it grows. Chapter 3, "Blocking the Sun," warns that solar could undercut its own economics, strain power grids, and struggle to displace ubiquitous fossil fuels.

It will take *innovation* in *financing and business models*, *solar technologies*, and *energy systems* for solar to avoid hitting a ceiling and instead reach its potential.

Chapter 1 Two Futures

The year is 2050, and the world is more polluted, unequal, and dangerous than ever. Megacities like New Delhi, Mexico City, and Lagos are suffocated by smog. More than a billion people around the world still lack access to reliable electricity. And climate change is serving up droughts, floods, and heat waves with alarming regularity.

The trouble is that fossil fuels continue to exert a stranglehold on the global economy. Coal and natural gas are still burned to produce most of the world's electricity and run most of its factories, spewing carbon dioxide and other climate-warming gases into the atmosphere. And oil still fuels a majority of cars and trucks, as well as almost every single airplane and ship on the planet, further polluting the air.

Much of this disastrous state of the world is a result of the solar power revolution sputtering out. Way back in 2016, solar photovoltaic (PV) panels, which convert sunlight into electricity, became the cheapest source of electricity on the planet.[1] Experts breathlessly prophesied that it was only a matter of time before solar PV dethroned fossil fuels—a bold claim for a technology that supplied less than 1 percent of the world's energy needs.

For a time, those rosy projections were vindicated. Over the next two decades, solar PV would soar in popularity. In developed countries, new homes came with sleek solar roofs, and in the poorest corners of the developing world, stand-alone solar systems gave millions of villagers with no connection to an electricity grid their first taste of modern energy. From Chile to China, more solar farms—vast fields of PV panels—sprouted than all other types of power plants combined. And as producers—mostly in Asia—churned out silicon-based panels year after year, they got better at shaving the technology's costs.

But sometime in the 2030s, solar's once-unstoppable growth slowed, leaving it far short of dethroning fossil fuels. Markets around the world saturated as demand for additional solar power dried up. On its face, this stagnation was puzzling: if solar PV kept getting cheaper, widening its competitive lead over fossil fuels, why did its expansion slow?

Part of the problem was that even as the cost of producing electricity from solar PV fell, the value of that electricity—the amount that a utility, for instance, was willing to pay for it to then send via the grid to meet the needs of homes and businesses—decreased even faster. The value diminished because a power source tied to unreliable sunshine quickly becomes a nuisance as it grows. PV panels produce power only when they receive sunlight, so nightfall (or even a passing cloud) can sideline them. Even before 2020, this intermittency caused problems in some regions that were early solar adopters. In California, for example, solar PV quickly rose to meet most of the state's power needs around lunchtime, when the sun was overhead. But then, adding a new solar panel, no matter how cheap, was worthless because when the state needed power—at dinnertime—the sun was setting. As a result, the gently declining cost of existing silicon solar PV technology was soon overtaken by the swift erosion of the value of the power the panels could produce.

Some countries—especially those that raced ahead to deploy solar PV projects—recognized that solar's value was in decline. But they were confident that lithium-ion batteries, which were also getting cheaper alongside PV panels, would come to the rescue. The falling cost of these batteries did indeed make it feasible to store some of the unused daytime solar power for later in the evening. Batteries, though, were not the panacea that many expected. It made economic sense to use them to store power for a few hours; but they were too expensive to use for smoothing out the day-to-day variations in solar PV output and certainly for handling the biggest energy storage need: squirreling away surplus solar energy from sunny months for use in gloomier ones.

Solar PV's growth also slowed because countries, especially in the developing world, failed to build out their electricity grids to keep up with the deployment of solar power. For example, India struggled to connect solar farms in distant deserts to its thirsty megacities. And when the government shifted focus to deploying solar panels on building rooftops, ramshackle urban grids buckled under the strain of absorbing sudden surges of solar power.[2]

Having leveled off, solar's contribution to the world's energy needs is respectable but limited today, at the mid-century mark. With the exception of wind power, other clean energy sources have not stepped in to pick up much of the slack. Wind power's rise has mirrored that of solar PV, and the two sister sources of renewable energy jointly produce a third of the world's electricity. But like solar PV, wind power is unreliable, so it too faces limits on its deployment.

More reliable sources of clean energy have disappointed. Nuclear power—politically radioactive—has declined from its glory days in the twentieth century to just a few remaining reactors in Asia today. New hydropower dams are just as unpopular. And various other potential clean energy sources—from geothermal to tidal power—remain mostly on the drawing board. As a result, the world still depends on fossil fuels to meet most of its electricity needs.

On top of this, many of the world's energy needs don't involve using electricity. Those needs are met almost exclusively by fossil fuels, and they have only grown as emerging economies have industrialized, with staggering consequences. Industrial facilities, like cement and steel plants, belch out soot from burning coal. Skyrocketing demand for transportation has also defiled the air and caused crippling congestion. Although fewer people own cars today than in decades past thanks to fleets of autonomous vehicles and convenient ridesharing, these advances have made it easier and cheaper than ever to get around; the resulting surge in travelers has packed more cars on the road at any given time.[3]

Many had hoped that electric vehicles might reduce local air pollution, and indeed they have risen to lead the pack in new vehicle sales. But over 1 billion petroleum-fueled cars and trucks still share the road with electric vehicles; and supposedly clean electric vehicles actually cause substantial pollution every time they charge up with electricity generated by fossil-fueled power plants. As a result, two-thirds of humanity face toxic air in miserable metropolises, in which global elites try to spend as little time as possible.

This would all be bad enough, but scientists predict it will only get worse because the cumulative carbon emissions from burning all those fossil fuels have set irreversible climate shifts in motion. It seems laughable that way back in 2015, countries around the world signed the Paris Climate Change Agreement, committing in all seriousness to limit global warming to 2°C. Just fifteen years later, those countries had already pumped enough greenhouse gases into the atmosphere to guarantee at least such a temperature rise.[4]

Climate change has already taken a toll around the world. Rising sea levels have spurred waves of mass migration from the floodplains of Bangladesh. Ocean acidification has decimated fisheries from Norway to Nicaragua. Droughts across Africa and the Middle East have left hundreds of millions in a persistent state of famine and water scarcity; Egypt has just declared war on Ethiopia for choking off its supply from the parched Nile river.[5]

Far from interceding, the United States has turned inward from the crumbling world order to weather superstorms on the Atlantic seaboard and extinguish the wildfires perpetually raging in the west. But the worst is yet to come. Miami and New Orleans will be underwater before the century is out. New York will be the new Bahrain of heatwaves.[6] For climate change is actually speeding up. The white ice sheets at the globe's poles have largely disappeared, leaving only darker ocean water that reflects less sunlight away and warms the Earth's surface even faster. Vast stores of greenhouse gases, once trapped by permafrost that has since melted, are escaping into the atmosphere from Siberia and the bottom of the ocean. Like a runaway train, the changing climate can't be stopped. Not now, nor for the next 10,000 years.[7]

Belated international efforts to drastically curb global emissions have stalled. Emergency negotiations at the United Nations over a global carbon tax don't stand a chance of finding common ground among bickering blocs. A corporate coalition of fossil fuel majors and heavy industries adamantly opposes what it calls draconian proposals to leave fossil fuels in the ground, arguing to great political effect that doing so would further impoverish the developing world. While the political theater has played out, entire countries—including the Marshall Islands, Tuvalu, and Fiji—have been swallowed whole by the Pacific Ocean.[8]

The time for decisive action is long past. With the benefit of hindsight, it is increasingly clear that the meteoric growth in solar power lulled governments into false confidence before their rude awakening to the solar slowdown. They had left the transition to clean energy on autopilot. Had they instead made a small course correction in those early days—by planning for, and investing in, the future—today's gloomy outlook might have been avoided.

A Brighter Future

The year is 2050; despite facing grave challenges, the world still controls its destiny. Nightmare scenarios of economic and humanitarian catastrophe—toward which the planet once hurtled—are off the table. The climate is undeniably changing, but at a manageable pace that has allowed countries to adapt. Now, the foremost priority of governments around the world is to find fulfilling employment for a global population of 10 billion in the era of artificial intelligence and the data economy.

The dramatic rise of clean energy has prevented climate change from spiraling out of control—and in the process powered economic growth and lifted the world's destitute out of darkness. For the first time in history, fossil fuels are on the wane. A dwindling number of plants still burn coal and natural gas to produce electricity and run factories, but their carbon emissions get captured and either used in industrial processes or stored deep underground. Oil still fuels a large percentage of global transportation, but that share falls every year as electricity and clean fuels are used instead.

Solar energy is the linchpin of this clean energy revolution. For 3,000 years, civilizations have yearned to harness the sun—an inexhaustible fireball that could power the world's energy needs thousands of times over. Finally, in recent decades, solar energy has risen relentlessly, clawing market share from fossil fuels. Today, solar supplies a third of global electricity; well before the century is out, most of the world's energy needs will be met by converting sunlight into electricity, heat, and portable fuels. When that happens, the twenty-first century will be remembered as the one in which humankind finally tamed the sun.

Obviously, today's solar technologies bear little resemblance to the quaint, silicon-based solar PV panels that China produced back in the opening decades of the twenty-first century. Those PV panels played an important role in establishing solar technology as a feasible source of energy. Their early success also reassured the world's biggest investors that it was safe to invest in clean energy projects. And they still reliably pump out electricity in some of the world's oldest solar parks.

But those original PV panels—heavy, ugly, and maxed out in terms of performance—evolved to become lightweight, attractive, and much more efficient at converting sunlight into electricity. By 2030, industrial printers were churning out rolls of solar PV coatings in a range of colors and transparencies. A decade later, solar-coating your house was as cheap as painting it.

Architects rejoiced. Today at the mid-century mark, most urban buildings are wrapped in electricity-generating solar materials that tint the windows, enliven the facade, and shrink the carbon footprint. Nearly free electricity has induced heavy industries to switch from burning fossil fuels to running off solar power. Solar PV isn't just powering glamorous urban buildings or massive industrial plants; PV materials are now light enough to be supported by flimsy shanty roofs in the slum outskirts of megacities in the developing world. And way outside the cities, even the poorest of the poor can easily afford solar power. Abject energy poverty has been eradicated—nearly every person on the planet has access to some electricity—although much work remains to address energy inequality.

Still, these wondrous solar PV coatings remain at the mercy of unreliable sunlight. Their trivial cost has helped mitigate this concern, making it economical, for example, to unroll a solar PV carpet over vast swathes of California's Mojave Desert and throw away excess power in the middle of the day. This, in effect, gives rise to a reliable power plant capable of producing a constant amount of electricity from late morning through early evening.

But solar PV still cannot supply California with power once the sun sets. Fortunately, that need has been met by a completely different solar technology that enjoyed a renaissance in the 2020s after analysts prematurely wrote it off as dead. Concentrated solar power plants, which employ armies of mirrors to focus the sun's rays to generate heat that can run a power plant, have improved dramatically in cost and performance. Most important, they are able to store the heat that they capture to produce power throughout the night. So, in tandem, PV coatings and concentrated solar power plants generate 24/7 electricity for a fraction of the cost of running fossil-fueled power plants.

In recent decades, the term "solar energy" has supplanted "solar power." That's because PV and other solar technologies not only generate electric power now, they also produce fuels that can store energy to be used where electricity is less practical. In the mid-2030s, firms began to mass-produce materials to convert sunlight directly into hydrogen fuel. Slowly but steadily, the makeup of the world's fuel mix has shifted toward clean solar fuels. Just as oil refineries convert crude oil into products like gasoline, jet fuel, and asphalt, so do solar refineries convert hydrogen into liquid fuels for vehicles, ships, and aircraft and into a whole range of other products, from fertilizer to plastics.

Hydrogen itself has become a popular fuel for cars and trucks. Petroleum-fueled vehicles are now a distant third-place choice, behind electric and hydrogen-fueled vehicles, neither of which contribute to local air pollution. As a result, even though urban denizens complain of ever-worsening traffic, air pollution levels peaked in 2040 and have been declining ever since.

Today's panoply of solar technologies is the result of farsighted decisions made over three decades ago in the public and private sectors to invest in innovation. The United States led this push and has profited handsomely as a result, now that the combined market for solar technologies is bigger than that for petroleum products. Just as America had surged past Saudi Arabia in 2013 to become the world's biggest oil producer, so too did it dethrone China twenty years later as the leading manufacturer of solar technologies. That was just as well—or else America might have developed a dangerous dependence on imports of Chinese energy products. Instead, the United States managed to achieve prosperity and energy security at the cost of a few billion dollars a year in additional funding for research into and development and demonstration of new technologies—a rounding error on the federal budget.[9]

Solar PV remains the most widespread method of harnessing the sun's energy even as other technologies, such as solar fuels, rise in popularity. To cope with the massive fluctuations of electricity from solar PV, countries have innovated in the design of their energy systems.

For example, countries have cooperated to build out continent-spanning power grids—the biggest ones are in Asia and North America—that connect solar PV in sun-drenched deserts with power-hungry cities. Not only are grids bigger, but they are smarter. They transmit signals to billions of Internet-connected devices—such as air conditioners, water heaters, and industrial machinery—that adjust their electricity demand on the fly to match the availability of solar PV supply. In addition, they can call upon various options to store intermittently produced solar energy, from batteries to hydropower reservoirs to underground wells. Grids can even intelligently decide when to charge up or draw down the millions of plugged-in electric vehicles that act as mobile batteries to back up solar PV.

Although solar energy has emerged as the star of the energy revolution, every star needs a supporting cast. Wind power has ably supplemented solar, rising steadily during this century. And the renaissance of nuclear power has shored up the supply of reliable electricity after governments around the world braved political headwinds to invest in a new generation of safer, cheaper reactors. Seeing the writing on the wall, fossil fuel companies have done their part as well, lavishly funding the development of technologies to capture and store the carbon emissions from the fossil-fueled plants that remain. They have even invested heavily in their own portfolios of renewable energy projects.

Despite the tremendous strides countries have made in reducing carbon emissions, the climate has still changed substantially. Again, solar energy offers hope for countries seeking to adapt. To ease water scarcity, countries have turned to cheap solar PV to run desalination plants that transform saltwater into freshwater. Concentrated solar power plants have also been repurposed in the developing world to power refrigeration, preserving badly needed food supplies and blunting famine.

The sobering scientific consensus predicts that the climate will continue to change for the foreseeable future. To stabilize it, governments are in final negotiations before unveiling a massive effort to suck carbon dioxide out of the atmosphere. Some of the countries hardest hit by climate change are clamoring for alternative approaches, like seeding the world's clouds to reflect more sunlight. Fortunately, governments can afford to deliberate carefully over whether and how to engineer the climate. Sharply reducing global carbon emissions from energy bought them time to do so.

Few would dispute that solar energy has emerged as one of the most important technologies—if not the most important one—of the twenty-first century. It may not have ensured victory over global challenges like climate change. But it has given the world a fighting chance.

The Sky's The Limit

The world may well be bound for the first of the two futures laid out here—and that's terrifying. But there is cause for optimism: the second future is not science fiction, but rather still an achievable goal. To arrive at it, the world must address the many challenges of realizing solar energy's sky-high potential—and that will require sharply increasing investment in innovation.

The reason that, for millennia, the sun has eluded humanity's best efforts to harness it—despite being the planet's most abundant energy source—is that its rays are terribly inconvenient to tap into. The amount of sunlight fluctuates wildly depending on cloud cover, time of day, and season of the year, whereas a barrel of oil or a ton of coal is a reliable store of energy to be used on demand. Like fossil fuels, sunlight is distributed unevenly. In some places it scorches the terrain; in others, it hides behind the clouds. Yet unlike the energy packed into dense fossil fuels, the sun's energy arrives much more spread out. Consequently, a field of solar panels typically requires hundreds of times more land to produce the same amount of power as does a power plant that burns natural gas.[10]

It will take human ingenuity to tame this troublesome energy source. Familiar solar PV panels that convert sunlight into electricity have made tremendous strides. In recent years, PV panels have gotten dramatically cheaper, and in 2016, solar PV projects attracted more investment globally than did any other type of power plant. But solar PV panels have a serious limitation: they only generate electricity when the sun shines. As a result, despite their early success as a niche energy source, they will struggle to dislodge convenient fossil fuels that offer on-demand energy.

And if the ongoing expansion of solar PV stalls, few clean energy alternatives to fossil fuels are on track to compensate. According to the International Energy Agency (IEA), twenty-three out of twenty-six clean energy technologies—from efficient industrial plants to nuclear reactors to clean fuels for trucks and planes—were being deployed too slowly as of 2017 to slash the world's carbon emissions enough to limit dangerous climate change. The remaining three—solar PV, wind power, and batteries (for the grid and in electric vehicles)—all enjoyed rapid commercial adoption.[11] But solar PV and wind are intermittent sources of electricity, and batteries can only do so much to smooth out their output. If solar PV stops expanding, slotting into a bit role in a clean energy ensemble, the first future could be in play. Realizing the second future instead will require solar energy to take center stage to make up for disappointing progress from other clean energy technologies.

Innovation is needed to make that happen. The solar industry will need new ways to attract vast sums of investment to fund solar's continued rise.

Countries will have to redesign their energy systems, starting with their electricity grids, to tolerate intermittent solar PV output. And scientists and engineers will need to develop the next generation of solar technologies—better suited to harnessing abundant but inconvenient sunlight to meet the world's diverse energy needs—to succeed today's PV panels.

These wondrous technologies are not mere fantasies. Early versions of all of them already exist. In the last five years, scientists at the lab bench have made rapid strides in creating efficient solar PV coatings from dirt-cheap materials.[12] Researchers are even further along in demonstrating the next generation of concentrated solar power plants, which could cost-effectively store sunlight in the form of heat to generate electricity night and day.[13] And recent prototype devices in the lab have achieved on a small scale what many scientists consider the holy grail: transforming sunlight into energy-dense fuels efficiently and with inexpensive materials.[14] Private investors are sinking real money into these technologies. For example, Bill Gates has launched a $1 billion investment fund and identified "solar paint" and "solar fuels" as two of the most important breakthrough clean energy technologies.[15]

Gates recognizes that harnessing the energy from the sun will probably be the single most important element of a clean energy transition. But he also knows that progress to date, though encouraging, is nowhere near sufficient to unlock the full potential of sunlight. The problem is that very few others have had a similar revelation.

Everybody's Doing It

A global push for innovation will require countries to realize that they're headed toward the first future and need to do something about it before it's too late. It doesn't help that the paths toward each future start out looking deceptively similar—both involve today's solar PV panels surging in popularity over the next decade or two—so it's not obvious which path the world is on right now.

Blissfully unaware of the two futures, countries around the world are jubilant at the arrival of cheap solar PV panels and focused today on installing them as fast as they can. They installed 50 percent more solar capacity in 2016 than in the prior year. And even though solar PV still supplied less than 2 percent of the world's electricity through 2016, that rapid growth has convinced governments that solar is on track to solve their most intractable problems.

They will be sorely disappointed if the first future materializes and solar's early growth hits a wall down the road. Whenever I've visited burgeoning solar markets—in Asia, the Middle East, or Latin America—I've left feeling unsettled about the gulf between the hopes that the first future would dash and the rewards that the second future would bestow.

New Delhi, India

We sipped chai on a verandah overlooking the expansive gardens of an ornate colonial relic, New Delhi's Imperial Hotel. Dressed in an immaculate pinstripe suit, complete with Hermès tie and a matching pocket square, my interlocutor explained his plan to meet India's rising energy demand with solar power. He radiated confidence as he remarked that his firm's track record of working with the government would guarantee it a slice of the growing solar pie. Left unspoken was the pedigree that backed Rahul Munjal, the scion of the Hero motorcycle empire that manufactures the dominant brand of two-wheelers in India.

Munjal isn't the only industrialist to venture into solar power; producers of everything from textiles to tractors have all made forays into the entirely unrelated solar power sector in India.[16,17] What's more, India's solar sector has attracted deep-pocketed foreign players as well, including the Japanese conglomerate Softbank.[18] These firms and investors are drawn by the prospect of powering India's expanding economy and by the Indian government's all-in bet on solar.

Prime Minister Narendra Modi has hailed solar as the "ultimate solution to India's energy problems."[19] As soon as he entered office in 2014, he announced an audacious target for solar power: by 2022, India would install 100 gigawatts (GW; a measure of how much electricity a power plant can pump out every second) of solar to provide roughly 10 percent of its electricity use. Starting from basically nothing, Modi was pledging to install in India more than half as many solar panels as existed in the entire world. He didn't waste time getting started. A year after he took office, annual deployment of solar PV in India more than doubled.

Modi is betting that the tumbling costs of solar PV—which fell by three-quarters between 2010 and 2017—will enable India to keep installing more of it. And his government plans to harness the versatility of PV

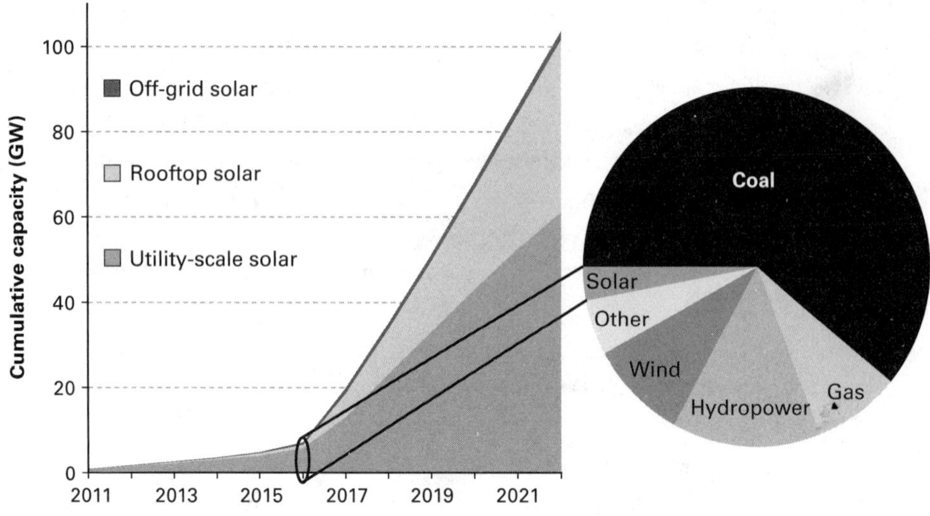

Figure 1.1

India's solar targets for 2022 and its electric power capacity mix in 2016. The chart on the left plots the Modi government's target for 100 GW of solar power generation capacity by 2022. The pie chart on the right breaks down India's electric power–generating capacity by source in 2016.

Source: Sivaram, Shrimali, and Reicher (2015), International Energy Agency.

installations—which can take the form of one panel or a million—to solve a whole range of pressing problems.

As figure 1.1 illustrates, India's 100-GW target breaks down into three categories. Most of the planned solar expansion will be in the form of utility-scale solar projects—massive solar farms sited in the sunniest areas—that are cheapest to build thanks to economies of scale. But over a third of the target is reserved for rooftop solar panels, distributed across India's crowded cities. A last sliver of the target is small, off-grid setups in rural villages having limited or no connectivity to the main power grid.[20]

One of the fastest-growing major economies in the world, India is hungry for power. As the population grows, farmers move to the cities, and a swelling middle class chases the energy-intensive trappings of a modern lifestyle, India could use four times as much power by 2040 as it does today. The government is betting that solar PV could displace coal power as its main engine of growth, and it has scrapped plans for new coal power plants.[21]

That's not all. The government has also pinned its hopes on solar to clear India's air. Beyond utility-scale solar plants substituting for polluting coal plants, rooftop solar panels are meant to replace household diesel power generators that cause urban smog. And Modi hopes to stamp out energy poverty with off-grid systems. That is long overdue in a country where nearly 300 million people lack any access to electricity and many more suffer from unreliable access.

Finally, the Modi government is banking on solar to meet India's international commitments as well. India is increasingly in the international spotlight because of its rising contribution to climate change. By midcentury, India could vault above China and the United States to become the world's biggest emitter of greenhouse gases. In response, the Modi government's 100-GW solar power target is the most ambitious part, by far, of its climate pledge under the 2015 Paris Agreement.

The problem is that Modi's wide-ranging wish list for solar—to power economic growth, clean the air, deliver energy access, and curb climate change—depends on a wildly optimistic extrapolation of solar's future growth. From 2012 to 2016, roughly 100,000 households gained access to electricity thanks to off-grid solar systems—but over 50 million households remained in the dark.[22,23] In 2016, total solar power capacity doubled, but coal still generated over 50 times as much electricity as did solar PV.[24] Even if India managed to achieve Modi's audacious 100-GW solar target, fossil fuels would still produce most of India's electricity. For solar to deliver what the government expects out of it, today's red-hot market will have to continue to grow for decades to come.

But that market could very well cool down. India has historically struggled to maintain its ailing power grid. If that trend continues, the grid may not be up to the task of transmitting power from faraway solar farms to growing cities or absorbing the swells and sags of unreliable solar power. And after an initial surge in solar PV installations, India might find little use for adding more; additional panels will not solve the problem of meeting electricity demand that peaks in the evenings. As a result, the nation might be left scrambling in search of other sources of cheap power to sustain its economic growth. That need might prompt it to double down on tried-and-true coal power, which would continue to foul India's air and drive its carbon emissions higher.[25] And outside of the electricity sector, other uses of fossil fuels could worsen air pollution in India's cities, with more petroleum-fueled scooters, cars, and lorries on track to crowd the streets while electric vehicles remain comparatively marginal.

The first future would be disastrous for India. And the stakes couldn't be higher for the planet. As the world's fastest-growing source of carbon emissions, India could make or break the quest to contain climate change.

Rokkasho, Aomori Prefecture, Japan

The northern tip of Honshu, the main island of Japan, is known for its picturesque peaks and hot springs. So it's a jarring change of scenery to emerge from the rolling countryside to find the forbidding gates of the Rokkasho Reprocessing Plant. The facility is designed to convert depleted fuel from Japan's nuclear reactors into fresh fuel to reduce the need for uranium imports. I'd been invited by the Japanese government to tour the plant, and although I wasn't allowed to take pictures, I still vividly remember the sprawling complex of chemical towers, labyrinthine pipework, and hulking centrifuges. It's an engineering marvel. After three decades and $25 billion in construction costs, Rokkasho is finally set to open in 2018.

Rokkasho is a symbol of a Japanese obsession: energy security. An island nation with negligible domestic energy resources, Japan has fretted about its energy security ever since the oil shocks of the 1970s. And for most of the last half-century, nuclear power has anchored its strategy to seize control of its energy supply. Yet even as Rokkasho prepares to start recycling nuclear fuel to end Japan's dependence on imports, most of its nuclear reactors have been shuttered. As a result, a desperate Japan is now looking to urgently ramp up its supply of solar power to achieve energy self-sufficiency.

Less than a decade ago, solar wasn't even on the table. In 2010, Japanese policymakers unveiled an ambitious plan to secure 70 percent of the country's energy needs from domestic sources by 2030.[26] The centerpiece of that plan was building enough nuclear reactors to supply half of Japan's power.

Disaster struck just a year later. In 2011, an earthquake and resulting tsunami caused three nuclear reactor meltdowns at Fukushima-Daiichi and the release of some radioactive material, forcing 164,000 residents to evacuate and deeply traumatizing the country.[27] Immediately, Japan shut down its entire fleet of nuclear reactors. Whereas nearly 40 percent of its power needs were met by local sources before the accident, that figure plunged to 12 percent in the aftermath of Fukushima (figure 1.2).[28] Now, to restart its nuclear plants, Japan must subject each reactor to a rigorous review process

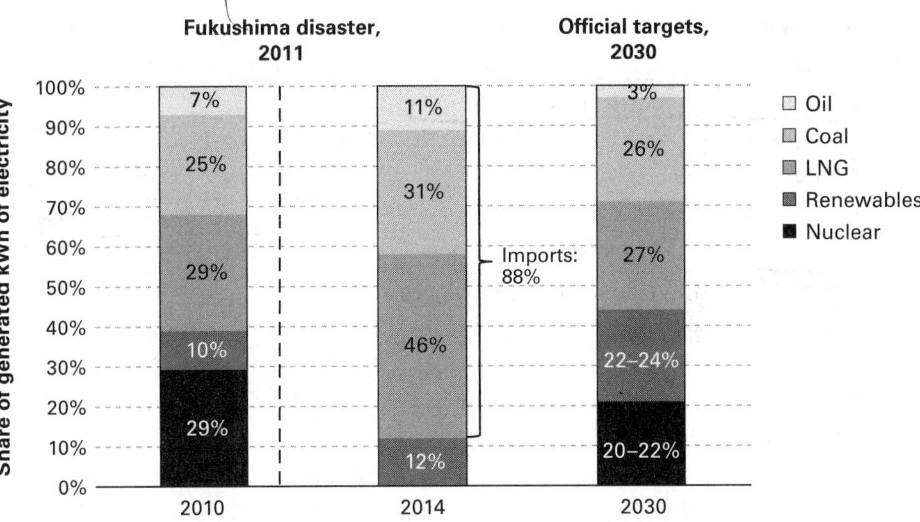

Figure 1.2

Japan's electricity mix before and after Fukushima. The bar on the left breaks down the sources of Japan's electricity in 2010, before the 2011 Fukushima disaster. The middle bar shows the mix of sources after the disaster in 2014. Finally, the bar on the right displays Japan's targeted electricity mix for 2030.
Source: Institute of Energy Economics, Japan.

and withstand grassroots legal challenges—through the end of 2016, it had managed to restart only four of nearly fifty reactors.[29]

To fill the void, the government has turned to renewables, such as solar and wind power. Thanks to generous public subsidies, Japan's solar market ballooned to become the third-biggest in the world in 2016.[30] By then, the cost of solar had fallen so steeply that the government was able to yank most of its subsidies and still expect healthy solar growth—it is aiming for solar power to supply 7 percent of its electricity by 2030. Some analysts are more bullish, anticipating that solar will actually hit 12 percent by 2030.[31] That would be remarkable, given that before Fukushima, Japan got less than 1 percent of its power from solar.

But even 12 percent won't be nearly enough to meet Japan's ultimate goal of securing most of its energy from domestic sources. That's because the government's forecast for nuclear power is probably wildly optimistic. The government faces stiff resistance from judges and the court of public opinion over restarting reactors. Building brand new ones, which will be needed to replace reactors at the end of their useful lives, is a political nonstarter. So, nuclear power might fall short of providing even 10 percent of Japan's electricity needs in coming decades.[32]

In the first future, solar power would slow down well before it could deliver meaningful energy security to Japan. Already, Japan's power utilities have warned that its balkanized grid may not be up to the task of integrating large quantities of intermittent solar power, and that the need for storage is growing.[33]

Still, Japan is taking baby steps toward realizing the second future. The government is third in the world in its funding for research and development (R&D) of advanced solar energy technologies.[34] And Japan is enthusiastic about setting up a nationwide hydrogen economy to slash fossil fuel imports and instead run its industries and vehicles off a fuel that could one day be produced from sunlight.

The symbolism was all around me as I left Rokkasho. Just as the nuclear reprocessing plant was now behind me, the era of rapid nuclear power expansion is probably behind Japan, for better or worse. A couple of minutes later, on the highway, I found, on my right, an array of storage tanks—a strategic petroleum reserve to protect Japan from foreign oil disruptions—and on my left, a solar farm. Those tableaus represent the two possible futures for Japan. The first would leave Japan at the mercy of foreign energy imports. But if Japan can invest in the innovation needed to realize the second future, the island nation can finally achieve the self-sufficiency that has long eluded it.

Mexico City, Mexico

Nervously clutching the conference room table in the Ministry of Energy, I hesitated before trying out the Spanish vocabulary I'd studied on the plane ride over. My host, the undersecretary of energy, patiently listened as I mangled my question: "How did Mexico manage to contract for some of the lowest-cost solar power in the world?"

Of course, he then answered in impeccable English, "We did it without government sweeteners. We ran an open auction, and solar beat out every other source including natural gas, plain and simple."

Cheap solar PV is sweeping through Latin America. Mexico's 2016 announcement of ultra-low solar prices came on the heels of similar announcements in Chile and Peru. This trend is prompting countries to breathe a sigh of relief, for the arrival of solar power could cushion Latin America from the ravages of climate change.

To see why, consider that Latin America, more than any other part of the world, depends on hydropower. Overall, hydropower supplies a majority of the region's power needs; the dependence rises to as much as 70 percent in some countries, such as Brazil. Yet climate change is inflicting droughts that are depleting reservoirs from Santiago to Sao Paolo; it's also melting the Andean glaciers that supply the mighty rivers of the Amazon.[35] As a result, the region faces chronic shortages of hydropower in the future.

As PV prices plummet, countries have seized the opportunity to make up the shortfall in hydropower with an equally clean and increasingly cheap power source. Now Latin America has emerged as one of the hottest solar markets around the world, poised to reach 10 percent of global solar PV demand by 2021, up from zero a decade earlier.[36]

Yet there are already warning signs that solar PV will face challenges in the region as more of it is deployed. For example, in Chile, a boom in solar PV installations led to a glut of power in the afternoon. As a result, the price that PV plants could fetch in the marketplace for the power that they produced was literally zero during those times.[37] And giving power away for free makes it impossible to repay the cost of constructing a solar PV plant, no matter how cheap that cost is.

Chile is a harbinger for what could happen across Latin America in the coming decades. Despite solar's rosy growth prospects today, its value to prospective electricity customers could sharply deteriorate as more of it comes online. And if solar's growth stalls in Latin America, consistent with the first future, the region could suffer from chronic power shortages as climate change wreaks havoc on hydropower plants.

For now, most in the region are simply content to ride the wave of cheap solar, although I did get the sense that a wary few are waiting for the other shoe to drop. Later in my day of meetings in Mexico City, another official remarked to me in Spanish, "When the charity is so great, even a saint wouldn't believe it." I had to look that one up—it turned out he was calling Mexico's solar boom too good to be true.

Dubai, United Arab Emirates

I arrived in Dubai all charged up. The Middle East Electricity Summit had invited me to give a keynote address about the future of solar power, so I'd prepared a detailed slideshow to share my vision. But once I got on stage, slide after slide detailing solar coatings on skyscrapers, slower rates of climate change, and cheap power for the developing world were met with yawns from the audience. I noticed several members fiddling with their headsets. Perhaps the live translation had stopped. Perhaps the electronics were more interesting than my speech.

Then, in unison, everyone perked up. I was making what I thought was just a minor point: in the near term, solar PV could offer Middle Eastern countries—notably Saudi Arabia—a way to burn less oil and gas at home and sell more of it abroad. Obviously, this wasn't part of my long-term vision: down the road, new solar technologies are supposed to replace fossil fuels.

But the crowd wanted to hear about how solar PV could goose fossil fuel profits (never mind the irony). The people who approached me after my talk were all businessmen with interests in Saudi Arabia, Kuwait, and Qatar. Those three are wealthy petrostates whose economies depend mostly on revenues from oil and gas. But they currently squander much of that oil and gas to generate power and sell it at a deep discount to domestic customers, encouraging wasteful consumption at home and foregoing export revenue abroad. Therefore, all three countries have launched ambitious solar programs to free up oil and gas for international sale at more lucrative prices.

In particular, Saudi Arabia has big plans for solar PV. In April 2017, the country announced an ambitious renewable energy program—a central component of its grand campaign to diversify its economy.[38] Following through on its solar plans could be crucial to keeping the country afloat. The kingdom consumes over one-quarter of the oil that it produces to generate electricity at home, limiting the amount that it can export abroad.[39] Constrained exports and sustained low oil prices have conspired to create yawning budget deficits for Saudi Arabia.

Whereas the rest of the world will be worse off in the first future, Saudi Arabia might be just fine. Even if it just derived a small fraction of its electricity from solar PV, the oil export revenue that it would gain might enable it to continue its lavish spending habits. Most important, in the first future, the world would remain addicted to oil—good news for the kingdom's coffers. Nevertheless, even Saudi Arabia would enjoy some benefits in the second future. Less extreme climate change would spare it from deadly heat waves, and improved solar technologies could make a transition to clean energy much cheaper at home, offsetting some of the pain from slowing global demand for Saudi oil.

Indeed, it is striking that even Saudi Arabia could find a silver lining in the second future, in which solar power would challenge fossil fuel dominance. In either future, there will be winners and losers. But there will be far more winners and many more prizes to go around if the world can realize the second future, not the first.

We've Seen This Movie Before

This isn't the first time that countries have pinned their hopes on a revolutionary clean energy technology to solve a range of their problems. The world would be wise to keep the nuclear industry's experience in mind as it tries to bridge the gap between solar's promise and today's realities.

Way back in 1954, Lewis Strauss, chairman of the U.S. Atomic Energy Commission, predicted that within a generation, nuclear power would be "too cheap to meter."[40] One of his successors, Glenn Seaborg, went further, predicting in 1969 that abundant nuclear power would alleviate water and food scarcity, power automated factories, and enable everyone to work a twenty-hour week.[41]

Yet those predictions would go unfulfilled. Nuclear did have a good run, rising rapidly in the second half of the twentieth century and achieving a 17.6 percent share of the world's power in 1996. But it would never surpass that figure. Ever since, nuclear's share of global electricity has steadily declined; it stood at around 10 percent in 2016.

What went wrong? One explanation is that accidents, activists, and ascending costs have plagued nuclear, stymying plans for new reactors across the developed world. From this perspective, the history of nuclear power has very little to do with how the future of solar power might unfold. It's hard to imagine a solar farm melting down and inciting a political backlash, and the costs of solar PV have steadily fallen and look set to continue doing so.

But there is a deeper reason that nuclear power may provide a cautionary tale for solar power. It is well documented that the technology in commercial nuclear reactors has stagnated. For over a half-century, nearly every nuclear plant built around the world has been a light-water reactor, a design that in rare instances, like Chernobyl or Fukushima, can allow a meltdown. Advanced designs that could be cheaper, more efficient, and meltdown-proof have remained on the drawing board for decades.[42]

Solar power might experience a similar technological stagnation. Nearly every single solar PV panel sold around the world is made of silicon. Over the last half-century, researchers and companies have brought silicon PV panels near their theoretical performance limits, in some cases converting over 20 percent of the sun's energy to electricity. Yes, every year solar panels get cheaper, but the gains are wrung from incremental optimization of manufacturing lines and supply chains, not breakthroughs in the lab.[43] At the same time, there is worryingly little investment in innovation. Massive firms in Asia, which dominate the industry, invest less than a penny from every dollar of revenue into R&D of new technologies.

If the technology stagnates, solar power is in danger of following in nuclear's footsteps, as occurs in the first vision of the future. Solar could also halt its expansion if countries (particularly those in the developing world) fail to build out their power grids and otherwise invest in ways to accommodate a rising share of power from solar. In those countries, the rise of solar could hit a ceiling sooner rather than later.

That vision of solar stalling is by no means a sure thing. Many argue that solar power will keep getting cheaper as more of it is produced and installed. What's more, the cost of batteries to store that power is falling in parallel, thanks in part to demand for electric vehicles. Some analysts even predict that the combined cost of solar panels and batteries might be cheaper than any fossil fuel alternative by 2030.[44] If that happens, they argue, neither technological change nor beefed-up power grids will be necessary for solar to continue growing.

But what if they're wrong? After the nuclear false start, the world is running out of time to switch over to clean energy. It doesn't help that global energy transitions take a very long time. As the energy scholar Vaclav Smil has pointed out, global energy transitions—for example, from wood to coal to oil—have each taken roughly a half-century.[45] If the world can zero out its carbon emissions within a half-century, then it stands a chance of avoiding catastrophic climate change.[46] But if the transition toward solar energy sputters by midcentury, there will be no opportunity for another do-over.

A particularly rosy 2016 study suggested that a clean energy transition could happen much faster—in just a decade or two—with the right support from policymakers.[47] And some argue that more sensible climate policies than the ones we have today are inevitable. Surely, they contend, the ravages of climate change will soon persuade governments around the world to enact regulations that put a price on carbon emissions. Such policies would improve the economic competitiveness of solar power even further and fuel its continued rise.

But do not bank on a carbon price coming to the rescue. So far, the few places that have instituted one, such as the European Union and California, have set the amount too low to matter.[48] Any push to set much higher prices on emissions could run into fierce political opposition from powerful entities like fossil fuel companies. Although several oil companies have come out in favor of a modest carbon price, they are unlikely to accede to a price high enough to seriously dent their bottom lines.

Switching Tracks

Policymakers can nonetheless help the world to switch tracks from the first future to the second. Targeted policy interventions to promote innovation are politically tractable and would yield outsize returns. But every year that the world dithers, diverting to the second track becomes much more expensive. Absent a decision to lay the groundwork needed to reach the second future *now*, the ride to a solar future could run out of steam.

The rest of this book will explore the promise of solar energy innovation and how to advance it. The remaining chapters in part I will set the stage, first by chronicling how far solar power has come, especially in the last decade. No longer a cottage industry, the solar industry is rapidly growing. Still, the barriers that solar PV has overcome to nip at the heels of fossil fuels are very different from the obstacles that stand in the way of solar energy upending fossil fuel supremacy. Achieving the latter will require three types of innovation.

As part II explains, firms can apply *financial and business model innovation* to do more with existing solar PV technology. Today, solar PV still struggles to woo the colossal investors who regularly finance fossil-fuel projects. With some financial engineering, the solar industry could gain access to massive pools of low-cost investment to deploy solar on an unprecedented scale. Similarly, even though villagers in Africa or India are willing to pay for solar power, off-grid solar has been slow to take off. Now, a new crop of entrepreneurs are deftly combining mobile phones, big data, and conventional PV panels to reach these customers and make a profit doing so. Prospects are rosy for these innovative financial and business models to fuel rapid solar deployment over the next decade.

Beyond that time horizon, *technological innovation* will be critical to continue solar's expansion, and part III reviews exciting advances in scientific labs around the world. Researchers are making progress on developing solar PV coatings, concentrated solar power plants, and generators of fuels from sunlight. These advances still face an uphill road to commercial success. Without much more support from the public and private sectors, academic researchers will struggle to bring their technologies to market.

Finally, part IV introduces *systemic innovation* that would refashion the world's energy systems to fully take advantage of abundant, but unreliable, solar PV output. Although doing so may be cost-effective, it will require shaking up sluggish industries and marshalling political courage. For example, change-averse power utilities need to be reformed before they will proactively equip electricity grids to cope with fluctuating solar power. And countries will need to be willing to take unpopular but prudent steps to support reliable generators, like nuclear reactors, that produce zero emissions while also compensating for intermittent solar power.

Public policy around the world can accelerate all three types of innovation. This book concludes by focusing on how the United States can provide global leadership through farsighted policies. Above all, U.S. policymakers should take steps to advance technological and systemic innovation, which are not proceeding as quickly as financial and business model innovation. In particular, they should sharply increase funding for the development of new technologies and investment in a more flexible power system.

Unfortunately, support for innovation in the United States has stagnated in recent decades, and funding for energy innovation in particular is in the crosshairs under President Donald J. Trump. The one solar policy likely to be enacted by the Trump administration, at the time of writing, was the erection of sweeping trade barriers to protect domestic manufacturers of solar cells and panels; but that policy would likely fail to encourage innovation and instead would dampen the U.S. solar market and probably incite trade retaliation from China. And on the international stage, the president will further damage U.S. credibility on energy and climate issues—and isolate America diplomatically—if he fulfills his pledge to withdraw the United States from the Paris Climate Change Agreement in 2020.

Abandoning a leadership role in making the transition to clean energy would be a grave mistake—especially when it comes to supporting innovation. Even though some investments—such as R&D into futuristic solar materials—may not pay off for years, the work has to be done now to ensure that the technology is ready when it is needed. What's more, failing to invest in innovation—and instead building walls to limit free trade—could cause the United States to get shut out of the rapidly expanding global solar market and forego a massive economic opportunity.

If, on the other hand, the United States acts now and inspires partners around the world to follow suit, its leadership could unlock the most abundant source of energy on Earth for generations to come.

Chapter 2 Coming of Age

In the fall of 2007, I was torn between two offers I couldn't pass up. One was to attend Stanford University, my dream school as far back as I could remember. The other offer was to stay on as a process engineer at a Silicon Valley start-up called Nanosolar that was going to change the world. The chief executive officer, a visionary entrepreneur from Germany named Martin Roscheisen, put his arm around me and told me in his booming voice, "Varun, it'll be just like Xerox PARC." He was referring to the legendary Palo Alto research park where the modern computer was invented.

Nanosolar had set out to commercialize a technology that it knew was just as revolutionary. The company had invented an alternative to the silicon solar panel: its idea was to use an inkjet printer to deposit a solar photovoltaic (PV) coating right onto unrolling spools of aluminum foil. The resulting solar foil would be flexible, lightweight, and cheap. At the time, silicon solar panels—in addition to their hefty weight, rigid shape, and ugly aesthetics—were expensive, making the cost of their electricity more than twice that from the grid.[1] Silicon was a costly commodity, and the process for manufacturing solar cells was adapted from that for producing expensive microchips. Roscheisen, formerly an Internet entrepreneur, planned to apply Silicon Valley's model of disruptive innovation to upend the lumbering solar industry.

It was an exhilarating time to be in solar. Al Gore's documentary *An Inconvenient Truth* had captivated the country. Investors were juiced at the prospect of red-hot market growth, running up the stock market valuations of early solar companies. At Nanosolar, the culture was infectiously optimistic. Around team lunches, we would dream about shipping cheap solar coatings to every corner of the developing world and carpeting remote deserts. We pulled all-nighters to prep prototype products for the CEO to show off to investors, reporters, and dignitaries, all of whom lapped up our vision. I reluctantly left the company to go to Stanford, but I eagerly kept tabs on the fundraising progress. In 2008, Nanosolar landed a $300 million venture capital round—the biggest of any company in Silicon Valley save Facebook.[2] The sky was the limit for next-generation solar technology.

Then the sky came crashing down. The price of PV panels plunged—between 2008 and 2013, it fell 80 percent—and a flood of cheap Chinese silicon panels washed away nearly the entire crop of American start-ups. To be sure, Silicon Valley shouldered part of the blame, as companies made questionable business decisions and investors lost patience in their portfolios. In Nanosolar's case, the firm scaled up manufacturing before it ironed out the kinks in its technology, and when the deluge of Chinese panels arrived, Nanosolar was in no position to compete. In 2013, it went belly up, selling off its assets piecemeal, for pennies on the dollar.

Amid the upheaval, though, something remarkable happened. Solar came of age. Two winners emerged from the brief and brutal price war that destroyed most solar producers across the United States and Europe. One was China, which established unchallenged dominance in the production of solar panels; it also became the world's largest market for their deployment. The other was silicon—long considered a stand-in material waiting to be replaced by a superior one. It surprised industry insiders by remaining the preeminent solar technology and pushing aside all other rivals. This partnership between China and silicon transformed the solar industry into a global powerhouse. In 2016, investors sank $116 billion into solar projects around the world, more than for any other power source, clean or dirty.[3]

It's about time. Humanity has dreamed of tapping the sun's potential for thousands of years, and the development of photovoltaics in the twentieth century offered a way to do just that. Solar initially took a back seat to nuclear energy, the poster child of the postwar era and focus of U.S. government support. That left early solar firms to hone PV technology in remote and exotic applications, like powering offshore oil platforms in the Gulf of Mexico, phone towers in the Australian Outback, and satellites out in space. Then, as Japan and Germany took the lead from the United States in supporting their domestic solar industries, solar PV started to gain traction in the early years of the twenty-first century. China's solar industry had modest beginnings, but when it finally got going, its competitors stood no chance.

Even though the solar industry is finally in the ascendant, it lost a vital element when Silicon Valley's start-ups failed. The surviving firms harbor no illusion that solar technology might change fundamentally. Rather, in each segment of the industry, all the way from upstream manufacturing to downstream deployment, firms are laser-focused on cutting costs rather than disrupting the current order. This approach looks set to fuel continued growth in the coming years, but it is not at all conducive to the innovation the industry needs to pursue to brighten solar's long-term prospects.

Three Millennia to Get Going

The abruptness of solar's recent rise is all the more pronounced given humankind's long history of trying, but not quite figuring out how, to turn it into a mainstream energy source. For most of that history, the focus was on the sun as an energy source for heating water rather than generating electricity. Although the silicon solar panel was invented more than sixty years ago, it is a newcomer in the context of humanity's millennia-old quest to harness the sun's energy.

Over 3,000 years ago, the Chinese used *yangsui*, or "burning mirrors," to focus sunlight to kindle a fire—the oldest-known human use of solar energy. In the seventh century BCE, the Chinese pioneered solar architecture, designing houses that faced south to admit light and heat from the sun during the winter months, whereas roof eaves kept out the higher sun in the summer months to moderate the temperature in hot weather. Solar architecture also flourished in the Mediterranean: Socrates delivered lectures on the subject in Greece in the fifth century BCE, and in the first century BCE, the Romans invented the *heliocaminus*, a glass room that used the greenhouse effect to warm public baths.[4]

Solar energy appealed to ancient civilizations for many of the same reasons it does now. Inhabitants of the Greek island Delos used solar architecture to minimize their energy use and improve their energy security in the event that they had trouble importing needed timber. And by the fourth century BCE, Chinese city-dwellers, who had deforested most of their surroundings and thus lacked firewood, turned to solar architecture to conserve energy and in turn preserve the environment. This reasoning was not confined to antiquity. After World War I, solar architecture became popular in Germany as a way to limit fuel dependence after the Allies occupied the coal-rich Ruhr district.[5]

The next level of sophistication in harnessing solar energy was to convert sunlight into mechanical work. In the first century CE, Hero of Alexandria built a solar siphon that heated air, which expanded to propel water from one chamber to another. Most other inventors focused on using sunlight to heat water instead to then perform mechanical work. A particularly audacious example was a 4-mile-long mirror designed by Leonardo da Vinci to heat a factory's boiler (he started building it but never finished).

Augustin Mouchot, a French mathematics professor, made the most impressive leaps forward in putting solar to work. He envisioned three uses of solar power that are still actively being developed today: driving a heat engine, generating electricity, and producing portable fuels. In 1874, he built the world's first solar engine in Tours, France, using an 8-foot conical mirror to focus the sun's energy on a boiler that drove a 1/2 horsepower engine (for reference, that's roughly enough to run some power tools in a modern woodworking shop). Then, in 1879, he figured out how to convert solar radiation into electricity by reflecting sunlight to heat the junction of two metals soldered together, generating an electric current. He used this electricity to split water into its constituent atoms—oxygen and hydrogen—intending to store the hydrogen as fuel. None of these three applications was cost-effective, though, and Mouchot soon abandoned his research—but he succeeded in inspiring modern uses of solar energy.[6]

The first form of solar energy to gain commercial traction was solar water heating. Around the turn of the twentieth century, solar water heaters proliferated in southern California, offering homeowners substantial savings over using coal or gas to heat their water. California would remain an important market, and by 1977, 60 percent of the state's pools would be heated by solar energy. In 1979, President Jimmy Carter installed a solar water heating system on the White House roof.[7]

International markets grew rapidly as well. By 1986, 60 percent of the population of Israel had adopted solar water heaters, as the government strongly encouraged energy conservation to limit the country's dependence on imported fuel. Similarly, the Japanese enthusiastically adopted solar water heaters, in some cases using them to heat popular public baths. But it is the Chinese who have fueled the most recent and pronounced boom; by 2010, China accounted for 70 percent of all solar water heaters worldwide. Around the world, the technology generates over 1 percent of all energy used for heating.[8]

Although solar water heating has experienced a respectable rise over the last century, it has been eclipsed by the explosive growth of solar-generated electricity—that is, solar power. (Note: The term "power" is often used interchangeably with "electricity." Its technical definition, however, is the amount of energy transferred per unit time.) There are two modern methods of transforming sunlight into electricity. First, concentrated solar power plants focus the sun's rays to heat water or another medium such as molten salts to ultimately produce steam that drives a generator. Second, solar PV panels, typically made of silicon, directly convert sunlight into electricity. Although both methods have roots in the late nineteenth century, major advances in the twentieth century enabled their commercialization.

Following Mouchot's invention of a solar engine, U.S. inventors made several advances that would ultimately underpin today's concentrated solar power plants. Around the turn of the twentieth century, American entrepreneurs went to great lengths to demonstrate new collector designs that concentrated sunlight to generate heat efficiently. In 1901, a bowl-shaped reflector, hooked up to a fifteen-horsepower engine, debuted at an ostrich farm in Pasadena, California. (The contraption was billed as an oddity among oddities.) Then, in 1911, Frank Shuman raised venture capital to build rows of *U*-shaped solar collectors in the Egyptian desert to drive irrigation systems. Decades later, in the 1970s, an American patented a scheme in which circular arrangements of heliostat mirrors would focus sunlight at a single point atop a central power tower.

Another advance was to store some of the heat for use when the sun went down. In 1904, a solar installation in Needles, Arizona, managed to power an engine 24/7 by storing some of the hot water for later. Together, progress in converting solar energy into heat and storing that heat inspired the concentrated solar power industry. Nowadays, new solar thermal plants increasingly use the power tower configuration and have built-in heat storage so that the plant can generate electricity around the clock.[9]

Still, because solar PV panels have recently fallen in cost much faster than concentrated solar power plants have, adoption of the former has accelerated, while adoption of the latter has slowed to a trickle. By the end of 2016, just 5 gigawatts (GW) of concentrated solar power capacity was online around the world, compared with over 300 GW of PV capacity.[10,11] The development of photovoltaics, which took place on a parallel track that also reached back into the nineteenth century, set the stage for the global solar industry as we know it today.

From Selenium to Silicon

The story of solar PV power starts in 1839, when the French physicist Edmond Becquerel discovered the photovoltaic effect. He immersed silver chloride in an acidic solution, illuminated it, and connected it to two electrodes, between which an electric voltage developed. Becquerel also noticed that his best results came from using blue or ultraviolet light, a phenomenon that he couldn't explain.

Forty years later, an English engineer, Willoughby Smith, discovered that selenium, a material known today as a semiconductor, became more conductive when exposed to light. Researchers at King's College London tested this discovery by exposing selenium to candlelight and then abruptly screening the candle; because the selenium's conductivity dropped immediately, they concluded that fast-moving light, rather than slow-acting heat, was the cause of the electrical activity. This behavior was entirely mysterious to scientists at the time, but that didn't stop an American inventor, Charles Fritts, from building the first solar panels out of selenium and installing them on a New York City roof in 1884.[12]

It was two more decades before Albert Einstein finally solved the mystery and explained how light was turning into electricity. In a 1905 paper that in time would win him the Nobel Prize in Physics, Einstein posited that light was composed of tiny packets—or photons—of energy.[13] Sometimes, he explained, a photon had enough energy to knock an electron out of its customary orbit around the nucleus of an atom in a metal or semiconductor, and that electron could then move freely. By freeing enough electrons, a stream of photons could generate an electric current.

Einstein's theory elegantly solved the pesky question of why only some colors of light produced an electric current. The energy of a photon depends on its color. Blue and violet photons have the highest energies in the rainbow; red photons have the lowest. Only some colors are energetic enough to kick electrons out of their orbits. Photons of the other colors sail right through a PV material. Which colors are absorbed rather than transmitted depends on the material.

But even though the theory had caught up with experimental reality, photovoltaics would remain a curious oddity for the next half-century. Writing in 1935, an executive at the American firm Westinghouse wrote presciently that selenium devices, which converted only 0.5 percent of the sun's energy into electricity, would need to get fifty times more efficient to become practical.[14] As it happens, today's state-of-the-art silicon PV cells are 26 percent efficient, roughly fifty times better than their selenium predecessors. (A solar PV cell is simply the basic building block of a solar panel. Cells can range in size from that of your fingernail to that of your hand. The former are typically research devices, whereas the latter are used in commercial solar panels. Panels are somewhat less efficient than individual cells because wiring cells together to make a panel can lead to various power losses.)

The first silicon cells weren't this efficient, of course. In 1953, Gerald Pearson and Calvin Fuller—researchers at Bell Laboratories who had helped invent the silicon transistor, the building block of the modern computer—realized that their device was highly sensitive to light. So they recruited Daryl Chapin, who was looking for a way to power remote telephone installations, and the trio built the first silicon solar PV cell. Although their first device was just 2.3 percent efficient, that blew selenium out of the water.[15] Chapin then doggedly worked to improve the silicon solar cell. The next year, in 1954, he unveiled a 6 percent efficient PV cell to great fanfare; the *New York Times* reported that the advance could lead to "the harnessing of the almost limitless energy of the sun for the uses of civilization."[16]

Peddler on the Roof

Unfortunately, the timing couldn't have been worse. The advent of silicon solar technology would be overshadowed by an even more heralded clean energy technology: nuclear power. That would leave the nascent solar industry to scour remote settings on and off the planet, peddling its wares. Indeed, the industry has been on something of a roller coaster ever since.

In 1953, President Dwight D. Eisenhower delivered his "Atoms for Peace" speech to the United Nations General Assembly, laying out his vision for "universal, efficient, and economic usage" of nuclear power.[17] This vision would captivate popular imagination about—and monopolize government support for—nuclear technology, eclipsing solar power. A sign of the stark contrast was the pageantry of the 1955 Atomic Conference in Geneva, which attracted heads of state. In comparison, the low-profile inaugural World Symposium on Applied Solar Energy, held three months later in Phoenix, Arizona, barely attracted media coverage.

At the time, solar PV technology was still prohibitively expensive—a 1-watt cell cost $286 to produce, implying a cost of $1.4 million for solar panels to power a single American home.[18] But the research and development (R&D) funding necessary to drive the cost down was not forthcoming because all eyes were on nuclear. During the 1950s, U.S. government funding for solar R&D was limited to $100,000 per year, whereas nuclear power received over $1 billion a year.[19] As a result, the use of solar PV technology for commercial power generation languished while nuclear power boomed—a reversal of modern trends.

But even as President Eisenhower pulled the rug out from under the fledgling solar industry with Atoms for Peace, just two years later, in 1955, he gave it new hope by announcing America's intentions to launch a satellite, kicking off the space race. Solar power quickly emerged as the only solution to keep satellites operating indefinitely—onboard batteries or fuel would run out after several days of use. The Soviets were first into space with their Sputnik satellites, but when the United States launched its Vanguard I satellite in 1958, its solar-powered radio lasted far longer.

Over the next decade, as the space program ballooned, it provided a steady stream of orders for solar panels, sustaining a $5–10 million market.[20] These crumbs enabled a few firms to invest in developing increasingly efficient solar panels because it was crucial to extract as much energy as possible from the limited number of panels that could be sent into space. Thanks to the space race, the fledgling solar industry slowly grew in size and sophistication.

The early applications of solar power on Earth itself were far from civilization. An advantage of solar over petroleum fuels or batteries was its low maintenance—you could leave a solar panel out for a decade or more and it could be trusted to generate power every day. That made it attractive for settings where routine maintenance was impractical. Thus, Australia used solar panels to power telecommunications repeaters and distant phone systems across the Outback; and Exxon financed its own company, the Solar Power Corporation, to deploy solar systems on its offshore oil rigs in the Gulf of Mexico in the 1970s.[21,22]

In fact, in an ironic twist, oil companies invested substantially in solar power at its outset. In addition to Exxon, the U.S. oil firms Mobil, Arco, and Amoco all had solar divisions. Arco made the biggest bet, investing over $200 million and building the first solar factory with an annual capacity greater than 1 megawatt (MW) in 1980; by 1988, it was the world's largest solar producer.

Oil companies had entered the space for a variety of reasons: Solar could be useful to their business operations by powering offshore platforms or service stations; the firms' versatile engineers were well suited to advancing the technology; and in Arco's case, the company's commitment to environmental stewardship drew it to solar.

But the American oil companies divested their solar portfolios by the 1990s, just as European oil producers started looking for a piece of the action. By the 1990s, British Petroleum (BP) and Royal Dutch Shell had cracked the list of the top four solar producers.[23] Yet ultimately, American companies—and, eventually, European companies by the 2000s—decided that solar was too far afield of their core business interests. Many also lost money on it, and nearly every firm left the sector. Today, however, as solar market forecasts predict rapid growth, some oil producers are expressing interest once again. Indeed, in 2011 a French oil major, Total, acquired a majority stake in a notable solar manufacturer and project developer, SunPower.

The solar industry got a big boost in the 1970s from the U.S. government as America reeled from spiking oil prices. Indeed, for a decade, the United States would build a commanding global lead in solar power. Following the Arab oil embargo of 1973, the price of oil quadrupled in the United States, and it tripled again by 1979 when the Iranian Revolution spooked world oil markets.

Facing gasoline shortages and economic malaise, the Carter administration shepherded incentives for solar power through Congress. These included increased support for R&D, tax credits of up to 30 percent to install solar panels and water heaters, and regulations requiring power utilities to purchase power from independent generators like solar farms. By 1980, Congress had authorized over $1 billion per year for solar incentives, including $150 million for solar PV R&D.[24] And the government's solar push established the preeminence of the American solar PV industry, which by the 1980s accounted for 85 percent of global PV sales.[25]

But U.S. dominance of both the solar panel production industry and the installation market was short-lived. The combination of the incoming

Reagan administration's ideology and a crash in oil prices in the 1980s led U.S. government support for solar to plunge. In 1985, Carter's solar tax credits lapsed, and by 1988, President Ronald Reagan and his administration had led Congress to slash R&D funding for photovoltaics by 75 percent compared with its 1980 peak.[26] President Reagan was partial to nuclear power, allergic to subsidies for uncompetitive energy sources like solar, and ideologically committed to funding only basic science research, rather than the applied R&D and demonstration projects supported by his predecessor.[27] Unfortunately, instead of making way for U.S. companies to privately fund applied R&D themselves, the withdrawal of government support simply drove American companies out of the market. For example, Mobil and Arco sold their solar divisions to German firms in the early 1990s.

In the vacuum created by the U.S. retreat from solar, Japan and Germany seized the opportunity to lead. In the 1990s, the Japanese government launched its own incentive programs—for example, to install 10,000 solar roofs around the country—and beefed up its R&D support. Thanks to the resulting strong domestic market and innovation, Japanese firms such as Kyocera, Sanyo, and Sharp surged to become leading global solar producers in the 1990s.[28]

By the 2000s, Germany had created the largest market in the world for the installation of solar power, and its firms challenged Japan's for dominance in solar PV production. In 2000, Germany passed landmark legislation that offered substantial incentives for new solar installations—a guaranteed premium price, or feed-in tariff, for which the owner of the installation could sell solar power to a utility over the next twenty years. Thus began Germany's *Energiewende* (energy transition). Over the next ten years, Germany's generous policy support would make it the world's largest solar market and almost singlehandedly underwrite the global PV manufacturing industry's growth.[29] By 2010, Germany accounted for nearly half of the global market for solar deployment.[30] As a result, solar panel production by Siemens, Q-Cells, and other German companies boomed to meet domestic demand.

Throughout the 1990s and 2000s, U.S. firms struggled to compete, squeezed by limited government support at home to improve solar PV technology or deploy more solar power. Nevertheless, thanks to Japan and Germany, solar grew into a multibillion dollar industry. Yet it was about to have an identity crisis.

Sunburned in Silicon Valley

The global solar industry had grown on the back of a single technology: the silicon solar panel. Yet for decades, scientists and entrepreneurs had been scouring the periodic table for alternative materials to silicon that could make solar power an even more compelling proposition. This schism set up a showdown between old and new technologies.

Scientists had long considered silicon a less than ideal material for a solar cell that was in use mostly out of convenience. Recall that the Bell Labs researchers who invented the modern solar cell used silicon because of the recent discovery of the silicon transistor—it was simple to repurpose that device, which the researchers had already designed equipment to produce, to act as a solar cell instead of a transistor. But silicon was known to be a weak absorber of light—that is, a particularly thick chunk of silicon is needed to absorb the same amount of light that a thin slice of other materials can absorb. On top of this, silicon absorbs more colors of light than other materials, but this broad absorption sacrifices much of the energy contained in blue and ultraviolet photons. Hence, silicon can never be as efficient as other materials that absorb fewer colors but harvest more of the energy from high-energy photons. Finally, producing high-purity silicon, in which the atoms are arranged in perfect, crystalline order and are thus most efficient in converting sunlight to electricity, requires expensive equipment, wastes a lot of silicon, and results in brittle wafers that break easily.

Recognizing these theoretical deficiencies, researchers hunted for alternatives. One of their earliest discoveries, in 1967, was not a different material, but rather a different form of silicon known as "amorphous silicon," which could be used to make flexible, thin photovoltaic films.[31] Making the films was cheaper and wasted less of the valuable silicon feedstock, but the resulting cells were often half as efficient as traditional crystalline cells. Ironically, they also tended to get worse during the first six months of exposure to sunlight before stabilizing—an unfortunate defect for a solar material! As a result, amorphous silicon solar never took off the way its backers had hoped, although it did carve out a niche as the material of choice for flexible or portable applications such as pocket calculators.

Another solar material that found a small market niche but struggled to achieve mainstream commercial success was gallium arsenide (GaAs), which is more efficient than crystalline silicon but quite expensive to produce. In

1970, Soviet scientists made the first highly efficient GaAs solar cells, and GaAs ultimately surpassed silicon as the material of choice for space applications by the 1990s because of its high efficiency. Because GaAs comes from a family of materials that are easy to stack on top of one another to harvest different colors of light most efficiently, the highest-performance solar cells today use GaAs and its cousins in multijunction solar cells—in the lab, these can exceed 40 percent efficiency. This is the technology that, for example, has powered NASA's rovers on Mars. Still, multijunction cells did not make much of a commercial impact on the terrestrial solar market because of their high production cost.

The most serious competition to silicon came from two thin-film materials—cadmium telluride (CdTe) and copper indium gallium (di)selenide (CIGS)—that stood out for their strong ability to absorb sunlight, the potential low cost of their manufacture, and the theoretically high efficiencies that they could achieve. Through the 1990s, these technologies waited in the wings while silicon continued to dominate the market. Researchers in the lab slowly pushed up thin-film efficiencies, but companies had little success selling panels in the marketplace. Finally, in the early 2000s, the American firm First Solar managed to rapidly ramp up production of CdTe panels, which were less efficient than silicon but also less costly to produce.

By 2006, it appeared as though thin films had arrived. When First Solar went public, it was valued at a (then) eye-popping $400 million. A Silicon Valley gold rush ensued, as venture capitalists poured money into start-ups developing thin-film solar that promised to drive down the cost of material inputs compared with that of expensive silicon solar cells. That's when Nanosolar—the company I worked for—took off, raising hundreds of millions of dollars to inkjet print thin-film solar on rolls of aluminum foil. Even more exotically, Solyndra planned to transform flat solar panels into cylindrical tubes that could absorb light from every direction. That vision earned it a whopping $1 billion in private investment, along with a $500 million loan guarantee in 2008 from the Barack Obama administration.

Many of the investors and entrepreneurs who drove the boom in solar start-ups had previously worked in Silicon Valley's venerated semiconductor industry. There, they had pioneered the equipment and technology to make highly complex silicon microchips for electronics. These semiconductor veterans saw the solar industry as a backwater—one that had simply borrowed decades-old equipment from semiconductor production lines to make mediocre solar panels.

One of these pioneers was my father. In 2008, high on Silicon Valley hubris, he left the semiconductor industry to start a new solar venture, Twin Creeks Technologies. Rather than choose an entirely new material, he opted to stick with silicon but try to use it more efficiently. So he and his team raised several hundred million dollars and built an awe-inspiring ion cannon—as big as a house—that could peel thin slices off silicon wafers and reuse the precious material more efficiently. The *New York Times* hailed the technology as "radical."[32]

Then silicon suddenly stopped being precious. A glut of production capacity in China plunged the price of polysilicon, the raw material input for silicon solar cells, from over $400 per kilogram (kg) in 2008 to $50/kg in 2010.[33] As a result, it was no longer necessary to economize on material costs with thin-film or thinner-silicon technologies.

Stuck with a product that cost $6.29 per watt to manufacture but only earned $3.42 per watt in the marketplace, Solyndra filed for bankruptcy in 2011, leaving taxpayers on the hook to cover a half-billion dollars of debt.[34] In 2012, Republican presidential nominee Mitt Romney assailed President Obama's bet on Solyndra as "a symbol of gross waste."[35] Over the next two years, both Twin Creeks Technologies and Nanosolar also ran out of money, as did nearly every other American solar start-up. Bruised venture capitalists slashed their cleantech portfolios, and solar became a dirty word in Silicon Valley. As for my father, he left solar behind to rejoin the semiconductor industry, where innovation was alive and well.

External shocks like falling silicon prices weren't the only reasons that the solar start-up bubble burst. As I've written with my colleagues Ben Gaddy and Frank O'Sullivan, investor expectations for these companies were likely unrealistic from the beginning. The start-ups had to develop new materials, customize the machinery to make those materials, design a new solar product, and cultivate a market for that product. And they had to do it all within three to five years because of the way that venture capital funds were structured to pay back their investors.[36] As a result, start-ups made costly mistakes, like racing to build expensive factories to mass-manufacture thin-film solar cells before they could reliably produce small batches of efficient cells.

Today, thin films limp along, accounting for less than 10 percent of the total market. Most of that is made by U.S.-headquartered First Solar. But even as Silicon Valley's technology revolution fizzled, the solar industry would experience a true coming of age, courtesy of China and its prodigious production of silicon solar panels.

China and Silicon: The Dream Team

In a curious twist, China's rise to dominance in the solar industry has its roots in the work of a scientist out in Australia. That scientist, Professor Martin Green of the University of New South Wales, is fondly regarded as the father of photovoltaics. In the 1970s, while the United States poured funding into PV research, Green salvaged equipment made to process semiconductors "from the scrap heap" in Australia to begin developing high-efficiency silicon solar cells.[37] When U.S. funding for solar dried up during the Reagan administration, Green's Australian research operation emerged as one of the best labs in the world. The scientific advances that he later made in the 1980s laid out the architecture for modern silicon solar panels. And Green's students would take that technology with them and create the Chinese solar companies that would take over the global industry.

Still, a quarter-century ago, Green's was a lonely voice arguing that silicon solar panels were the future. Writing in 1993, he remarked:

> Since silicon introduced the photovoltaic era over 40 years ago, silicon solar cells have been the "workhorse" of the photovoltaic industry. Many, including the present author, have assumed that this has been a stop-gap measure while the photovoltaic community, with widely different levels of patience, awaited the arrival of a more ideal material.
>
> . . . rather than being a stop-gap, silicon has the potential to become the ultimate photovoltaic solution . . . [Silicon's] strengths lie in the presently established market position, the on-going improvements to the technology, and the remaining scope for future improvement and the sustainability of silicon-based technology.[38]

In contrast to the accelerated timelines of Silicon Valley start-ups that tried to perfect thin film technologies in just a few years, silicon technology matured over several decades. In the 1970s, the U.S. satellite company COMSAT figured out how to carve microscopic pyramids on the surface of silicon solar cells to ensure that incoming light rays bounced around instead of being reflected away and were ultimately absorbed. These cells were known as "black cells" because they absorbed all visible light and could thus achieve efficiencies in excess of 17 percent.[39]

Then Professor Green took over. Starting in the 1980s, his lab unveiled a remarkable series of improvements to silicon solar cells, pushing them to over 25 percent efficiency by the turn of the twenty-first century (see figure 2.1).[40,41] Even today, top silicon manufacturers are switching their production lines over to replicate Green's cell architecture—a design known as PERC—to boost their efficiencies.[42]

In parallel, private firms also made important advances. For example, firms boosted the reliability of silicon panels, improving their economics. In 1982, Arco offered a five-year warranty for its solar panels; by the 1990s, BP was offering a twenty-year warranty.[43] Quadrupling the lifetime of a solar

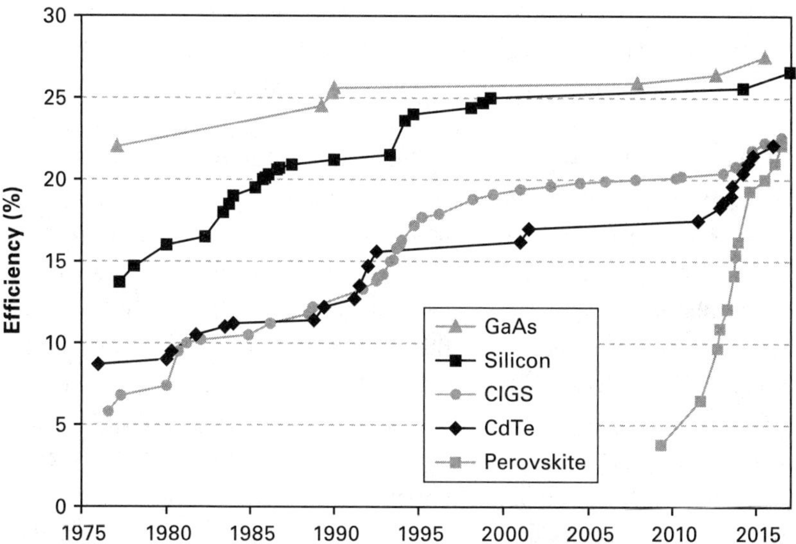

Figure 2.1

Efficiencies of various solar PV technologies. In the last half-century, scientists have progressively increased the efficiencies—or the percentage of the energy delivered by the sun at high noon that can be converted into electricity—of solar cells constructed and tested in the laboratory. This chart plots the increase over time in the efficiencies of silicon and GaAs, which are traditional wafer technologies; CIGS and CdTe, which are thin films; and perovskite, an emerging solar technology (this technology is discussed in detail in chapter 6).

Source: National Renewable Energy Laboratory (NREL).

panel meant that the panel's power could be sold for many more years, making it easier to ultimately pay back the panel's up-front cost. This effect was just as powerful for the competitiveness of solar PV as increasing the efficiency of converting sunlight to electricity.

There was even a Silicon Valley solar success story a decade before the thin films debacle. As industry pioneer Dick Swanson tells the story, in 2001 he was ready to commercialize the highly efficient silicon solar panels that his start-up, SunPower, had developed. But for several years, nary an investor had showed any interest in funding solar power. So the company was about to run out of money and was preparing to lay off half the company. Then Swanson reconnected with an old Stanford classmate: T. J. Rodgers, CEO of Cypress Semiconductor, a well-known chipmaker in the Valley. On hearing Swanson's pitch, Rodgers wrote SunPower a personal check for $750,000 to prevent the layoffs. Cypress went on to acquire SunPower, supplying the investment and manufacturing expertise to scale up production. As of 2016, SunPower still manufactures the most efficient silicon solar panels on the market.

Building on this progress—including improvements to silicon cell technology in the laboratory and the accumulation of expertise and equipment in the global solar industry—Chinese companies entered the sector. Students from Professor Green's lab fanned out across China to start or join silicon solar firms. One former doctoral student, Shi Zhengrong, founded Suntech, which became the world's largest manufacturer of solar cells.[44] And other students from Green's lab went on to become executives at every major Chinese solar producer. In addition to importing technical knowledge, Chinese companies took advantage of foreign equipment to set up their factories. From the late twentieth century through the early 2000s, they bought turnkey solar production lines from American and Canadian semiconductor firms and later sourced equipment from Germany and South Korea.[45] And through joint ventures with foreign companies, some Chinese firms honed their factories to produce reliable and long-lived solar panels.[46] Not all of China's contributions to solar were borrowed from abroad, though. Chinese producers invested heavily in making their factories more efficient than foreign facilities and wringing every last cent out of their supply chains.

In 2005, China was still a minor player in the solar industry, accounting for just 11 percent of global solar production. The Chinese government considered solar too expensive for widespread domestic use and minimally supported its deployment. But over the next five years, it enthusiastically supported the expansion of its fledgling manufacturing industry. Subsidies poured in from the central and provincial governments to depress the cost of raw materials, energy, land, and components.[47] And Chinese firms enjoyed a free-flowing stream of low- to no-cost loans to scale up production and defer any need for profits.[48,49]

China also benefited heavily from subsidies in the developed world. As domestic solar panel production boomed, over 90 percent was exported between 2005 and 2010, mostly to European countries with generous deployment incentives. In addition to Germany's feed-in tariff, Spain and Italy offered abundant incentives. In Spain, incentives sometimes covered half the cost of a solar installation, and by 2009, the share of solar in Spain's power mix was the highest in the world. By 2010, Chinese companies produced nearly half the world's solar panels, and only 6 percent were sold to its own sluggish domestic market.[50]

But by then, there were already warning signs that China could not continue to expand its domestic manufacturing capacity at the expense of the developed world indefinitely. Thanks in part to government subsidies for domestic solar factories, China built up massive production overcapacity all along the solar supply chain, from the raw polysilicon through the finished solar panel.[51] On top of this, European countries reeling from the Great Recession yanked their solar subsidies. Germany's target for solar deployment in 2020 sank by a factor of ten; Spain slashed its incentives by nearly half.[52]

Combined, overcapacity and subsidy cuts drove solar producers in China and elsewhere to wage an all-out price war to win scarce customer demand. As a result, panel prices dropped 30 percent just from 2009 to 2010; they fell by half again by 2013.[53] In response, the Chinese government scrambled to create a market for the domestic industry that it had created.[54] (Helping out domestic producers probably is not the only reason for China's push to deploy solar at home; others include its desire to cut down on air pollution in its cities.) As a result, China has shifted the focus of its public policies away from subsidizing the production of solar panels to funding their deployment at home. In 2013, China dethroned Germany as the largest market for solar panels in the world, and by 2016, it accounted for nearly half of global panel sales (figure 2.2).[55]

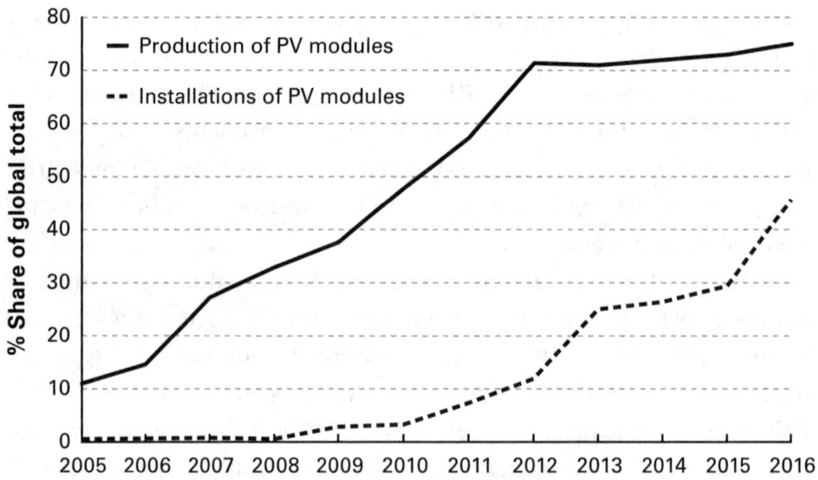

Figure 2.2

Chinese share of solar PV production and deployment. Comparison of China's rising domestic share of global PV panel production (panels are also known as "modules," and production quantities are measured in gigawatts of power-generating capacity) with its more recently rising domestic share of global solar PV installations (also measured in gigawatts of power-generating capacity). Note that Chinese production statistics include Taiwanese production, which accounted for roughly 12 percent of global solar PV cell and panel production in 2016. Chinese firms have shifted substantial manufacturing activities off the mainland, including to Taiwan and Malaysia, to avoid U.S. and E.U. anti-dumping tariffs.

Source: Center for Study of Science, Technology and Policy; Fraunhofer Institute.

The precipitous decline in panel prices upended the global solar industry, wiping out not only the crop of Silicon Valley upstarts but also established solar producers across the developed world. Whereas in 2007, solar PV production was somewhat evenly divided among China, Japan, Germany, and the rest of the world, over 80 percent of solar production was happening in Asia a decade later, mostly in China.[56]

In particular, 2011 saw an industry shakeout that crippled the U.S. and European industries. Several American and European solar producers went bankrupt between 2010 and 2012, unable to compete with the flood of cheap Chinese panels. Belatedly, both the United States and the European Union sued China for violating international trade laws by dumping its panels below cost on global markets. But the punitive tariffs that they imposed on Chinese imports were too little and too late to revive failed Western solar firms.

Chinese firms suffered as well, booking negative profit margins as they tried to ride out the glut in production capacity. The extension of $47 billion in lines of credit from the China Development Bank in 2010–2011 helped keep many Chinese manufacturers afloat.[57] But the largesse didn't last, as the Chinese government pivoted to providing incentives for deploying solar rather than producing it, causing major Chinese firms to go bust or merge with competitors. For example, Suntech, once the world's largest solar producer, went bankrupt in 2013.[58] When the dust settled from the global industry upheaval, China had emerged as the world's largest producer and consumer of solar PV, almost all of which is made of silicon. That dominance is unlikely to be challenged anytime soon.

State of the Industry

Now that the solar industry has come of age, it is poised to continue growing rapidly. In the face of relentlessly falling costs and declining public subsidies, companies are just trying to stay afloat while expanding quickly enough to keep up with global market growth. This dynamic implies that the basic structure of the industry should stay relatively stable because firms are making minimal investments in revolutionary technologies. (See box 2.1 for an overview of terms and concepts used in today's solar industry.)

Throughout all the upheaval, bankruptcies, and price swings of recent decades, the solar industry and market has grown consistently and rapidly. Over the two decades leading up to 2016, global annual PV production grew at an annual pace of roughly 40 percent. Solar now supplies more than 2 percent of global electricity demand. And despite short-term swings, long-term solar panel costs have regularly fallen as total solar production has risen—by roughly 20 percent for every doubling of cumulative production.[61] This regular reduction has been dubbed "Swanson's Law" (although Dick Swanson, founder of SunPower, will tell anyone who will listen that Paul Maycock at the U.S. Department of Energy (DOE) noticed this trend first, and Swanson just popularized it later).

From 1980 to 2001, while Professor Green was churning out new and improved solar cell designs, improvements in PV efficiency drove cost

Box 2.1
Solar Photovoltaic Power 101

At the heart of a solar PV power system is the solar panel (also referred to in the industry as a solar module). Figure 2.3 breaks out the components of a solar panel. Sandwiched between layers of glass and polymers is an array of solar cells, which are typically made of silicon and convert sunlight into electricity.

Next, figure 2.4 depicts a typical residential solar system. Solar panels mounted on a roof absorb sunlight and convert it to direct current (DC) electricity. However, because the grid runs on alternating current (AC) electricity, the output from the solar panels runs through a device called an inverter that changes DC to AC. Some of that AC electricity now can power appliances in

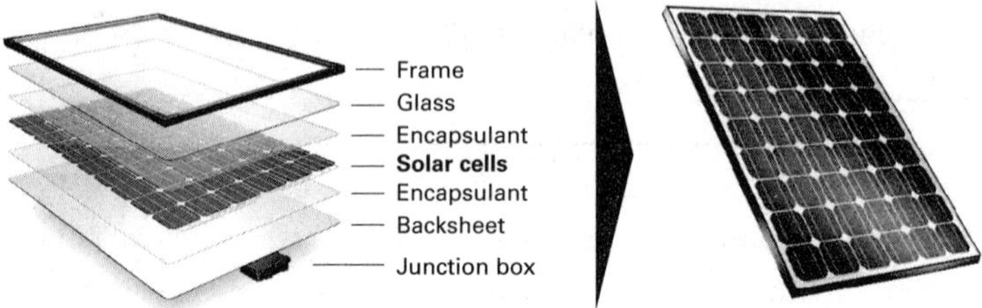

Figure 2.3
Components of a typical solar PV panel.
Source: DuPont.

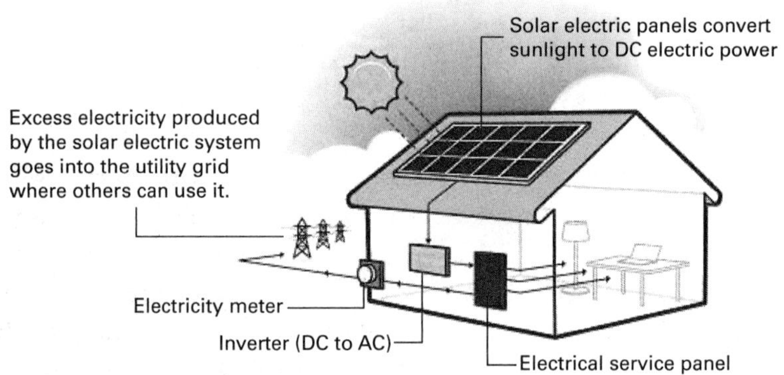

Figure 2.4
How a residential solar PV system connects to the grid.
Source: New York State Energy Research and Development Agency.

Box 2.1 (continued)

the home. And if the solar panels produce more electricity than the home needs at any given moment, the excess can be sold to the main grid.

The amount of energy per second that a solar panel can produce when the sun is directly overhead is called its power generating capacity, measured in watts (W) of electric power. A single panel can typically produce 250–350 W. And the average U.S. home solar system is roughly rated at 5,000 W, or 5 kilowatts (kW). [Note: a megawatt (MW) is 1 million watts, and a gigawatt (GW) is 1 billion watts.] Residential systems are just one use of solar power. As figure 2.5 illustrates, there are four major markets, divided by the typical size of a solar system:

- Utility-scale installations range from several to several hundred megawatts of generation capacity.
- Commercial and industrial installations typically are smaller than 2 MW.
- Residential installations are typically below 50 kW.
- Off-grid installations, which are deployed where the central power grid does not reach, can be as small as a single panel.

As figure 2.5 shows, the solar power sector can be divided into the downstream deployment of solar panels in these four markets and their upstream manufacturing. Manufacturing a solar panel starts with mining and refining polysilicon, which is then melted into long, cylindrical ingots and sliced into thin wafers. These wafers of high-purity silicon are then turned into solar

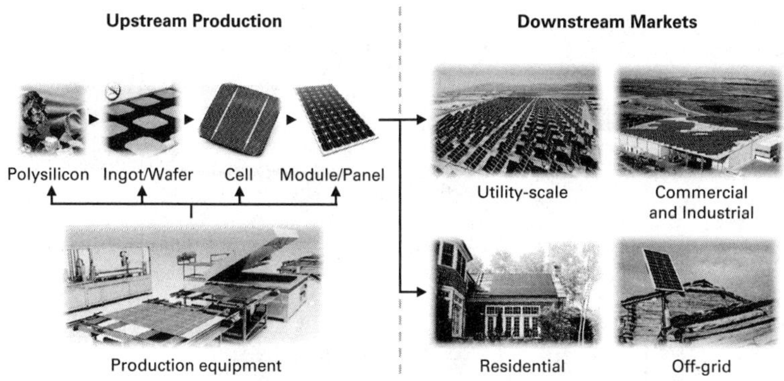

Figure 2.5
Solar PV upstream production and downstream markets.
Source: Images from Wikimedia Commons.

(continued)

Box 2.1 (continued)

cells, which convert sunlight into electricity. Finally, solar cells are arranged in an array and sealed together into a solar panel.

The solar industry comprises a diverse set of firms. One important category is upstream producers (or, interchangeably, manufacturers) of solar equipment, components, and panels. Another category is downstream developers that shepherd a solar project through its various stages of design, financing, construction, and operation. Some vertically integrated firms perform multiple upstream steps and even have divisions that deploy solar panels into downstream markets as well.

The cost of solar power has fallen substantially in recent years and looks set to continue doing so. The simplest way to measure cost is to divide the up-front cost of a solar installation by its rated capacity in watts. The top chart in figure 2.6 plots the cost per watt of solar installations in the United States (excluding any government subsidies). The larger the solar installation, the lower the cost per watt, thanks in part to economies of scale.

The bottom chart focuses on the cheapest segment—utility-scale solar—and breaks out its projected costs through 2020. By the end of the decade, the cost of a utility-scale solar installation is forecast to be less than $1/W, and the solar panel itself will account for less than half of the total cost. The rest of the cost will come from associated hardware, like inverters that connect

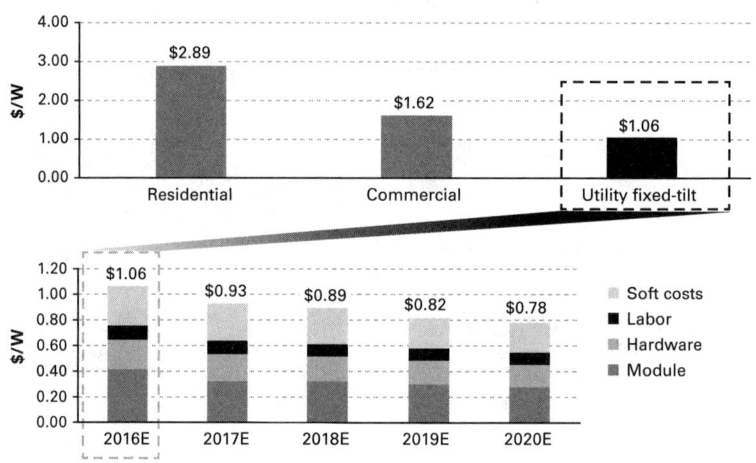

Figure 2.6
The falling cost of solar PV. Projections exclude potential 2018 U.S. tariffs. Source: GTM Research (2017).

Box 2.1 (continued)

panels to the grid, electronics, and mounting system, as well as labor costs and other soft costs, like securing permits and financing.[59]

Still, the cost per watt of capacity is not a useful measure to assess the cost competitiveness of solar power. Whereas fossil-fueled power plants can produce power at their rated capacity indefinitely, a solar panel can produce close to its rated wattage only under peak sunlight, around midday. Because on average there is much less sunlight over the course of each day, solar installations produce much less power on average than their rated capacity. A residential solar system in the United States typically produces only a fifth of the energy over the course of a year that it would if it continuously produced at its rated power. That figure can rise to over one-third for some utility-scale systems if their solar panels are equipped with single-axis trackers, which follow the sun as it moves throughout the day. Increasingly, developers are opting for this configuration.

A better way to assess the economics of solar power is to compare the cost of the electric energy, rather than power, that it produces with the cost of the same amount of energy from other sources. Electric energy is measured by the kilowatt-hour (kWh), a kilowatt of power output sustained for one hour [1,000 kWh amount to a megawatt-hour (MWh)]. Calculating this cost entails spreading out the up-front cost of a solar installation over the energy that it produces over its lifetime, taking into account the time value of money. The investment bank Lazard calculated that the cost of utility-scale solar was in some cases lower than $50 per MWh in 2016, comparable with the cost of electricity from the cheapest fossil fuel (natural gas).[60] Still, as chapter 3 explains, even a low cost per kilowatt-hour can fall short of making solar competitive if the cost of solar exceeds the value that it provides.

declines. But since then, performance improvements have stopped driving declining costs. Rather, those declines have happened because firms have achieved economies of scale from mass production, and they have learned to wring costs out of their manufacturing processes and supply chains.[62] On top of this, the costs of deploying thousands of solar panels in the desert or a dozen of them on a roof have also fallen regularly, as installers and developers around the world have gained experience and devised clever ways to install solar more cheaply. As solar becomes more widespread, these trends should continue to drive down the installed cost of solar.

At the same time, competition will only get fiercer across the entire solar value chain. In the early 2000s, the most lucrative segments of the solar industry were upstream, especially in the production of polysilicon. But when the glut of Chinese factories producing polysilicon, cells, and panels came online, prices for all of these products plunged, squeezing profits out of the entire upstream value chain.[63]

Now profits for firms in the downstream deployment of solar are being squeezed as well, partly from intensifying competition and partly because of a global decline in incentive payments for solar power. Historically, governments have supported the deployment of solar in three major ways. One, they have used mandates to require utilities to procure a certain share of their power from renewable sources such as solar power. Two, they have subsidized the construction of solar installations, for example through tax credits that reduce solar's up-front cost. And three, they have paid for the energy that solar produces at a premium rate. For example, through feed-in tariffs or another policy known as "net metering," homes and businesses sell power to the grid, often at higher rates than the power would fetch on the open market.

Feed-in tariffs in particular have been central to spurring the deployment of solar power, and in 2015, they were the most popular policy instrument to promote renewable energy in the world.[64] But around the world, countries are replacing feed-in tariffs, which guarantee the same, high payments to every supplier of solar electricity, with reverse auctions in which developers bid against one another to offer the lowest price for which they will agree to sell solar power for the next fifteen to twenty years. By pitting firms against one another, this policy shift has dramatically reduced the contract price for which developers can sell their power, squeezing their profits.[65] Even Germany, which pioneered feed-in tariffs, has switched to reverse auctions, which is fiscally prudent for Germany, but disastrous for the profit margins of solar developers.

Even as profits are being squeezed across the solar value chain, global prospects for solar deployment around the world have never been stronger. A string of record-low prices for solar projects around the world has encouraged governments to set ever-more-ambitious deployment targets. Beginning in Dubai in 2015, with a then-unheard-of bid by a Saudi developer to build a project and sell power for 6 cents per kilowatt-hour (kWh), subsequent government tenders in Peru, Mexico, and Chile plunged prices below 3 cents/kWh. Then, in late 2016, Abu Dhabi seized the title of cheapest solar at 2.4 cents/kWh (figure 2.7).[66] Then, in late 2017, the kingdom of Saudi

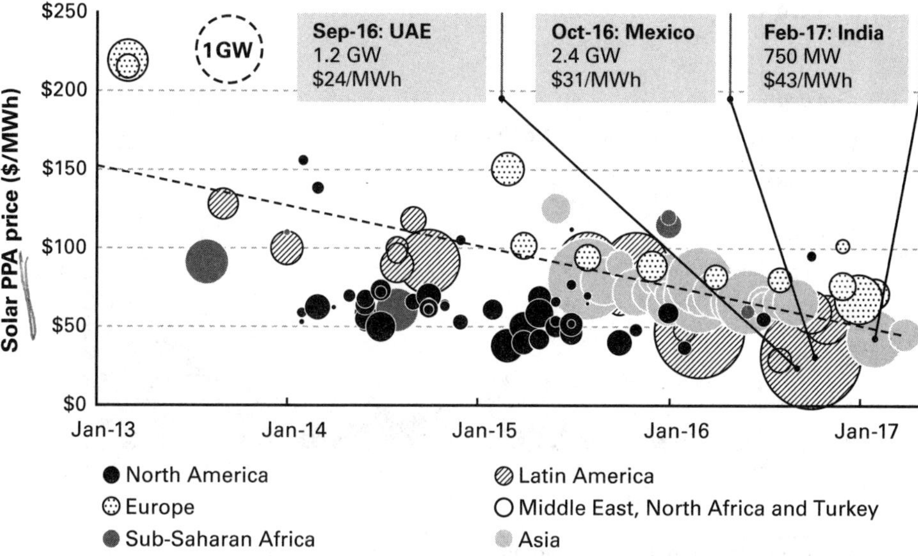

Figure 2.7

Recent prices for solar PV power purchase agreements (PPAs) around the world. Each circle represents the price for which a developer of a utility-scale solar project has agreed to sell electricity through a PPA contract with a customer (for example, a utility that will buy the electricity and distribute it to homes and businesses). The size of each circle represents the power-generating capacity, in megawatts or gigawatts, of that particular solar installation. The shading of each circle denotes the region of the world where the project has been, or will be, built. The dashed line approximates the average downward trend of PPA prices over time.
Source: GTM Research (2017).

Arabia seized the crown for cheapest solar at 1.79 cents/kWh (possibly with the aid of incentives).

Recognizing ongoing cost declines, market analysts are bullish about solar's deployment prospects on every continent save Antarctica. Bloomberg New Energy Finance projects that by 2040, the cost of solar PV will plummet by two-thirds, and as a result, solar will account for 17 percent of total electricity generation (see figure 2.8). This would be especially impressive, given that electricity demand is projected to grow rapidly in emerging economies, driven by urbanization, economic growth, and the rise of new sources of demand such as electric vehicles. So, if Bloomberg's forecast is right, solar will grow by more than 1,500 percent through 2040, and more than 40 percent of that growth will occur in China and India, which are poised for

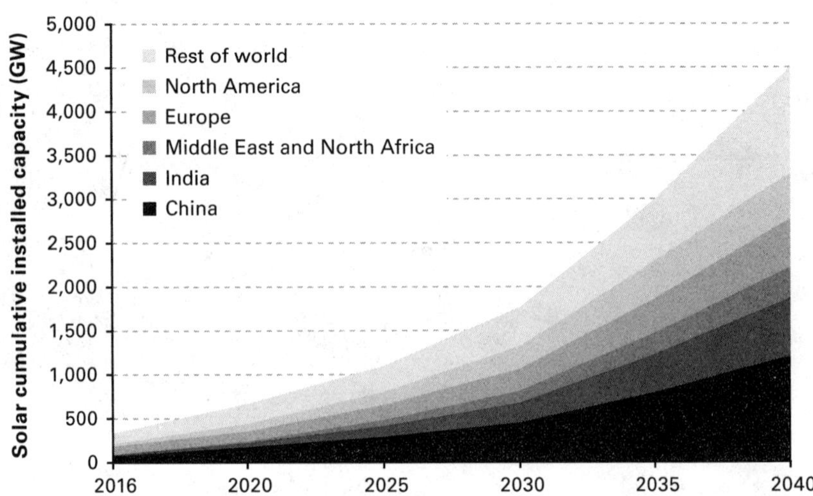

Figure 2.8

Projections for global solar deployment. This chart plots the expected growth in the installed solar PV capacity (measured in gigawatts) in major countries and regions around the world between 2016 and 2040.

Source: Bloomberg New Energy Finance (2017).

explosions in solar PV deployment. Strikingly, these installations will come in all sizes, not just in the form of massive solar farms. The 4,500 GW of solar in 2040 is projected to break down 70–30 between utility-scale solar farms and distributed solar installations that span off-grid projects and residential and commercial rooftops.[67]

Still, the scarcity of profits and recent upheaval in the industry has instilled in firms a conservative, low-risk approach to the future. Indeed, the solar industry today is a far cry from the vision that Martin Roscheisen sold me on when he put his arm around me at Nanosolar and spoke glowingly of the coming technology revolution. Today, barely any investment is flowing toward post-silicon solar materials, as the existing industry structure, organized around silicon, crystallizes. Polysilicon producers are focused on maximizing the purity of silicon. Ingot and wafer manufacturers then ensure that no scrap is left unused as they deliver increasingly thin silicon wafers down the chain. And cell and panel manufacturers are intent on nudging up the efficiency of their products while minimizing the expense of the materials and factory operations that go into making them.

Downstream, developers and financiers of solar installations fixated on meeting falling cost targets will trust only existing silicon technology that has been thoroughly vetted. Solar industry associations trumpet their road map for a steady upward march of solar panel efficiency as a sign of the industry's innovative zeal.[68] But the reality is that the average efficiency of a silicon solar panel will increase each year for the next decade simply as more producers switch from low- to high-purity silicon and to more efficient cell architectures that have already been invented.

To be sure, the industry will continue to see incremental innovation. Inverters, which connect solar panels to the grid, will get smarter and less expensive. Project developers will devise ingenious configurations for how to lay out and mount solar panels to minimize wiring costs and electrical losses. Companies are already using drones to aerially monitor the operations of solar farms and cut down on labor costs.

Yet the fact remains that the industry spends on average just 1 percent of its annual revenues on R&D—a measly sum in comparison with most advanced industries. In 2017, researchers at Stanford University reported that Chinese solar companies are beginning to spend more on R&D collaborations with Western researchers and coinvesting with the Chinese government in new technologies. But it is still the case that most of these firms' R&D expenses remain targeted at incrementally improving existing silicon technology. Technology disruption is simply not the aspiration for most Chinese firms. Rather, their preferred route to a better market position has been vertical or horizontal consolidation.[69]

It's clear, now that China and silicon have won the day, that the solar industry plans to steer clear of disruptive innovation. The industry has come of age. Yet, that dearth of innovation should be deeply worrying to anyone hoping for a solar-powered future.

Chapter 3 Blocking the Sun

At 9:45 a.m. on March 20, 2015, electricity grid operators in Germany scanned the heavens, praying for clouds. To their dismay, they had an unobstructed view as the moon inexorably drifted toward the sun. Because of the good weather, solar panels all over the country were already pumping out electricity. But over the next two hours, more than 70 percent of Germany's solar power installations, which ordinarily would provide a quarter of the country's peak daytime power, would be knocked offline by a total solar eclipse before rushing right back online.[1] Grid operators braced to maintain a consistent electricity supply across the country and avoid blackouts.

It didn't have to be this way. In Italy, where the level of solar power has soared in recent years, operators disconnected all major solar installations from the grid before the eclipse hit, to prevent a sudden loss of, and subsequent surge in, solar power from wreaking havoc on the grid. But Germany was determined to confront the eclipse. Leaving its vast solar fleet operational would represent a high-profile test of the *Energiewende*. So, with typical German rigor, grid operators prepared for months to recruit every manner of generator—coal, natural gas, biomass, nuclear, and hydroelectric power plants—assembling a backup fleet with twice as much reserve capacity as normal. And they coordinated plans with neighboring countries so that Germany could rely on resources outside its borders to compensate for the sudden dip in solar production.[2,3]

Two hours later, German grid operators were popping champagne—their preparations had paid off, and the grid had sailed through the eclipse without any noticeable blip felt by consumers. TenneT, a company that operates a part of the southern German grid with the highest solar penetration, triumphantly tweeted, "Energiewende: 1, Solar Eclipse: 0."[4] News outlets around the world hailed Germany's success as a harbinger for solar's inevitable rise and a smooth transition to clean energy.

But very few noticed the much more telling remark by the head of TenneT's control system, Peter Hoffman, who would have to manage the grid long after the media moved on from celebrating Germany's triumph over the eclipse. Peering into his crystal ball, Hoffman mused, "What we see as a crisis [today] will be a daily phenomenon in 10 years."[5]

That's because much more solar is on the way, bringing with it wild swings in power output that could increase the risk of blackouts. In 2016, there were enough solar photovoltaic (PV) panels to supply a quarter of Germany's power if all the panels produced at full output simultaneously. But taking into account the parts of the day when solar produces little or no power, solar panels accounted for less than 7 percent of Germany's annual electricity. In the future that German politicians envision, the share of electricity generated by solar PV will more than quadruple to 30 percent by midcentury.[6] That increase would lead to huge fluctuations in the instantaneous power supply to the grid whenever clouds happen to roll in—shifts as volatile as the weather.

That volatility would bear out Hoffman's ominous prediction that crisis today could be commonplace tomorrow. If, in the future, solar were to supply Germany with nearly a third of its electricity over the year, that would mean it would account for virtually all of Germany's power on most sunny afternoons. In that case, sudden clouds would reduce the flow of electricity to the grid much more than the 2015 eclipse did. And whereas Germany's grid operators had months to prepare for the 2015 eclipse, they'll have to respond to clouds within hours, if not minutes. The extensive preparation that it took for Germany to sail through the eclipse should be a warning sign that managing the rise of solar could be expensive for utilities and fraught with peril.

Looking past Germany's momentary victory over the eclipse, the costs of renewable energy's increasing share are coming into focus. As more and more solar and wind generators have come online, their output has upended power markets, crashing the price at which power companies can sell electricity to the grid and putting financial strain on those firms that own fossil-fueled and nuclear power plants. To compensate for the rise in fluctuating renewable energy, Germany has invested in a fleet of expensive backup plants to maintain grid reliability.[7] Over the next five years, consumers will foot the bill as Germany invests $20 billion in building transmission lines, upgrading local distribution grids, and installing smart grid technology, partly to accommodate even more renewable energy.[8]

Given the sophistication of its grid and its ability to invest in grid upgrades, Germany is better equipped than less wealthy countries, such as India, to confront the challenges inherent in rapidly adding solar capacity. Still, rich or poor, countries will confront dizzying costs and complexity if they seek to ramp up their levels of solar power. They have no choice but to try, however. To limit catastrophic climate change, the world is likely going to need solar power to provide at least a third of all electricity by midcentury. That expansion, though, will lead to challenges even more daunting than those of the past.

Already, countries around the world are abandoning subsidy-driven models of financing solar power, like the feed-in tariffs in the early years of Germany's *Energiewende*. Instead, they will need to unlock vast pools of private capital to ramp up solar deployment. The trouble is, the world's biggest investors have so far ignored solar power; if they don't reach into their deep pockets, solar's advance could stall.

Even if an investment surge accelerates the construction of new solar capacity, though, solar PV's rise could be its own undoing. As the cost of generating solar power steadily falls, the value of consuming that electricity could fall even faster as more of it connects to the grid. The value could drop both because additional solar panels would supply power in excess of customer demand in the middle of the day and because high levels of solar power would strain power grids around the world, requiring costly solutions. This so-called "value deflation" could plunge solar's value below the gently falling cost of producing it, thereby undermining the economic benefits of adding more solar power. Then solar's current economic appeal would turn out to be a mere illusion—a poor predictor of solar's future prospects.

Innovation offers a way forward, and as box 3.1 elaborates below, it comes in many different flavors. Financial and business model innovation can unlock massive amounts of capital to continue deploying solar power around the world over the next decade or two. In addition, technological innovation can enable the cost of solar power to fall much more quickly than it has been dropping, allowing solar to remain competitive even as its value tumbles. Finally, broader, systemic innovation can boost the value

Box 3.1
Introduction to Innovation

According to the Austrian economist Josef Schumpeter (1883–1950), an *innovation* is a technological product or process that has been commercialized, or brought to market, for the first time.[a] He distinguished innovation from *invention,* which is the first development of a technology. Therefore, even if a firm does not invent a technology, it can *innovate* by successfully introducing that technology into the marketplace. (In addition to referring to a technology that has been commercialized, the term *innovation* can refer to the act of innovating.)

Schumpeter's definition of innovation might today be called *technological innovation.* More recently, scholars have introduced other types of innovation. These uses retain the core definition that *innovation* means the introduction of something that is adopted in a real-world context for the first time. Examples include:

- **Financial innovation:** Popularization of financial instruments, institutions, or markets that are new to a particular sector.[b]
- **Business model innovation:** Introduction of product offerings, revenue models, or operational practices that are new to a particular sector.[c]
- **Systemic innovation:** Implementation of novel approaches to designing a particular system. An energy system includes physical infrastructure (e.g., the power grid), economic markets (e.g., wholesale power markets), and public policies (e.g., regulations that govern power utilities).[d]

Notes

a. Adam B. Jaffe, Richard G. Newell, and Robert N. Stavins, "Technological Change and the Environment," in K-G Maler and J. R. Vincent (eds.), *Handbook of Environmental Economics,* Volume 1 (Amsterdam, Netherlands: Elsevier Science B.V., 2003): 461–516.

b. This is based on the *Financial Times* Lexicon definition of financial innovation, http://lexicon.ft.com/Term?term=financial-innovation.

c. See Karan Girotra and Serguei Netessine, "Four Paths to Business Model Innovation," *Harvard Business Review* (July/August 2014): https://hbr.org/2014/07/four-paths-to-business-model-innovation.

d. See Theocharis D. Tsoutsos and Yeoryios A. Stamboulis, "The Sustainable Diffusion of Renewable Energy Technologies as an Example of an Innovation-Focused Policy," *Technovation* 25 (2005): doi:10.1016/j.technovation.2003.12.003.

that solar provides. Altogether, the three types of innovation can safeguard solar's economic appeal indefinitely. What's more, they can enable solar to serve needs outside those traditionally met by electricity, which is an essential step toward harnessing the sun to satisfy a majority of humanity's energy needs sometime this century.

How Much Solar Does the World Really Need?

In 2015, Tesla founder and CEO Elon Musk quipped, "We have this handy fusion reactor in the sky called the sun. You don't have to do anything. It just works. It shows up every day and produces ridiculous amounts of power."[9]

Indeed, the sun is far and away the most potent energy source available for human use, and the world will need to harness much more of it than it currently does to transition away from fossil fuels. Our star produces 2 billion times as much energy as the sliver of light that eventually reaches the Earth, yet that sliver delivers over 10,000 times the power that the world needs. For the United States, that means that in theory, solar panels covering just 1 percent of the land area in Texas could supply all domestic power demand. Yet solar accounted for about 1 percent of total U.S. electricity generation in 2016.[10] Globally, solar accounted for only around 1.5 percent of all electricity in 2016. Clearly the sun's abundant energy is vastly underutilized.

Of course, the world's existing energy mix does not ignore the sun—quite the contrary. Fossil fuels like oil, gas, and coal—which supply over 80 percent of the world's primary energy—are ancient stores of solar energy. They are the remnants of organisms such as plankton that used photosynthesis to store solar energy as chemical bonds. Eons of crushing and heating below layers of rock transformed them into the energy-dense fuels that we use today.

Another 10 percent of the world's energy comes from burning biomass like wood or manure that exists thanks to sunlight, photosynthesis, and the food chain. The sun is also responsible for wind energy, heating up the Earth's atmosphere and causing air currents, which wind turbines then can convert to power. And the sun's heat drives the hydrological cycle, evaporating water that falls as rain into rivers and lakes and can spin hydroelectric turbines to produce electricity. Three other energy sources don't come from the sun. Of these, two sources—tidal energy caused by the moon's gravity and heat energy from the Earth's hot and radioactive core and sliding tectonic plates—are difficult to harness and have largely been ignored. The remaining source, the nuclear energy in atoms of uranium created from the explosions of distant stars, accounts for a few percent of global primary energy demand. So nearly all of the energy that the world uses today comes from the sun in some form or another.

But direct use of solar energy will need to increase rapidly to enable a transition from fossil fuels. The first priority is to increase the amount of electricity generated by solar power. This increase is needed because scientists who study the possible pathways to limiting climate change firmly agree that carbon emissions from the electric power sector must fall by between 80 and 100 percent by the middle of the century. This goal is known as "deep decarbonization" of the power sector.[11] And renewable solar and wind power are the most promising options to do most of the heavy lifting, taking into account economic and political considerations.

Decarbonizing the electricity sector first makes sense for other reasons as well. For one, economical sources of clean electricity exist already, whereas it is wickedly difficult to replace the fossil fuels that run other sectors. In the industrial sector, for instance, affordable options are very limited for replacing the coal and natural gas that are burned to provide process heat for plants and refineries. And in the transportation sector, oil exerts a vice grip, accounting for over 90 percent of the energy that cars, trucks, planes, and ships use. Currently, few alternative fuels for those uses are commercially viable.

The tiny but growing electric vehicle fleet suggests that electricity might be a viable alternative fuel for transportation sector. So, not only is decarbonizing electricity the least difficult way to start reducing global emissions from energy, it may also be a way to reduce emissions from other sectors that have not traditionally used electricity.

Another reason to decarbonize electricity is that demand for it is expected to grow rapidly. Economies around the world are starting to use electricity for activities that historically have relied on other energy carriers (for example, electric engines displace petroleum fuel in vehicle propulsion; electric heat pumps displace natural gas in the heating of homes and businesses; and electric arc furnaces displace coal in the production of iron and steel). On top of this, population growth and urbanization will lead to more people demanding access to modern energy. By midcentury, the International Energy Agency (IEA) forecasts that demand for electricity could double. Even in a best-case scenario, in which the world steeply ramps up energy efficiency measures, electricity demand would rise by 80 percent.[12]

Zero-carbon power sources will be needed to supply all or nearly all the world's growing power demand by 2050. But how much of that could solar power provide? Some estimates in the academic literature are extremely optimistic, arguing that nearly 100 percent of global electricity can feasibly and cost-effectively come from solar and wind power by midcentury.[13] This projection is probably a fantasy, and other studies argue forcefully that the costs of relying entirely on intermittent renewable energy would be astronomical.[14,15]

On the other end of the spectrum, the IEA is much more conservative about prospects for solar and wind power. In its projection of what the global electricity mix needs to look like in 2050 to give the world a chance at limiting global warming to 2°C, solar power—a combination of solar PV and concentrated solar power (CSP) plants—would provide just 20 percent of the world's electricity. Adding the contribution from wind power would bring the total share of solar and wind to a little over one-third of the global electricity mix by midcentury. Although this projection is more conservative than others in the literature, it would still increase the share of solar and wind contributed in 2016 by a factor of more than six (figure 3.1).[16]

Many other sources of power would also be in the IEA's recommended mix. Two assumptions stand out: One, the world will be able to build over three times as much nuclear capacity as currently exists; and two, every coal-fired power plant that doesn't get shut down will be retrofitted with equipment to capture and store its carbon emissions. On its face, this plan seems sound in that it is based on a diversified portfolio of zero-carbon resources. Also, because both nuclear and fossil plants are widely used in today's power sector, building them into the future electricity mix would be least disruptive to the status quo.

But it would be very risky to bet on this route to decarbonizing the power sector. Tripling nuclear capacity could be tough, given that nuclear power's share of global electricity supply actually declined over the last decade as a result of high costs and political opposition.[17] Betting that carbon capture and storage from fossil plants can take off is even riskier; only a handful of demonstrations exist around the world—most of them very expensive. The

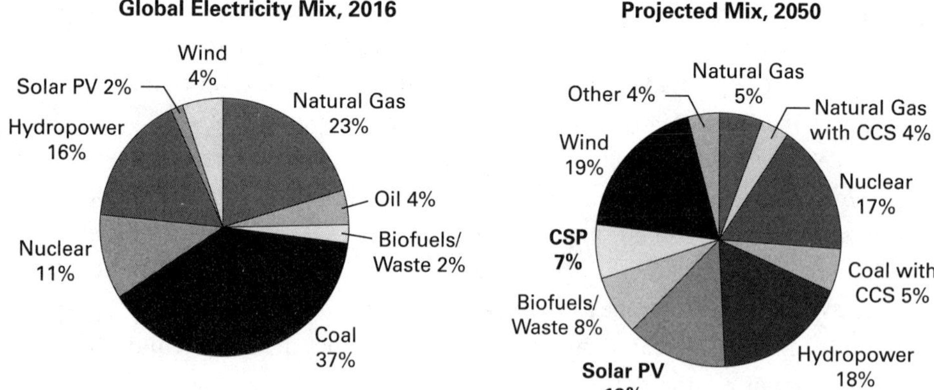

Figure 3.1

Current global electricity mix and one proposal to decarbonize it. The left pie chart displays the world's electricity mix in 2016. The right chart displays the IEA's projection for the mix in 2050, in a scenario that keeps the world on track to limit global warming to 2°C. The combination of solar PV and concentrated solar power (CSP) represents the share of global electricity that solar energy is projected to contribute. "CCS" refers to carbon capture and sequestration from fossil-fuel power plants.
Source: International Energy Agency (IEA), U.S. Energy Information Administration, World Energy Council.

risks, however, do not make it acceptable to give up on these sources. Both nuclear and fossil plants with carbon capture and storage could provide reliable power that would make it easier and cheaper to supplement the intermittent output from wind and solar.

A wise approach would be to plan for the worst case, in which these two sources do not get scaled up rapidly. One way to do so would be to plan for solar and wind to collectively contribute a majority of the world's electricity supply by midcentury. Across a range of different assumptions about how technology costs will evolve—and under the assumption that nuclear power and carbon capture cannot be meaningfully scaled up—the most economical way to decarbonize the power sector is for solar power to contribute at least one-third (and, under some assumptions, over one-half) of global electricity by 2050.[18]

A global target for solar to provide one-third of the electricity mix is roughly equal in percentage terms to Germany's midcentury target. Yet achieving the target on a global scale will be far harder. Whereas Germany needs to quadruple its solar penetration to hit its target, the rest of the world would have to boost its solar penetration from below 2 percent in 2016 to upward of 30 percent by 2050. And solar power will have to expand its slice of the global electricity pie while at the same time keeping up with a growing pie that could double by midcentury. Finally, to achieve a one-third solar penetration on average around the world, some regions will need to achieve even more than that proportion to make up for other regions that underperform.

Recognizing the magnitude of the challenge, one might ask why it's a good idea to plan for a future that could require multiplying global solar capacity thirtyfold or more. Wouldn't just tripling nuclear capacity be an easier route to decarbonization? Quite possibly, from a technical perspective. But solar power has two advantages that argue strongly in its favor. One, its cost continues to decline substantially—by contrast, nuclear reactors have barely fallen in cost in recent decades and, in some places, have even gotten more expensive.[19] Two, solar power does not face the stiff political obstacles that obstruct nuclear power. In fact, a growing political constituency enthusiastically supports deploying more solar power.

As ambitious as the midcentury target for solar to supply one-third of the world's electricity is, the ultimate potential for solar energy to meet humanity's energy needs is even grander because it is far and away the most abundant energy source on Earth. Estimates of solar's technical potential, or how much sunlight could feasibly be converted to energy, subject to environmental, geographic, and technical constraints, can vary by a factor of over 100.[20] But even so, solar is in a league of its own, with the technical capacity to supply the world's power needs many times over.[21]

So sometime in the second half of the 21st century, the most logical goal is for solar to become the world's primary energy source, accounting for a majority of its energy demand.[22] Getting there will necessarily entail much more than solar PV panels that convert sunlight to energy. It will require ways to convert sunlight to portable fuels and to heat. And it will demand reimagined energy systems, configured to connect the sun's energy with the world's energy needs.

Achieving this vision may sound daunting, but Elon Musk is confident that the world will get there. His prophecy: "The primary means of energy generation is going to be solar. It will at least be a plurality, and probably be a slight majority in the long term."

Capital Crunch

The most immediate obstacle to the continued rise of solar is that the world's biggest investors have so far passed it over as a major investment opportunity. This trend is worrying because almost the entire cost of a solar project comes up front, whereas the revenues trickle in through sales of power. Solar power can't become a mainstream power source, rising over an order of magnitude from its current level of providing less than 2 percent of the world's electricity, without tapping into vast pools of private capital to finance its up-front costs.

In the developed world, private investment is important because even though taxpayers may have assented to (or failed to notice) generous solar subsidies when solar was a niche energy source, they will be loath to underwrite solar at a much larger scale. For example, the subsidy-driven model of Germany's *Energiewende* successfully incubated the fledgling solar industry, but today over a quarter of an average German household's power bill is a surcharge to subsidize renewable energy, up from 5 percent a decade ago.[23] Consumers are unlikely to tolerate paying much more, and the government has already slashed subsidies for new solar projects. In the developing world, where government assistance is scarce to begin with, unsubsidized private investment is crucial for solar to take off in those markets from the get-go.

This capital gap isn't readily apparent from statistics of the rise in funding for solar power. In 2016, the most funding for any power generation technology, clean or dirty, went to solar, to the tune of $116 billion.[24,25] The investment drove the installation of over 70 gigawatts (GW) of solar capacity globally that year (up 20 percent from 2015), as solar continued to drop in cost to become the cheapest source of generation—below wind, coal, and gas—in emerging economies, including China, India, and Brazil.[26] From the numbers, it certainly sounds like solar investment is booming.

But the magnitude of funding available from the sources that have brought solar to where it is today pales in comparison to what solar will need in coming decades. Investment will need to be almost double what it is currently on pace to reach by 2040 if the world is to limit global warming to 2°C, according to Bloomberg New Energy Finance (BNEF). In other words, more than $2.5 trillion of additional investment will be needed for solar power over and above what it looks like investors are prepared to plow into the sector. Compounding this challenge, as interest rates creep up in the United States and elsewhere, cheap money could become less abundant.[27]

Existing sources of capital may provide only up to a third of the funds that solar will need by 2040.[28] In the United States, most solar projects are financed in an arcane way known as tax equity finance. In essence, because the federal government offers a 30 percent tax credit for solar installations, big banks and other corporations that pay billions of dollars in taxes agree to invest in solar power projects and use government incentives to reduce their tax bill. The tax credit is set to ramp down starting in 2020. And the possibility of corporate tax reform under the Trump administration could reduce investor appetite for the tax credits still further. Thus, tax equity investors, who have financed the bulk of the 25 GW of solar in the United States, will likely be unwilling to up the ante and fund the next several hundred gigawatts.

In Europe, public incentives have also underpinned solar financing, encouraging utilities, private equity investors, and infrastructure funds to inject capital into solar projects.[29] But such public incentives are drying up in Europe, even while countries target achieving a manyfold increase in solar capacity.

Across the developing world, both national and international development banks have been crucial in infusing capital to jump-start investment in solar energy.[30] Yet, development bank resources are inadequate to support the next phase of solar's growth, which will require an influx of capital in the developing world. For example, in 2016, the Asian Development Bank agreed to spend a half-billion dollars to help India finance rooftop solar power, a major, multi-year deal.[31] India, however, is going to need roughly 200 times that amount of money—$100 billion—to meet its goal of 100 GW of solar capacity by 2022. Its hunger for capital will not end there, given that its 2030 target is 250 GW of installed solar nationally. The Climate Policy Initiative (CPI) projects, however, that without new sources of capital, India will miss its 2022 funding target by roughly 30 percent.[32]

The only investors with pockets deep enough to bankroll the next phase of solar's growth are institutional investors. These investors include pension funds, insurance funds, and sovereign wealth funds, and they collectively manage over $100 trillion.[33] For them, the few trillion dollars needed for solar to explode on the world energy scene is small change. The problem is that currently only 1 percent of that gargantuan sum is invested in infrastructure globally, and even less supports low-carbon infrastructure. Indeed, just 2.5 percent of all clean energy assets were financed by institutional investors from 2004 to 2011.[34]

A casual observer might wonder why institutional investors haven't already piled into solar power projects. These investors have a strong demand for long-dated, yield-oriented investments—that is, ways to park their money for long periods of time and receive healthy, recurring payments for doing so. Solar power projects appear to fit that investment profile. They have historically been safe bets. Investors could sign long-term contracts to sell electricity at a locked-in rate to local utilities and enjoy preferential treatment in electricity markets thanks to favorable public policy. What's more, once a solar power plant is built, it just sits there, harnessing sunlight and generating income by selling electricity. Very little can go wrong with it, in comparison with more complicated power plants like fossil-fueled or nuclear plants.

The problem is that institutional investors find it difficult to invest directly in solar power projects. Rather, they end up having to invest through intermediaries, such as private equity funds. But these funds are set up to make riskier bets and realize higher returns than the lower-risk, lower-return proposition of a boring solar project. This constraint limits the number of solar projects that private equity funds will invest in and, in turn, limits the investment that institutional investors can make in solar projects through intermediaries.

Even though many solar projects are in theory ideal investment opportunities for institutional investors, practical hang-ups prevent them from investing their capital directly in those projects. These colossal investors have two stipulations when assembling their portfolios, both of which solar currently violates. The first is liquidity—that is, the ability to buy and sell their investments quickly on the market. Liquidity enables an investor to make an investment without paying a significant premium over the market price and to sell off an investment without having to offer a significant discount below the market price. The second stipulation is that institutional investors want to invest large chunks of money at one time, rather than having to make many small investments. They work this way because they have the capacity to scrutinize only a limited number of investments.

The easiest way to satisfy both stipulations is to invest in listed securities, that is, stocks and bonds listed on public exchanges. This approach offers liquidity—it is straightforward to buy or sell securities on large exchanges—and it is possible to invest large sums in a diversified portfolio. To avoid having to perform due diligence on every stock or bond in which an investor has exposure, investors can invest in index funds, which themselves are listed securities that aggregate lots of individual stocks or bonds. Overall, institutional investors invest 80–90 percent of their portfolios in listed securities.[35]

For the most part, solar power projects fail to meet either of the criteria that institutional investors demand. There is no way to buy or sell solar power projects, similar to trading stocks on a public exchange, so an investment in a solar power project can be illiquid for years or even decades. And institutional investors often employ too few staff to justify conducting extensive diligence on individual projects, each of which may require only tens of millions of dollars of investment.

Despite the challenges, institutional investors are not uninterested in investing in renewable energy. In fact, some are getting creative in finding investment opportunities in the sector. For example, Abu Dhabi's sovereign wealth fund invested hundreds of millions of dollars in Renew Power, India's biggest solar company. And investors from the University of California's endowment to the New Zealand pension fund have pooled resources to invest in clean energy companies around the world.[36,37] By and large, though, these promising investments are drops in the bucket—nowhere near the trillions that will be needed to scale up solar.

Although most of the investment needs are for grid-connected solar systems, capital is also badly needed to scale up off-grid solar systems to deliver electricity to some of the more than 1 billion people around the world who lack it. Right now, most investors perceive off-grid solar for poor, rural populations as a high-risk, low-reward opportunity. As a result, the few projects that do receive private financing get it on unfavorable terms, with high interest rates for loans that must be paid back in short order.[38]

So far, international institutions such as the World Bank and nonprofit philanthropies have valiantly funded off-grid projects to supplement the dearth of private capital. As a result, more than 120 million people worldwide enjoy some sort of solar energy—mostly solar-powered lanterns, but also systems of solar panels and batteries to provide such basic energy needs as lighting and cell-phone charging. To realize the full potential of off-grid solar systems to reduce energy poverty, though, investment must surge by a factor of 250, from just $200 million today to over $50 billion annually.[39] If institutional investors were wary of investing on a per-project basis in solar farms, they certainly will want no part of investing in individual rural solar home systems.

Whether on-grid or off-grid, scaling up solar power in the coming years will require massive investment. The approaches that have turned solar into a $100 billion annual market will not be enough going forward; the leap to trillions of dollars of investment will require fresh ideas and new players. Fortunately, progress on that front is accelerating. The industry is devising new ways to make solar investments liquid and painless for institutional investors, and entrepreneurs are introducing business models to connect unelectrified populations with investors looking for healthy returns. The good news is that these developments could propel solar power to overcome its impending capital crunch. The bad news, however, is that even bigger obstacles stand in the way of solar's continued rise.

Undone by Success

In 2013, Chile looked like an ideal match for solar power. The country's economy was booming on the back of its expanding mining industry, which supplied a third of the world's copper. But mining is electricity-intensive, and Chile has no domestic oil, gas, or coal with which to generate power. To make matters worse, since 2004, neighboring Argentina has periodically throttled natural gas exports to Chile. In the absence of power from fossil fuels, the mines turned to hydropower to meet most of their needs.[40,41] But droughts started to dry up Chile's existing hydropower reservoirs, and new dams ran into strong public opposition.[42,43] Amid all these woes, solar power in the sun-drenched Atacama Desert stood out as an abundant source of electricity, right next to the mines.

The value proposition looked so strong that solar developers in Chile made an audacious bet to offer solar power into the electricity market with no long-term price guarantee at all. This move bucked conventional wisdom in the industry. In standard practice around the world, a solar developer signs a power-purchase agreement with a customer, such as a utility or an industrial power user. Under this agreement, that customer, called an "off-taker," agrees to purchase power from the solar plant at an agreed-upon price for several years (often fifteen or more). The developer benefits from the guarantee of cash flows for many years into the future, and the guarantee also makes it easier to raise capital from lenders and investors to foot the up-front bill. The customer benefits from locking in a long-term power price, even as other sources of electricity are likely to get more expensive over time. To abandon the power-purchase agreement and instead operate a solar farm as a "merchant plant," which sells its power at a price that fluctuates every hour in the marketplace (known as the "wholesale power market"), was solar heresy.

But in Chile, developers reasoned that power prices were virtually guaranteed to stay high, given the host of challenges confronting other power sources. And the copper industry, a mainstay of the Chilean economy, wasn't going anywhere. So when miners balked at signing long-term power-purchase agreements, developers still managed to raise capital for merchant solar projects to sell into Chilean power markets, where electricity prices were steep.

Then those prices crashed. Worldwide, the commodity boom contracted, and copper prices halved between 2013 and 2016, reducing the demand for electricity.[44] Over the same period, droughts spared Chile, so its hydropower plants ran at full capacity, oversupplying electricity markets. On top of this, the rush to add solar—including over 1 GW in 2015—added even more supply to markets facing shrinking demand.[45]

As a result, Chile literally gave power away, with prices hitting zero in the afternoon (when solar production was highest) on a majority of days in 2015 and 2016.[46] That slashed revenues for merchant solar plants, whose developers scurried to find customers to sign power-purchase agreements to provide income security. Developers of new projects have signed long-term contracts at any cost to avoid the calamity that befell merchant plants. In August 2016, a Spanish developer agreed to a long-term contract to supply Chilean utilities with power for just 2.9 cents per kilowatt-hour, setting a new world record (although that record would last just a month before an auction in Abu Dhabi went still lower).[47]

Chile offers a window into the economic woes that solar could face as more of it comes online. Because the power output from a solar panel cannot be controlled (in power system parlance, solar is known as a "nondispatchable" resource), all the solar panels in the same geographical area will produce power when the sun is overhead, flooding the market. In Chile, it took a demand-reducing economic downturn on top of a solar supply glut to bring prices to zero. But at higher penetrations of solar power, excess supply alone will be enough to make solar power worthless. This value deflation problem could halt solar's rise down the road. It's a counterintuitive penalty that the industry will incur for being too successful at adding solar capacity.

Not so fast, retort skeptics of this prediction. They rightly point out that the Chilean trend of merchant solar power is a global aberration, and elsewhere in the world the power-purchase agreement contract structure has protected solar from fluctuating power prices.[48] For example, in Germany, rising levels of solar electricity have hurt the bottom lines of fossil and nuclear reactors rather than undercutting solar revenues. Just as in Chile, Germany's wholesale power prices have fallen by two-thirds since 2008 as more renewable energy has come online. Sometimes when there is an oversupply of solar and wind power, power prices even go negative.

On its face, the skeptics' argument appears convincing—indeed, in Germany, solar's rise is hurting every other generator, but not solar itself. Although power markets are complex systems, a 2016 study unambiguously concluded that the rise in renewable energy is the largest driver of the plunge in wholesale power prices.[49] This drop is disastrous for other power plants that rely on higher power prices to pay for fuel (coal and gas plants) and to pay down tremendous capital costs (nuclear plants). But solar power is protected in the German power market by incentives that boost solar income even as revenues from wholesale power markets fall. As a result, German power utilities, which have traditionally owned fossil-fueled and nuclear plants, have experienced major financial distress. In 2015, one of the two major utilities, E.ON, reported its largest loss ever, at $8 billion.[50] Both E.ON and RWE, another major German utility, have attempted to cut their losses by splitting off their fossil-fueled and nuclear plants, retaining the more lucrative renewable energy portfolios.[51] The lesson from this, some have argued, is that even though solar will upend power markets as it becomes ubiquitous, its profitability will remain unscathed as other types of generators suffer.

Yet this argument is myopic. Even if subsidy regimes protect solar today, they are unlikely to last as higher solar penetration makes them more expensive. Already, Germany has enacted reforms that sometimes reduce the price that solar generators are paid if wholesale prices are low.[52] Fundamentally, rising solar penetrations degrade the value that solar offers to the electricity grid, regardless of the revenue that a particular policy paradigm guarantees solar owners.

This value deflation will reduce solar's economic competitiveness in the long run. If power-purchase agreements persist as the dominant way to finance solar, the long-term price that new solar projects will be able to secure from offtakers will fall. If long-term contracts give way to merchant arrangements, as happened in Chile, solar's profits could evaporate even faster. The market is already moving in this direction; some utilities in the United States are pushing to reduce the duration of the power-purchase agreements that they sign.

Regardless of the near-term effects of the contracting arrangement, the profitability of solar power in the long term will be dictated by its underlying economic value in markets around the world. And that value will fall as more solar connects to the grid, following simple principles of supply and demand.

Shayle Kann at GTM Research and I have surveyed the early evidence of value deflation around the world, as well as various economic models of how bad it could get as solar's penetration increases toward the target of supplying one-third of global power demand.[53] In figure 3.2, we plot the power market prices that solar generators would receive in California, Texas, and Germany if they were not protected by long-term contracts or subsidies. This approach measures the deflating economic value that solar offers the grid as its penetration rises. The results are stark. When a grid relies on solar power for 15 percent of its total energy needs, the value of solar falls by more than half. At 30 percent solar power, solar's value declines by more than two-thirds in a simulation of California's power market.

Because solar generates most of its energy during just a few hours of the day, even if it accounts for a moderate share of the power grid's annual energy—say 20 percent—it can account for an enormous share of the *instantaneous* power in the middle of the day (in some cases, up to 100 percent). That high share magnifies the value deflation effect during those hours.

This phenomenon is not restricted to the three markets displayed in figure 3.2. For example, in Italy, where solar penetration approached 10 percent in 2016, peak power prices have shifted from daytime to nighttime. There, gas generators, which are dispatchable and can run whenever demand is highest, can take advantage of higher prices and actually increase their value to the grid. But nondispatchable solar has become less and less valuable.[54]

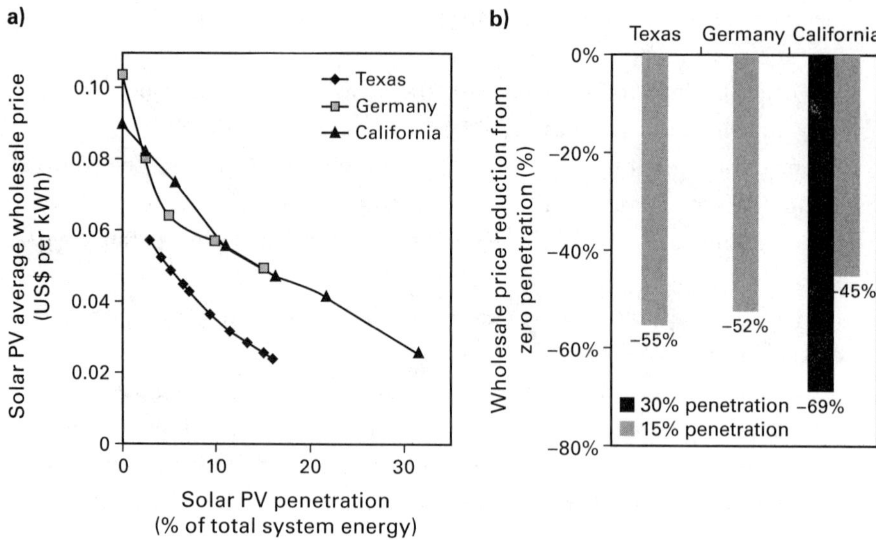

Figure 3.2

Solar PV value deflation. Panel (a) displays the results of three different simulations of power grids in different parts of the world that forecast the falling value of electricity produced by solar PV projects as the penetration of solar PV increases. (Penetration is measured as the percentage of the annual demand for electric energy, measured in kilowatt-hours, supplied by solar PV.) Panel (b) plots solar PV value deflation at 15 percent and 30 percent solar PV penetration, compared with no penetration.
Source: Figure reprinted with permission from Sivaram and Kann (2016).

That solar is more vulnerable to value deflation than dispatchable generators is an important insight. All power generators—even fossil-fueled ones—will suffer from lower profits if too many of them are added to the grid and bring excess electricity online at all hours. But solar PV will experience much more severe value deflation for every additional increment of electricity that it generates because its power output cannot be shifted to another part of the day. Therefore, a glut of solar supply can build up rapidly in the middle of the day.

Still, most parts of the world may not experience solar value deflation for several years. That delay makes it especially dangerous because the seeds of value deflation are unwittingly being sown today, whereas its effects will become stark only down the road. So, even as rapid solar deployment today invites breathless projections of exponential growth, it is worth noting that solar's trajectory is also consistent with logistic growth (known colloquially as an "S-curve"). In this kind of trajectory, solar's rise would peter out in a couple of decades as it hits a penetration ceiling well before reaching the midcentury target of powering a third of global demand. Panel (a) in figure 3.3 plots one study's grim scenario of logistic growth, in which the combined capacity of solar and wind power level off after 2030, so that they contribute only around 10 percent of the world's electricity needs.

Panel (b) shows that of the five countries with the largest shares of electricity from solar PV, four—Italy, Greece, Germany, and Spain—have already seen their shares stop rising after they reached 5–10 percent. (The fifth country, Japan, did not experience a slowdown in solar growth in 2016, though it had reached only 5 percent solar penetration. The clearest exception to the trend of slowing solar growth is California—a country-sized

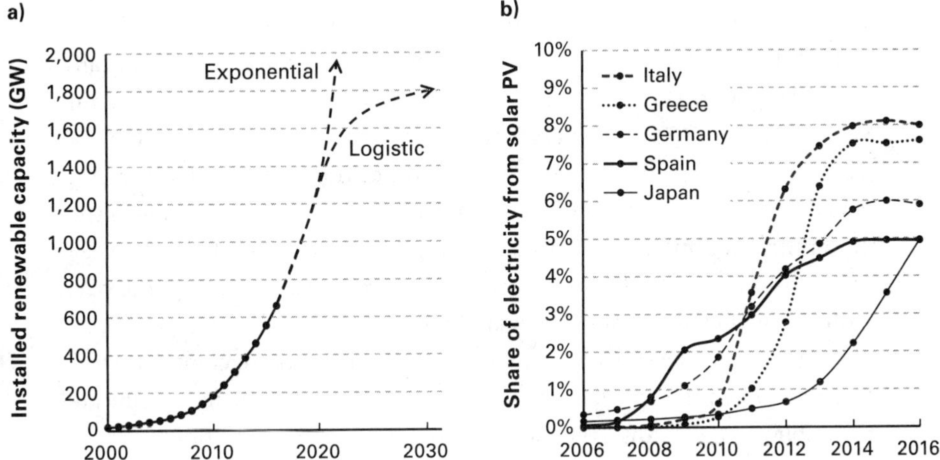

Figure 3.3
Exponential and logistic growth for renewable energy. In panel (a), the plotted points through 2017 represent the actual installed capacity, in gigawatts, of global wind and solar power installations. The dashed lines are exponential and logistic extrapolations of the trend that best fit the existing data. Both extrapolations pass through the value in 2020 that was the average prediction from a group of experts. Panel (b) displays the share of electricity from solar PV in the five countries with the highest solar penetrations over the decade from 2006 to 2016.
Source: Panel (a) adapted from Hansen et al. (2017); panel (b) generated from data in BP Statistical Review 2017 and compiled by Keith Pickering.

economy—where solar has broken through the 10 percent barrier to supply nearly 14 percent of the state's electricity in 2016.[55] Nevertheless, warning signs that solar's rise may be unsustainable are emerging even in California, as the next section details.) If countries, especially in the developing world, experience a slowdown in solar growth similar to that in Europe, then the world's slim window to decarbonize the power sector will slam shut.

If It Quacks Like a Duck . . .

Oversupplying electricity markets is just one way that a surfeit of solar could sink its value. Adding more solar PV to the grid could force other generators to pick up a greater amount of the slack at times when solar stops producing. It could also destabilize the power grid, which is normally self-correcting. The hidden costs of maintaining the power system's reliability as the contribution of solar rises further tarnish the economic appeal of solar power. The state of California is already finding this out the hard way.

In 2013, the state, which had raced to a nationwide head start in installing solar power, started to ring alarm bells. The California Independent System Operator (CAISO), which operates the state's transmission grid, published a vivid chart displaying the evolution of the demands that the grid would face in the future (see figure 3.4). Each year, a new curve graphed the power that Californian consumers would expect the grid to deliver after they had consumed all of the solar power generated in the middle of the day. Plotted together, the various curves took on the unmistakable shape of . . . a duck. Excited to have boiled a complex concept down to a tractable bath toy, CAISO adopted the "duck curve" as the mascot of its campaign to educate the public about the difficulties of the renewable energy transition.

In 2012, when less than 3,000 megawatts (MW) of solar capacity existed in California, that curve had some gentle bumps, reflecting variations within the day of how much energy consumers use. Then, in 2013, the state nearly doubled its solar capacity. Because solar matched up well with consumer demand for power, it soaked up the usual rise in power consumption through midday and left a flat daytime demand profile for the rest of the generators serving California's grid to supply.[56]

But then, CAISO predicted, more solar on the grid would produce increasing amounts of power during the day, reducing the net daytime demand. That reduction would form the duck's belly. Especially on a cool spring day

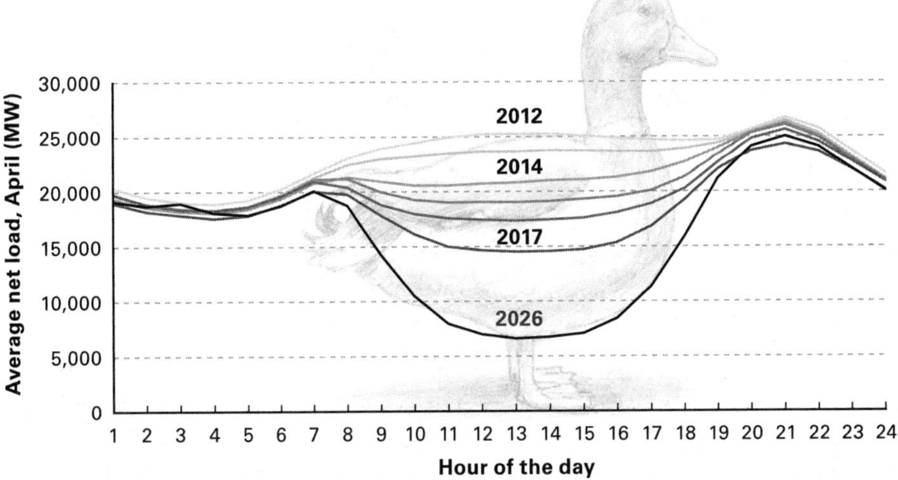

Figure 3.4

California's duck curve. This is an updated version of the original figure created by the California grid operator (CAISO) to predict the increasing strain on California's grid as the penetration of solar power increased. CAISO's original projection of a more than 1,000 MW/h ramp requirement in 2020 arrived three years ahead of schedule. By 2026, the requirement could be more than 4,000 MW/h.

Sources: GTM Research, CAISO, and Wood Mackenzie.

in April—too brisk for air conditioning but sunny enough for solar panels to churn out power—the duck's belly would deepen at midday. But then the sun would set, just as millions of Californians returned home from work. And at the same time in the evening, solar power production would plunge as power demand would surge, forming the duck's head. Altogether, by 2020 CAISO predicted that this would result in a mammoth "ramp," or change in output from all the other, nonsolar generators of more than 13,000 MW in the evening.

As it turned out, CAISO's projection came true—but in 2017, rather than in 2020—and it's only getting worse. The reason that grid operators obsess over the duck curve is that it places onerous, destructive demands on the nonsolar generators serving the grid. Meeting the ramp requirement from the duck's belly to its head requires an army of power plants—mostly fueled by natural gas—that are idling until the late afternoon, when they all have to start rapidly injecting power into the grid. This inefficient use of resources is expensive, entailing paying a fleet of generators to wait around until they are needed. And repeating this cycle every day induces wear and tear in power plants that are much happier if they are producing a steadier output with gentle changes.[57] None of these costs show up in the sticker price of solar panels, but solar imposes them on the grid nevertheless. Several studies have aimed to quantify these costs, and a typical estimate is that solar becomes up to 50 percent more expensive when the additional costs of integrating it onto the grid are taken into account.[58]

Other problems emerge as the duck gets fatter and taller. When the duck's belly—the remaining load after using up all the produced solar energy—dips below a certain level, other power plants that are much less flexible than natural gas plants need to be turned off. California has few of these other plants to worry about because the state is heavily reliant on natural gas plants, barely uses any energy generated by coal power, and is on track to shut down its last nuclear reactor. But elsewhere, power grids often rely on coal and nuclear plants for a large chunk of dependable, "baseload" power—it is expensive and disruptive to stop and restart those plants to accommodate excess solar energy on the grid.

Sometimes the pain that solar inflicts on other generators can rebound on solar itself. If it proves impossible or uneconomic to shut down baseload plants, grid operators may be forced to curtail, or throw away, excess solar power, often with no compensation. In 2017, this problem struck in California when the state got hit by a perfect storm, so to speak. After an extended drought, torrential downpours caused state reservoirs to overflow and run hydroelectric turbines at full tilt. This increase in hydropower combined with the surplus of solar power to produce so much oversupply that CAISO warned it might have to throw away electricity from a third of California's solar panels.[59]

California's solar generators get paid even when the power they produce goes unused. In China, by contrast, solar generators traditionally have not been paid when the grid operator curtails their output. Nearly 10 percent of all solar power in China was curtailed in 2016, and the proportion exceeded 30 percent in some provinces.[60] Things are getting a little better in China, where in 2016, the government ordered its utilities to compensate solar owners at least partially for curtailment. But in Europe, solar could be in trouble. Previously, solar and wind generators enjoyed an advantage known as "priority dispatch," under which other generators had to shut down first if the grid experienced excess power supply. But in 2016, the European Union announced new rules eliminating this special status for renewables and opening them up to curtailment.[61] Those rules did not decide the issue of whether solar owners will get paid if they are curtailed. Regardless of who foots the bill, curtailment creates costs, and the situation worsens as solar's penetration rises.

In addition to imposing costs on the grid, rising solar penetration could make the grid less reliable. California already faces challenges integrating intermittent renewable energy, but at 60 percent penetration of wind and solar power, CAISO frets that the whole grid could shut down if one of its conventional fossil-fueled power plants malfunctions. The 60 percent level may seem a long way off, but California's goal is for 50 percent renewable energy by 2030, and 60 percent soon thereafter—at least half of which would likely come from solar power.[62]

Historically, the grid has achieved reliability through a characteristic called "inertia." Conventional power plants all basically operate via the same principle—the heat from burning fossil fuels (or fission of nuclear fuels) is used to spin a shaft that runs an electrical generator. All the conventional generators connected to the grid have heavy masses spinning at the exact same speed, keeping the frequency of the power flowing through the grid very close to 60 Hz. When one generator breaks down, threatening to drag down the frequency of the grid, the inertia of the rest of the spinning generators pulls the frequency back up and gives grid operators time to ramp up a backup plant to fill the generation gap. But solar power has no moving parts. In other words, it has no inertia. So a grid dominated by solar could be at heightened risk of blackout owing to the lack of the built-in safety mechanism that the traditional grid's inertia offered.

Rising levels of solar can inflict still more problems on the grid, both at the local and global scales. If too many homeowners in a particular neighborhood install solar on their roofs and try to sell their power to the grid, they can overload local distribution circuits that were designed to deliver power from the grid to consumers, not the other way around. If there happens to be a momentary flicker in the power flows on one of these circuits, the inverters that connect rooftop solar panels to the grid can shut off, all at once, causing a blackout from an otherwise self-correcting blip.[63] At the global scale, too much solar can lead to temporary surges that a country's power grid can't handle and has to shunt across an international border.

For example, Germany's neighbors—Hungary, Poland, the Czech Republic, and Slovakia—have all complained that unexpected surplus power from Germany has compromised the healthy functioning of their own grids.

All of these issues are daunting headaches that are on track to accompany the rise of solar. So far, only a few frontier markets—most notably, California and Germany—have experienced them. But if solar is to increase its penetration around the world, it will impose economic and technical costs on power grids everywhere.

Necessity Is the Mother of Innovation

This array of obstacles to solar's rise might appear daunting, but none of them is intractable. What solar energy needs to surmount each one is innovation. Financial and business model innovation can drive massive amounts of investment in solar power, avoiding a capital crunch, and technological and systemic innovation can ensure that the cost of solar power remains lower than the value it provides, even as much more solar comes online.

In the near term, financial and business model innovation could expand the reach of existing solar PV technology. New financing techniques—likely borrowed from other sectors, but novel to renewable energy projects—could make it easier for institutional investors to plow vast sums of capital into solar power. And new business models, especially in the poorest parts of the world, could enable solar power to reach places that the traditional power grid has missed.

As more investment results in greater deployment of solar power projects around the world, an important knock-on effect will be continued declines in the cost of producing solar power. Rising solar deployment will drive demand for greater production of solar panels, which should reduce their cost of production. As figure 3.5 illustrates, solar panels have gotten cheaper as more of them have been produced worldwide, enabling panel producers to shave their costs by harnessing economies of scale and honing their production processes. And as more solar power projects are deployed in a particular region, it will become cheaper to bring the next one online because local firms will learn to reduce the costs of installing and permitting new projects.[64] So, if an influx of investment can support the deployment of solar power around the world, solar's costs should continue to fall. And by making it easier for the world's biggest investors to invest in solar

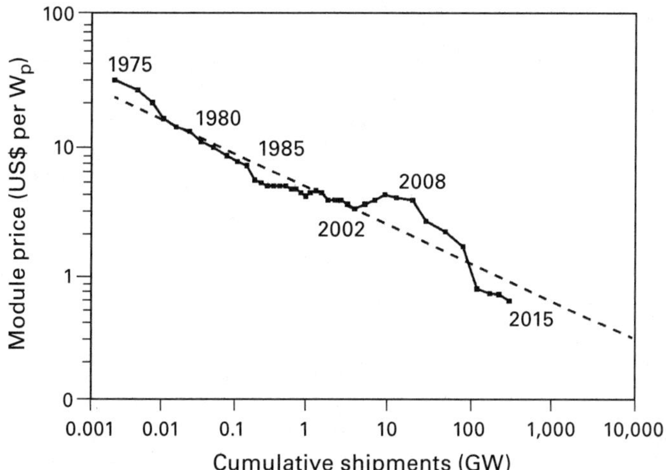

Figure 3.5

Historical and projected solar PV panel price declines. This chart displays the falling price of solar PV panels over time (the *y*-axis is logarithmic, so a straight line is actually an exponential decrease in cost over time). From 1975 to 2015, the price per watt of a solar PV panel fell approximately 18 percent for every doubling of cumulative production. Extrapolating the line that best fits the historical data through 2015 suggests that a solar PV panel could fall below $0.25/W after roughly 10,000 GW of panels have been cumulatively produced.

Source: Figure reprinted with permission from Sivaram and Kann (2016).

power, financial and business model innovation could unlock a virtuous cycle. Greater investment flows into the sector would drive down the cost of solar power, which in turn would make investing in solar even more attractive.

But that may not be enough. Making today's silicon solar PV technology cheaper by deploying more of it will result in important progress toward a midcentury target for solar to supply one-third of the world's electricity. In isolation, however, the cost of solar power is a meaningless quantity when it comes to determining whether it is economical to install more of it. As panel (1) on the left of figure 3.6 illustrates, even if the cost of solar falls as a result of increasing deployment, its value might fall even faster. That's because the more solar that is installed, the less that the electricity it generates in the middle of the day is needed. On top of this, higher levels of solar power strain the rest of the electricity system, imposing costs or, equivalently, reducing solar's value.

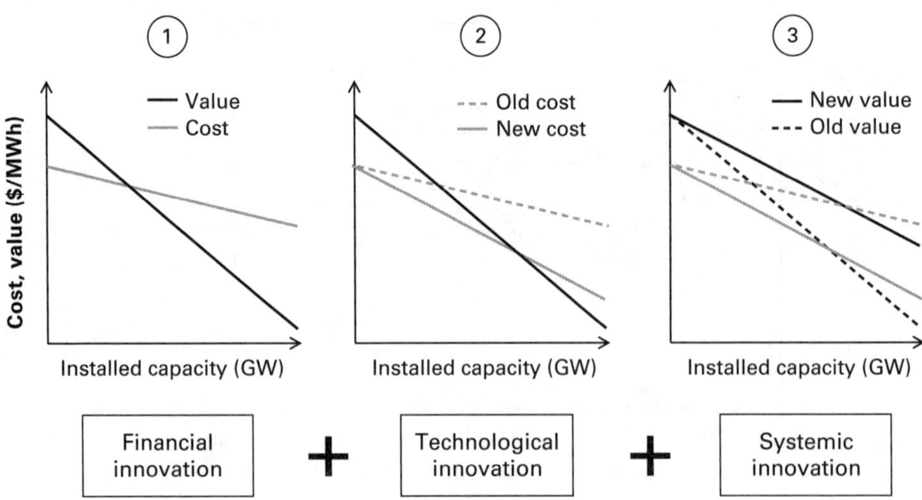

Figure 3.6
How three types of innovation can preserve solar's economic appeal. These three schematic graphs illustrate the effect of innovation on the global average cost and value of the next unit of electricity from solar PV panels as the total installed solar PV capacity increases worldwide.

At some point, it may not make sense to install another solar project because the electricity that it would generate would be worth less than the cost to deploy the project in the first place. Shayle Kann and I published a rough calculation suggesting that if solar PV met 30 percent of electricity demand, then the cost of a fully installed, utility-scale solar PV farm would need to plunge to 25 cents per watt to remain economical. We concluded that projects based on silicon solar PV panels are unlikely to achieve that target.[65] I do not mean to imply that existing technology has no chance of meeting this target. Bloomberg projects that the cost of solar power could fall by two-thirds by 2040, which is within striking distance of the three-quarters decline that we forecast solar will need to achieve. But the best available evidence today suggests a strong likelihood that the cost of electricity from existing solar PV technology will not be able to fall fast enough to stay below its value as PV penetration rises.

Here is where technological innovation comes in. Already, in laboratories around the world, scientists are making advances in developing highly efficient PV coatings made out of very inexpensive elements. Not only could such coatings be cheaper than solar panels based on existing silicon technology, but they could also reduce the land, equipment, labor, and other associated costs of installation. As panel (2) of figure 3.6 illustrates, if such PV technologies gain traction in the marketplace, they could sharply reduce the cost of electricity from solar projects. Then, the pace of solar cost reductions would be much faster than the gentle declines from rising deployment of existing technology. As a result, much more solar could be installed before the falling value caught up with the falling cost.

Yet, even superior solar PV technologies would generate electricity only based on how much sunlight there was—so the value of the electricity would still fall rapidly as a function of increasing solar deployment. Fortunately, other novel technologies, as well as a third type of innovation, systemic innovation, could arrest solar's declining value. Panel (3) shows the combined effect of all three types of innovation on the cost and value of electricity from solar installations. In addition to the faster cost declines carried over from panel (2), the value in panel (3) falls less quickly, such that cost remains below value no matter how much solar is deployed. In that case, solar's economic appeal remains strong even as its penetration rises. Importantly, note that the new, gently sloping line denoting solar's value in panel (3) would still intersect with the original cost line from panel (1) if enough solar capacity were installed. In other words, systemic innovation alone, without technological innovation, is insufficient. The lesson is that all three types of innovation are needed to make costs fall faster and value fall slower, thereby ensuring that cost remains below value as solar penetration rises.

How might it be possible to beat back value deflation even as more solar is installed? First, in addition to cheap PV coatings, technological innovation can serve up new solar technologies that feature built-in energy storage to turn intermittent sunlight into a reliable source of energy. For example, the next generation of concentrated solar power plants that convert the sun's rays into heat could store that heat throughout the night to generate electricity 24/7 efficiently and cheaply. Other technologies could store sunlight in the form of fuels to displace fossil fuels in activities that do not use electricity. Doing so will be essential to meeting the long-term target of supplying a majority of humanity's energy needs with solar energy sometime this century.

Still, intermittent solar PV will probably remain the leading method of harnessing sunlight for the foreseeable future. And that means that systemic innovation—refashioning the systems in which solar PV is embedded—will be essential to preventing solar's value from nose-diving as its penetration rises. This innovation has to start with power grids, which today are ill equipped to handle the fluctuating output from solar PV. Much larger power grids would have an easier time of matching volatile solar supply with diverse sources of demand, and a glut of solar on one part of the grid could be shipped to another time zone when it was in higher demand. And smarter grids could alert electricity consumers to continually tailor the consumption of their homes and businesses to better match with solar output.

To shore up the deteriorating value of solar photovoltaics, this revamped power grid will need to be connected to a diverse mix of power plants and energy storage resources. Solar itself will need to become a better citizen of the grid, and smart inverters—the electronic devices that connect solar power to the grid—could re-create the inertia that today's solar panels fail to supply to the grid.[66] On top of this, reliable, zero-carbon power plants like nuclear reactors and fossil-fueled plants that capture and store their carbon emissions could adjust their power output to compensate for swings in solar power. Deploying nuclear and fossil-fueled plants could face political, economic, and technical obstacles, though, so solar PV will also depend on various technologies, like batteries and hydroelectric reservoirs, to store its energy for when it is needed most.

A final element of systemic innovation to countervail value deflation is the integration of sectors that traditionally have not used electricity—such as the transportation and heating sectors—altering those sectors so that they derive some of their needs from electricity instead of from burning fossil fuels.[67] For example, fleets of electric vehicles plugging into the grid could actually serve as mobile batteries to store solar power and slim down the fattening duck curve.[68] The possibilities don't end there. Indeed, as freshwater becomes increasingly scarce as a result of climate change, solar-powered desalination could kill two birds with one stone—providing fresh water and storing excess solar power in the form of water.

All these examples of systemic innovation could prop up the value of electricity from increasingly abundant solar PV. But none of them is a silver bullet. For instance, despite all the hype around the falling cost of lithium-ion batteries (the same ones used in power cell phones and electric vehicles and which are now increasingly being used to back up the power grid), battery storage still makes up roughly 1 percent of the total energy storage on grids around the world. The rest is mostly in the form of hydropower facilities that have existed for decades and store energy by pumping water uphill.[69] Moreover, batteries are great for buffering short-term variations in the output of solar power, but their economics and functionality are ill suited to store energy for periods much longer than a few hours—and solar's output varies strongly by season. So although the use of batteries may grow rapidly, they'll be only part of the solution to combatting solar value deflation.

Systemic innovation is also limited in how much it can preserve solar's value. One study set out to find the limits of strategies to fight value deflation by forecasting California's future grid with rose-tinted glasses. The study's extremely ambitious scenario assumed that the cost of storage would fall 80 percent faster than expected by 2030, and that consumers would respond like robots to instantly changing power prices set by utilities to better align electricity demand with fluctuating solar supply. The researchers found that less than half of the value deflation caused by high solar penetration would disappear.[70] So without technological innovation to make solar PV much cheaper, systemic innovation may not be enough to prevent solar's value from falling below its costs.

The safest strategy, then, is to bet on all three types of innovation, recognizing that each has an important role to play in decreasing the costs of solar power, preserving its value, and ensuring that its rise continues uninterrupted. The good news is that financial and business model innovation appears to be proceeding rapidly, so chances are good that massive pools of new investment will help push existing technology to its limits. That achievement could also benefit new technologies, which—once they mature and can be commercialized—could enjoy ready access to sophisticated markets and investors.

But the bad news is that technological and systemic innovation is lagging. This is particularly true of technological innovation, which needs far more investment from both governments and private firms in order to flourish. Systemic innovation also requires policymakers around the world to take action, for example by investing in upgrading power grids and reworking regulations to encourage a diverse set of zero-carbon sources to complement solar power. If they can muster the political will to invest in all three forms of innovation, a bright future awaits, in which solar becomes humanity's primary energy source.

PART II TEACHING AN OLD TECHNOLOGY NEW TRICKS

Highlights

- The expanding deployment of existing solar photovoltaic (PV) panels could hit a ceiling, falling short of the midcentury target of supplying a third of global power needs. But for the next decade, while new technologies emerge and scale up, existing ones could make substantial progress toward the target, supplying a double-digit percentage share of global electricity demand. *Financial and business model innovations are on track to make this possible.*
- For installed solar PV capacity to grow by an order of magnitude, it will need massive amounts of new capital investment, on the scale of many trillions of dollars. Those sums are pocket change for deep-pocketed institutional investors, like pension or insurance funds. Chapter 4, "Chasing Capital," reports on how the solar industry is starting to apply the financial engineering used to fund cars, homes, or oil pipelines to finance solar projects of every size. And large companies that have historically owned fossil-fueled power plants are reorienting their business models to target solar, serving as conduits that direct abundant investor capital toward the right projects. Public policy can speed these activities up through providing judicious incentives or assurances to skittish investors, but governments should avoid creating long-term dependencies.
- In addition, existing solar technologies are poised to make progress on one of the most intractable challenges obstructing economic development: energy access. Across sub-Saharan Africa and South Asia, more than a billion people still lack access to electricity. But entrepreneurs are scaling up innovative business models that harness cheaper PV panels, more

energy-efficient appliances, and virtually ubiquitous cell phones to sign up droves of new electricity customers. Chapter 5, "From Charity Case to Business Case," profiles some of the nimble start-ups, from East Africa to India, marketing off-grid solar power that rural villagers can pay for by cell phone. In some cases, off-grid solar PV is powering microgrids, which connect whole communities and one day could link up with the main grid—if it ever arrives. Again, policymakers should take care not to create dependencies on public policy; the first order of business is actually for the government to get out of the way of vibrant private innovation.

Chapter 4 Chasing Capital

Through the first half of 2015, SunEdison looked unstoppable. A developer of massive, utility-scale solar projects, the company was surfing a wave of expansion in renewable energy markets around the world. Over the past decade, the global installed capacity of solar had risen from just 4 gigawatts (GW) to nearly 200 GW. And yet solar had just breached the 1 percent threshold as a share of the world's electricity, implying decades worth of growth to come.[1]

Recognizing the market's inexorable growth, SunEdison signed contracts around the world, from Asia to Africa to Latin America, to build massive solar farms. It also went on a buying binge between 2014 and 2015, spending nearly $5 billion on acquiring a global wind energy developer and a major U.S. installer of rooftop solar. Financial analysts parroted SunEdison's executives, who called the company the next energy "supermajor."[2] That characterization was speculative, but not wildly so: in July of that year, the company's market value would peak at over $9 billion.[3] CEO Ahmad Chatila had Exxon, the world's biggest oil company, in his sights, remarking: "Their market cap is around $400 billion. That's what we're going after."[4]

That spring, I invited Chatila to share his grand vision for the future at a lunch roundtable at the Council on Foreign Relations. He gave an optimistic and inspiring talk. Afterward, as we debriefed, I asked why he had moved the company away from developing solar technology to instead financing and building projects with off-the-shelf solar panels. Chatila's response surprised me, given that he was an engineer by training, with decades of experience in Silicon Valley's research-intensive microchip industry. Exiting the solar manufacturing business was the best decision he had ever made, he assured me, because the engineering behind solar panels wasn't where the value lay.

The future of the industry, he contended, was the development of ingenious ways to raise the necessary up-front capital to construct new solar projects. In fact, in the early 2000s, SunEdison had invented the "solar-as-a-service" business model, in which the company would take out loans to construct large solar installations for its commercial clients, who would then pay for the generated power for decades to come. Now SunEdison would pin its strategy for the future on a new financial innovation: the YieldCo.

The YieldCo was a seductive idea. Simply put, it is a collection of renewable energy projects packaged into a company that is publicly listed. By selling shares on the stock market, this company then can raise capital to purchase new renewable energy projects. A liquid investment that any retail or institutional investor can trade, YieldCos offered the tantalizing prospect of deepening the capital pool available to fund solar power.

What's more, SunEdison realized that by creating a YieldCo, it would create a customer that would purchase the solar projects SunEdison developed and supply the funds to build even more projects. Enamored by the model, SunEdison actually created two YieldCos—one focused on projects in the United States and another that would buy up projects across the developing world—and it aggressively advertised shares in these new companies to stock market investors. Investors gobbled up the shares, wooed by SunEdison's promises of soaring stock prices and fat dividends. A few market analysts wondered aloud if the YieldCo model was too good to be true, but most ignored the naysayers; SunEdison assumed that its YieldCos would supply the cash it needed to continue its breakneck growth.[5]

As it turned out, the model was indeed too good to be true. Just a year after I hosted its triumphant CEO, SunEdison completed an astonishingly fast fall from grace, declaring bankruptcy under the crushing weight of its $16 billion debt load (figure 4.1). Spooked by a perfect storm of unfortunate events—including a crash in the price of oil and rumblings from the U.S. Federal Reserve about an interest rate hike—investors had dumped their YieldCo holdings. The share prices of SunEdison's two YieldCos tumbled, undercutting the YieldCos' ability to purchase projects from their parent. SunEdison would later face lawsuits for plundering the remaining cash of the ostensibly independent YieldCos to make its debt payments.[6] Once the cash flows from the YieldCos dried up, SunEdison was left with no option but to fold.

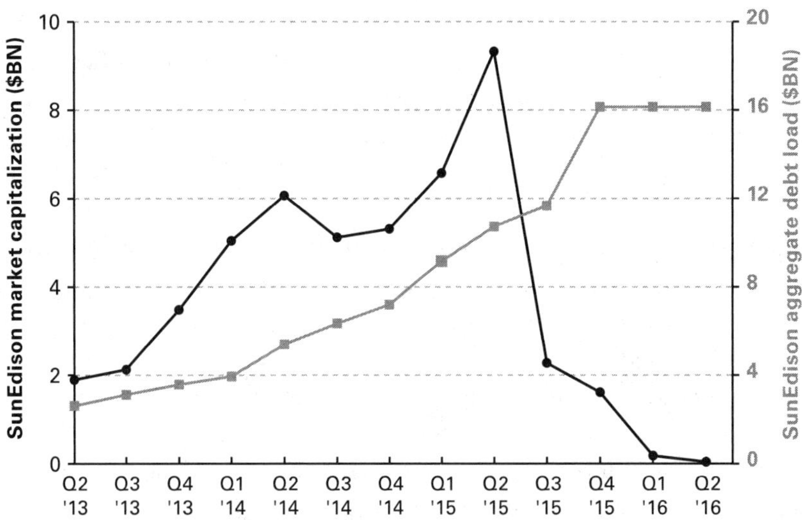

Figure 4.1

SunEdison's market value crushed by mounting debt. The left *y*-axis measures SunEdison's market value (filled circles), which peaked at nearly \$10 billion in 2015 before the company declared bankruptcy in April 2016. The right *y*-axis measures the company debt burden (filled squares), which soared to more than \$16 billion as SunEdison acquired companies and expanded its project pipeline around the world. Source: Bloomberg.

In the wake of SunEdison's collapse, analysts scrambled to determine what went wrong. Was this the end of financial engineering in solar? Was it simply unrealistic to expect that a solar energy supermajor might rise up to challenge conventional fossil fuel supermajors? The right answer to both questions is no. SunEdison flopped because of its overly aggressive growth strategy, questionable governance of its YieldCos, and rash accumulation of debt.

But Chatila was not wrong in his conviction that financial innovation could enable the solar industry to rapidly scale up the deployment of existing solar panel technology. SunEdison's mistakes were its own, but they do not contradict the broader wisdom of finding ways to enable new investors to fund solar projects that line up well with their investment criteria. And although its failure is a setback for the industry, SunEdison will not be the last ascendant solar company with the potential to rival the oil majors.

In fact, although a rapidly growing solar sector needs more funding than its current investors can provide, there is reason to be optimistic that financial and business model innovation will deliver trillions of dollars of new investment in the coming decades. Fundamentally, projects based on existing solar technology are remarkably safe investments. Today's solar photovoltaic (PV) installations are simple infrastructure projects that, once built, produce power for decades. And solar's costs are falling predictably, making the business case increasingly compelling. Given these characteristics, solar power lines up well with the needs of deep-pocketed institutional investors around the world. All of this suggests that it is only a matter of time before new approaches dramatically expand the pool of capital available to fund solar power.

The financial innovation needed to expand this pool of capital does not require reinventing the wheel. Under Schumpeter's paradigm (see box 3.1 in chapter 3), an innovation is an invention that has been brought to market. So adapting novel financial instruments from other sectors and popularizing them for the first time in the solar sector exemplifies financial innovation. According to New York's energy czar, Richard Kauffman, there is plenty of inspiration to be drawn from other sectors of the economy to augment funding sources for solar projects:

> Projects in the [United States] rely upon an old-fashioned and anachronistic form of financing that is different than how other parts of the U.S. economy are financed. Rather than use bond or stock markets, projects depend on non-capital market sources of so-called tax equity, bank debt, and private equity where rates of return can approach typical private equity rates of return of 12–15 percent. [New strategies] . . . don't require going to the lab; they involve applying financing techniques that have already been invented and are used widely in other parts of the economy, but have not yet been applied to this sector.[7]

Kauffman is suggesting that by tapping public capital markets, the solar industry can finance projects at a lower cost of capital—the rate of return demanded by the investors who provide the capital—than it can using funds from its existing, private sources.

To deploy solar projects, the industry needs to recruit two types of capital: equity capital and debt capital. Investors provide equity capital to a company in return for an ownership stake, and they provide debt capital in return for a promise to be paid back at a later date with interest. The cheapest equity capital can be raised on public stock markets, through which investors purchase stakes in listed companies and earn returns through increases in share prices or dividend payouts. And even more than equity, the industry needs debt capital, which tends to be cheaper than equity capital and therefore represents the majority of infrastructure funding. The cheapest debt capital can be raised on public bond markets, through which investors can make loans for a predetermined period and receive interest payments in the meantime. Accessing these two public capital markets would connect the solar industry to a broad range of investors, including deep-pocketed institutional investors hungry to fund infrastructure.

To tap public stock markets, the industry can emulate a strategy applied by the oil and gas industry to raise public equity capital for infrastructure projects, such as transcontinental pipelines. Indeed, the YieldCo was originally modeled after a common financial vehicle from the oil and gas industry. Clearly, this imitation was not entirely successful, but the industry is already working on tweaks to attract capital for solar projects without running the risk of another SunEdison-esque implosion. To access public bond markets, especially to fund small, distributed solar projects through debt capital, the industry can employ the strategy that the real estate and automobile industries use to make owning a home or driving a car affordable to millions of Americans: bundle a diverse portfolio of consumer loans into a tradable security attractive to investors. Ironically, that strategy, known as "securitization," was the culprit behind the Great Recession of 2009. But by meticulously collecting and analyzing data from solar projects to ensure that investors can accurately assess the risk they won't be paid back, the industry can safely and profitably take advantage of securitization.

But it will take more than deep-pocketed investors to speed the deployment of solar PV projects. The oil and gas industry benefits from supermajors who use their substantial balance sheets to identify and develop new projects. Similarly, large corporations will need to undertake the initial risk of developing solar installations and serving as a conduit to direct capital from wealthy investors to worthy projects. The power sector has such behemoths, but only some of them are in a position to embrace solar. In the United States, regulated electric utilities—which own and operate the grid and are subject to strict government scrutiny—are often fixated on the potential threat from distributed solar power. By contrast, unregulated power companies in the United States and abroad are aggressively seeking investment opportunities in solar, most in utility-scale projects. And even corporations outside the energy sector, including technology giants such as Google and Microsoft, are beginning to invest in solar power in a big way.

The private sector must be front and center in financing solar power. But the public sector has an important role to play as well. If governments intelligently deploy their resources—which are scarce compared to solar's capital needs—they can mobilize much more funding from the private sector. State and local governments have already unveiled a variety of innovative approaches to encourage private investment flows, for example by marshalling public borrowing power to direct capital toward solar. National governments around the world are also rolling out initiatives to attract capital, such as by helping foreign investors hedge against the risk of local currency depreciation. And multinational institutions, including the World Bank, are deploying credit enhancement mechanisms, which make the terms of investing in solar power more attractive. Importantly, governments should avoid indiscriminate incentives that make solar power dependent on public funds. Only if solar projects have the potential to be profitable will financial engineering and public incentives succeed in unlocking large flows of private capital.

The proliferation of innovative approaches for directing capital toward solar power is a promising start. Perhaps from the ashes of SunEdison's flameout will emerge a genuine solar supermajor.

Toward YieldCo 2.0

The example from the oil and gas industry that inspired renewable energy YieldCos was a decades-old financial vehicle known as the "Master Limited Partnership (MLP)." An MLP pools together a diversified portfolio of oil and gas infrastructure assets, such as pipelines and processing facilities. Investors then can buy shares of MLPs on the stock market. MLPs get special treatment under the U.S. tax code: they pay no corporate tax and can distribute the revenue generated by their oil and gas assets directly to shareholders as dividends. MLPs are hugely popular because they are liquid (i.e., investors can readily trade their shares on the stock market), they diversify risk through pooling many assets, and shareholders can expect reliable dividends. In 2016, publicly listed MLPs were worth roughly a half-trillion dollars.[8]

If solar power projects could be bundled together into MLPs and listed on public stock markets, the industry would be able to tap into nearly limitless pools of equity capital, just as the oil and gas industry has. That's because the world's largest investors are hungry for new opportunities to invest in infrastructure—so much so that from 2013 to 2017, the number of institutional investors holding infrastructure assets more than doubled.[9] Investors that are even more active, such as private equity funds, are also looking for stable infrastructure investments (witness a $40 billion partnership in 2017 between the Public Investment Fund, a Saudi Arabian sovereign wealth fund, and Blackstone, a private equity investor, that is structured for long-term infrastructure holdings.[10])

Infrastructure investors seek opportunities to park their capital and harvest reliable income for several years or even decades without having to worry about reinvesting their money in new assets. Solar PV projects fit the bill. Yet they can't be bundled into MLPs because of U.S. tax code restrictions enacted thirty years ago, well before it became clear that investors would have much appetite for including solar power projects in their portfolios. After oil and gas companies formed the first MLPs in the 1980s, the practice caught on in unrelated sectors—the Boston Celtics even became an MLP—because of the resulting tax benefits. Seeking to block tax evasion but also encourage some forms of investment, in 1987, Congress restricted the scope of MLP income to activities such as the production and transportation of depletable natural resources. More recently, as renewable energy has grown in importance, lawmakers have tried in vain to amend the U.S. tax code. In 2012, Senators Chris Coons (D-DE) and Jerry Moran (R-KS) introduced a bipartisan bill, the MLP Parity Act, to allow MLPs to include renewable energy assets, but the legislation never passed.[11]

Undeterred, some energy companies devised the YieldCo structure as a way to approximate an MLP. In 2013, the American power company NRG listed the first public YieldCo, NRG Yield, setting off a wave of fifteen U.S. and European YieldCo offerings over the next two years.[12] They all followed the basic MLP model by bundling together a diverse portfolio of renewable energy projects, listing on the stock market, and paying quarterly dividends to shareholders. Most YieldCos held a portfolio of large, utility-scale solar and wind energy projects, although some ventured into owning smaller, rooftop solar installations as well.

Soon the European and American YieldCos began to diverge in their approaches. European YieldCos were basically holding companies, offering investors little more than a convenient way to invest in a bundle of renewable energy projects. But American companies had ambitious plans for the YieldCos that they created. Some of those firms, such as NRG and Nextera, owned conventional power plants and saw solar and wind projects as an attractive way to diversify their assets. Others were pure-play solar developers, such as SunEdison, SunPower, and First Solar, who wanted to stake out their share of a growing solar market. Both kinds of firms saw their YieldCos not only as a way to bring more capital into the solar industry, but also as a way to goose their own growth.

This motivation led to a clever partnership between parent sponsors (such as NRG or SunEdison) and their YieldCo children. Here's how it worked. The sponsor would create a publicly listed YieldCo—advertised as an independent company—but retain some degree of control over its operations, such as through a majority ownership stake or board seats. Then the sponsor and the YieldCo would split up the low- and high-risk aspects of developing a renewable energy project. The sponsor would take on high-risk activities, like obtaining land and government permits, building a solar farm, and finding a long-term buyer for the power. The YieldCo, by contrast, would undertake the lower-risk activities of owning and operating a diverse portfolio of projects.

This separation of high- and low-risk activities, then, would allow both sponsor and YieldCo to make money when the YieldCo purchased a project from its parent. The sponsor would sell newly constructed projects at a high-enough price tag to return its investors a healthy premium for the risk that they had assumed. But the YieldCo would view the same price tag as affordable because its shareholders would not demand hefty returns on a low-risk investment. In fact, shareholders saw the reliable dividends—payouts from the sale of solar power produced by the projects that YieldCos owned—as a terrific alternative to the near-zero returns from U.S. government bonds and other safe investments.[13]

So far, so good. But sponsors oversold the potential of their YieldCos to investors—a tactic that ultimately doomed the model. No sponsor went as far as SunEdison in spinning the fantasy that YieldCos would mint money for their investors. Not only could shareholders in its first YieldCo expect reliable dividends, SunEdison promised, but they could also look forward to surging growth in those dividends—north of 30 percent a year.[14]

How could such gains be achieved, given that the dividends should have merely reflected the stable revenue streams of the underlying solar projects?

Well, SunEdison insisted, it was possible because its YieldCos would continue to buy new projects, which would generate new revenues. SunEdison assured investors that those new projects would be "accretive"—that is, they would increase the YieldCos' value, boosting share prices and enabling the YieldCos to raise even more cheap money on public markets to buy more projects. The model was a frenetic upward spiral—a virtuous cycle that guaranteed that everyone would make money.[15]

Investors lapped it all up. Most of them were major investors in oil and gas MLPs and salivated at the prospect of a familiar investment vehicle with jaw-dropping growth prospects. By the summer of 2015, they had bid up YieldCo market values to a collective $28 billion, over double their market debut.[16] But the euphoria didn't last long: Just as YieldCo values spiraled upward, so too were they vulnerable to a vicious downward cycle. If their share prices dropped, the dividend yields would necessarily rise, and the YieldCo no longer could afford to buy expensive solar projects from the parent developer and still pay their shareholders the expected dividends. This stagnation would depress share prices further and continue the downward spiral.

That the transition from upward to downward spiral happened in July 2015 was a matter of happenstance—a confluence of random events that by themselves should not have had much of an effect on the solar industry. Nevertheless, it was the perfect storm. Oil prices crashed by 20 percent, spooking the MLP investors who had piled into YieldCos; panicked, they sold off both the MLPs and YieldCos. This sell-off may not have been totally rational—after all, solar projects produce electricity, and oil fuels vehicles. The two do not often compete, and they basically never do in the United States (although some countries, such as Saudi Arabia, do use oil to generate power).

Investors were also spooked by statements from U.S. Federal Reserve policymakers who all but guaranteed an imminent hike in interest rates. A rate hike would mean that YieldCos would face competition from government bonds and other safe investments, whose returns suddenly would be more attractive. On top of all this, four YieldCos issued shares worth $2 billion in June and July, pumping a new supply of YieldCo stock into the market just as skittish investors did not want it anymore. As a result, YieldCo share prices plunged (figure 4.2). Both of SunEdison's YieldCos would lose over 80 percent of their market value over the next six months. SunEdison's demise

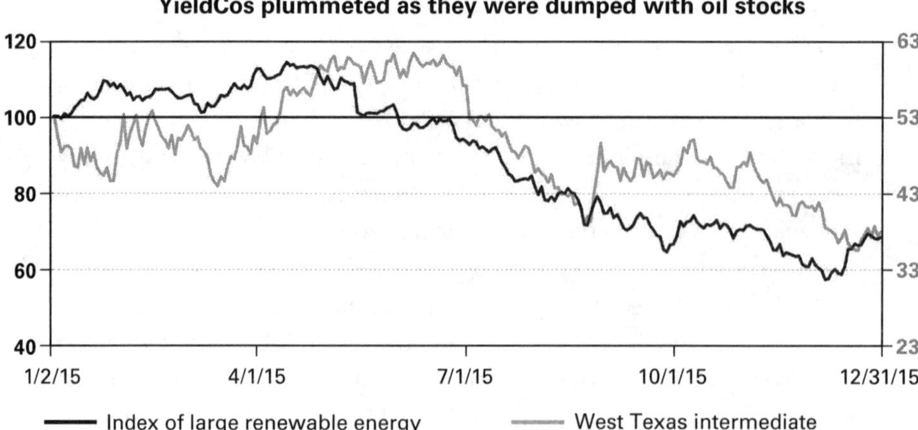

Figure 4.2

Crash in 2015 oil prices and U.S. YieldCo market values. The left *y*-axis measures a weighted average of YieldCo share prices on the stock market, which increased by 15 percent in the first half of 2015 before shedding half their value later that year. The right *y*-axis measures the price of oil in the United States, which increased above $60 per barrel in April 2015 before crashing to less than $40 per barrel.
Source: Sivaram (2016).

followed shortly thereafter, when it could no longer service the mountain of debt that it had taken on to build solar projects that its YieldCos no longer could afford to buy.[17]

Ironically, throughout this period of upheaval, solar power projects remained fundamentally attractive investments because falling costs made them even more economically competitive. But, by pursuing rapid growth, U.S. YieldCos managed to nullify this basic advantage of a portfolio of solar projects as being a safe haven from the volatile stock market. By relying on the growth-driven upward spiral, YieldCo sponsors baked rising share prices into the YieldCo business model. In doing so, they made the success of a YieldCo more dependent on whether the rest of the market was rising or falling. By one estimate, this additional risk added a hefty 2 percentage points to the cost of YieldCo equity, making it harder for them to raise low-cost capital.[18]

Sponsors also managed to convert another potential YieldCo strength into a weakness by exerting their control over YieldCo business decisions.

In theory, YieldCos should be low-risk vehicles that own and operate existing projects, isolated from the higher risk that project developers assume. But some sponsors, such as SunEdison, forced their YieldCos to guarantee that they would purchase projects before they were complete, thus transferring the associated construction risk. Moreover, when times got tough for SunEdison, it tried to raid the cash holdings of its global YieldCo. When the YieldCo's management protested, SunEdison overhauled the YieldCo's board of directors. Magically, the new board immediately agreed to transfer $150 million to SunEdison.[19] But by tying its YieldCos to its own volatile fortunes, SunEdison further swelled the risk of what should have been a boring, independent holding company.

Since the bubble burst, the share prices of surviving American YieldCos have become much more comparable to their European cousins, which have steadily maintained modest valuations. In particular, YieldCos in the United Kingdom have followed a much less ambitious model that could serve as a more stable vehicle for use around the world. U.K. YieldCos tend not to be affiliated with a particular sponsor, insulating them from external meddling. And they are designed to grow very modestly, in line with inflation, rather than to gobble up new projects to fuel share price and dividend growth. Finally, they rely less heavily on debt than their U.S. counterparts did, further reducing risk.

Not everything is perfect about these vehicles. In particular, U.K. YieldCos tend to have limited diversity in the projects that they own. Still, the general contours of the U.K. YieldCo—a modest holding company that offers a liquid investment opportunity in safe renewable energy assets—are promising. And the model is not confined just to the developed world. For example, in India, firms are looking to publicly list infrastructure investment trusts that could house solar projects, among other assets. Having learned from the U.S. YieldCo crash, Indian regulators are imposing rules that would prevent a single sponsor from exerting too much control over these vehicles.[20]

Some analysts have proposed taking a step further to create a YieldCo 2.0 that would solve all the problems of the initial U.S. version. The Climate Policy Initiative calls such a financial vehicle a "Clean Energy Investment Trust." It would largely resemble a European YieldCo, but it would bundle together a much broader pool of renewable energy projects (probably across international borders and from multiple different developers) to build a diversified portfolio without reliance on a single sponsor. Deep-pocketed institutional investors would be involved from the earliest stages of forming this vehicle to ensure that it would have low management fees, would distribute all the revenues from the underlying projects back to investors, and would be forbidden from adding new projects and chasing growth.[21]

In the future, publicly traded vehicles (the moniker "YieldCo" may go out of fashion, but the underlying concept should endure) might raise cheap equity capital for a diverse range of solar assets, not just utility-scale solar farms. Although the first generation of such vehicles largely focused on raising equity capital for large-scale projects, the strategy of bundling assets into a holding company in which stock market investors can buy ownership stakes works just as well for smaller, distributed assets, such as rooftop solar. And if they proliferate, YieldCos may also specialize, each one catering to a different market niche.[22]

The bright side of the YieldCo 1.0 fiasco is that the solar industry has learned its lesson and is moving toward financial vehicles that could attract new investors without adding undesirable risks to the sector. And back in the United States, in addition to redesigning the YieldCo model, solar firms are redoubling their efforts to convince Congress to alter the tax code to make it legal for renewable energy projects to be housed within MLPs. They are also lobbying lawmakers to make it legal to include renewable energy projects in real estate investment trusts (REITs). Both of these moves would enable tried-and-true financial vehicles to be used to direct capital toward solar power.[23]

The solar industry is maturing after a tumultuous boom-and-bust cycle. As it contemplates revising its strategy to tap public markets for equity capital, it now appears to be on track to balance financial innovation with a lower risk appetite, which is promising. But what about debt capital? SunEdison found itself crushed under its mounting debt load. Can the broader solar industry avoid the perils of too much leverage while still using financial engineering to expand the available pool of capital?

Securitization Blanket

At first blush, it might be unsettling that the financial trick that some solar companies are using to attract cheaper debt capital is the same maneuver that helped cause the Great Recession. Investment banks used that trick, securitization, to bundle, slice, and dice subprime mortgage loans from around the country. They managed to hoodwink the ratings agencies into certifying that the resulting high-risk derivatives were low-risk, but no amount of financial engineering could take garbage in and spit anything but garbage out. When this reality became clear, the global economy collapsed.

But there is good reason to be optimistic that securitization won't end in disaster when it comes to financing distributed solar installations on the roofs of homes and businesses. There's nothing intrinsically wrong with securitization, which is a general term that just refers to pooling many assets together to create securities that investors can then buy and trade. In fact, the process of bundling together a diverse portfolio of loans is a tried-and-true way to reduce risk. By carefully vetting each of the underlying loans, one can be confident that they won't all go bad at once.

Beginning in the 1970s, banks began to securitize mortgage loans, bundling them together to create mortgage-backed securities, which investors then could purchase. In subsequent decades, these securities gave rise to the more general category of asset-backed securities, which offer investors an opportunity to invest in everything from auto and student loans to Domino's Pizza franchise royalties.

In the run-up to the financial crisis, Wall Street abused securitization by packaging subprime mortgage-backed securities together into an arcane entity known as a "collateralized debt obligation." But since the crash, federal regulators have reined in these abuses, and asset-backed security markets are thriving again. Today, the U.S. mortgage-backed security market is worth about $9 trillion, and the asset-backed security market is worth $1.4 trillion. Attracting these enormous sums of capital has made it possible for Americans to engage in activities with an up-front cost they wouldn't normally be able to afford. For example, only 14 percent of consumers bought cars outright in 2015. Instead, 55 percent took out an auto loan, and a further 31 percent drove off the lot without actually owning the car, thanks to an auto lease.[24] Car companies finance loans and leases for consumers and then sell asset-backed securities on bond markets, freeing up capital to provide even more loans and leases. (Some analysts have warned, however, that rising subprime auto lending has inflated a dangerous auto asset-backed security bubble, waiting to pop.[25])

The auto industry's success in promoting car leases and loans could be a model for the solar industry—provided that it scrupulously avoids risky lending practices. Indeed, the two asset categories are comparably valued—in 2015, the average U.S. car sold for a little more than $30,000, and the average residential solar installation in California cost around $20,000.[26,27] And as is true in the auto industry, both leases and loans play important roles in financing distributed solar installations. In 2016, roughly half of all residential solar in the United States was leased by companies that, like SolarCity (now part of Tesla), retained ownership over the installations; the other half was owned by customers, who typically took out loans to finance the up-front cost. As the cost of solar falls, customers are increasingly choosing to own, rather than lease, their solar systems; by 2019, two-thirds of new customers are projected to own their solar systems.[28] But the capacity of solar providers to offer loans to customers is limited by their modest balance sheets.

That's where securitization comes in. The stable cash flow from customers making monthly payments over multiple decades makes distributed solar investments a natural fit for institutional investors.[29] If solar providers can sell securitized loans and leases to investors, they can expand rapidly to serve enormous untapped distributed solar markets. One meticulous 2015 study of buildings across the United States found that rooftop solar has the technical potential to power 40 percent of national electricity demand.[30] That figure is an extreme upper bound, but it gives a sense of how much room rooftop solar has to grow from its present role supplying just a fraction of a percent of U.S. power. And as the cost of rooftop solar has fallen, the number of U.S. homes and businesses installing solar has risen, driving annual market growth of more than 40 percent from 2008 to 2014.[31] Today, there is twice as much solar capacity on residential rooftops than on larger buildings.[32] And substantial untapped potential remains, although growth has been limited by the availability of financing.

Outside of the United States, there is also tremendous potential to expand rooftop solar, both in the developed and developing world. In particular, India has set an aggressive target of 40 GW of rooftop solar by 2022. But there, too, limited access to finance remains the biggest barrier to rooftop solar growth.[33]

In the United States, securitization to raise debt capital to deploy distributed solar is gaining momentum. From 2013 to 2016, distributed solar providers, led by SolarCity, raised more than $1 billion by selling securities backed by residential solar assets on bond markets.[34] In a securitization, a

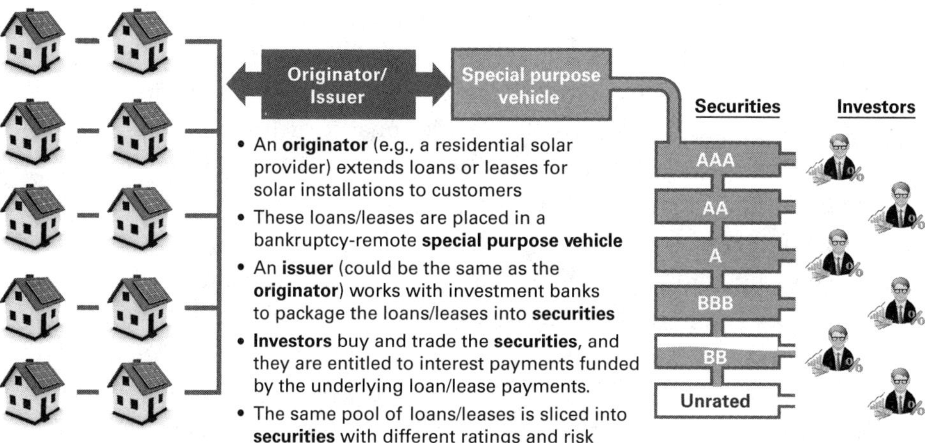

Originator/
Issuer
Special purpose
vehicle
Securities
Investors
• An **originator** (e.g., a residential solar provider) extends loans or leases for solar installations to customers
• These loans/leases are placed in a bankruptcy-remote **special purpose vehicle**
• An **issuer** (could be the same as the **originator**) works with investment banks to package the loans/leases into **securities**
• **Investors** buy and trade the **securities**, and they are entitled to interest payments funded by the underlying loan/lease payments.
• The same pool of loans/leases is sliced into **securities** with different ratings and risk
AAA
AA
A
BBB
BB
Unrated

Figure 4.3

How solar securitization works. (Note that the ratings of the securities on the right side are aspirational—through 2016, no solar securitization has resulted in the issuance of AA- or higher-rated bonds.)

solar provider bundles a diverse portfolio of loans for rooftop solar installations into a special-purpose vehicle, which is a way to protect the loans even if the solar provider were to go bankrupt (figure 4.3). Then the provider issues securities to fixed-income investors, who receive interest payments funded by the cash flow from the underlying loans. And with the loans off the solar provider's books, the provider is free to finance new solar installations.

As securitization grows in popularity, some companies, such as Mosaic Solar, are focusing exclusively on securitizing loans for solar installed by other providers.[35] A good sign that investors are getting comfortable with securitization is the steady increase in the advance rate (the percentage of the value of the underlying loans that investors are willing to buy in the form of securities). Between 2013 and 2016, the advance rate for new solar securitizations climbed from 62 percent to 75 percent. At those levels, it is starting to approach the advance rates of over 90 percent for auto and mortgage securitizations, with which investors are intimately familiar.[36]

Moreover, an innovative approach, called "warehousing," has emerged to fill the capital gap to get solar installations up and running in the first place so that securitization can then proceed. This strategy entails raising capital from investors and donors to fund several developers to construct a portfolio, or warehouse, of rooftop solar projects and sign contracts with customers to make monthly loan or lease payments. Once the warehouse is assembled, it can issue securities and pay back the warehouse investors. In 2014, Connecticut's Green Bank helped finance such a warehouse, demonstrating the role that the public sector can play in mobilizing private finance. Now international development banks are looking to deploy the warehousing strategy in the developing world to raise the capital needed to build rooftop projects and make it possible to securitize them.[37]

Nevertheless, there are still obstacles to more widespread use of securitization as a way of financing distributed solar installations. As interest rates creep up in the United States, the yields on newly issued solar securities also have risen—from 4.8 percent to 6.25 percent between 2013 and 2016. This uptick makes it more expensive to raise capital, which might dampen the growth of distributed solar. Moreover, few companies have a large and diverse enough portfolio of solar assets to do their own securitization. Until smaller solar providers begin to pool their assets together and jointly securitize them, then, the market for these securities may remain small and illiquid, which is undesirable for prospective investors.

Regulatory changes could also slow the momentum behind securitization. In most U.S. states, owners of distributed solar power can send excess power that they don't consume on site to the grid, canceling out some of the power that they consume from the grid at other times, like at night. The rule that allows this is called "net metering," and utilities hate it. Because owners of solar power get to reduce their bills by the amount of energy, in kilowatt-hours, that they send to the grid, the utilities argue—correctly—that those consumers avoid paying for the construction and operation of the grid. Yet they still depend on that grid when their solar panels produce less power than they need.

In several states, utilities have lobbied furiously to amend net metering to reduce the rate at which excess solar power is compensated for or add charges to solar owners' bills to cover the costs of the grid. In some places, such as Arizona, they have succeeded, dampening the growth of residential solar. If more states roll back net metering, consumers in those states would save less money on their monthly utility bills by installing solar power. That reduction might make it harder for them to make their monthly loan or lease payments, lowering the income that an asset-backed security might generate for investors. In this way, regulatory changes might reduce the appeal of new securitizations.

A final risk facing securitization is counterintuitive: the price of solar installations actually might be falling too fast. The price of a U.S. residential solar installation halved between 2009 and 2015, from $8 to $4 per watt.[38] If this trend continues, customers may be unwilling to continue paying loan payments on an asset whose market value has plunged only a few years after it was installed.

Fortunately, the rise of big data may both enable securitization and prevent it from turning into a bubble that abruptly bursts. To drive down the risk of investing in portfolios of distributed solar projects, investors will need as much evidence as possible that the solar installations perform as expected over their full lifetimes and that customers reliably make their monthly loan or lease payments. Some firms are beginning to provide exactly this data. For example, kWh Analytics has built a database of several hundred thousand operating solar projects around the United States.[39] It has then taken that database to major insurance firms, which have agreed to offer insurance against the solar systems producing less energy than expected.

The insurance firms are happy to participate, having seen reams of data confirming that solar projects do indeed produce as much electricity over a year as the models predict. Assured that the solar projects will work as intended, investors in securitized solar loans need only worry about solar owners defaulting on their loans—a risk that is straightforwardly quantified for home or auto loans and should not unnerve bond markets or ratings agencies.

As more data become available, investors will gain access to a wealth of evidence that enables them to correctly price the risk of solar securities without exaggerating that risk. Evidence is the best way to ensure that solar securitization grows through responsible investing rather than speculation. With more data, solar PV panels could transform from a niche product in need of specialty financing to a totally normal household accessory. One firm, Sunlight Financial, thinks that one day, it could be as easy to finance rooftop solar panels through a home equity line of credit as it is to buy furniture or renovate your bathroom.

I have been focusing on financing for rooftop solar PV projects, but such projects are not the most cost-effective way to deploy solar power or reduce greenhouse gas emissions. In the United States, the average cost of a utility-scale solar plant in 2016 was $1.06 per watt, whereas that of a residential solar project was $2.89 per watt (solar PV projects on commercial and industrial rooftops achieve some economies of scale and are therefore cheaper than residential rooftop projects).[40] Some argue that rooftop solar power brings additional benefits to the grid, for example by reducing power losses over transmission lines when solar produces power near where it is used, or by avoiding the need to invest in expensive new grid infrastructure by lightening the load on the grid. These benefits are possible in theory, but in reality, rooftop solar is often more likely to increase rather than relieve strain on the grid. For example, one study of California determined that only if rooftop solar were located on a specific 10 percent of the grid could it help avoid costly grid infrastructure upgrades.[41] More commonly, solar can overload equipment designed to deliver power from the grid to the consumer when a rooftop solar system feeds power back to the grid.[42] This does not mean that distributed solar systems are necessarily uneconomical. Larger distributed systems—for example those mounted at ground-level in urban areas at the scale of a few megawatts—can enjoy economies of scale and feed their power directly to electrical substations that can handle the influx of power instead of overloading neighborhood circuitry.

Rooftop solar, however, often enjoys strong political support, partly because it tends to create more local jobs than larger solar project sizes. Taking consumer preferences and political realities into account, it is likely that rooftop solar will inevitably feature prominently in the total mix of solar capacity as the industry grows, regardless of the theoretically optimal mix. And that optimal mix could shift thanks to technology; future rooftop solar projects connected to the grid through smart inverters could, for example, provide greater benefits to the grid than rooftop solar currently provides.

Although utility-scale solar is already much cheaper than rooftop solar, the economics of utility-scale installations could improve even further with more debt financing. And just as for rooftop solar, the rise of data could unlock cheap debt capital for utility-scale solar as well. Utility-scale projects are large enough that companies are able to raise project financing without bundling many projects together. Still, the winning strategy should look similar for utility-scale solar plants as for distributed solar projects: convince investors that the risk of a solar project is low in order to obtain low-cost loans. If insurance companies are willing to insure the power production from a large solar installation that is contracted to sell its power to a credible offtaker (a customer for the electricity unlikely to renege on the contract, such as a utility that will transmit solar power to homes and businesses), then potential investors can have high confidence that the project's cash flows will cover interest payments on the debt.

This scenario is analogous to how the electric power industry derisks natural gas power plants to raise cheap debt finance. Firms will purchase financial hedges to lock in the long-term cost of input fuel and the price of output electricity, which is basically taking out an insurance policy that the plant will make as much profit as expected.[43] That insurance allows the firm building the plant to raise cheap debt capital from investors who are satisfied that the project has a low risk.

Beyond enabling such derisking insurance, data could reduce the cost of debt capital for a diverse set of projects, from rooftop to utility-scale solar.[44] With good enough data on how much revenue a project in a certain region will earn, a firm might even be able to raise debt capital based on a promise to build a solar farm on a parcel of land, similar to how the oil and gas industry can raise capital to drill wells by convincing investors of the value of their reserves.[45] Down the road, the next step is to expand high-quality data collection to developing countries, where skittish investors need hard data to get comfortable with plowing their capital into markets having both high growth potential and high perceived risks.

Searching for a Supermajor

On the table in front of me lay nearly four sumptuous dumplings—*nearly* four because I'd managed to steal a bite of only one. Between my clumsy grasp on the chopsticks and the torrent of questions that I was trying to answer, I didn't have much chance to dig into the meal. I was ensconced in a luxuriously wood-paneled dining room of the historic Hong Kong Gentlemen's Club, where the executive team of China Light and Power (CLP) was grilling me about the current state of solar power markets around the world in 2016 and their prospects for the future. My answers could influence the company's solar expansion plans. The mouthwatering dumplings were going to have to wait.

CLP, one of the biggest electric power businesses in Asia, with operations in several countries, traditionally has owned power plants that run on fossil fuels, mostly coal. But as the CEO, Richard Lancaster, was fervently arguing from across the table, times were changing thanks to the falling cost of renewable energy and policy breakthroughs like the Paris Agreement on climate change. In 2007, CLP made a pioneering pledge to cut its carbon intensity (i.e., the carbon emissions per unit of generated power) by 75 percent by 2050. That's probably the most ambitious target of any major power company in the world. To meet it, CLP is aggressively deploying renewable energy in China, India, and other markets, while divesting some of its fossil plants.[46] Although most of its renewable investments have been in wind power, the plummeting cost of solar had caught CLP's attention. Hence its interest in understanding burgeoning solar markets across Asia, and my growling stomach.

Companies with CLP's size and reach could be as crucial to the future of solar power as the deep-pocketed investors that solar will need to attract. CLP owns more than $25 billion worth of power plants, but only 16 percent of them are renewable generators.[47] Such companies have an enormous balance sheet and appetite to transform their holdings in the coming years. Crucially, they are willing to take risks to develop projects that, once constructed, turn into ripe investment opportunities where institutional investors can park their money.

This process happens all the time in the oil and gas industry. In that sector, supermajors with big balance sheets are able to make big bets on large infrastructure projects. Because their balance sheets comprise debt and equity from the world's biggest investors, the supermajors are in effect acting as conduits for that capital, directing it to fuel the industry's growth.[48]

SunEdison grew so fast, and took on so much debt, because it was trying to replicate this strategy. Ultimately, its demise was a reminder that the company was a long way off from achieving the necessary scale to really act as a supermajor. Perhaps another pure-play solar company will adopt a more measured growth strategy and gradually fill that role a decade or more in the future. But right now, large electric power companies looking to diversify from fossil fuels are the best-positioned entities to transform their business models and don the mantle of solar supermajors.

Actually, this view applies only to some firms in the electric power sector. Electric power companies come in two major flavors, a result of a push for deregulation around the world. For much of the twentieth century, there was largely only one type: the vertically integrated utility. These utilities owned both power plants and the transmission lines and distribution infrastructure to deliver power to their customers, and they enjoyed a monopoly over a limited service territory to sell their power. Then, around the turn of the century, markets across North America and Europe started to deregulate—that is, they no longer awarded a monopoly to a single utility over all power-related activities. This deregulation led to a restructuring of the industry. State-regulated utilities still retained monopolies to own and operate the power grid in their service territory. But competitive markets sprang up, in which private companies that owned power plants would sell their power, and regulated utilities would buy it. These two types of firms—regulated utilities that have a monopoly over the power grid in a limited area and unregulated companies that own power plants, often in multiple countries—are responding to the rise of solar in very different ways.

The regulated utilities are unlikely to become solar supermajors. Their opinion of utility-scale solar tends to be blandly positive because they can buy cheap electricity from solar farms (although state mandates might require them to buy more than they know what to do with). They reserve their strongest opinions for distributed solar, which they tend to view with suspicion and sometimes fear.

Regulated utilities in the United States are the ones that are lobbying to roll back net metering. One of their fears is the so-called death spiral, in which customers install rooftop solar, reduce their bills, and cause nonsolar customer bills to rise to cover the costs of the grid. This rise, in turn, makes solar a more attractive proposition than buying electricity from the grid, leading to even more customers reducing their bills and raising the bills of the remaining, dwindling pool. The prospect of fewer and fewer customers buying electricity that flows through the grid makes utilities that own the grid view solar as a competitive threat.

In addition to distributed solar, a new trend called "community solar" appears threatening to utilities. In community solar, consumers can band together to collectively own or lease a larger-scale solar installation. In many U.S. states, consumers then can use net metering to offset their power purchases from the grid with power generated by the community solar project. But the economics of a large-scale solar project are often much better than those of a small rooftop installation. So net metering provides extremely generous compensation for community solar consumers, slashing their electricity bills and accelerating the death spiral. Indeed, community solar has shot up, accounting for nearly 5 percent of annual U.S. solar installations in 2017 from next to nothing in 2015.[49]

With their attention focused on stopping distributed solar from eating into their customer base, regulated utilities are making only limited inroads into becoming players in the growing solar industry. And, utilities that might be interested in making the leap will have a hard time doing so. In deregulated states with competitive wholesale power markets, regulated utilities are not allowed to develop and own large solar power projects that sell power into the wholesale market. Instead, regulated utilities have tended to sign power purchase agreements with developers of large solar projects, often to meet obligations under state renewable energy mandates. Moreover, it is tricky for regulated utilities to market and install distributed solar because they might run afoul of antitrust laws owing to their monopoly status within their service territory.[50]

Still, there are some models for regulated utilities to pursue business model innovation and capture some of the value in the growing solar market. For example, utilities have reams of data on the customers in their service territory, whereas acquiring customers is an increasing component of the costs that distributed solar providers face.[51] By partnering with solar providers and taking a cut of their sales, utilities can make money even as more customers install distributed solar.[52] They can even make it easier for customers to pay for clean energy upgrades, such as solar panels or energy-efficient home retrofits, in installments as part of their monthly electric bill.[53]

In contrast to their regulated cousins, unregulated power companies are eagerly expanding into solar. In the United States, regulated utilities are often subsidiaries of holding companies who own other, unregulated subsidiaries that are free to build power plants and sell power into competitive markets. Many of these unregulated counterparts of regulated utilities—such as Duke Energy Renewables, Southern Power, Berkshire Hathaway Energy Renewables, and NextEra Energy Resources—are investing heavily in solar power. In fact, through 2016, half of all utility-scale solar projects in the United States were owned by unregulated subsidiaries of utility holding companies, and analysts forecast that they will further increase their share of the U.S. solar market.[54] Many of these companies have historically owned fossil fuel generators, but they are now piling into the cheapest power-generation source in the United States—solar power.

Similar trends are occurring abroad. Companies that have historically owned conventional power plants are driving a boom in solar investment. Enel, formerly Italy's national utility, which has expanded into a global powerhouse since Italy deregulated its power sector, bid aggressively to develop solar projects across Latin America at record low prices.[55] But it is

Chinese firms—for instance, CLP in Hong Kong and China Three Gorges Corporation on the mainland—that dominate investments in solar around the world.[56] All these power companies have enormous balance sheets, which they are starting to use as a conduit to channel investment toward solar power.

Although electric power companies looking to diversify from fossil fuels are the most likely candidates for solar supermajors, they are not the only corporate players tempted by solar power. A recent entrant to the industry, the Japanese technology giant Softbank, has made an enormous bet on solar power. Led by Japan's richest man, Masayoshi Son, Softbank leaped into solar after Japan's Fukushima disaster, developing 500 MW of solar in the country and then pledging $20 billion to invest in India. In late 2015, I sat down in New Delhi with the CEO of Softbank's energy subsidiary, Raman Nanda, a tall, charismatic, Oxford-educated McKinsey veteran. I remember wondering to myself whether his blue-chip pedigree might hinder him from succeeding in the rough-and-tumble atmosphere of India's business world. He soon dispelled my doubts. The next day, when I arrived for a meeting in the energy ministry, I ran into Raman, who was making the rounds before bidding in a major government auction. A few days later, Softbank won a major contract to build a utility-scale PV project in the Indian state of Andhra Pradesh. Within a year, Raman triumphantly sent me a Google Earth satellite photo of three adjacent project sites. Two were barren—waiting to be built on by slow-moving local firms—but Softbank's site already brimmed with 350 MW of installed solar panels.

Aside from Softbank, other global technology companies have entered the renewable energy business. As of 2016, Apple, Google, and Amazon had all created energy subsidiaries and were aggressively investing in powering their data centers with wind and solar power to reduce exposure to volatile and rising electricity costs.[57] Outside the tech world, MGM Resorts, which owns much of the Las Vegas strip, defected from NV Energy, the regulated utility owned by Warren Buffett. MGM plans to double its consumption of renewable energy now that it can go out and arrange its own power contracts for fifteen casinos that are no longer captive utility customers.[58] That trend could accelerate—three-quarters of the *Fortune* 100 companies have set renewable energy or sustainability targets. And corporations accounted for over one-fifth of renewable energy added to the U.S. grid in 2015, up from virtually none in 2012.[59]

Rising corporate interest could add another headache for regulated utilities, which are already distraught over losing residential customers to distributed solar and could now face an exodus of corporate consumers to utility-scale solar. Indeed, it is ironic that regulated utilities are a lonely category of firms that are not cashing in on the solar boom. Aside from them, a remarkably diverse assortment of corporations is investing in solar. Comprising unregulated power companies, tech titans, retailers like Walmart, and industrial giants like Dow Chemical, this myriad of firms may actually represent a new model to power the growth of solar, making the supermajor model that worked so well for oil and gas obsolete. That a wave of corporations is willing to alter their business models to invest in solar is a promising sign for the industry's future.

Public-Sector Training Wheels

To date, governments and international institutions have played important roles in directing capital toward solar power. Many argue that the public sector will continue to be integral, as the solar industry seeks new sources of capital from new investors and firms to fuel its continued growth. Indeed, public entities at a range of levels, from municipal governments to international development banks, have already unveiled innovative financial tools to mobilize private funding. Although public dollars are scarce, they can unlock much more private capital if deployed intelligently. So in the near term, the public sector could play a substantial role in attracting new private capital. But in the longer term, beyond five to ten years, the public sector will have been successful if it makes itself obsolete. A truly successful solar industry will continue to grow entirely through private capital flows and efficient markets.

The public sector has its work cut out for it on this score. It has provided roughly 15 percent of all funding to date for renewable energy. Given the vast amounts of capital needed to finance the growth of solar into a mainstream energy source, the proportion of public funding will certainly not increase. More likely, in fact, it will have to decrease under the constraints of public budgets. So, somehow, the public sector will need to do more with less, mobilizing more private capital with proportionally less public funding.

That is a tall order. McKinsey estimates that globally, there is a $1.5 trillion annual gap between current spending and the spending required to build the power-sector infrastructure needed to rapidly reduce greenhouse gas emissions. Most of that gap is in emerging economies.[60] But at the same time, because institutional investors are hungry for stable, long-term cash-flow, the Organisation for Economic Co-operation and Development (OECD) estimates that pension funds and insurance companies could invest $2.8 trillion per year in clean energy (see figure 4.4).[61] And a growing share of the investment community is motivated by sustainability mandates. In other words, investors are just waiting to be matched with the right projects and to get comfortable with investing in solar. The public sector's role is just to provide the training wheels for the private sector to ultimately drive solar's growth all by itself in the future.

Multilateral development banks (MDBs) have led the way to date, and they still have some tricks up their sleeves. MDBs like the World Bank are most effective when they reduce the risk that investors face when investing in solar projects. One tool that they can use is to provide loan guarantees, which reduce the concern that a private investor might have about being paid back for supplying a loan to build a solar project. Guarantees can take various forms. One type protects against political risks such as government expropriation of assets. Another guards against offtaker risk, making a lender whole if a solar project goes insolvent because its customer (for example, a utility) reneges on a contract to purchase solar power. Although MDB guarantees are common, only 4 percent of them are used to help finance renewable energy. Of that, the majority goes to hydropower projects, and just 7 percent goes to solar, so there is plenty of room for MDBs to expand their use of guarantees to encourage more solar investment.[62]

An MDB can also crowd in private investment through a strategy known as "loan syndication," in which the bank leads a coalition of investors to finance a solar project. These investors might have been too wary of investing by themselves, but they are happy to do so with the security that many other investors, led by an MDB that conducts most of the due diligence, are jointly undertaking the risk with them. For example, in Jordan, the International Finance Corporation (IFC), an arm of the World Bank Group, brought together a consortium of banks in 2014 to provide more than $200 million in loans to seven solar projects.[63] Going forward, both loan syndication and guarantees are promising and inexpensive approaches for MDBs to ease new institutional investors into financing solar, especially in emerging markets.

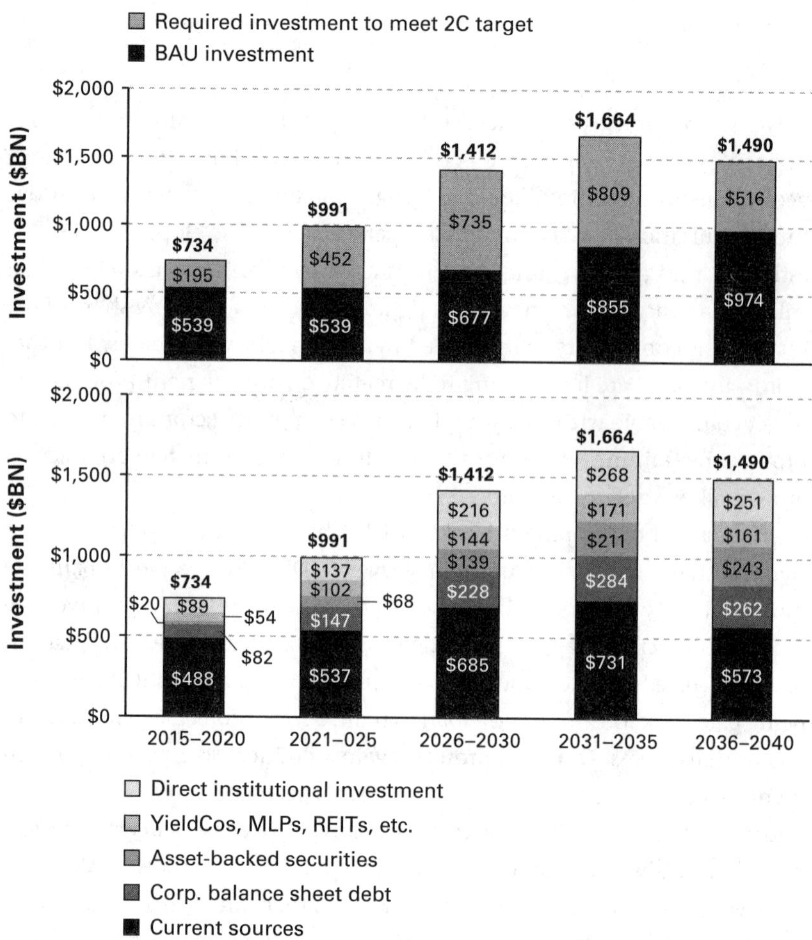

Figure 4.4

Required investment levels in solar power to limit climate change. The top chart plots levels of investment in solar energy under a business-as-usual (BAU) scenario and compares those levels with higher ones needed through 2040 to keep the world on track to limit global warming to 2°C. The bottom chart provides a viable breakdown of these required investment levels by source. Currently, private bank loans and direct equity investments by, for example, private equity funds are the most common sources of capital. But in the future, new sources of debt and equity capital will be needed. Raising corporate balance sheet debt and asset-backed securitization are ways to direct debt capital from public debt markets toward utility-scale and distributed solar projects. Equity capital can come from vehicles like YieldCos that enable investors to buy shares of a portfolio of renewable energy projects on public stock markets. Finally, although deep-pocketed institutional investors invest most of their capital in public markets, they also have substantial capacity to provide both debt and equity capital directly, through direct loans and ownership stakes in projects.
Source: Bloomberg New Energy Finance (2016).

In addition to MDBs, governments around the world are rolling out innovative ways to crowd in private funding for clean energy. For example, the New York Green Bank offers loans at market rates to solar projects that make economic sense but aren't yet considered mainstream enough for private banks to fund.

One strategy that MDBs devised but that governments soon adopted is to issue "green bonds."[64] In essence, these are just like normal bonds that investors can buy and trade, but their proceeds must be used for sustainable projects. Governments at every level—national, state/provincial, and municipal—now regularly issue these bonds to raise funding at low cost that can be used for clean energy projects. Green bonds are a good example of how the public sector can catalyze private activity that soon becomes self-sustaining. Now utilities, corporations, and banks are all issuing green bonds. In 2016, green bonds worth over $100 billion were issued and certified to meet a set of principles created by large banks that allow the bonds to be labeled "green." In addition, unlabeled bonds worth nearly $600 billion that mostly financed sustainability projects were issued.[65]

In the developing world in particular, the public sector will need to provide incentives or guarantees to embolden private investors who are often unfamiliar with emerging markets and wary of the heightened risks. But developing countries' governments may be strapped for cash. The incentives that they do choose must be extremely efficient at mobilizing many private dollars for every dollar of public finance.

India provides a good example of this imperative, requiring massive infusions of capital to meet its solar goals. To encourage domestic investors to provide loans at decent terms, the Indian government can scale up its use of partial credit guarantees, which reduce a local bank's exposure to default.[66] To attract foreign investors, the government has announced plans to roll out a currency-hedging facility. Currency risk spooks foreign investors who do not want the solar projects they have financed to become less valuable in, for example, U.S. dollars. This risk can add up to seven percentage points to the minimum rate of return that investors will tolerate, preventing them from investing in otherwise attractive solar projects.[67] But by offering to share some of the currency risk with foreign investors, the government could increase the number of projects that make business sense for those investors to fund.

Other risks that chill the investment climate relate to India's dysfunctional energy sector. Its electricity utilities are in bad financial shape, raising fears that they might renege on contracts to purchase power from solar projects. They also have failed to invest in upgrading the grid, which might not be able to handle an influx of solar power. If the Indian government could successfully reform the energy sector, possibly deregulating its utilities as much of the developed world has, it would substantially reduce the risks facing investors in solar projects.

Those sorts of structural economic reforms, which can enable solar power projects to be profitable even without incentives, should be the first priority of governments across the developing world. Indeed, the appropriate role for the public sector is to provide training wheels for private investors in solar, not to create dependence on a public crutch.

The decade ahead is a crucial one for the solar industry. To fund its rise as a mainstream energy contender, the industry will need to tap into the largest capital pools in the world. It will take financial engineering to coax institutional investors to trust solar with their capital, and the public sector may have to provide training wheels for a limited period. But already the capital has started flowing, and major corporations have begun to act as conduits to direct that capital toward solar projects around the world. So, despite the massive scale of the need for investment in solar power over the coming decades—on the order of trillions of dollars—there is good reason to be optimistic that financial and business model innovation will rise to the challenge.

Chapter 5 From Charity Case to Business Case

At the edge of Tarangire National Park, known for its elephant herds and iconic baobab trees, lies the Tanzanian town of Babati. The town itself is picturesque, framed against the distant Mount Kwaraa and adjacent to a lake teeming with fish (who scatter every so often when a submerged hippo surfaces for air). Here in Babati, Grace—a young mother of three—lives with her husband, Patrick, in a one-room brick house.

Grace dreams of sending her children to the prestigious University of Dar es Salaam, 600 kilometers to the east. There, they might train as doctors, engineers, or civil servants. But securing admission is no small feat, so Grace takes her children every evening to the town market, where the lights from street vendor stalls illuminate their schoolwork. When their concentration wanes amid the chaos of the market, Grace brings them home, where they squint next to a kerosene lamp that fills the room with soot and smoke. To afford kerosene refills, Grace carefully stockpiles roughly $8 per month.

Around this time, Patrick tends to discover that his cell phone battery is out of charge and treks into town to a communal charging kiosk. His small farming business demands that he stay in close contact with vendors in the neighboring village. Aside from coordinating logistics with them at odd hours, he constantly checks market prices and executes transactions via mobile money payments through his cell phone. To keep his phone charged, Patrick forks over around $4 per month.

When one day a salesman knocks on the door, advertising a compact solar-powered system that will run three LED lightbulbs and charge a phone, Grace is understandably skeptical. But the man, a sales agent sent by the aptly named Off-Grid Electric, offers to immediately slash the family's monthly energy spending from $12 to $5 per month. On top of replacing the noxious kerosene fumes and inconvenient charging trips, the solar system—a 12-watt panel hooked up to a battery and a charge controller, plus three light-emitting diode (LED) lights—comes with free maintenance and service for as long as the family uses the system. It goes without saying that payments are made by mobile money. If they are not made on time, the system will shut down remotely.

Six months later, Grace and her family are hooked. They plan to upgrade to the $15 per month plan to supersize their solar system and outfit a new room they are building with two more LED lights, a radio, and a television. And Grace is eyeing a brand new offering—an electric sewing machine with which she can start her own small tailoring business. For its part, Off-Grid Electric is in the red, having spent nearly $200 on the components, distribution, and marketing of the solar system. But it expects full payback in three years—faster if Grace and her family complete their planned upgrade to a pricier service tier. And the company sees many more households like Grace's in its existing service territory in Tanzania and Rwanda, as well as in future target markets across sub-Saharan Africa.

Started in 2011 by business school graduates from Oxford University, Off-Grid Electric soon attracted funding from SolarCity (now part of Tesla) and its venture capital investors. SolarCity had launched the residential solar market in the United States by offering solar systems on lease to customers happy to pay monthly power payments rather than foot solar's high up-front capital cost. And Off-Grid Electric was poised to apply that same strategy in the developing world.

Through 2016, Off-Grid Electric raised more than $60 million to meet its target of bringing electricity to 100,000 households in Africa by 2019.[1] The company is not alone; a torrent of investment in recent years has funded start-ups across Africa and Asia to deliver electricity to the more than 1 billion people who lack it. This chapter tells the unfolding story of how innovative business models for providing off-grid electricity to individual homes or larger communities could enable existing solar technology to make a dent in one of the most intractable barriers to ending extreme poverty around the world.

A remarkable confluence of trends is upending conventional wisdom about whether off-grid solutions can improve energy access. Historically, virtually all the progress in bringing electricity to those who have lacked it has been made through extending the reach of centralized power grids.

But, as a by-product of the rapidly growing global solar market and the falling costs of PV panels, stand-alone solar PV systems—unconnected to the main grid—suddenly have become cost-competitive with kerosene, diesel, and biomass, on which most of the world's poorest populations currently subsist. Aiding the favorable economics of solar systems are plunges in the prices of home appliances, from lights to fans to televisions, that are ultra-energy-efficient. Simultaneously, the rise of cell phones and mobile banking has made electricity access to charge phones even more desirable, while at the same time offering a way for customers to pay for it.[2]

Lumbering national power utilities have been slow to notice these changes. But nimble entrepreneurs, recognizing an opportunity, have flocked to off-grid solar. They are designing an assortment of business models to offer the world's poor their first taste of electricity while cashing in on their untapped willingness to pay for it.

The vast majority of this entrepreneurial activity is happening in sub-Saharan Africa and South Asia, which together encompass 95 percent of the world's unelectrified population. But there is a stark contrast between the evolution of the off-grid solar markets in each region. In the East African countries of Kenya, Tanzania, and Rwanda—the epicenter of the off-grid solar boom—companies have fanned out to remote villages without having to worry about government oversight or restrictive regulations. They have won over customers by promising to reduce the cost of their energy while improving its quality. And they have done so knowing the risks of operating in lawless regions where contracts are practically worthless. Thanks to their clever use of technology—such as when they remotely deactivate solar systems in response to delinquent mobile payments—they've gotten by just fine without government oversight.

In India, by contrast, pure economics and safety are not the only factors that companies have to consider. There, rural villagers enjoy government subsidies for purchasing kerosene, which keeps the price of that fuel artificially low. And, until recently, federal restrictions on mobile banking meant that Indian companies had to collect electricity payments from customers in person—a costly and unreliable endeavor. In consequence, the inroads made by off-grid solar have been more modest. Now that the government has relaxed those restrictions, prospects have improved for India's off-grid solar market to take off in the way that Africa's markets have.

In both laissez-faire and highly regulated environments, a range of inventive business models has flourished. Off-Grid Electric exemplifies the hottest model for enabling people at the bottom of the economic pyramid to finance solar power: Pay-As-You-Go (PAYG). In 2016, international investors funded PAYG start-ups to the tune of over $200 million.[3] As is true of residential solar in the United States (see chapter 4), securitization might hold the key to unlocking vast pools of capital from abroad that can finance the up-front cost of PAYG projects.

In addition to clever financial engineering, off-grid solar providers are offering a diverse array of products that span from systems with a single solar panel to microgrids serving hundreds of homes and businesses. The versatility of the solar panel means that it can be used in myriad different configurations and system sizes. In addition to serving isolated, off-grid communities, solar microgrids could improve the quality of electricity service for those whose grid connection is frustratingly unreliable, for example in urban areas served by a dilapidated central grid.

The public sector has important roles to play in enabling off-grid solar to improve energy access. First, governments must take care not to impede markets, as the Indian government has done through its kerosene subsidy and restrictions on mobile banking. Second, governments and international financial institutions should be careful to tailor their interventions to test off-grid solar business models that can eventually be self-sustaining, rather than create a dependency on public funds. Third, governments should coordinate efforts to expand central grids with entrepreneurial activity to deploy off-grid solar systems, ensuring that the grid is a complement—not a competitor—to off-grid solar. Fourth, they should use public procurement to further drive down the cost of off-grid system components, like energy-efficient appliances. And, finally, governments can help by developing a trained workforce to support a thriving off-grid solar sector.

When Past Is Not Prologue

Despite its recent growth, off-grid solar is not free of controversy. Some development experts argue that it is a distraction, diverting resources and attention from concerted efforts to extend a country's central grid and encourage people to move into cities where power grids make the most economic sense. Together, these two strategies have accounted for virtually all the progress over the last century in delivering electricity to those who did not previously have it. Because off-grid solutions have had little success in improving energy access in the past, they contend, strategies for the future should largely ignore off-grid solar.

The critics hold that off-grid solutions are bound to fail for two reasons. First, power from the grid is much cheaper than power from off-grid sources because the grid benefits from economies of scale, whereas decentralized alternatives do not.[4] Todd Moss at the Center for Global Development has argued forcefully against directing U.S. development aid in Africa toward off-grid solar projects. He contends that for the same number of dollars ($10 billion), the United States could attract several times as much private investment in centralized natural gas–fired power plants that would bring electricity to 90 million people than would be invested in off-grid solar systems that would serve just 20 million.[5] The right course of action is a no-brainer, according to Moss, and the hype over off-grid solar is not only distracting, but damaging. (This analysis did cause a stir, and some have quibbled with its methodology.[6])

The second reason that many experts discount off-grid solar is that it fails to put the world's poorest on a ladder to modern energy access. Various programs to distribute solar-powered lanterns, solar cookstoves, or rooftop solar panels have marginally improved quality of life. But these steps can be dead ends, the experts say, rather than on-ramps, for integrating people at the bottom of the pyramid into the modern economy.[7] Becoming productive members of that economy, and reaping its benefits, tend to go hand in hand with a threshold level of annual electricity consumption—on the order of several thousand kilowatt-hours per capita, which far exceeds the amount of electricity that simple off-grid solar systems can deliver. Morgan Bazilian at the World Bank argues that on top of increasing the number of people with an electrical connection, it is crucial to increase the quantity of electricity used in homes and businesses to power economic growth.[8]

Taking all this into account, Ted Nordhaus, Shaiyra Devi, and Alex Trembath at the Breakthrough Institute argue that "decentralized renewable and off-grid energy technologies . . . cannot, however, substitute for energy and other infrastructure necessary to support industrial-scale economic enterprise. Microfinance, microenterprise, and microenergy are no substitute for industry, infrastructure, and grid electricity."[9]

I respect the judgment of these experts, and, through many conversations, they have certainly convinced me that off-grid solar has played a negligible role in the tremendous progress made to date in lifting people out of poverty in the industrializing world. But I am not convinced that past is prologue. The confluence of trends mentioned earlier—cheaper solar photovoltaics, appliances, and batteries; the rise of mobile phones and banking; and entrepreneurs tying it all together with innovative business models—has enabled a new generation of off-grid solutions that are more economical and can power a broader range of uses than earlier systems.

Considering these newer trends, one recent study concluded that off-grid solar systems could bring meaningful electricity access to over 1 billion people by 2030. That study also concluded that the majority of gains in energy access would still come from extending the reach of central grids. But working in tandem, it noted, off-grid solutions and efforts to extend central grids could deliver reliable electricity to 3 billion people by 2030, offsetting population growth to achieve near-universal energy access.[10]

This outlook reconciles competing views holding either that off-grid solar is a silver bullet or that it is a distraction. In many countries where governments have struggled to build centralized grid infrastructure, off-grid solar can probably play an important, albeit not exclusive, role. It can provide electricity to extremely remote areas that the grid may never reach, it can offer a stopgap during delays in grid extension, and it can supplement grid power in areas with a grid connection but unreliable service, as is often the case in urban outskirts. This view recognizes that to help put countries on the path to economic prosperity, off-grid solar will need to serve as a stepping-stone, not an impediment, to modern levels of energy access.

The scale of the energy access problem implies that solving it will take an all-of-the-above strategy. Around the world, over 1 billion people still lack access to any electricity—and many more lack access to reliable electricity. Figure 5.1 makes it clear that areas of limited access are concentrated in sub-Saharan Africa and South Asia. Although the problem might appear more acute in sub-Saharan Africa, the sheer population size in South Asia means that although three-quarters of Indians have access to electricity, India, in fact, still accounts for the largest unelectrified population in absolute numbers, at 263 million. Nigeria is a distant second (75 million), followed by Ethiopia (67 million) and Bangladesh (62 million).[11]

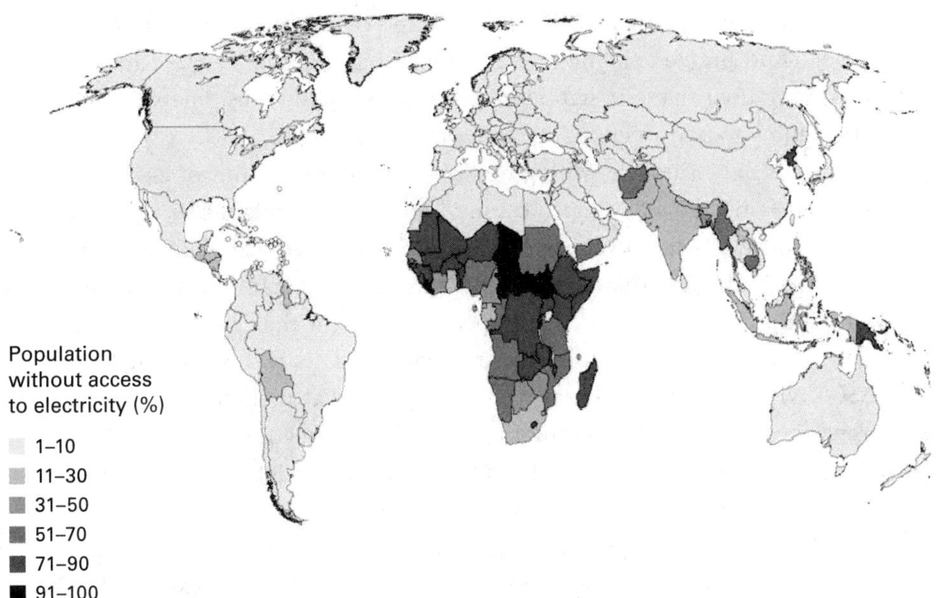

Figure 5.1
Global distribution of populations without access to electricity.
Source: World Bank.

And the number of people with electricity access is on track to increase, as population growth in unconnected areas adds to the totals, especially in sub-Saharan Africa, which (excluding South Africa) has less generating capacity than Sweden. It might not be realistic to expect governments to extend the grid to substantially increase energy access. For example, achieving 70 percent access to electricity in sub-Saharan Africa would require countries to double the annual investment in their power sectors from \$7.5 billion to \$15 billion in the near term; in the long run, more than \$1 trillion in investment could be needed to meet the power demands.[12] Cash-strapped governments are unlikely to pull off such a feat.

But off-grid options financed almost entirely by the private sector might play a role in filling the gap. Contrary to received wisdom, people at the bottom of the pyramid are not necessarily too poor to pay for energy. In fact, those without access to electricity spend about \$27 billion every year just on lighting and mobile phone charging. But their current sources of energy have clear drawbacks. In addition to being expensive, light from kerosene lamps or candles is poor quality and causes deadly indoor air pollution. And phone charging can often entail arduous treks, like Patrick's, to a communal charging station miles away. Many such customers are able and willing to pay for electricity access at home.[13]

Surprisingly, they are willing to pay much more per unit of electricity than customers in a developed country. An American might balk at power prices above 20 cents/kWh (the average U.S. retail electricity price is about 12 cents/kWh). But that figure is meaningless to African village-dwellers who are willing to pay over $100 per year to light their homes at night, and 20 cents for every phone charge. That translates to a whopping $30–$50/kWh of electricity—more than 100 times what their counterparts in developed countries are willing to pay. So even though off-grid electricity is more expensive than power from the grid, it can still be much less than what customers are willing to pay.[14]

Even so, to date off-grid systems—often set up to burn fossil fuels—have had limited traction and been confined to niche markets. For example, on small islands in Indonesia and the Philippines, where grid extension is not a viable option, communities continue to use portable diesel generators to power microgrids. And the African country of Mali has deployed more than 200 isolated, diesel-powered microgrids. (Many in the industry use "microgrid" and "minigrid" interchangeably, whereas others assume that the latter is larger than the former. This book uses only the term "microgrid" to mean an isolated grid of any size that is not connected to the main grid.)

Yet the appeal of off-grid systems has recently improved. With the fall in technology costs, solar has emerged as an increasingly viable option to complement or replace diesel. This is an attractive entry point for solar, which can piggyback on the existing infrastructure of already-built microgrids in remote areas.[15] In addition to slotting solar power into existing microgrids that were previously served by diesel, firms have developed an array of solar systems to reach customers currently without access to grid or off-grid electricity. These systems range in size from just a few watts—known as "picosolar" systems—to several kilowatts and more in the form of microgrids that network together entire communities. All these variants have started to grow rapidly. Pico-solar systems of less than 10 W might power one or two lights and perhaps charge a phone; 44 million of them had been sold as of 2015, up from basically none five years earlier.

Larger systems have recently grown even more rapidly in generation capacity. Solar home systems (SHSs) might be as large as 300 W and combine solar panels, a battery (traditionally a lead-acid battery like the one in your car, but increasingly it will be a lithium-ion battery as the costs fall), electronics, and appliances to provide energy services to a single household. In addition to lighting and phone charging, these energy services might include powering a television, ceiling fan, radio, or even a refrigerator. The rise of the PAYG business model has boosted SHS sales in the last five years, and by the end of 2015, over a half-million households across Africa and Asia had an SHS.[16]

A final off-grid segment that has experienced recent growth relies on microgrids in the range of several kilowatts to several megawatts in size to network multiple households or businesses together. These systems might be hybrids, in that they include not only solar power and batteries but also wind turbines, diesel generators, and other power sources.[17] These systems have begun to spread across Africa and Asia. Overall, the rise of off-grid solar has split roughly evenly, in terms of capacity, between the two regions.[18]

Already, in some countries, off-grid solar is making a real dent in the energy access problem, and its rapid growth suggests that it will have even more of an impact in the years ahead. Nowhere is the promise of off-grid solar more apparent than in Bangladesh. One of the world's most densely populated countries, Bangladesh has 163 million residents, half of which lived without power in 2003. Since then, the proportion of the population without access to electricity has plunged to just 20 percent. About two-thirds of that improvement came from efforts to connect customers to the central grid, and the remaining third happened thanks to a dramatic increase in off-grid solar systems.[19] By 2014, Bangladesh's 3 million SHSs represented half of all the off-grid solar systems around the world.[20]

To be sure, Bangladesh has not completely solved the energy access problem. It took World Bank subsidies and government coordination to roll out this ambitious program. And households with SHSs still have limits on the energy services that their systems are equipped to provide. But as technology costs fall, the off-grid industry could become self-sustaining. And as appliances become more energy-efficient, the same solar panel will be able to provide higher-quality energy services. So, the case of Bangladesh might offer a glimpse into the future role that off-grid solar can play in improving energy access around the world. It certainly cannot carry the entire burden of electrification alone. But past may not be prologue, and off-grid solutions might play a much more meaningful role in the coming decades than they have over the past century.

Paying for PAYG

The rise of Pay-As-You-Go offerings for off-grid solar home systems is finally tapping into the willingness of those without any grid access to pay handsome sums for a small quantity of electricity. The early success of PAYG—mostly in Africa to date, though Asia is catching up—echoes in some ways the rise of the residential solar market in the United States in 2008. There, the advent of the solar lease, offered to customers who would make monthly payments for solar power, tapped into customers' latent willingness to pay for solar power without footing the steep up-front cost of a PV system. And just as U.S. firms had to then find ways to tap into financial markets, creative entrepreneurs offering PAYG off-grid solar systems must also find ways to source the capital needed to construct their projects so that their customers can pay in small installments. If they can successfully scale up, not only could PAYG solar bring power to those who have never had it, but it could also unlock the power of credit to transform them into modern consumers.

The PAYG model for off-grid solar traces its roots to the telecommunications sector in East Africa. In 2007, Safaricom, Kenya's largest mobile network operator, launched a revolutionary mobile payment service called M-PESA. Customers eagerly used the service, which has since become a mainstay of the economy, to transfer cash via phone for everything from salaries to taxi rides. Then two of the executives behind M-PESA realized that the platform could enable customers to pay for electricity, and they founded M-KOPA in 2011 to deploy and finance small SHSs.[21]

M-KOPA estimated that off-grid Kenyan households were spending nearly $300 a year on kerosene-based lighting and mobile phone charging, whereas they would save $750 over the first four years of paying 45 cents a day for an SHS.[22] This value proposition has proven irresistible, and in just four years, M-KOPA managed to reach over 300,000 households in Kenya, Tanzania, and Uganda. Still, as the first player in the market, M-KOPA chose to offer very small systems (under 10 W) that offer limited energy services beyond basic lighting and phone charging.

Subsequent players have gone bigger. Mobisol, which operates in Tanzania and Rwanda, markets SHSs that are 80–200 W; it leads the market in terms of installed solar power capacity, having deployed more than 5 MW of off-grid solar in East Africa as of 2016.[23] Its systems can power a wide range of appliances, including televisions, radios, irons, and stoves. Moreover, Mobisol's customers can use a larger SHS to earn a livelihood—for example by powering electric hair clippers—which in turn enables them to pay for their power more reliably. A whole host of solar providers offering SHS sizes between those of M-KOPA and Mobisol, such as Off-Grid Electric, has sprung up in East Africa. As competition saturates the initial markets, firms are expanding to new places, such as Nigeria and Ethiopia, to serve the massive untapped demand for electricity there.

In addition to offering differently sized systems, PAYG firms vary in their level of vertical integration. At one extreme, Off-Grid Electric designs and provides its own SHSs, complete with appliance offerings. It also operates its own distribution, sales, and service channels. This approach enables it to learn about its customer preferences and quickly update its system offerings in response. At the other extreme, Azuri, a PAYG player that offers smaller SHS systems, recognized that a whole network of distributors already existed to deliver consumer goods (such as shampoo) to far-flung regions and decided to piggyback on that network to distribute the components of its solar systems. Similarly, another start-up, d.light, has chosen to outsource product distribution completely and focus on what it perceives as the higher-margin business of designing and operating their solar-powered lighting products.

Although PAYG providers vary in their product offerings and scope of activities, they are united in their use of technology to collect payments and remotely operate solar systems (see figure 5.2 for an overview of the PAYG model). In general, customers make monthly payments via mobile money platforms like M-PESA. And providers use mobile networks to collect a wealth of data from their solar systems remotely, monitoring equipment performance and detecting maintenance needs.[24] Being able to shut down the solar system remotely if payments are delinquent also spares providers the cost of operating a far-flung network of collection agents to collect payments manually.

To offer customers the option of making monthly payments for an SHS with little to no money down, off-grid solar providers need to raise capital

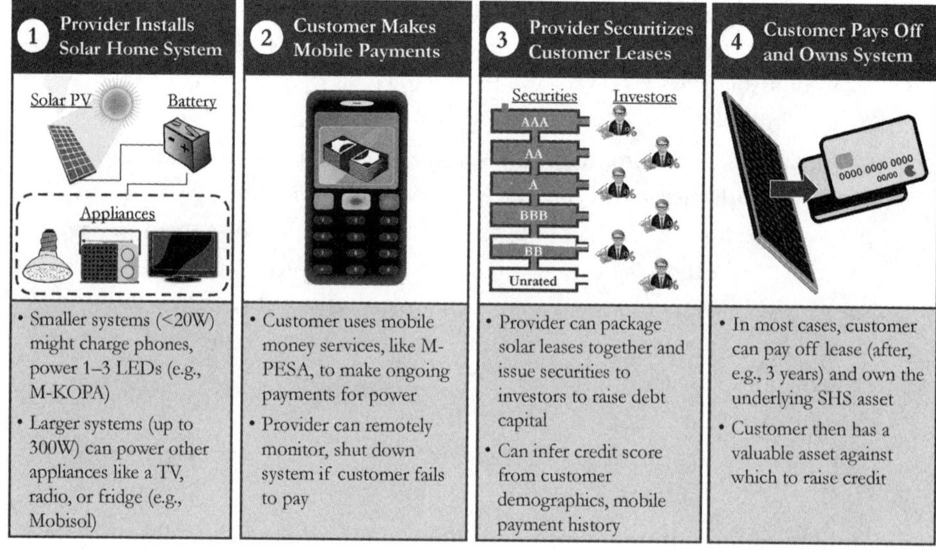

1 Provider Installs Solar Home System
Solar PV
Battery
Appliances
• Smaller systems (<20W) might charge phones, power 1–3 LEDs (e.g., M-KOPA)
• Larger systems (up to 300W) can power other appliances like a TV, radio, or fridge (e.g., Mobisol)
2 Customer Makes Mobile Payments
• Customer uses mobile money services, like M-PESA, to make ongoing payments for power
• Provider can remotely monitor, shut down system if customer fails to pay
3 Provider Securitizes Customer Leases
Securities
Investors
AAA
AA
A
BBB
BB
Unrated
• Provider can package solar leases together and issue securities to investors to raise debt capital
• Can infer credit score from customer demographics, mobile payment history
4 Customer Pays Off and Owns System
0000 0000 0000
00/00
• In most cases, customer can pay off lease (after, e.g., 3 years) and own the underlying SHS asset
• Customer then has a valuable asset against which to raise credit

Figure 5.2
How the PAYG model works.

to cover the up-front cost of the systems. Recall from the previous chapter that the cheapest way to raise debt capital to cover the majority of the cost of a U.S. residential solar system is to bundle a portfolio of the assets together and issue securities on public bond markets. The exact same logic applies to the off-grid, developing-world case, albeit with some twists. If providers can raise debt capital to cover most of the cost of a portfolio of off-grid SHSs, they can free up funds to build more systems.

But there are some stark differences between a Californian homeowner and a Rwandan farmer. The former has a well-defined credit score, possesses valuable assets, and enjoys a rule of law that protects the sanctity of a lease contract. By contrast, the latter has no assets or credit score and might live outside the reach of the law. Existing microfinance offerings have had only limited success at bringing financial services to those outside the global financial system.[25,26]

Even so, start-ups have figured out how to make a portfolio of leases to low-income Africans seem attractive to international fixed-income investors. In late 2015, the British start-up BBOXX announced the world's first securitization of off-grid solar assets, raising a half-million dollars at a

21 percent interest rate. It was a modest start, but more recent offerings have improved those terms.[27] And it's not just off-grid solar providers jumping into the financing fray. One start-up, a peer-to-peer lending marketplace called Lendable, modeled on Lending Club and based in Kenya, is growing rapidly by enabling you or me to invest in unsecured consumer debt in Africa to finance off-grid solar systems.

How can these companies make such investments attractive to their international clientele? The answer, as is the case for solar in developed countries, is data. Solar providers are building massive databases of where their customers live and whether they pay on time. At the same time, telecom firms have extensive histories tracing how often customers pay their cell phone bills on time. Putting all this data together, often through partnerships among financiers, solar providers, and telecom firms, can yield highly accurate predictions of whether an off-grid customer will reliably make lease payments for an SHS. Using these inferred credit scores, issuers of off-grid solar securities might achieve high ratings and low interest rates one day, attracting much more capital to the sector.

If these novel financing strategies work, they could fund widespread deployment of off-grid systems, which in turn could unlock economic opportunities beyond just solar. Most providers offer customers a lease-to-own option, under which they pay off an SHS over a period of time (often around three years) and subsequently own it. This payment approach represents a dramatic shift in the nature of off-grid household energy expenditures. Whereas in the past, households would basically throw money away by purchasing kerosene refills that would quickly be used up, now every monthly power payment goes toward ownership of a valuable asset.

Once customers own an SHS, they can then use it as collateral to raise credit. On top of this, their payment history and inferred credit score could make it cheaper to borrow money in the future. Recognizing that good customers could represent a source of more business, many solar providers have ambitions well beyond offering a basic SHS. They might offer an enhanced SHS with better appliances that the customer can buy with credit; down the line, they might even sell nonenergy products. Ultimately, they envision the customer gradually upgrading to higher-quality energy services and greater purchasing power. That projection is partly predicated on customers like Grace and Patrick using energy to power their livelihoods and generate income. But it is also based on the tremendous potential of providing credit for customers who traditionally have not been able to access it.

Still, for all the promise of the PAYG model, daunting obstacles remain. Among them, limited access to finance is foremost. Even though some providers are starting to tap into securitization, the floodgates of international debt capital have not yet opened. To enable a steady stream of funds, providers need to deploy off-grid solar systems in the first place before packaging them up to market to investors. That requires working capital, which funds the construction of solar projects and the operations of a business while it waits to receive funds from its customers. The scarcity of working capital has emerged as a major bottleneck, hindering the growth of the off-grid solar sector. The World Bank has stepped in to provide low-cost debt to fund some of firms' working capital needs, which is a good start.[28]

Another promising development is the loosening of government restrictions in India on mobile banking, which have held the country back even as PAYG has started to take off in Africa. Finally, in late 2015, the Reserve Bank of India started issuing banking licenses to telecom operators, enabling them to offer mobile payment services.[29] Without mobile banking, few firms had dared to try the PAYG business model in India. One of the rare firms that did, Simpa Networks, had to rely on a network of vendors and kiosks to sell refills for customers SHS power subscriptions.[30] Going forward, if mobile banking takes off, firms will be able to scale back on expensive networks of collection agents, making it possible to offer affordable PAYG packages with convenient payment options.

Microgrids, Macro-Impact

As exciting as the PAYG-fueled surge in SHS deployment is, systems that power only a single household are inherently limited. They are expensive (though they may seem reasonable compared to the exorbitant cost of kerosene), owing to their lack of economies of scale. And although companies are increasing the power output of their SHS offerings and pairing solar with an increasing range of low-power appliances, the energy services that these systems can offer customers are limited. So although they may have an important role to play in delivering power to the poorest of the poor, they cannot yet offer the full benefits of modern energy access.

The story is different for solar-powered microgrids. Because such systems can be networked together to serve a whole community, they can power a much wider range of energy services than can an SHS, and they produce comparatively cheaper power owing to economies of scale. And just as start-ups have employed PAYG offerings to jumpstart the SHS market, firms are also popularizing new ways to fund more complex solar projects, and their innovative business models are fueling a rise in microgrids. To be clear, PAYG can be—and has been—used to make microgrid power affordable to customers; but further innovations are needed to finance microgrids, which are larger and more complex than SHSs. Such microgrids could deliver modern power access to areas where it is prohibitively expensive to extend the grid—indeed, they already have been used to electrify villages in the Himalayas.[31]

Down the road, microgrids in remote areas could be integrated into the main grid, once it arrives. Indeed, microgrids are not just promising for off-grid areas; they also could boost power reliability in areas nominally served by the grid but that suffer from chronic blackouts. Their versatility suggests that microgrids are an ideal investment to put those with limited energy access on the ladder to a modern standard of living.

Microgrids comprise three subsystems. First is the power-generation subsystem, which typically has a capacity of (much) less than 15 MW, and even as little as a few hundred watts. In addition to solar panels, a solar-powered microgrid might enlist a small wind turbine, diesel generators, and batteries to supplement and smooth out the solar generation.[32] Second is a distribution subsystem that delivers electricity from the generators to the microgrid's users. Third is a subsystem consisting of the equipment and appliances with which customers access and consume the microgrid's electricity—this might include a ceiling fan, as well as the electrical meter that measures how much power a household uses.

In rural settings in the developing world, where microgrids primarily aim to increase energy access, these three subsystems suffice to define a microgrid. But microgrids are also gaining popularity in the developed world for a very different reason: They can enhance the reliability and resilience of the electricity supply by continuing to operate even if there's a problem with the main grid. In this context, the definition of a microgrid has an added layer. According to the U.S. Department of Energy (DOE), a microgrid is defined as a semi-autonomous "group of interconnected loads [equipment that uses electricity] and distributed energy sources within clearly defined electrical boundaries that act as a single controllable entity with respect to the grid."[33]

Even when isolated from the main grid, microgrids are considerably more complicated and expensive than SHSs. Given this complexity, start-ups operating in the developing world must devise innovative business models to deploy solar microgrids. Many providers are using a PAYG model, relying on monthly mobile payments—once the system is up and running, they argue, each customer's payment should be much less for power from a microgrid than from an SHS because of economies of scale.[34] But first, a microgrid provider must finance the high capital cost of setting up the generation sources, distribution infrastructure, and customer equipment. And its survival depends on reliably collecting payments from most of or all the microgrid's customers. In a rural community, a failed harvest might prevent an entire community from paying on time, which could torpedo the economics of the microgrid.

For this reason, other innovative elements have to supplement the PAYG business model. A popular option secures an "anchor client," which will provide reliable payments to lower the cash-flow risk of a microgrid. In India, OMC Power, which is a leader in deploying this model, constructs microgrids near remote cell-phone towers. Those towers typically rely on expensive diesel generators, so their owners are open to switching to a cheaper option. And, because of India's booming use of mobile phones, telecom firms operating towers are typically safe bets to be reliable, paying power customers and thus to serve as the anchor client. If such a client provides the majority of the revenue that the microgrid needs, then the remaining microgrid power capacity that it doesn't use can be sold to a nearby community using a PAYG model.[35]

Some researchers have demonstrated that adding another business client—such as a flour mill—can further reduce the risk that a microgrid provider will lose money.[36] This strategy of diversifying revenue streams can enable start-ups to reduce the risk that investors perceive in financing the relatively higher up-front cost of microgrids compared with SHSs.

In addition to carefully choosing a microgrid's clientele, firms must make an important choice between using alternating current (AC) or direct current (DC) electricity. On the one hand, the former is compatible with the main grid's standard, making it possible to eventually link microgrids and macrogrids. But the latter is more efficient and cheaper and might be ideal for supplementing an unreliable main grid.

The AC versus DC debate is not new. Indeed, it dates back more than a century, to the birth of the power system and a stormy debate between Thomas Edison and Nikola Tesla, two pioneers of electricity. Edison backed DC, which is an intuitive form of electricity analogous to a steady stream of water. In fact, Edison publicly electrocuted farm animals to demonstrate that high-voltage AC power was lethal. But Tesla, who favored AC, which involves electric current switching direction many times a second, ultimately won this debate.

Tesla's arguments made sense for the twentieth century. At the time, it was possible to send AC power over long distances without incurring high losses along the way by using high-voltage AC. With twentieth-century technology, it was straightforward to increase the voltage of AC power coming out of a generator, send it along a high-voltage transmission line, and reduce the voltage to a safe level on the other side to distribute to customers. By contrast, the voltage of DC electricity could not easily be changed, so DC power could not travel very far. As a result, grids around the world still use AC power.

Compatibility with that standard provides an argument for using AC for a microgrid: if the grid eventually reaches an area that is served by an AC microgrid, that microgrid can simply join the main grid rather than trying to compete with it. Several microgrid start-ups—among them, Powerhive in Kenya—have adopted this AC model. Governments are often supportive because they can partner with such start-ups to electrify remote areas with microgrids before the main grid eventually arrives. In Kenya, regulators granted Powerhive the country's first-ever license to sell power in defined rural areas.[37]

But, AC makes less sense than DC in the twenty-first century. Thanks to advances in power electronics technology, the cost of changing the voltage of DC electricity has plummeted, so DC can be sent over long distances with low losses. Plus, in the future, customers will increasingly use DC electricity to power such items as modern lights, digital devices, and electric vehicles. Meeting those needs by converting AC to DC electricity is inefficient. Power utilities, however, are lumbering giants overseeing enormous networks of expensive infrastructure, so it is unlikely that central grids will switch over to DC anytime soon.

The case is different for firms building microgrids today. First, microgrids do not typically need to deliver electricity over long distances. The short distance neutralizes the main advantage of AC over DC (which really is not even an advantage anymore). Second, solar-powered microgrids in particular are better suited for DC than AC because solar produces DC power, and batteries store and discharge DC power. Third, the most energy-efficient appliances—LED lights, televisions, radios, and fans, for instance—all use DC power. Running a customer's appliances, then, requires an AC solar-powered microgrid to have equipment that converts the solar or battery power from DC to AC and then back from AC to DC. In these repeated conversions, some of the electricity is lost, often around 5 percent to 20 percent.[38] By contrast, an all-DC microgrid can be much more efficient.[39]

All these factors can make DC solar microgrids cost less than half as much as their AC counterparts. But the most dramatic improvements in the economics of the former have come from the plunging costs and soaring performance of highly efficient DC appliances. From 2009 to 2015, the cost of LED lights fell by a factor of more than ten; over the same span, the amount of light emitted by a bulb more than doubled.[40] This trend, moreover, will continue. Figure 5.3 tracks falling appliance costs for SHSs, but the trend is equally applicable for solar microgrids. Between 2014 and 2020, solar systems are projected to nearly halve in cost, and most of that improvement will come from cheaper, more efficient appliances.

Researchers in India have run computer simulations to compare the costs of using AC and DC solar-powered microgrids to power household energy use. They found that a DC microgrid required nearly three times less electricity, incurring less than half the cost, compared to a household with less efficient appliances connected to an AC microgrid that suffered from conversion losses.[41]

AC advocates argue that these DC benefits are trumped by AC microgrids' ability to link up with the main grid, which is crucial to ultimately provide access to modern energy. But a grid connection by no means guarantees modern energy access. Consider that in addition to the 1.1 billion people worldwide who have no access to electricity, up to another billion have a grid connection but face frustratingly unreliable service.[42] And having consistent access to power can matter just as much as having any power at all. One study found that the increase in satisfaction from receiving seven

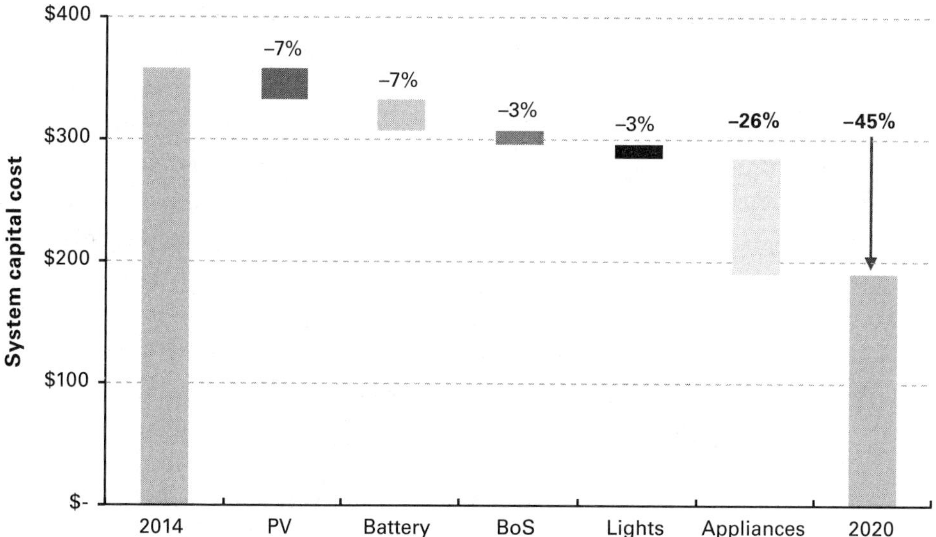

Figure 5.3

Current and forecast cost of an SHS. Comparison of the total capital cost of an off-grid SHS powered by a 25 W PV panel in 2014 with that of an equivalent system in 2020, breaking out the cost savings by system component.

Source: Bloomberg New Energy Finance (2016).

extra hours of electricity access per day was similar to that from gaining an electricity connection in the first place.[43] Indeed, in rural Karnataka, in southern India, researchers found that in many rural areas where the grid had finally arrived, local residents still preferred off-grid generators because the grid power was unreliable.[44] And cities—already home to a majority of the global population—will increasingly confront the most pressing energy access challenges. In urban and peri-urban areas on the outskirts of metropolitan areas, aging power grids incapable of absorbing population growth are set to face chronic blackouts.

DC microgrids could ameliorate that worrying situation. In fact, in Bihar—India's most densely populated state, with over 100 million people—a team of researchers from the Indian Institute of Technology has deployed DC microgrids to improve urban energy access. Their goal is to equip 100,000 homes with a DC microgrid powered by a solar panel and battery, and also connected to the grid through a device that converts incoming AC grid power to DC electricity.

They anticipate that when the grid cannot meet customer demand—which happens often in Bihar, the state with the biggest deficit between power supply and demand—a brownout will cut up to 90 percent of the grid power. But the remaining 10 percent, along with the power from the solar panel and battery, should be enough to power a whole range of DC appliances: five fans, eight lights, two small televisions, several cell phone and tablet chargers, and a laptop charger. Thanks to DC microgrids, these households will have uninterrupted access to a range of modern energy services, even though only 10 percent of the grid electricity might be available at any given time. And although in this particular deployment, each household gets its own DC microgrid, the researchers are linking households together in another project in Rajasthan, making it possible to reallocate limited resources even more efficiently to meet demand.[45]

In fact, the process of DC microgrid formation and networking could lead to a brand new paradigm in how power systems are built, turning the conventional model on its head. In that model, utilities use a top-down planning process, forecasting demand and building a network of power lines and equipment to meet those needs. But in a DC microgrid future, networks might arise organically, from the bottom up.[46,47]

This theory is known as "swarm electrification," and the researcher who conceived the term, Sebastian Groh, likens a bottom-up electricity network to a "swarm of fish," in which "there is no central intelligence, and the fish work together to create unity." His company, ME SOLshare, is making it possible for the 4 million households in Bangladesh with DC SHSs to connect to one another and trade electricity. Using peer-to-peer mobile payments—securely logged using blockchain technology, which is also used to authenticate Bitcoin transactions—homes can participate in a bottom-up marketplace, dynamically balancing supply and demand across a self-assembled DC microgrid. This concept could work in any place with a high population density—Bangladesh is an ideal starting point, with a population of 160 million squished into an area the size of New York State.[48]

Clearly, DC microgrids could enable a wealth of new ways to improve energy access. If innovative firms can successfully scale up their demonstrations, Edison might have the last laugh in the AC versus DC debate after all.

The Double-Edged Sword of Public Intervention

Many examples of off-grid business model innovation—whether the rise of PAYG solar systems in Africa or swarm electrification in Bangladesh—avoid relying on the public sector. This is just as well, because weak governments and dysfunctional state-owned power firms are partly to blame for the dismal progress of electrification. Better to circumvent the government altogether, entrepreneurs reason, and focus on delivering a valuable product to customers that needs no public assistance. So far, this strategy has worked best wherever there is minimal government regulation. Hence, in Africa, start-ups have been able to rapidly scale up on the back of mobile payment systems. But, as noted previously, government restrictions on mobile banking in India prevented similar market growth.

So, the first order of business is getting government out of the way of innovation, and that requires eliminating distortionary policies. The biggest of these is India's kerosene subsidy, which artificially depresses the price of kerosene and makes it more difficult for off-grid solar to compete. More than 70 percent of the savings that customers realize from switching from kerosene to solar in Africa are eliminated by subsidies in India.[49] Unfortunately, the subsidies are politically popular, so politicians are loath to cut them. They are, however, indefensible—rather than alleviating poverty, as policymakers might intend, kerosene subsidies lock people without access to power into dependence on a fuel source that is expensive, produces low-quality light, and emits lethal fumes. They have also held back the growth of off-grid solar in Asia compared to its rapid clip in Africa.

Although kerosene subsidies are the most prominent example of policy malpractice, other distortionary policies also threaten the ability of off-grid solar firms to gain traction. Another example in India is artificially low electricity prices, which are politically popular with residential customers. These subsidies make it harder for solar firms to market off-grid systems that would supplement grid power in areas with unreliable electricity service. And these subsidies also bankrupt utilities, making it tougher for them to upgrade the ailing power grid.

Trade barriers are another good example of distortionary policy. One of the reasons that off-grid solar has taken off in East Africa is that tariffs and import duties there are relatively low, which enables Off-Grid Electric and other firms to import components of their solar systems from all over the world and move them freely between their bases of operation in Tanzania and Rwanda. In West Africa, by contrast, higher tariffs and duties make it more complicated and expensive to operate a global supply chain, ultimately raising the cost of off-grid solar. So a lesson for countries seeking to harness off-grid solar to improve domestic energy access is to tear down trade barriers that might artificially increase the cost of solar systems.

Getting governments out of the way of innovation is a foundational requirement in order for public policy to enable off-grid solar deployment, but for the sector to flourish, it will need active support. The most important role that governments can play is in crafting a national plan for energy access that helps off-grid solar firms focus their efforts most effectively. Without such a plan, firms marketing SHSs or solar microgrids in remote areas might fear getting put out of business when the grid finally does arrive. For example, a survey conducted in India found that companies' fear of the main grid arriving was the most commonly cited barrier to the development of microgrids in the country.[50]

By contrast, if the government maps out the areas where it is most feasible to extend the grid, while carving out regions that might more economically be served by off-grid solutions, then it can minimize the risk of competition between the two solutions. And by clearly articulating technical standards for how to interconnect microgrids with the main grid, governments can help off-grid solar firms plan for eventual grid extension and thus prevent them from losing their investment.[51]

Many countries have begun to do this. One of the most exciting examples is Nigeria, which has the second-largest unelectrified population in the world. The government plans to electrify 75 percent of the country by 2020 and is banking on off-grid solar to complement its grid extension efforts. The government is designating some areas—those that might be sparsely populated, hilly, or otherwise very expensive to serve with new transmission lines—as optimal for stand-alone SHSs or isolated solar microgrids. It has designated other areas as targets for extending the central grid. Finally, it has chosen some areas, such as those where a grid connection exists but is weak or unreliable, as best suited for microgrids to shore up electricity access in the near term, with the option for the government to eventually extend the grid and link up with the microgrids in the future.

If and when that happens, the government has pledged to compensate microgrid providers, either buying their infrastructure outright or allowing them to continue operating as local distributors for electricity from the merged main grid and microgrid.[52] To create these geographical designations, Nigeria has taken advantage of studies that marshal computer simulations to predict which regions are best served by microgrids, the main grid, or both (see figure 5.4).[53] And by articulating this overall vision, the public sector is

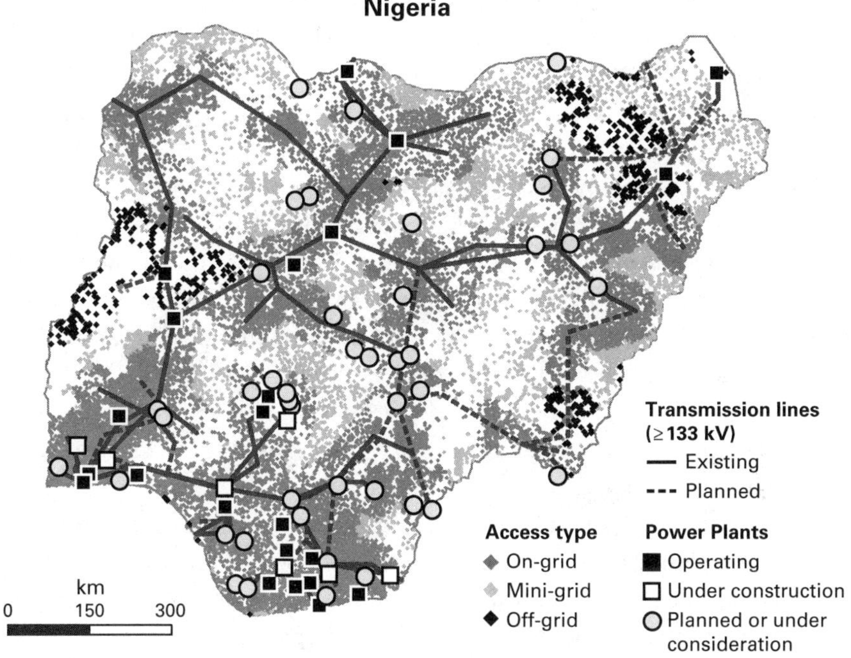

Figure 5.4

Using microgrids and main grid extensions to electrify Nigeria. This map, based on research conducted at the Royal Institute of Technology in Sweden, depicts the optimal deployment of different strategies to achieve universal electrification in Nigeria. The dark gray regions are areas where the main grid currently operates or could feasibly be extended. The light gray regions are remote, possibly sparsely populated areas where it does not make economic sense to extend the main grid. And the black areas are targets to deploy microgrids (likely powered by solar), which could initially provide energy access without the main grid, but to which the main grid might ultimately connect.

Source: Reprinted from International Energy Agency (IEA) (2014), and originally published in Mentis et al. (2015).

able to provide certainty to off-grid solar providers and encourage them to fill needs that are beyond the government's capacity.

Another way that governments can promote off-grid solar growth is by driving down the technology costs of off-grid systems. India has excelled at this. In fact, the Indian government can take much of the credit for the recent plunge in LED prices, and its strategy could work well to lower the cost of other DC appliances. To reduce technology costs, the government, through an agency called Energy Efficiency Services Limited (EESL), has purchased LED lightbulbs in massive quantities, enabling it to distribute and sell them for very low prices. Through the end of 2016, the agency had sold more than 200 million bulbs and driven their prices in India down below those in the West.[54] And major suppliers, including Phillips, have competed aggressively—and frantically worked to improve their products—in order to win lucrative bulk contracts with EESL.

Saurabh Kumar, EESL's director, excitedly informed me over breakfast one day that the next technology he was targeting was air conditioners. If India can drive down the cost and increase the efficiency of air conditioning, which could be the single largest driver of India's electricity demand in the coming decades, it could bring modern energy access to hundreds of millions of people without vastly increasing India's carbon emissions. And by purchasing other DC appliances in bulk, it could make the DC microgrid an even more affordable proposition.

Yet another need that the public sector can help fill is the dearth of trained professionals to install and service solar systems.[55] Governments can fund centers to train electrical technicians, for example. Off-Grid Electric and other companies already train some service professionals in house, but start-ups by themselves have been unable to train enough professionals to meet the sector's exploding demand.

Finally, the public sector can help jump-start the off-grid solar industry by providing access to low-cost capital. In particular, both governments and international financial institutions such as the World Bank can help provide working capital—the funds that an off-grid provider needs to build up its inventory and construct solar systems. In the long term, the industry should be self-sustaining, in that solar providers should be able to tap into capital markets, for example through securitization, to finance PAYG solar services for customers. But just to set the industry on a trajectory for self-sustaining growth, the public sector might provide low-cost working capital loans or grants.[56] Again, this support should resemble training wheels, not a permanent crutch.

Together, a strategy of dismantling distortionary policies and implementing enabling ones is the best way to support the nascent off-grid solar industry. The combination of supportive public policies and vibrant business-model innovation could provide hope—and a pathway toward modern energy access—for Grace's family and countless others like it.

PART III REINVENTING SOLAR

Highlights

- The trend is clear: Solar installations based on existing silicon photovoltaic (PV) technology should expand their market penetration over the next decade. But beyond then, their growth could hit a ceiling. Meeting solar's midcentury target of powering one-third of global electricity demand will require dirt-cheap solar and cost-effective storage of the electricity it produces. For humanity to meet the longer-term goal of meeting a majority of its overall energy needs by harnessing sunlight, it will need to devise ways of converting solar energy into fuel. The technologies for meeting both goals do not exist at commercial scale today. *Technological innovation* is therefore urgent.
- Today, silicon technology dominates the commercial solar PV market, but researchers in academic laboratories around the world are making rapid advances in tomorrow's solar PV materials. Chapter 6, "Revolution by Evolution," explores the brief history and meteoric ascent of solar cells made of perovskite, a material that could enable manufacture of cheap, highly efficient solar coatings that could be unspooled from a printer much as newspaper is printed. Perovskite currently has taken the lead among emerging PV technologies, and even more radical ideas and materials are on the drawing board. Because revolutionary technologies face steep barriers to enter the marketplace, it might be easier to find an evolutionary route from today's PV technologies to tomorrow's. One promising approach to do just that is to layer perovskite on top of silicon, piggybacking an emerging technology on top of the established incumbent.

- Solar PV technology—whatever the material—converts sunlight instantaneously into electricity. It would be much more useful to instead squirrel away the sun's energy to be used on demand. Chapter 7, "Stashing Sunshine," reports on the rapid progress scientists are making on converting sunlight into more convenient stores of energy. For example, artificial leaf technology already outperforms natural photosynthesis and can generate fuels that could one day replace oil. Still another way to store the sun's energy is in the form of heat. So scientists are working to upgrade the technology behind concentrated solar power plants to focus the sun's rays to higher temperatures than ever before, enabling these plants to run 24/7.

Chapter 6 Revolution by Evolution

Wintertime's arrival in England adds an unpleasant chill to already dreary, drizzly days. So, I wasn't surprised at the resigned mood in the conference room as a motley crew of graduate students and postdocs shuffled in for a weekly lab meeting in 2011. Many of us hailed from much balmier climates—California, Spain, Italy, even the Caribbean islands. We were all here, amid the dreaming spires of Oxford University, to learn from Professor Henry Snaith, an up-and-coming scientist studying brand new materials for solar power.

Henry—he insists on being called by his first name—is not your average physics prof. A former rugby player at Cambridge University, he's energetic, athletic, and competitive; once he took our lab skiing in the Alps, beat us down every run, and made fun of the slower folks (okay, just me). He's also gregarious and charming, especially when discussing his work. And he's equally comfortable in the lab or at a cocktail party. Most important, he is a brilliant scientist with a spooky intuition about how materials behave at the nanoscale, in the realm of atoms and electrons.

Not surprisingly, Henry earned attention from renowned scientists early in his career. He studied under Professor Sir Richard Friend at the famed Cavendish Laboratory at Cambridge, and he went on to pursue postdoctoral research in Switzerland under Professor Michael Grätzel, another venerated researcher. He was still a post-doc when our lab held its routine weekly meeting on that dreary day, a young scientist with a solid pedigree and fewer than 3,000 citations to his papers.[1] Over the next four years, Henry would amass ten times that many citations, ascending to become the second-most-cited scientist in the *world* in 2015.[2] As it turned out, that lab meeting was anything but routine.

Mike Lee, one of my fellow graduate students, unveiled a startling discovery. At Henry's behest, he had flown to Japan to track down a chemical recipe that researchers at Tokyo University had invented for making novel solar cells. Then, back at Oxford and working late at night, a bleary-eyed Mike mistakenly flipped two of the chemical concentrations on his recipe. The mistake yielded a solar PV cell that was more than 10 percent efficient—able to convert more than 10 percent of the sun's energy striking it into electricity.

Compared to the record silicon solar cell efficiency of more than 25 percent, Mike's number was unremarkable. But it was a major jump for a material not already in commercial use. Our lab (as well as a scattered assortment of researchers around the world) was trying to get away from silicon's limitations, such as the need for expensive manufacturing equipment and the brittle quality of silicon wafers that resulted in rigid, ugly panels. With the right material, we thought, a cheap inkjet printer might be able to produce rolls of flexible, efficient solar PV coatings. Flexible coatings would make it possible to put energy-producing materials on parts of buildings that cannot support solar panels and might increase solar's aesthetic appeal as well. After more than a decade of trying, the best result that anyone had achieved was 7 percent efficiency. Mike had managed to get to more than 10 percent using a brand new material that he had stumbled on and not yet optimized—the equivalent of nailing a bulls-eye in darts while blindfolded. As the results sank in, our team of stunned researchers salivated, confident that concerted development of the material should make it possible to improve efficiency to 20 percent and well beyond.

The material Mike had tweaked to such dramatic effect is known as "perovskite" ("pear-AHV-skite"). Unlike their silicon counterparts, perovskite solar cells are simple to make at the lab bench. They are also remarkably versatile, enabling flexible, colorful, semitransparent, and lightweight variants. Once Mike's results became public, the idea that they could have these properties and also be highly efficient at absorbing sunlight and converting it into electricity sparked a solar gold rush.

Our lab had a head start, as Henry smartly deployed the rest of us to learn as much about this material as we could while he and Mike prepared an announcement to the world for the prestigious pages of *Science* magazine.[3] In those early days, our little group of researchers resembled kids in a playground, with perovskite all to ourselves. I was elated that perovskite acted like fairy dust on all my existing experiments, turning kooky solar cell designs into respectable devices. But Henry would gently prod me to recognize that perovskite was much more than a fairy-dust accessory to another experiment—it was the main event itself. Our monopoly over research into Henry's perovskite ended a year later in 2012, when the rest of the scientific community read about the technology, and researchers around the world dumped their previous projects to pile onto the field.

This flurry led to flourishing international collaboration—but also fierce competition. The most intriguing subplot has been the rivalry between Henry's lab and that of his former mentor, Michael Grätzel. Once, my colleague Sam Stranks discovered that Grätzel and his colleagues were racing to beat Sam to press with a research result that Sam had independently obtained weeks earlier and presented at a conference. Henry and Sam worked around the clock to prepare their own manuscript and win the scoop. Ultimately, *Science* published the two results side by side.

Beyond conferring credit to both teams, the simultaneous publication was a powerful signal that perovskites are such an important breakthrough that they merit the extra column inches in top journals that cover a myriad of other scientific fields.

In fact, just from 2012 to 2016, nearly thirty articles discussing perovskite solar were published in the top two scientific journals, *Science* and *Nature*. For a scientist, publishing in *Science* or *Nature* is akin to an actor receiving an Oscar nomination. And the surest way to publish a prestigious article relating to solar is to set a new efficiency world record. Responding to this incentive and the prospect of revolutionizing solar technology, scientists from around the world—most recently in South Korea—have pushed up the efficiency of perovskite solar cells faster than that of any other solar technology in history (reaching more than 22 percent by 2016).[4]

If you're surprised that you haven't heard of perovskite, don't be. Outside the rarefied world of academia, where researchers confer celebrity status on the latest efficiency holder, very few people understand how remarkable this new material is. Some in the silicon-dominated solar industry may be aware of perovskite, but they are not worried about it challenging silicon's primacy. At least in the short term, they are entirely justified. The frenzy in academic circles surrounding cell efficiency has very little to do with making a commercial product that will survive outside for years or even decades, as current silicon panels regularly do. In the lab, scientists attempt to break the efficiency record by cherry-picking the best result from tests of hundreds of tiny slivers of solar material a fraction of the size of your fingernail under a special lamp simulating perfect noontime sunshine.

Realizing what it will take to bring the technology closer to commercialization, academics have recently started to build bigger perovskite cells, subject them to real-world heat and moisture conditions, and test how long they survive. But the cells may never leave the lab unless investors become interested in them. Investors, however, are skittish about funding solar startups, having lost their shirts in the Silicon Valley clean technology boom and bust from 2006 to 2011. As long as investors and the solar industry continue to ignore academia, perovskite and other new solar technologies could well remain lab-bench novelties.

Such neglect could be disastrous for solar power's long-term prospects. Chapters 4 and 5, on financial and business model innovation, explained how existing solar technology can flourish by accessing vast untapped pools of low-cost capital. That approach, on its own, might work for a decade, or maybe even two. But solar must do more than attract investment in existing technologies to meet the midcentury target of supplying a third of the world's power. As described in chapter 3, solar will have to surmount its plummeting value as its penetration increases—the value deflation effect already manifest in Germany and California—as well as the strain on power grids that must integrate an intermittent generation source. Once solar power ascends to provide a double-digit percentage of global electricity, these obstacles could prevent it from delivering a larger share of the world's electricity, even if the cost of silicon-based solar PV systems continues the rate of decline it has enjoyed over the last half-century.

To avoid a growth slowdown, solar PV will need to become still cheaper. And to do that, it has to become more efficient than silicon may ever allow. That's why a group of leading solar scientists insisted in 2016 that solar research is not finished, arguing:

> While [the] spectacular success [of solar photovoltaics (PV)] should be celebrated, many PV researchers have recently been dismayed to see shrinking public PV research and development (R&D) funding (both in the US and in other countries) . . . For higher penetration of the market, PV systems must cost even less to cover the additional costs of storage or transmission so that solar generation can be dispatched to cost-effectively meet electricity demand more broadly in both time and space.[5]

Fortunately, exciting research on many fronts has potential to improve the performance of solar PV and make it much cheaper. Future technologies lie on a spectrum from evolutionary to revolutionary.[6] Evolutionary improvements to existing technologies have a better shot at making a commercial debut in the near term—remember that a successful innovation is one that makes it to market. And the most promising evolutionary option right now is for perovskite or other materials to literally piggyback right on top of existing silicon solar panels. Combining silicon with perovskite would boost the efficiency of existing panels, while largely leaving the existing production process and the finished product the same, maximizing the chances of market acceptance.

But down the road, revolutionary concepts that look nothing like today's PV panels will be needed, and those advances require investment right now so they can ultimately bring massive benefits. The evolutionary route can lead to a revolution. For example, layering perovskite on top of silicon in the near term can eventually make it feasible to produce even more efficient and versatile all-perovskite solar coatings, smashing through the limits that constrain silicon technology.

Although perovskite is the lab leader, it does have potential drawbacks, and it isn't the only promising solar material out there. Other approaches—including organic and quantum dot solar cells—come with their own unique advantages. They present the possibility of a virtually limitless range of color, transparency, and flexibility, as well as theoretically unmatched efficiency.

All these new technologies could enable a range of applications. They could coat weak shanty roofs in urban slums, power forward-deployed military operations, and give architects a diverse palette for designing beautiful, energy-efficient buildings. Highly efficient solar tarps might carpet deserts; Home Depot might sell solar paint as cheaply as wallpaper. And, new technologies could even make it feasible to realize an idea generally dismissed as science fiction: space-based solar power, which would harness a 24/7 supply of sunlight and beam power down to the Earth's surface.

Right now, we don't know which solar technologies and which applications will be needed to transform today's fossil fuel–dominated power system. So, it makes eminent sense to pack our technological quiver with as many potent arrows as possible. Henry Snaith knows that tall barriers stand in the way of any upstart that aims to challenge silicon's dominance over the solar industry. But that hasn't stopped him from trying. He's founded a start-up, Oxford PV, which has generated the most buzz of any solar start-up in years. He can't do it alone, though. It will take scientists, entrepreneurs, investors, corporations, and—importantly—policymakers to help emerging solar technologies have their day in the sun.

From Photons to Electrons

To understand what it takes to maximize the efficiency of PV cells, consider how silicon cells convert incoming sunlight into electricity. Solar electricity production involves two of nature's elementary particles: the photon and the electron. Photons are wispy particles of light, and a photon's energy is directly related to what color it is. For example, blue photons have more energy than red ones; invisible ultraviolet photons have even higher energy, whereas infrared photons—also invisible—are low energy. Electrons are negatively charged particles that surround the positively charged nucleus of an atom.

A solar cell recruits both of these particles by transferring the energy from each incoming photon to an electron. Once endowed with an energy boost, the electron can break free from its host atom and exit the solar cell. The stream of electrons leaving the solar cell represents electricity, and the amount of energy pumped out by the solar cell depends on two values. First, the "electric voltage" is tied to how much energy is in each electron that flows out of the solar cell. Second, the "electric current" depends on the total number of electrons leaving the solar cell each moment. The power output of a solar cell—how much electric energy it pumps out every second—is just the voltage multiplied by the current.

So, if a solar cell could transfer all the energy from every single incoming photon to an electron, and make sure that every energized electron left the solar cell to do useful electrical work, it would maximize its electric voltage, current, and power output and be 100 percent efficient. But even the very best silicon cells can muster only a quarter of that figure. Why? Silicon is a semiconductor—a material that can switch back and forth between a conductor of electricity and an insulator, making it possible for electrons to toggle between staying put and moving around when photons strike them. And, semiconductors have a fundamental feature that limits their efficiency: the more photons the cell absorbs, the less energy per photon it can transfer to each electron. In other words, there is a trade-off between the maximum current and the voltage that a solar cell can produce, even though both quantities matter for the cell's power output. The more current there is, the less voltage, and the more voltage, the less current. Because electrical output is simply voltage multiplied by current, 100 percent efficiency remains out of reach.

The voltage-current trade-off stems from a property of semiconductors called the "bandgap": the amount of energy that an electron needs to break free from its host atom and contribute to the cell's electric output. A photon with less energy than the bandgap will pass right through the solar cell. A photon with more energy than the bandgap can transfer only a bandgap's worth of energy to an electron—the rest of the photon's energy gets wasted as heat.

Think of a particular semiconductor's bandgap as the amount of force needed to get ketchup flowing from a stuck bottle. Tapping the bottom too lightly won't do anything to get the ketchup flowing (analogous to a low-energy photon passing right through the solar cell). Hitting it with the perfect amount of force will transfer just enough energy to get the ketchup flowing (like a photon with energy equal to the bandgap setting an electron free to flow out of the solar cell). And hitting the bottle with a sledgehammer will also get the ketchup flowing—but at the cost of expending a lot of energy to heave the hammer and wasting most of that energy (like a high-energy, ultraviolet photon transferring a bit of its energy to an electron and then dissipating a lot of heat).

To achieve high efficiency, scientists have to choose a material with an optimal bandgap. If the bandgap is too high, most photons will lack the energy needed to eject electrons and will pass right through the solar cell, failing to generate much electric current. If the bandgap is too low, most photons will set electrons free but only transfer a dribble of energy to each one, resulting in a low voltage. Silicon happens to have a decent bandgap somewhere in the middle, although it is a little lower than that of more ideal semiconductors, such as gallium arsenide, which is used to make more efficient solar cells but is too expensive to have commercial success. Theoretical models indicate that silicon's highest efficiency is about 29 percent—a couple percentage points lower than that of gallium arsenide.

Despite more than a half-century of development, silicon has topped out at just above 26 percent efficiency, below its theoretical maximum. Why? The reason lies in the journey that an electron takes from being liberated by a photon to successfully exiting the solar cell. It turns out that the path is filled with perilous potholes, and electrons behave like drunk drivers. If a mobile electron runs into an obstacle or a trap, it loses as wasted heat some of or all the energy imparted by the photon. A solar material that is a perfect crystal lattice—that is, its atoms are perfectly arranged in a repeating pattern—will pose no obstacles to electrons careering across the lattice toward an external circuit. But real-life crystals tend to have defects or impurities that can impede an electron's journey. So, it takes expensive equipment and temperatures above 1,000°C to produce high-purity silicon with very few defects. Those defects that remain, as well as ones at the interfaces between silicon and other layers of the finished solar cell, prevent some fraction of electrons from reaching the external circuit, reducing the efficiency of real cells below their theoretical limit.

This process is summarized in figure 6.1, which walks through the various losses that a silicon solar cell incurs in trying to convert sunlight into electricity. The *x*-axis shows the range of different photon energies, or colors, emitted by the sun. And for each color, the *y*-axis value sums up the energy from all the photons that pass through a 1-m^2 box every second, otherwise known as the "power density" for that color.

The area of "atmospheric losses" represents the power that is lost as sunlight travels from outer space through the Earth's atmosphere, and photons

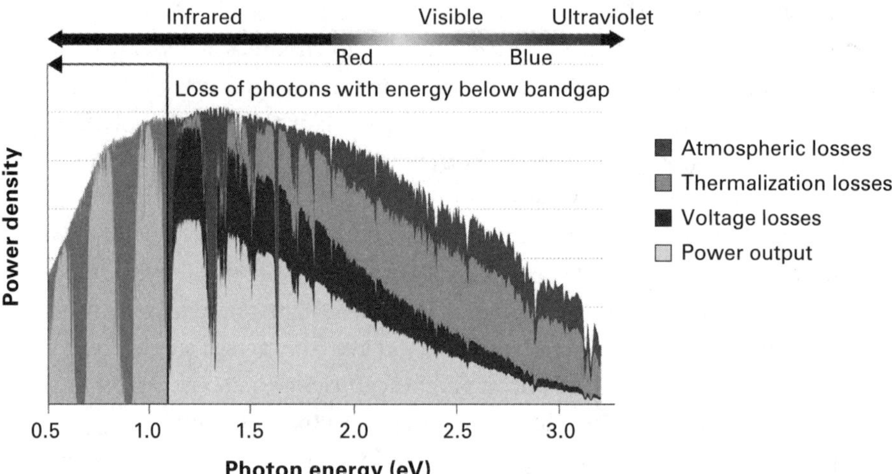

Figure 6.1

Harnessing sunlight with a silicon solar cell. This graph displays the total energy embodied in sunlight and the various losses incurred by a silicon solar cell in converting sunlight to electricity.

bump into air molecules before reaching a solar cell on the Earth's surface. Now the solar cell starts to rack up losses. Every photon below the bandgap of silicon, which is 1.1 eV ("eV," or "electron-volt" is just a measure of energy appropriate for a tiny particle like an electron) passes right through the solar cell. Every photon above the bandgap transfers only a bandgap's worth of energy to an electron, wasting the rest as heat. Thus, after these "thermalization losses," the silicon solar cell's electrons already have less than half the energy that the sun's photons brought to the Earth's surface. From there, electrons lose more energy as they zig and zag their drunken route toward the exit, bumping into crystalline defects and traps as they go. Those "voltage losses" further reduce the electric power output of the solar cell. What's left—the area labeled "power output"—represents an efficiency of just 25 percent or less of the sunlight incident on the solar cell.

For decades, the received wisdom among experts was that it would take high-temperature processing and expensive equipment to prepare high-purity crystalline materials, as silicon is, to maximize the efficiency of solar cells. Getting to 30 percent efficiency and beyond was a commercial non-starter because exotic approaches, such as stacking layers of semiconductor on top of each other to capture more of the solar spectrum, have traditionally been prohibitively expensive. But perovskite technology has shattered both of those conventional assumptions, forcing scientists to rethink whether silicon is indeed the best technology out there.

Say That Ten Times Fast

Even though it is a seemingly foreign, tongue-twisting term, perovskite isn't anything new to scientists, especially not geologists. The term applies to a particular crystal structure; various minerals that take the perovskite structure are abundant below the Earth's surface. What Mike fabricated at Oxford, though, was a synthetic perovskite, rather than a naturally occurring one. His creation incorporated inorganic atoms, as is usual in natural perovskites, with organic molecules. High-efficiency solar cells are normally made of inorganic materials. Such materials include silicon and gallium arsenide—traditional materials that are produced in wafers that can be turned into discrete solar cells—as well as materials such as cadmium telluride (CdTe) and copper indium gallium (di)selenide (CIGS) that can be deposited as continuous, thin films. Organic polymers are used in plastics, among other applications, and have historically been considered inefficient and unreliable solar materials, though they are easier to work with and cheaper than their inorganic counterparts. As it turns out, perovskite is a hybrid that combines the best elements of its inorganic and organic constituents.

One of the remarkable characteristics of perovskite is that it naturally coalesces into near-perfect crystals without much effort at all. To make perovskite materials in the lab, researchers will mix up the chemical constituents of the perovskite and dispense a few drops onto a spinning slide. Then, just like tide pools at the beach leave behind salt crystals, the evaporating solvents leave a film of perovskite crystals that are ready to guide drunken electrons safely to their off-ramps from a solar cell. Researchers are still working hard to improve perovskite crystal quality, and their improvements to date are a big reason why the efficiency of perovskite solar cells more than doubled from 2012 to 2016.[7]

Perovskites can be produced at low temperatures, which makes it possible to deposit them on flexible materials like plastics or ultrathin metal meshes.[8] By contrast, making a silicon solar cell requires heating it to temperatures that rule out most flexible substrates. Flexibility is out of the question for current commercial silicon technology anyway, because silicon wafers are so brittle that they crack at the slightest stress. (I did a stint working on a silicon production line, and I snapped countless wafers when unpacking them, picking them up, and, in one instance, sneezing on one.)

Another advantage that perovskite has over silicon is an adjustable bandgap. Whereas silicon's bandgap is fixed at a suboptimal, infrared 1.1 eV, scientists can adjust the perovskite bandgap by tweaking its chemical composition. That flexibility opens up the tantalizing possibility of cheap, multijunction solar cells that stack semiconductors of different bandgaps on top of one another to capture more of the solar spectrum than silicon can. Whereas a single material is limited to a maximum theoretical efficiency of 33 percent, a two-layer solar cell's ceiling is 44 percent, and adding a third layer gets it all the way up to 50 percent.[9]

Here's how such a multijunction cell works, considering just a two-layer, or tandem, cell for simplicity. The top layer has a high bandgap, so it absorbs visible and ultraviolet photons and harvests a large amount of energy per photon. The bottom layer has a lower bandgap, ideal for absorbing lower-energy photons. The infrared photons that pass right through the top layer get absorbed by the bottom layer. Because the high-energy photons have already been harvested, their energy does not get wasted as it would if the cell consisted of a low-bandgap layer alone. Thus, the layering mitigates the trade-off between absorbing more photons and harvesting as much energy per photon as possible.

Already, researchers have developed high-bandgap (about 1.7 eV) perovskites to layer on top of a silicon cell.[10] Although the record efficiency for such a tandem device (nearly 24 percent as of 2017) was less than the record for a conventional silicon cell, these devices will almost certainly surpass silicon's efficiency in the near future as researchers continue to optimize them.[11] Others have made a flexible tandem cell by combining perovskite and CIGS layers.[12] And in 2016, Dr. Tomas Leijtens at Stanford managed to combine two perovskites into a tandem device that was more than 20 percent efficient.[13] (Tomas, a tall, blond Dutchman, was formerly a graduate student with me, so I can attest that behind his nonchalant surfer look is a brilliant scientific mind.) All-perovskite multijunction cells, with two, three, or even more layers, could shatter efficiency records in the future and convert more than a third of the sun's energy to electricity.[14]

But in the nearer term, combining perovskites with silicon (figure 6.2) is the most promising research avenue—evolutionary, not revolutionary. Not everyone agrees that perovskites can provide a meaningful boost on top of silicon, but the results to date are promising.[15] In press interviews, Henry has disclosed that his company, Oxford PV, can boost the efficiency of commercial silicon solar panels by a third with a perovskite coating.[16] And although Oxford PV is out in front, other start-ups, such as in the United States and China, are racing to catch up.

If layering perovskite on top of silicon works, it could pay off handsomely. The factory equipment needed to deposit a perovskite layer would represent just a small fraction of the cost of a silicon solar cell production line. The gains would far outweigh that small cost. More efficient panels would be much cheaper per watt. Many associated costs of building solar projects, such as land and labor, would fall as well because fewer panels would be needed to produce the same power. Most important, the final product would look just like existing silicon solar panels that investors and customers are comfortable with. Overnight, this product would become the best deal on the market.

Perovskites are not quite there yet, and much work needs to be done to improve their commercial viability. Because of the skewed incentives

HOW IT WORKS

Two Are Better Than One

Rather than competing commercially, silicon and perovskite solar cells could operate together, converting sunlight into electricity with greater efficiency than the technologies achieve alone. In a tandem cell (right), a perovskite layer and silicon layer connect, generating electrons that have higher voltage and more energy than either material creates on its own. Perovskite and silicon also convert different wavelengths of sunlight (below), putting more of the spectrum to work.

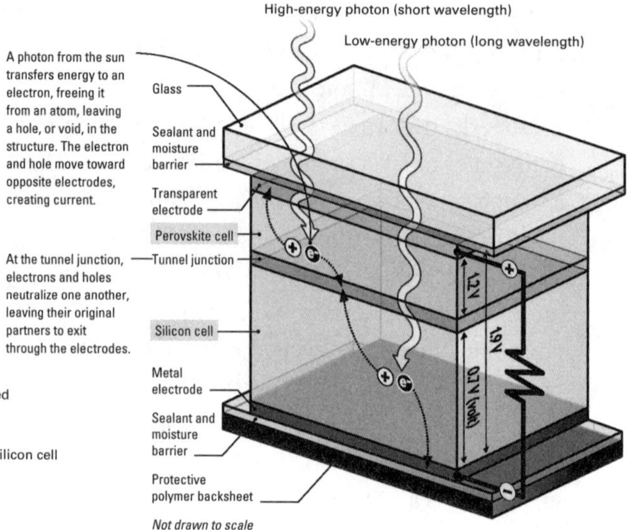
High-energy photon (short wavelength)
Low-energy photon (long wavelength)
A photon from the sun transfers energy to an electron, freeing it from an atom, leaving a hole, or void, in the structure. The electron and hole move toward opposite electrodes, creating current.
At the tunnel junction, electrons and holes neutralize one another, leaving their original partners to exit through the electrodes.
Glass
Sealant and moisture barrier
Transparent electrode
Perovskite cell
Tunnel junction
Silicon cell
Metal electrode
Sealant and moisture barrier
Protective polymer backsheet
Not drawn to scale
1.2V
1.9V
0.7V (volt)

Solar spectrum
High
Energy
Low
Short Wavelength Long
Additional energy converted by perovskite cell
Energy converted by silicon cell

Figure 6.2
How a tandem perovskite/silicon cell works.
Source: Image reprinted with permission from Sivaram, Stranks, and Snaith (2015).

of academia, most attention is focused on tweaking the chemical formula of perovskite to maximize its efficiency—new world records are guaranteed airing in prestigious journals.[17,18] But just as important is proving that they can last, and poor durability has been the Achilles' heel of perovskite solar cells. Some argue that one of the elements found in many perovskite formulations—iodine—destabilizes the cell from within.[19] Others have demonstrated that sunlight—yes, *sunlight,* the thing that a solar cell is supposed to receive—can degrade a perovskite solar cell (although it recovers in the dark).[20]

Fortunately, scientists have started to design perovskite for durability as well as for peak efficiency. Several groups have demonstrated perovskite cells that remain stable during more than a month of testing. In one study, encasing perovskite in epoxy resin (similar to the glue used to bond together pieces of wood) safeguarded it from ordinarily deadly moisture over several months of storage in a hot and humid room.[21] In 2017, researchers reengineered perovskites, using a brand new architecture that saw no degradation after more than a year.[22] The efficiency of their device was just 11 percent, but the team's durability-first attitude is promising, given that to attract significant investment, scientists will need proof that perovskite solar cells can survive in the real world for years, or even decades. As unglamorous as it is, extended field testing in harsh, outdoor environments will be a prerequisite for the technology to move toward commercialization.

Just as important, scientists must demonstrate that they can make perovskites that are much larger than the sliver-sized prototypes in the lab. They need, therefore, to come up with methods for depositing uniform, defect-free perovskites over larger areas. In 2016, an Australian group at Professor Martin Green's PV center made a 12 percent efficient solar cell that was about as big as the palm of a hand.[23] Then in 2017, researchers in the U.S. National Renewable Energy Laboratory (NREL) made four fingernail-sized cells using a special perovskite ink and linked them together to make a 13 percent mini-panel.[24]

These studies are promising; still, the efficiencies they achieved substantially lag the 20 percent efficiency that other scientists have managed to achieve on a single fingernail-sized cell.[25,26] But they are far from the last word. One of my former classmates from Stanford, Joel Jean, is leading a new initiative at the Massachusetts Institute of Technology (MIT) to help researchers transform their tiny perovskite cells into large-scale, lightweight, flexible, and highly efficient solar panels for use in the developing world.[27]

A theoretical final drawback of perovskite may have little basis in reality, but could loom large in consumers' imaginations. Because perovskite contains lead, it might be perceived as unsafe. This lead content is unlikely to pose any health hazard. After all, the amount in a perovskite solar panel is the same as in an equivalent volume of dirt.[28] Moreover, if perovskites make their debut layered on top of silicon, then the various sealing layers inside a conventional panel will virtually guarantee that no lead will be able to escape.

Nevertheless, the presence of a toxic element might well provoke public concern. A good example of what to expect comes from First Solar's experience. That firm manufactures cadmium telluride solar panels containing the toxic element cadmium, and it has faced opposition from communities near the deserts that host its utility-scale installations.[29] To assuage their fears, First Solar has demonstrated that their panels would not discharge toxic cadmium even in a wildfire of 1,000°C. Down the road, any perovskite firm will have to do similar stress testing of their product, and any plans to seal in the perovskite with something flimsier than glass could complicate safety demonstrations.

One promising route might be to eliminate the lead from perovskite altogether, as Dr. Nakita Noel has proved can be done by replacing lead with tin (Nakita was also a fellow graduate student; I remember her best for her colorful Trinidadian slang and perfectionist experimental design).[30] Unfortunately, so far tin-based perovskites are less efficient than lead-based ones, so there remains a clear trade-off between high efficiency and use of nontoxic materials.[31] Still, the meteoric rise of perovskite efficiencies and Henry's inspired business decision to piggyback on silicon rather than confront it head on are reasons to be optimistic that perovskite will transition from invention to innovation—advancing from the lab into the world at large.

Alternatives to the Alternative

Even though perovskite is the undisputed leader in emerging PV technologies, its drawbacks create an opening for other contenders to shine. One is organic PV. Organic electronics have already made a splash in other fields. For example, your television or smartphone might have a screen lit up by vibrant organic light-emitting diodes. Today, organic solar cells cannot match perovskite cells in efficiency, but they are rapidly improving.

Organic solar cells also have some exciting advantages—at least in theory. They can be produced with no toxic materials at all. They are extremely versatile, able to take on the full range of colors and transparencies.[32] (It's possible to create perovskites of different colors as well, but organics rule when it comes to versatility.) Like perovskites, organic solar cells can be produced at low temperatures on flexible substrates, and they can be extremely lightweight.[33] They also have adjustable bandgaps, making organic tandem devices possible as well.[34]

Organic solar cells have a long way to go to catch either perovskite or silicon, however. Recently, researchers have improved the notoriously poor stability of organic solar cells by introducing novel materials, but much more proof is needed that these cells can last in the real world.[35] And the best efficiency of organic solar cells as of 2017 was still only around 12 percent, in large part because organic materials make for quite treacherous terrain for an electron to travel across.

Researchers have tried to increase the surface area and decrease the volume of these materials—a move somewhat akin to replacing logs of firewood with kindling—but doing that just adds surface traps that can doom an electron's journey. Researchers are toying with more radical ways to improve organic solar cell efficiencies—such as relying on a quantum effect in which electrons are teleported out of the cell, obviating the need to fix all the potholes in an electron's path—but those prospects are way down the road.[36]

Another exciting material for solar cells, "quantum dots," could harness many more aspects of quantum mechanics. As the celebrated (and irreverent) physicist Richard Feynman quipped, "Nobody understands quantum mechanics." Physics gets weird on the scale of nanometers (for reference, a nanometer is about the width of two silicon atoms)—and that weirdness is exactly what quantum dot solar cells would harness.

Quantum dots are semiconductor particles that are only a few nanometers in diameter. Many of their properties, including their bandgap, depend on their exact size, so scientists can manufacture quantum dots with a range of bandgaps just by making them bigger or smaller. And like perovskite or organic solar cells, it is possible to make quantum dot solar cells at low temperatures at the lab bench, opening up possibilities for flexible, lightweight solar coatings.[37] In fact, academics are even starting to combine technologies. For example, researchers recently created quantum dots out of perovskite to make a solar cell with greater than 10 percent efficiency.[38]

Although the record quantum dot solar cell efficiency was only around 13 percent as of 2017, investigators have some tricks up their sleeves to raise that number. Here is where things get weird. First, quantum dots may be able to transfer the energy from a single photon to two or more electrons (a process known as "multiple exciton generation"), which would be less wasteful of photons with energy way above the bandgap. So instead of obliterating a single ketchup bottle with a sledgehammer, think of distributing the sledgehammer's force across many ketchup bottles to get lots of ketchup flowing.

A second quantum way to avoid wasting high photon energies is to transfer more than a bandgap's worth of energy from a photon to a single electron and extract the excess from the solar cell before it is released as heat (this is known as the "hot carrier" strategy). Some researchers have even proposed using a coating of quantum dots to absorb high-energy photons and emit twice as many low-energy photons to a solar cell waiting below in order to harness them more efficiently.[39] Although these effects have been observed in the lab, using them to improve cell efficiency is far off on the horizon.

A final way to take advantage of the weirdness of quantum dots is something called "plasmonic resonance." If the quantum dots are just the right size, incoming light waves will jiggle their electrons at just the right frequency to transfer energy with very high efficiency.[40] Think of this as somewhat similar to an opera singer hitting the exact right note that shatters a champagne flute: very effective energy transfer—though a little messy.

All of these are exciting prospects for a new generation of solar technologies. Figure 6.3 plots the rise in efficiencies for several different solar materials side by side, showing the rapid progress across the board. Whereas

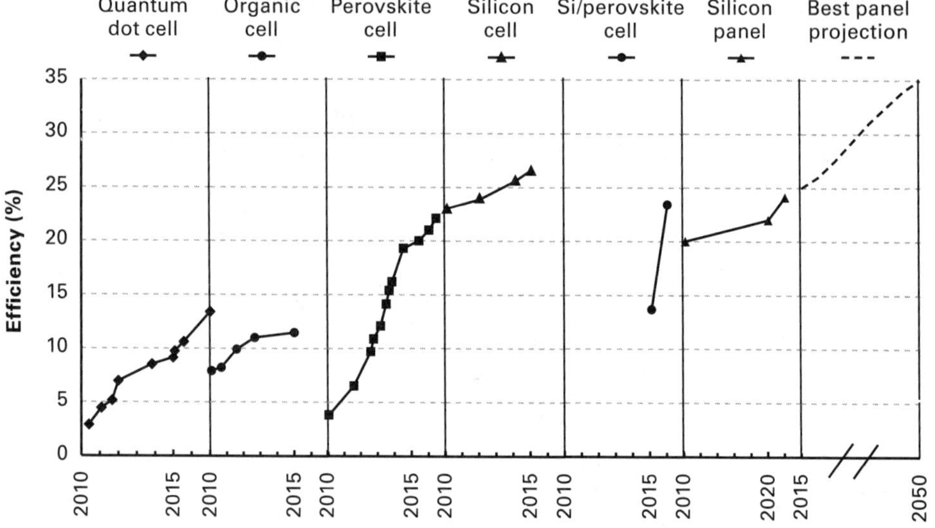

Figure 6.3

Comparison of solar PV efficiency across different technologies. The first six panels chart the progress in record efficiencies for solar cells and panels made of different materials between 2010 and 2017. The rightmost panel projects the efficiency for the best, commercially available solar panel by 2050 (it is likely that this solar panel will consist of multiple semiconductor layers; it might also combine emerging and existing technologies).

Source: Historical record efficiency data from NREL and industry reports. Future projection from Albrecht and Rech (2017).

the five plots on the left display the efficiencies of different solar cells, the two plots on the right show the efficiencies of full panels composed of many cells. The efficiencies of panels are lower than those of cells because of power losses that accompany putting cells together, and because bad cells drag down the performance of good ones. Even taking such losses into account, panel efficiencies could rise dramatically in the coming decades. The final plot on the right displays one study's projection of how new technologies could increase the efficiency of commercial solar PV panels. That projection sees panel efficiency hitting 35 percent—roughly double the average panel efficiency in 2016—by midcentury.

But are academics barking up the wrong tree? Is higher efficiency even necessary? Does the world really need rolls of flexible and lightweight solar coatings? Or are today's silicon panels already up to the task of providing cheap solar power in the twenty-first century? Answering these questions requires delving into the possible applications of new technologies and understanding whether they can add value to existing markets and unlock brand new ones.

One Size Doesn't Fit All

The assertion that silicon solar panels are all the world needs for solar to flourish implicitly makes a huge bet: that silicon panels can be cheap, modular, and versatile enough to serve a wider range of uses than they do today. But this is unlikely. Even in solar's core markets today—utility-scale and rooftop installations—higher-efficiency panels than those sold now could substantially reduce costs, which is crucial to securing solar's competitiveness when value deflation sets in at high penetrations. And there are other markets for which today's silicon PV panels are inadequate, such as in places in both the developed and developing worlds where roofs are weak, in areas where military operations are carried out, and even in outer space.

For today's solar PV markets, however, it isn't obvious why silicon needs replacing, not least because silicon solar panels keep getting cheaper. For decades, they have fallen in cost regularly by roughly 20 percent for every doubling of total production, as producers incrementally shave their costs as they gain scale and experience. This pattern makes it possible to roughly forecast costs well into the future by making some assumptions about the continued growth of solar production.[41] A 2017 study forecasts that the total cumulative solar capacity around the world could hit 8 terawatts (or 8,000 gigawatts) in 2030. By then, the average solar panel would cost $0.25 per watt of rated capacity, thanks to lower-cost production, incrementally better efficiencies, and longer panel lifetimes.[42]

On top of this, there will likely be declines in the associated costs to install a solar PV project, including other hardware, land, labor, and soft costs such as permitting and financing. Recently, the U.S. Department of Energy (DOE) released a road map incorporating all those reductions. In 2030, the study found, electricity from a utility-scale solar PV plant might cost just 3 cents per kilowatt-hour (figure 6.4), roughly half its cost in 2016.[43]

The problem, my colleague Shayle Kann and I have argued, is that even halving solar PV's costs probably won't be enough. That would still leave the cost of electricity from solar PV roughly double the level needed to

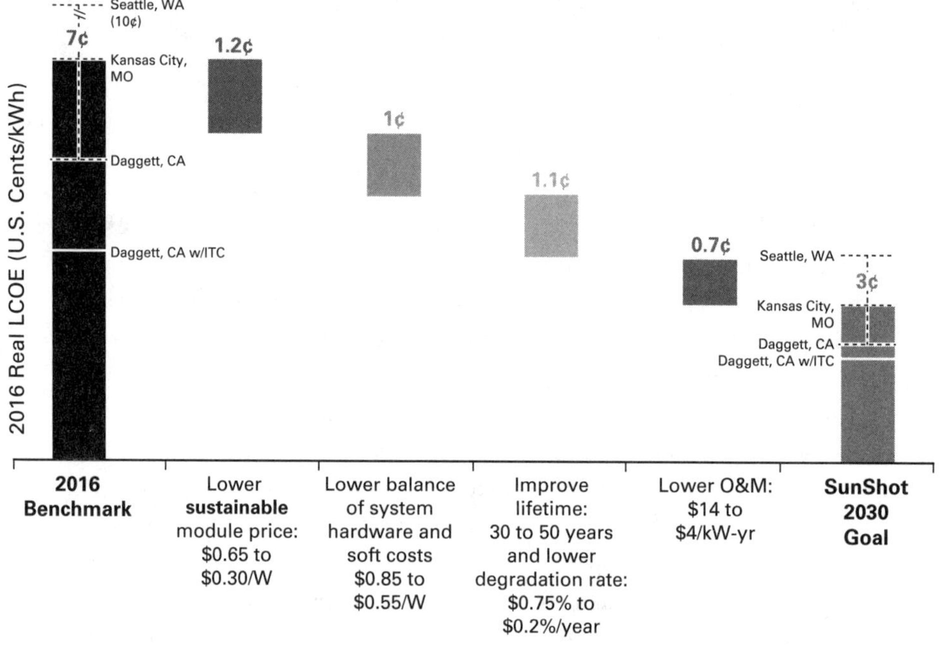

Figure 6.4

The DOE SunShot 2030 cost road map for solar power. Comparison of the cost of a fully installed utility-scale solar PV installation in 2016 with one in 2030, based on projected declines in the costs of PV system components and maintenance as well as longer PV panel lifetimes.

Source: DOE (2016).

outpace value deflation, which sharply reduces the economic value of each additional kilowatt-hour of electricity from solar PV as more of it connects to the grid.[44]

Some observers contend that replacing silicon solar panels with some other material won't solve the devaluation problem because the panel represents only a fraction of the costs of a utility-scale solar PV installation. Indeed, as the MIT Energy Initiative has reported, "Reducing the cost of [solar panels] by half only reduces estimated costs by about 15% for the utility-scale projects we analyze, and 9% for the residential-scale projects." The Initiative's report concluded that trying to improve solar panel efficiency beyond 15 percent is just wasted effort.[45]

But others disagree strongly. In fact, Martin Green—who, remember, predicted the dominance of silicon solar back when that was a very lonely view—argues that higher efficiencies can make a big difference to solar's long-term prospects.[46] In the near term, he predicts that the industry will try to max out the efficiency of silicon solar panels, using a design that he invented in Australia decades ago. But down the road, firms that can increase the efficiency even more, for example, by using perovskite-silicon or even perovskite-perovskite tandem cells, will have a big advantage. In addition to lowering panel costs, higher panel efficiencies enable solar installations to pump out more power with fewer panels. And needing fewer panels reduces the land, labor, and equipment costs of a solar project. This math applies to utility-scale applications and is even more important for installations on rooftops with limited areas, which put space at a premium.

Higher efficiencies are not the only advantage that new technologies offer. Shattering the existing paradigm of heavy, rigid panels would also broaden solar's appeal. Historically, installers often had to choose performance over flexibility. Thin films of "amorphous" silicon, which has low crystallinity, were good enough for powering calculators or camping equipment, but not for much else because they were very inefficient. But in being flexible, lightweight, *and* highly efficient, perovskites and other emerging technologies could extend the uses of solar in existing markets and make inroads into new ones.

The new materials—perovskites, organics, and quantum dots—all share the prospect of being printed on flexible substrates en masse, much as reams of newspapers are spooled through high-volume printers. The ease of transporting solar rolls would reduce logistics and shipping costs across the industry. Then, the ability to unroll solar tarps out in the desert, with minimal equipment to secure them, could slash the cost of utility-scale solar.

The elastic solar materials that have already been demonstrated in the lab could be deployed in new types of terrain, such as shifting landfills or uneven hillsides. In distributed markets, solar paint could be far cheaper and more aesthetic than existing rooftop panels, as could solar materials integrated into buildings in new ways. Tesla has already announced solar roof shingles that cleverly conceal silicon cells in expensive roofing materials. If it can switch to the high efficiencies and stunning versatility of new materials in the lab, it could make even more appealing and affordable products for the mass market.

The first new market for innovative materials might be rooftop solar for the developing world. An estimated 1 billion people in the developing world live in urban slums, mostly under roofs too weak to support heavy silicon solar panels.[47] In the best cases, these roofs are made from thin sheets of metal, and in the worst cases, they are flimsy textiles that barely offer shelter. Most of these people also lack access to reliable energy. Therefore, flexible, elastic rolls of highly efficient solar coatings could make it possible for these populations to power their own needs and perhaps even feed surplus power into the grid.[48] Importantly, researchers in academia and industry will need to develop sealants to protect the solar rolls from moisture, dust, and wear, and they will need to develop ways to anchor flexible PV to makeshift roofs and durably connect electrical cables. All of this will require engineering innovation beyond just the core solar material innovation that academic labs are currently pursuing.

The versatility of new technologies could also enable the integration of solar and building materials in a variety of ways. In densely populated urban areas, roof space for solar panels is constrained. But skyscraper windows and building facades receive plenty of direct and diffuse sunlight over the course of the day. Making it possible to convert some of that sunlight—which otherwise might heat up building interiors and increase power demand for running air conditioners—into power could offset a building's energy use. Already, researchers in the lab have developed semitransparent perovskite cells that produce electricity with 13 percent efficiency while keeping out 85 percent of the heat that would pass through a window in the absence of the cells.[49] And because new materials can take on a range of colors and transparencies, building-integrated PV could enhance, rather than constrain, an architect's palette—think of power-generating stained glass, for instance.

The military would also be an eager customer for new solar technologies. Whereas a gallon of diesel fuel might cost consumers $3 at the pump, it can cost the military fifteen times as much in the field once the cost of fuel convoys and their protection is factored in.[50] If, rather than refueling diesel generators to power a base in Afghanistan, the military could instead easily transport lightweight rolls of solar film that it could unroll and deploy, it would save money—and maybe lives, too.

But for me—a science fiction junkie—the most exciting prospect of all is truly out of this world. Recall that the strongest solar radiation is actually in outer space, before the molecules in the Earth's atmosphere absorb a chunk of the energy in sunlight. And, obviously, there is no such thing as nighttime in outer space—the sun shines 24/7. So, there is ten times as much solar energy to harness outside the Earth's atmosphere compared with at the surface, taking into account the lack of seasons, weather, variable daylight, or atmospheric losses.[51] Would it be possible to construct massive solar farms in outer space and somehow send the energy back down to Earth, providing massive amounts of 24/7 power?

This idea is not as far-fetched as you might imagine. In fact, Japan is very serious about building an orbital solar power satellite. Its goal is to lead an international consortium to build a satellite that can pump out 1 GW—which would weigh more than 10,000 tons and measure several kilometers across—in the 2030s. As hard as setting up the satellite would be, Japan is focusing on the even tougher challenge of beaming power back down to Earth via microwave radiation, which a several-hundred-meter receiving station on Earth would turn into electricity. Elon Musk is dismissive of the idea because of the conversion losses from sunlight to power to microwaves to power again. But Japan's space agency believes that the abundance of 24/7 power in space could more than compensate for the losses.[52]

New solar materials could go a long way toward making an orbital solar power satellite viable. Lightweight, highly efficient, and foldable or rollable solar film could be much easier to launch into space. In addition to solar material innovation, there are at least five other categories of innovation needed to realize the solar power satellite vision. These include "wireless power transmission, space transportation, construction of large structures in orbit, satellite attitude and orbit control . . . and power management."[53]

Perhaps these challenges are collectively too daunting to surmount, especially in an affordable way. But the Japanese attitude is the right one when it comes to imagining the future of solar technology: remarkable advances become possible by pouring attention and resources into innovation.

Escaping Lock-In

Unfortunately, the industry as a whole takes a dim view of innovation. In other industries, such as the semiconductor industry from which solar descended, Intel and other large corporations routinely spend up to 20 percent of their revenue on R&D. In solar, that figure is more like 4 percent to 7 percent for a U.S. firm, such as First Solar, and around 1 percent for Chinese firms. Recently, both Chinese corporate and government funding for solar technology innovation has risen, but it remains well below U.S. levels.[54]

As long as China retains its stranglehold on the solar industry, the country is unlikely to abandon the silicon technology that has vaulted its firms to the forefront of the global industry. Indeed, most in the industry view silicon solar panels as the end point of a half-century of innovation. Now, the industry is focused on ruthless cost-cutting, from the upstream production of polysilicon to the downstream deployment of silicon panel–based installations. And because the factories that make solar panels, including the facilities and equipment to produce high-purity silicon and PV cells, carry a high price tag, firms are reluctant to change course once they sink large amounts of capital into the ground.[55]

This tendency puts the industry at risk of suffering a technology lock-in, entrenching the dominance of silicon solar PV. The economic theory of lock-in explains that an incumbent, dominant technology gets an advantage against emerging technology upstarts. Even if the upstarts might have the potential to cost less and perform better upon further development and scale production, they may flounder in a free market that favors first movers.[56] By 2030, the cost of electricity from silicon solar PV projects could halve, making silicon an even more formidable incumbent. Although far superior technologies would be even cheaper, efficient, and more versatile if they were commercialized, the world might get stuck with only incrementally better silicon panels. Those silicon panels might not be up to the task of defeating the most problematic form of lock-in—namely, the world's dependence on fossil fuels.

Might lock-in be happening right now? There is no way to tell. Silicon may fall more rapidly in cost than currently anticipated, and value deflation might turn out to be less severe than today's best simulations suggest. And if indeed solar is destined for lock-in, that will become clear only in retrospect. That was the case for nuclear power, for which it's now possible to point out the fateful decision that led to disastrous lock-in.

Following World War II, U.S. Navy admiral Hyman Rickover chose one of several potential nuclear reactor designs being investigated at the time, the light-water reactor, to power American submarines. Because the design worked, he then chose it again to power aircraft carriers and, ultimately, civilian nuclear power plants.[57] The rest of this story of path-dependence is history. Today over 90 percent of all nuclear plants around the world are light-water reactors, owing to aggressive U.S. export and nonproliferation policies in the 20th century. Never mind that these reactors can melt down and are expensive to build, nor that several of the other designs that Admiral Rickover passed over might be better options but have been stymied to date because of the dominance of the light-water reactor.[58]

Some signs suggest that solar power could be headed toward a nuclear-like lock-in. The fall in silicon solar panel prices is beneficial in the short term. But the drop makes it harder for emerging technologies that might not be cost-competitive before economies of scale kick in at mass production to break into the market in the long run.

What's more, the financial innovation discussed in chapters 4 and 5 could aid this lock-in. Silicon solar projects might soon be able to tap into public capital markets and access cheap finance, thanks to the existence of decades of performance data and thirty-year manufacturer warranties. That ability would add another cost advantage to silicon over emerging technology competitors that public investors, having just gotten comfortable with silicon technology, would be loath to bet on. As a result, financial innovation could act as a barrier, rather than a bridge, to technological innovation.

Public policy can exacerbate lock-in as well. In the nuclear case, by applying rules that were customized for light water reactors, U.S. nuclear regulators have made it very difficult for firms to deploy new reactor designs. And in solar, policies that are ostensibly technology-neutral and subsidize all solar technologies actually implicitly tilt the playing field against emerging technologies. For example, developers building solar projects in the United

States are much more likely to use federal tax credits to deploy silicon solar PV rather than try to build projects based on emerging technologies that may not yet be ready for prime time. And state-level renewable energy mandates are monopolized by silicon solar at the expense of emerging technologies. These policies expand silicon's advantage and make it even harder to break into the market.

They also create political constituencies that attempt to entrench the first-generation technology. In the case of silicon, public policies such as federal tax credits have bred armies of lobbyists who aim to support the extension of those policies.[59] They were successful in 2015, when Congress extended the tax credits for both solar and wind power. To be sure, political coalitions that support silicon solar PV and other clean energy technologies are important forces behind a transition away from fossil fuels. Some scholars have argued that they might be the crucial players to pressure governments to pass carbon pricing policies, which enjoy widespread support from economists.[60] But in advocating narrow policy interventions that support mature clean energy technologies over emerging ones, these coalitions could also contribute to technology lock-in.

Vanquishing lock-in will take a combination of public policy interventions and private-sector ingenuity. Intervening in the market is difficult, both technically and politically—just ask the officials who disbursed a loan guarantee to Solyndra. Chapter 10, on U.S. policy recommendations, will delve into ways that the government can reduce lock-in barriers to innovation most effectively. These include ramping up spending on R&D, funding first-of-their-kind field demonstration projects, and making it easier for private firms to use public research facilities to reduce the costs of developing new technologies.

But it will also take approaches like the business model of Henry's firm, Oxford PV, to gradually bring new technologies into the solar industry. Henry's approach—to put a perovskite layer on top of existing silicon cells, adding a minor step to an otherwise undisturbed production process—is an evolution en route to a revolution. In the near term, Oxford PV could succeed at wooing Chinese solar panel manufacturers to use its technology and boost silicon panel efficiency by one-third. But once firms amass experience at manufacturing perovskite layers at scale, they could then consider manufacturing all-perovskite solar cells. And that could be a viable commercial route toward the high-efficiency, flexible, lightweight, and aesthetically pleasing solar rolls that academics dream of.

I hope Henry succeeds. (In case you are wondering, I have no financial interest in his venture.) But it will probably take many more companies like his to improve the odds of commercial technology advancing. Fortunately, there is no shortage of great ideas out there. To reach its massive potential, solar will require them to win the support they deserve.

Chapter 7 Stashing Sunshine

In early 2012, the Japanese automaker Toyota found itself at a crossroads. A year before, it had been sitting pretty, having sold more new cars than any competitor. But the 2011 Fukushima disaster was a blow to business. The price of electricity to run Toyota's factories surged after Japan shut down its fleet of nuclear reactors; domestic suppliers couldn't deliver parts on time; and the yen spiked, raising the price of Toyota's exports to the rest of the world. The firm's net profits plunged by half, and it watched helplessly as the U.S. automaker General Motors and the German car company Volkswagen raced ahead of it in sales.[1]

Yoshikazu Tanaka, a senior Toyota engineer, recalls fretting, "There is only extinction ahead if no action is taken." At the time, Tanaka was in charge of the Toyota Prius plug-in hybrid, a variant on the original, high-mileage Prius that launched the hybrid revolution. Toyota had sold more than a million Prius cars in each of the U.S. and Japanese markets, and Tanaka's plug-in hybrid Prius gave customers the new option of charging up with electricity at home in addition to refueling with gasoline at a gas station. Despite its present woes, Toyota still owned the greenest brand in the industry, and it was poised to take a big next step to capitalize on that lead.

Presumably that step would be to launch a fully electric vehicle (EV) with no gas tank. All electric seemed to be the way of the future globally. In 2008, U.S. president Barack Obama had announced a splashy goal: put 1 million EVs on the road by 2015. China upped the ante in 2012, pledging to introduce 5 million EVs by 2020. The same year, Tesla launched its Model S sedan to critical acclaim, breaking the ratings scale of the venerable *Consumer Reports* magazine. Electric cars looked as if they might finally break petroleum's stranglehold as the fuel of choice for passenger vehicles.

Imagine Tanaka's surprise when his executives assigned him to lead the design of a brand-new, ecofriendly car with nowhere to store petroleum, but also nowhere to plug into the power grid, either. Instead, he was asked to bring to market the Toyota Mirai—whose name literally means "future" in Japanese—a car that would run on hydrogen as its fuel, and to accomplish the job on a shoestring budget. Tanaka—a mild-mannered, bespectacled engineer with a gently receding hairline—began running 5 kilometers a day right before lunch just to cope with the stress.

Elon Musk, Tesla's founder, would deride Toyota's bet on hydrogen, sneering, "If you're going to pick an energy source mechanism, hydrogen is an incredibly dumb one to pick."[2] But by 2015, when Toyota unveiled the Mirai, EVs had lost some of their luster. A plunge in oil prices in 2014 from a high of over $100 to less than $50 per barrel had juiced consumer demand for gas-guzzlers and undercut the case for EVs. Promptly, EVs fell as a share of new vehicles, dropping from 3.5 percent to 2.9 percent in the United States.[3] The United States missed President Obama's million-EV target by a whopping 60 percent. As of 2017, China, too, was on track to substantially miss its 2020 target, especially once it ratcheted back EV subsidies.[4] Toyota was not alone in seeking to forge an alternative path—the Japanese government was behind its champion automaker. Prime Minister Shinzo Abe later declared, "a hydrogen society of the future is about to begin here in Japan."[5]

In 2015, with Toyota having regained its crown as the world's biggest automaker, Tanaka argued that the Mirai, rather than the EV, was the logical descendant of the Prius. Indeed, he had repurposed many of the same components from the Prius—including its electric motor, which was powered by using hydrogen fuel to generate electricity—for the Mirai.[6] But more important, the Mirai retained a crucial design feature of the Prius that all-electric cars had abandoned: the ability to fuel up (with hydrogen) in under five minutes. That feature, coupled with a 340-mile range on a single tank, would make owning a Mirai similar to owning a conventional gasoline-fueled vehicle. Toyota was betting that most consumers would be reluctant to buy an EV with a limited range and long recharging time.

Toyota could be right that EVs may be slow to take off and challenge conventional vehicles, which have a massive head start. In 2016, global annual sales of petroleum-fueled vehicles grew more than 3 percent, to nearly 90 million.[7] New EV releases—such as Chevy's Bolt and Tesla's Model 3, each of which can travel more than 200 miles on a single charge—might increase the rate of EV adoption. Many more all-electric models are on the way; Volvo announced in 2017 that it would only make electric or hybrid vehicles beginning in 2019. But EVs are starting way behind conventional vehicles, having accounted for less than 1 percent of total vehicle sales in 2016.

The market challenges faced by EVs point to an even bigger challenge. If the planet is going to decarbonize, the task will not be accomplished solely by eliminating fossil fuels from electricity generation and powering on-road vehicles with electricity instead of oil derivatives. Most of the world's energy demand is not met by electricity but by burning other fuels, the most prevalent of which is oil. So, decarbonization will require replacing oil—the most widely-used energy source on the planet—with storable fuels that have no carbon footprint.

Yet oil is so popular, especially in the transportation and industrial sectors, because it and fuels derived from it are remarkably convenient. For example, gasoline packs eighty times as much energy into the same volume as taken up by the lithium-ion batteries that power electronics and EVs. In fact, a single gallon of gasoline has enough energy to charge your iPhone every day for 20 years. And transporting oil around the globe in massive tankers adds just a few cents to the cost of that gallon of gasoline.

What is more, many forms of transportation—including heavy-duty trucking, shipping, and aviation—depend on the high energy density, portability, and reliability of fossil fuels. (Indeed, when a solar-powered plane finally circumnavigated the globe for the first time ever, the trip took more than a year because bad weather kept grounding the plane.[8]) Applications that cannot be electrified readily, if at all, account for 40 percent of global transportation energy demand.[9]

The challenges for electrification don't end there. Global industrial energy use, which is twice that of transportation and accounts for half of the world's energy demand, relies on electricity for less than 15 percent of its needs. It is often cheaper to burn fossil fuels for heat to run industrial processes than it is to pay for electricity to produce the same heat.[10]

If electricity serves only a minority of the world's energy demand, then how can humanity possibly harness the sun's energy to power a majority of its needs sometime this century? Rapid financial and technological innovation in the field of solar photovoltaics (PV) alone cannot resolve this quandary. In addition, innovation is needed to develop and commercialize alternative technologies that stash sunshine by converting it into convenient stores of energy that can be used where PV can't.

The production of hydrogen fuel from sunlight is one of those technologies. The Toyota Mirai is just the tip of the iceberg when it comes to the potential for hydrogen to replace fossil fuels. In addition to fueling cars, hydrogen could fuel trucks and provide heat for industrial uses. And solar-produced hydrogen would solve that pesky problem of intermittent sunlight, acting as a store of energy that can be used on demand, in contrast to solar PV, which produces power only when the sun is shining.

Scientists seeking inspiration for converting sunlight into fuel have found it all around them—in the form of plants, which harness solar energy to produce fuel through photosynthesis, a process that includes splitting water to make hydrogen. Plants are an imperfect model, because photosynthesis is a highly inefficient method of energy conversion. So, scientists have copied some of the basic principles but ditched many of the details in a quest to produce an artificial leaf that will exploit sunlight to generate hydrogen fuel from water. In 2015, researchers developed a prototype device that produced hydrogen with respectable efficiency and the potential for low cost once the technology is improved and reaches manufacturing scale. Just as important, the device neither broke down immediately nor exploded. Although this breakthrough still leaves plenty of challenges on the road to commercialization, it is an encouraging sign of progress.

Yet hydrogen is far from a shoo-in as oil's replacement. In the realm of cars, for instance, consumers will not switch to hydrogen vehicles en masse unless they have convenient access to hydrogen-refueling stations, which don't yet exist. If stations did exist, supplies of cheap hydrogen would need to be generated and transported to them at a scale rivaling that of today's massive petroleum sector. Recognizing this reality, Toyota is hedging its bets. It announced in 2017 that it hoped within five years to commercialize a new type of battery (known as an "all-solid-state battery") that would enable an EV to charge up in a few minutes and travel farther than today's EVs on a single charge.[11]

In light of the drawbacks of hydrogen, scientists have embarked on a much tougher quest: cost-effectively converting sunlight into liquid fuels that can substitute readily for today's fossil fuels. If such a process were to use as a raw material carbon dioxide from power plant exhausts, or even from the atmosphere, as an input, then burning the output fuel to produce energy would be carbon-neutral. But the chemistry involved in producing convenient, carbon-based fuels is far more complex than the comparatively simpler task of splitting water to produce hydrogen. Still, researchers are undeterred, and a breakthrough in 2016 harnessed the complex metabolisms of bacteria to do the hard work of producing usable fuel.

Technologies to convert sunlight to fuels could store intermittent solar energy one day, something that solar PV cannot do. Another way to crack the storage nut is to convert the sun's energy into storable heat. Already, some concentrated solar power (CSP) plants on the market can store energy throughout the night and generate electricity hours after the sun has set. Yet CSP growth has stalled owing to its high cost compared with solar PV. To drive down the cost of CSP plants equipped with storage, researchers are attempting to concentrate sunlight to realize previously unreachable high temperatures. Greater efficiency combined with cheap and long-lasting thermal storage could boost the profits of these plants and enable them to stabilize the power grid in response to rising PV penetration, storing excess energy produced at sunny times of the day and making it available when needed later on.

To reach solar's potential, all these non-PV technologies—including convenient solar-generated fuels and CSP plants that generate electricity 24/7—will need to advance dramatically. And it won't do to wait to make the requisite investments until an urgent need for them arises. Technology development can take decades, and even pumping gobs of money into innovation at the last minute will compress those timelines to just a limited extent. Only with long-term planning and a willingness to incur costs up front can countries around the world reap the massive rewards of innovation down the road.

For its part, Toyota is probably crossing its fingers that the artificial leaf can graduate from the lab bench to a commercial scale. Aside from betting big on hydrogen, the automaker has pledged to slash emissions from its cars in 2050 by 90 percent. And without a way to generate hydrogen or liquid fuels from a clean source like sunlight, its advertised zero-emission Mirai would be just a mirage.

"No Bugs, No Wires"

I was a little nervous on my flight to Los Angeles. This would be the first time that I had hosted an academic scientist to address members of the Council on Foreign Relations. And to be perfectly honest, I worried that my guest might feel like a fish out of water over dinner in Beverly Hills, surrounded by a cosmopolitan collection of executives and ex-ambassadors.

I shouldn't have worried. My guest, Nathan "Nate" Lewis, a professor at the California Institute of Technology (Caltech), is a rarity among scientists for his ability to condense complex concepts into memorable soundbites and weave a compelling narrative that drives home the immense importance of his various research strands. Nate kicked off his remarks on the future of solar power with this pithy refrain: "Can't store? No power after four." That failing, he argued forcefully, makes it an urgent need to develop technologies able to store the sun's energy in a fuel that can be used when needed. His preferred route, an integrated solar fuel generator, is an elegant device that takes in water and sunlight and spits out gaseous hydrogen and oxygen. It would be as simple as that, Nate reassured the spellbound roundtable attendees: "No bugs, no wires."

By that, Nate meant that his device would avoid all the messiness of real biological systems ("no bugs"). It would also sidestep the complications and costs that arise when wiring together separate devices in a piecemeal approach to producing hydrogen fuel. His vision was to create a simple, elegant hydrogen generator that would outperform nature's best plants.

Plants, for all their success, are actually terrible at converting sunlight into energy. Even if you don't know anything about how photosynthesis works, you can tell from the leaves' green color that totally efficient energy conversion might not be a plant's top priority (black leaves would be much better at absorbing the sun's rays). The green chloroplasts in leaf cells function well enough for a plant's needs. They perform complex chemical reactions that, fueled by the sun's energy, turn carbon dioxide and water into the energy-storing sugars needed for such activities as surviving and reproducing. When all is said and done, the most efficient plants convert barely 1 percent of the incoming sunlight into stored energy.

Vegetation nonetheless offers a generic model for turning sunlight into fuel. Early on in photosynthesis, plants split water and generate hydrogen and oxygen—the oxygen goes into the atmosphere, while the hydrogen feeds into subsequent chemical reactions. The way plants accomplish this water-splitting is instructive. The first lesson is that they separate the two half-reactions of producing oxygen and hydrogen between two different areas, known as photosystem I and photosystem II. Evolution was no pyromaniac, and this design choice prevents hydrogen from spontaneously combusting in the presence of oxygen. Second, each of the photosystems where light is absorbed also contains catalysts, or molecules that speed up the respective half-reaction. Indeed, we can thank the manganese catalyst that accelerates a plant's production of oxygen for all the oxygen in the Earth's atmosphere. Third, plants separate the two half-reactions with a membrane that not only keeps hydrogen and oxygen apart, but also allows charged ions to pass through it, which is important to avoid an imbalance of charge that would halt the two half-reactions.

Researchers developing solar fuel generators likewise need to put together five components. Two photoelectrodes immersed in water absorb light energy to perform each of the two half-reactions to split water. Two catalysts speed up each of those half-reactions. And a membrane stops the whole contraption—called a "photoelectrochemical cell (PEC)"—from exploding.

But the similarities end there. As Nate likes to say, after taking inspiration from feathered birds, humans ditched the feathers and invented the 747. Unlike plants, PECs of the future probably will not use two green photoelectrodes that compete with each other to absorb the same part of the sun's spectrum. Rather, one of them—the anode, which creates oxygen from water—should harness high-energy photons, letting the low-energy photons pass through it to be absorbed by the one below—the cathode, which produces hydrogen. This design is reminiscent of the way tandem solar PV cells comprising multiple semiconductor layers work, such as a high-bandgap perovskite stacked on top of low-bandgap silicon.

Wait, you might ask—if a PEC is similar to a solar PV cell, why not use the latter to split water? Indeed, solar PV panels are much more commercially advanced, and a well-known device called an "electrolyzer" can use PV-generated electricity to split water and produce hydrogen. Large-scale PV is already a reality, as are large-scale electrolyzers, which have been used for decades at the High Aswan Dam in Egypt to supply hydrogen for fertilizer production.[12] Given rapid cost declines in photovoltaics, hooking solar PV panels up to an electrolyzer might seem like an economical way to produce hydrogen today, rather than waiting for an elusive artificial leaf.

But this approach would violate Nate's mantra of "no wires," which he swears by for good reason. Economic analysis reveals that the PV + electrolyzer approach would produce hydrogen costing more than $10 per kilogram (fortunately for those of us more accustomed to judging the price of fuel at the pump, 1 gallon of gasoline is almost exactly equivalent to 1 kilogram of hydrogen in terms of energy content). By contrast, the cost of producing hydrogen using natural gas—the most popular way to do it today, though obviously not a zero-emission method—is around one-sixth of that figure. And, of course, the most important cost target, the price at the pump, was somewhere less than $3 per gallon in the United States in 2017.[13]

The wired approach is so expensive in part because the electrolyzer runs during only about 25 percent of the day, while the sun is shining and the solar PV panels are providing their peak electricity output. Paying off the capital cost of the electrolyzer, therefore, takes four times as long as would be needed if it were running at full output all the time. Also, the electrolyzers require expensive catalysts, whereas the two-layered, integrated design of a PEC allows it to function with cheap catalysts (thanks to requiring low current density).

Beating the cost of producing hydrogen with natural gas—let alone that of gasoline—will require a PEC that uses extremely cheap and abundant materials for all five of its major components. But that's not all it has to do. To succeed in a big way, it needs to be not only cheap, but also safe, robust, and efficient. Unfortunately, so far researchers have only managed to create PECs with no more than three of those four characteristics. Like Bill Murray trying to plug gopher holes in *Caddyshack*, fixing one problem tends to spawn another.

Start with safety. To prevent hydrogen and oxygen from combining and exploding, a PEC needs a membrane that separates the two half-reactions. But the half-reaction that produces oxygen from water also turns that water acidic, whereas the half-reaction that produces hydrogen turns nearby water basic. Acids are what digest food in your stomach, and bases clean your drain. If safety weren't a concern and the membrane could be eliminated, the acidic and basic water would neutralize each other. But with the membrane in place, scientists have to find materials for photoelectrodes and catalysts that do not get dissolved or corroded in acidic or basic media. That demand rules out the many cheap materials that wouldn't survive under such conditions.[14] Therefore, making a PEC out of cheap materials and equipping it with a membrane to ensure safety can lead to it failing the robustness test. Gopher alert!

Next, consider a PEC's efficiency—the amount of the sun's energy that the device converts into energy stored as hydrogen. Efficiency depends on how well the photoelectrodes collectively absorb sunlight and how fast the two half-reactions split water. With carefully chosen photoelectrode bandgaps and catalysts, a PEC can theoretically achieve more than 30 percent efficiency.[15] Expensive semiconductors offer a diverse buffet of bandgaps to choose from, but cheap materials—especially those having a high bandgap—present a far more limited menu. Similarly, precious metal catalysts such as platinum are great at speeding up reactions, but they are rare and costly. So again, plugging the efficiency gopher hole leads to another problem—high cost—poking its head out.

So, Nate realized that, just as Bill Murray went after all the gopher holes at once using dynamite, he, too, would have to upgrade his research arsenal (ideally with better results). As the founding director of the Joint Center for Artificial Photosynthesis (JCAP) at the U.S. Department of Energy (DOE), Nate wanted to shake up the way that the federal government pursued research. So, JCAP convened an interdisciplinary group of scientists and coordinated their efforts toward the ultimate goal of creating a safe, efficient, robust, and cheap integrated solar fuel generator.[16] It also threw massive computational power at the problem of finding materials that could satisfy all four criteria, systematically simulating thousands of compounds and testing out the most promising candidates in the lab.[17] This strategy turned traditional science on its head. Rather than laboriously sifting through existing materials hoping to find one that fits the application, this materials-by-design paradigm started from the end goal and worked backward to create the right materials.

Good old scientific intuition has also played an important role in the research process—as has a little luck. Two examples stand out. First, Nate's group, with collaborators at Penn State University, found inspiration in the catalysts used in oil refineries to strip the air-polluting sulfur out of petroleum products. These catalysts are cheap, use abundant elements, and are terrific at speeding up the half-reaction that produces hydrogen.[18,19] (Unfortunately, researchers are still looking for a cheap, effective catalyst for the oxygen-producing half-reaction.)

Second, researchers in Nate's lab accidentally coated their samples with a thin layer of titanium dioxide and found a surprising result. Titanium dioxide is the key ingredient in sunscreen, so one might expect it to block sunlight. Instead, this ultrathin coating let light in while protecting the photoelectrodes and catalysts from being eaten away by the basic solution—which, remember, is corrosive like a drain cleaner.[20]

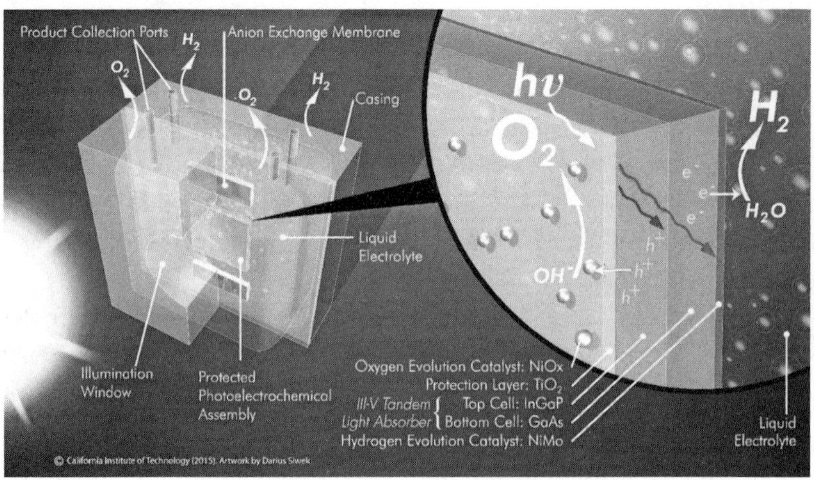

Figure 7.1

Diagram of JCAP's 10-percent-efficient PEC prototype. This illustration displays the architecture of an integrated solar fuel generator that uses sunlight to split water into hydrogen and oxygen, which are collected from ports on opposite sides of a membrane that keeps the two half-reactions separate. These reactions occur at the center of the device (inset), at the two photoelectrodes, each of which is coated with a catalyst that speeds up the relevant half-reaction.

Source: Reprinted with permission from the California Institute of Technology.

Together, the borrowed insight from the oil industry and the accidental sunscreen discovery allowed Nate and the JCAP research teams to make a breakthrough. In 2015, JCAP announced an integrated solar fuel generator that was over 10 percent efficient at converting sunlight into hydrogen fuel.[21] By itself, the efficiency was pedestrian—others had reached 22 percent for the efficiency of a PEC.[22] But the JCAP device used cheap, Earth-abundant catalysts, and it was able to pump out hydrogen over two days of continuous operation (figure 7.1). As a proof of concept, it teased the possibility of a commercially viable product down the road.

Many research needs remain unaddressed. For example, the JCAP device used expensive semiconductors for the photoelectrodes borrowed from previous solar PV cell record holders. The next step might be to take a more recent page out of the PV playbook and use perovskites as cheap but efficient light absorbers—perovskite-based PECs have already reached over 12 percent efficiency.[23] And perovskite/silicon tandem structures, which are the front-runners for the next generation of solar PV panels, might also show the way to 20 percent efficient PECs and beyond.[24]

If and when this technology leads to a commercial product, it is unlikely to look anything like the leaves that inspired it. Nate envisions a tarp, rolled out across a vast expanse to soak up the sun's rays, with drainpipes to collect the hydrogen that it produces. That is a far cry from the 1-cm^2 prototype that JCAP created, but, listening to Nate's vision, it's hard not to dream big.

The Holy Grail

Across the country from Nate Lewis, another acclaimed scientist is also on a quest to commercialize an artificial leaf. Like Nate, Dan Nocera at Harvard University deftly combines science and communication, moonlighting as a science celebrity—something of a Carl Sagan for solar fuels. He has a knack for connecting with diverse audiences, from American Physical Society scientific gatherings to the Aspen Institute's hobnobbing summits. If his crowd is dining on steak, he'll warm them up by asking: "What did you just chew? The sun! The beef was just the energy of sunlight."[25]

In 2011, Nocera took the world by storm by announcing that he had invented the artificial leaf. His preferred demonstration was to plop the device, which looked like a dark postage stamp, into a glass of water. At that point, it started to bubble up hydrogen and oxygen on either side (though only converting a tiny percentage of the incoming solar energy into hydrogen).[26] Despite its simplicity, the artificial leaf was the culmination of his life's work of thirty years, from his days as a graduate student at Caltech. Having made the breakthrough, Nocera set out to bring his new technology to market.

Unfortunately, he was about to learn the lesson that almost every other Silicon Valley clean energy start-up learned: the really hard part comes *after* making an exciting lab discovery. He would later lament, "I did a holy grail of science. Great! That doesn't mean I did a holy grail of technology. And that's what scientists and professors don't get."[27] His start-up, Sun Catalytix, ended up pivoting away from solar fuel to develop batteries to store energy for the power grid instead (Lockheed bought the company for an undisclosed amount in 2014).

But, the experience hasn't stopped him from chasing holy grails. In fact, Nocera has since switched to chasing an even harder target: harnessing sunlight, water, and carbon dioxide to produce liquid, carbon-based fuels that could be drop-in replacements for petroleum products. The prospective benefits of such a technology are compelling. Liquid fuels already have enormous global infrastructure networks, including storage facilities, transcontinental pipelines, and oil supertankers, not to mention ubiquitous filling stations around the world. A device that could transform sunlight into fuels that are already commonly used could piggyback on that infrastructure.

Currently, the most promising route for making carbon-based fuels from sunlight involves solar-generated hydrogen as an intermediary. Hydrogen is the easiest fuel to make from sunlight—though doing so is still wickedly complicated—and well-understood industrial processes are able to then combine hydrogen with carbon dioxide to produce a range of useful fuels known as hydrocarbons.[28]

A daunting challenge, though, is the need to obtain pure carbon dioxide to combine with the hydrogen to produce hydrocarbon fuels. The flip side of this challenge is an opportunity: the production of carbon-based fuels could consume carbon dioxide emitted by coal and natural gas power plants, as well as such industrial facilities as oil refineries and cement plants, that otherwise would escape into the atmosphere and contribute to global warming. But obtaining pure carbon dioxide cost-effectively is difficult, especially because the exhaust from fossil-fueled plants contains a whole mix of unsavory gases that need to be separated. Various technologies to perform this task exist, from treating the exhaust with a solution that selectively grabs carbon dioxide molecules to using a membrane that separates different gases. But all of them are costly at present and can have other side effects, such as reducing the efficiency of a power plant.[29]

If scientists can solve the twin problems of cost-effectively generating hydrogen from sunlight and capturing carbon dioxide from fossil fuel plants, however, then a diverse range of solar fuels would be in reach. Figure 7.2 envisions solar fuels displacing petroleum across various sectors, from powering vehicles to producing plastics. Solar-generated hydrogen could be used directly as a transportation fuel for vehicles like the Toyota Mirai. Or it could be combined with carbon dioxide in a facility that might be called a "solar refinery," to create the same range of hydrocarbon fuels that are produced today in oil refineries and then used in a range of industries and as transport fuels.

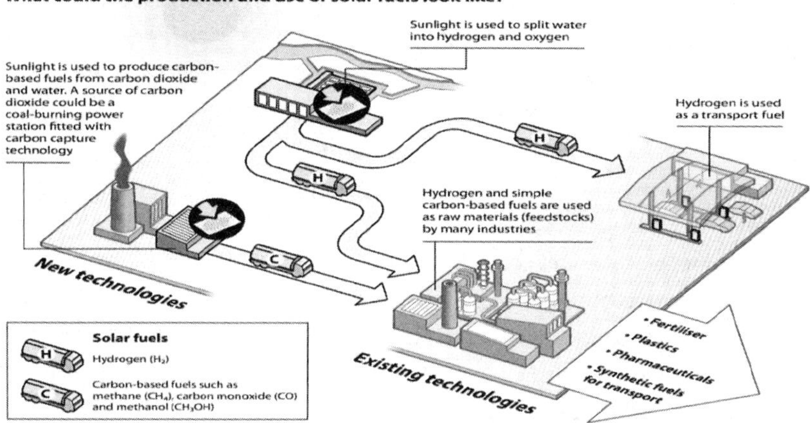

Figure 7.2
A vision of the hydrogen economy.
Source: Reprinted with permission from the Royal Society of Chemistry.

As futuristic as all of that sounds, Nocera wants to do something even harder. He wants to bypass hydrogen production and use sunlight, water, and carbon dioxide to produce carbon-containing fuels directly. If this maneuver could be done cost-effectively and at scale, it would be the most efficient, single-shot method of storing sunlight in the most convenient fuels known to humankind.

From a scientific point of view, this task looks nearly impossible. Just splitting water to generate hydrogen and oxygen is hard enough—that reaction is known as a "four-electron reaction," in which four electrons change energy levels or switch from one atom to another. But to create the simplest hydrocarbon—single-carbon methane, which makes up natural gas—requires shuffling eight electrons, a far more complex proposition. Harnessing sunlight to directly create carbon-based fuels will require the discovery of even more new materials to absorb light and catalyze chemical reactions.[30]

As a result, a commercial technology to make carbon-based fuels directly from solar energy is much further away than one that can produce hydrogen. Still, some exciting research breakthroughs have recently materialized. In an example of scientific cross-pollination, one of these breakthroughs relies on perovskite to power the production of carbon-based fuel from sunlight, water, and carbon dioxide. Although this device achieved a record efficiency of 6.5 percent, it relied on very expensive elements—iridium and gold—to catalyze speedy chemical reactions.[31]

Professor Peidong Yang of the University of California, Berkeley, had a different idea: using bacteria as catalysts. He knew that nature uses intricate enzymes as catalysts in photosynthesis; even though those enzymes often break down in the process of converting sunlight into complex sugars, plant cells can either rebuild or replace them. Yang realized that genetically engineered bacteria could behave similarly after being equipped with an arsenal of potent enzymes.[32] He then pioneered a hybrid approach that split water with an inorganic catalyst to make hydrogen, as other artificial leaf technologies do, and then fed the hydrogen to bacteria, which combined it with carbon dioxide to produce methane.[33]

Nocera then took Yang's research one step further. Whereas Yang's setup produced only methane, Nocera sought to produce a much wider array of liquid fuels at higher efficiency. His hybrid device used a solar PV cell to run a current that, in the presence of an inorganic catalyst, would split water. Then, the resulting hydrogen would be fed, along with pure carbon dioxide, to microbes that could produce various fuels.[34] The bugs were terrific at converting carbon dioxide and hydrogen into a variety of fuels, but unfortunately they were incompatible with the inorganic catalyst, which produced forms of reactive oxygen that destroyed the bacteria's DNA.

Then in 2016, Nocera and colleagues published a paper in *Science* triumphantly announcing a new catalyst. A cobalt-phosphorus alloy, this catalyst not only left the bacteria unharmed, but also self-assembled out of solution, mimicking the self-healing catalysts found in nature.[35] With the catalyst and bacteria working together in harmony, Nocera's device was able to achieve 10 percent efficiency in converting sunlight into alcohol fuels. Nocera reports that the bugs should be able to produce several other carbon-containing molecules for a range of applications from fueling vehicles to producing plastics.[36] And he followed this up by demonstrating in 2017 that a hybrid catalyst-plus-bacteria approach could fix nitrogen in the atmosphere to produce ammonia.[37] That is a tantalizing discovery because over 1 percent of global energy is used today in the production of ammonia to fertilize crops and feed the world. Nocera's prototype suggests that one day, sunlight could power that process rather than fossil fuels.

Nocera's breakthrough violates both halves of Nate Lewis's mantra—"no bugs, no wires." The jury is still out on whether that's a good idea. Indeed, bacteria are quite finicky, sensitive to the acidity and temperature of their environment, and thus tough to design around. Smart money, for now, is on devices that harness sunlight to produce hydrogen advancing faster than those that try to produce complex carbon-based fuels. But, by combining modern materials with nature's wizardry, researchers may yet leapfrog simple hydrogen in pursuit of a viable route to the ultimate holy grail: 100 percent clean, drop-in replacements for fossil fuels.

Heating Up

For all their promise, solar fuels—hydrogen or even carbon-containing liquid fuels—are far from commercial reality. But concentrated solar power (CSP), which uses sunlight to generate heat that can then produce electricity on demand, is already at commercial scale, with the potential to store the sun's energy and supplement the intermittent output of solar PV.

CSP's benefits are less tantalizing than those of solar fuels. CSP-generated heat can be stored for only a few hours, unlike the long-term storage that fuels offer, and CSP feeds power back into the electricity grid, leaving unsolved the problem of fueling unelectrified transportation and industrial uses. In the near term, though, a combination of solar PV and concentrated solar power—with the latter providing badly needed storage—is the best bet to meet the midcentury target of 30 percent solar in the global electricity mix.

And yet in recent years, prospects for the CSP industry have looked about as grim as for the downward-spiraling streamers at the troubled Ivanpah CSP plant in California's Mojave Desert. A "streamer" is what workers at the plant call a bird unlucky enough to venture into the "flux field" in the air above the plant's 5 square miles of sunlight-concentrating mirrors.[38] More than 2,000 birds succumb to this grisly fate yearly, catching fire and falling to Earth.[39] Buffeted by strident environmental criticism, Ivanpah's operators have tried everything to keep the birds away, from spewing respiratory irritants to broadcasting pre-recorded shrieks. They have had limited success—and the birds aren't even the plant's biggest headache.

That distinction goes to the difficulties that the plant has faced in ramping up to its rated power production. In contrast to a simple PV plant consisting of panels bolted to the ground, Ivanpah relies on hundreds of thousands of mirrors to track the sun across the sky and perfectly focus their energy on the same point atop a massive tower nearly 500 feet high. The energy superheats steam, which can then be piped to spin a turbine and generate power. When a slight misalignment caused the mirrors to target the wrong point on one of its three towers in 2016, the tower caught fire, melting its metal pipes.[40] This and other engineering snafus prevented the plant from delivering the quantity of power that it had promised in its contract with a California utility. Faced with a shortfall in revenue in 2016, the plant neared a shutdown shortly after its expensive construction, which had cost $2.2 billion and had been largely backed by a U.S. government loan guarantee.

Ivanpah's woes reflected those of the broader industry. From 2011 to 2014, the CSP industry grew at a rapid clip of over 40 percent annually.[41] But much of that growth reflected the completion of projects that were conceived before the crash in the price of power from solar PV projects. Since 2014, new CSP projects have slowed to a crawl because the cost of constructing CSP plants has not come down nearly as fast as the cost of utility-scale solar PV farms. That is true, at least, when gauged by the costs per generated kilowatt-hour of electricity—irrespective of when those kilowatt-hours are produced. Whereas the lowest-cost electricity provided by a U.S. CSP plant in 2016 was nearly 12 cents per kilowatt-hour, the cheapest electricity from a utility-scale solar PV plant was less than 5 cents per kilowatt-hour.[42] Firms in the sector struggled to cope with the abrupt market slowdown. In 2016, Abengoa, a Spanish company hailed by President Obama for building projects in Arizona and California, looked as though it was headed for the largest corporate bankruptcy in Spanish history.[43]

Since then, the industry's outlook has improved a bit. In 2017, Ivanpah finally managed to boost its power output up to the levels that it had promised to deliver to the utility, avoiding a plant shutdown.[44] Abengoa narrowly escaped bankruptcy through a restructuring deal with its creditors.[45] And market analysts have forecast a slow but steady growth rate of 10 percent annually through the end of the decade.[46]

The key to CSP's recovery and future growth is storage. Nearly every plant on the drawing board or under construction in the United States and abroad has built-in storage. And the amount of storage at these plants is growing. In the past, plants would have stored at most six hours of power in the form of heat, so they could continue generating after the sun went down. But the 110-megawatt (MW) Crescent Dunes plant in Nevada, which opened in late 2015, can store up to ten hours of power and run throughout the night.[47] And the same firm plans to open a hybrid solar plant in Chile in 2019 that will generate PV power by day while stowing heat from CSP in its fourteen hours of thermal storage to drive electricity production by night.

Storage is so important because it differentiates CSP from PV. Even if PV is cheaper per kilowatt-hour, CSP becomes competitive when factoring in the value of "dispatchability," or the ability to produce power on demand. This will matter more and more as PV penetration increases on power grids. One study projects that in California, once wind and solar power account for at least a third of the electricity mix, the value of a kilowatt-hour from a CSP plant with six hours of thermal storage could be more than double that from a PV plant.

The value is better because CSP with storage can sidestep value deflation. Whereas PV plants will be forced to produce power when the grid needs it least, CSP plants can store up the extra energy and discharge it when demand is greatest—and get paid for the excess instead of wasting it. Today, power markets in the United States and elsewhere offer some compensation for dispatchability, but less than its true value to the grid. In the future, however, as the strain on the grid rises from PV penetration, regulators and utilities will face increasing pressure to incentivize dispatchable resources, like CSP, to come online. Over time, then, CSP is likely to enjoy economic tailwinds stemming from its storage capabilities. One study forecasts that although PV will race ahead in deployment, CSP will ultimately catch up as the need for storage grows more acute; by the end of the century, PV and CSP together could supply a majority of the world's power.[48]

Yet CSP systems with thermal storage still need to become cheaper and more efficient before the technology can truly take off. That will require—you guessed it—technological innovation. One consistent theme runs through the various strands of research and development (R&D) currently underway to improve CSP technology: raising the temperature. If a future CSP plant were to run at much higher temperatures than today's systems, it could store more energy and produce more power at a lower cost. But cranking up the heat will require solving some thorny technical challenges.

Fundamentally, CSP works by concentrating the sun's energy to heat up a heat transfer fluid, which can rise in temperature, is easy to move through pipes, and can convert its heat into mechanical work to spin a turbine (or transfer its heat to another fluid, called the "working fluid," that can do the mechanical work). Suppose that steam is the heat transfer fluid in a CSP plant—although many other fluids, such as synthetic oil and molten salts, can be used as well. The first step in this CSP plant's cycle is to focus the sun's rays to vaporize pressurized water to produce high-pressure steam. The steam is then piped to a turbine, where it expands and cools, and in doing so transfers its energy to spin the turbine, which in turn generates electricity. Low-pressure steam is then further cooled so it condenses back to liquid water and can start the cycle anew.

High temperatures are so important in part because the efficiency of the electricity generator depends on the temperature difference between the hot and cold stages of the working fluid. Heating steam to a higher temperature before it reaches the turbine, as well as cooling it down more after it expands, will increase the efficiency of converting heat energy into electricity. Also, higher temperatures enable better energy storage. The heat-transfer fluid can be stowed in a tank for later use or can transfer its energy to another thermal storage material. Higher temperatures make the process of storing and releasing energy more efficient and extend how long the heat can be used to generate power. Together, these two advantages could reduce the cost of power generation and storage from CSP.

Textbooks traditionally teach that four different configurations can allow a CSP plant to harvest sunlight. But only one can achieve high temperatures and store energy and is therefore likely to have a future. Two designs—parabolic troughs and linear Fresnel collectors—use mirrors to concentrate sunlight onto a long pipe, an arrangement that generally limits temperatures to less than 400°C. The third, the Stirling Dish Engine, can reach a high temperature of 800°C but lacks the scale to enable storage, limiting its commercial future. Not surprisingly, then, new CSP projects are increasingly slated to use the "power tower" configuration, on which Ivanpah is based. By arranging a whole field of mirrors, or "heliostats," to reflect and focus the sun's rays on a single point at the top of a tower, CSP can theoretically achieve very high temperatures (figure 7.3). It also has the scale to enable cost-effective thermal energy storage.[49]

Reality has not yet caught up with theory. Today's power towers are limited to temperatures below 600°C. To reach higher temperatures than are possible with water, many of these plants use molten salts as the

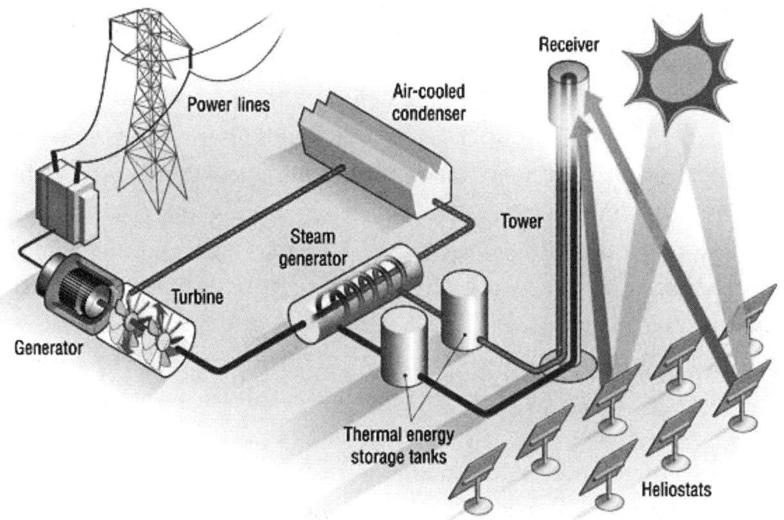

Figure 7.3
How a CSP power tower works. This schematic illustrates how an array of heliostats focuses sunlight on a receiver at the top of a tower, imparting the sun's energy to a heat-transfer fluid. The hot fluid can be stored for later use (or its heat can be transferred to another energy-storage medium). To generate electricity, the stored heat is used to heat steam that then runs a steam turbine to produce electricity, the voltage of which can then be increased by a transformer so the power can be transmitted over long distances. In future designs, supercritical carbon dioxide could replace steam as the working fluid that drives a turbine, in order to enable a higher operating temperature and greater efficiency of generating electricity.
Source: DOE Sunshot Program.

heat-transfer fluid. Unfortunately, the most commonly used molten salts, called "nitrates," break down near 600°C, precluding them from reaching a higher temperature. In consequence, when the molten salts transfer their energy to steam, that steam is cooler than it would be in a power plant fired by natural gas or other fossil fuels. Lower-temperature operation makes the CSP generator, which converts only 40 percent of the heat captured from sunlight into electricity, less efficient than a natural gas power plant, which can reach 60 percent efficiency at converting the heat from burning gas into electricity. When the accounting also includes energy lost from converting sunlight into heat by using concentrating mirrors, today's power towers can convert between 20 percent and 24 percent of the incoming solar energy into electricity.

Researchers are pursuing several options to raise that figure. The first step is to break through the temperature barrier of current molten salts. Versions called "chlorides" could surmount the 600°C barrier, reaching 700°C or even higher.[50] Alternatively, researchers at Sandia National Laboratory in New Mexico have invented an elegant "falling-particle receiver," which showers a stream of hard, sandlike particles from the top of the tower through the focal point of the concentrated solar rays to heat them. The Sandia researchers have managed to heat those particles to 700°C—breaking through the conventional molten salt barrier—and they expect that they can reach as high as 1,200°C. To get there, though, they will have to design a container for those particles that can withstand the extreme heat. The concept is elegant because the falling stream of hot particles is versatile: it can be diverted to transfer heat either to the working fluid of a turbine (to generate electricity) or to a storage tank, where the particles can remain at high temperature, for nighttime use. Capping off this design is a bucket elevator that recirculates cool sand back to the top of the tower for reheating.[51]

These high temperatures would unlock newly efficient ways to run the generator. For example, at temperatures greater than 700°C, it becomes possible to replace steam with "supercritical" carbon dioxide (at high-temperature and high-pressure) as the working fluid to turn a turbine. Supercritical carbon dioxide is always a gas even as it heats up or cools down, so it avoids the expensive energy losses involved in having to vaporize liquid water to make steam. Researchers expect that this strategy could increase the efficiency of converting heat energy to 55 percent, nearly on par with a natural gas plant. And that increased efficiency of power generation would translate to a reduction in cost—possibly by 40 percent, making CSP with built-in storage an affordable 6 cents per kilowatt-hour (figure 7.4).[52]

In this chapter, I have emphasized hybrid solutions for generating fuel from sunlight. Hybrid technology can also enhance CSP. Two hybrid approaches to improve CSP efficiency are being explored—one for the near term and one for further down the road.

In the near term, a viable way to get to high temperatures is to combine CSP and natural gas. Mirrors could concentrate and focus the sun's energy on compressed air, heating it up to 800°C, and that air could then be heated further to 1,200°C by burning natural gas. This extremely hot, compressed air would then be able to turn one turbine to generate electricity, and then the exhaust heat at around 650°C could be recovered to turn

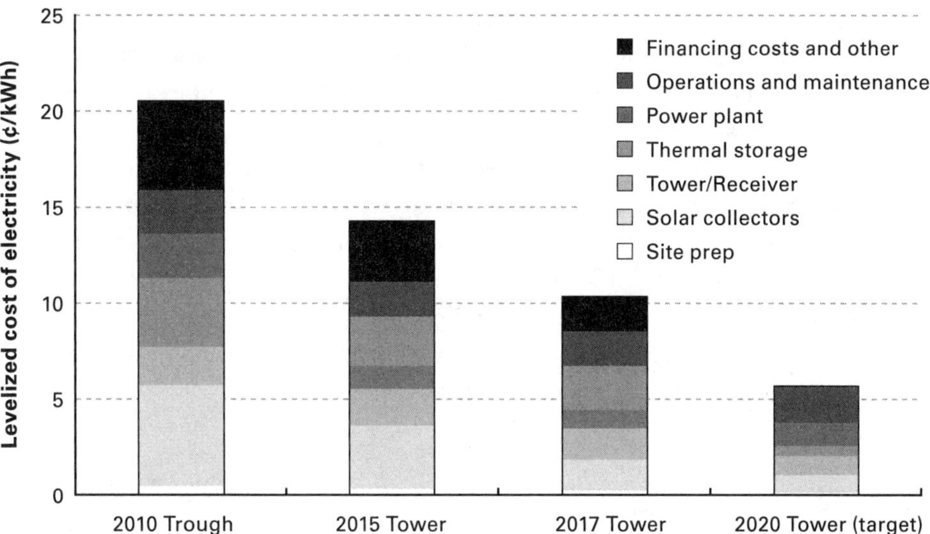

Figure 7.4

Historical and targeted costs of CSP. The first bar shows the various costs that composed the total cost per kilowatt-hour of electricity of a parabolic trough CSP plant in the United States in 2010. The second and third bars display the costs for power-tower CSP plants in 2015 and 2017. Finally, the fourth bar displays the DOE's targeted cost for a power-tower CSP plant that operates at a higher temperature and uses supercritical carbon dioxide as the working fluid.
Source: DOE Sunshot Program.

a second turbine and generate even more power. Known as a "combined cycle," this highly efficient method resembles the way that modern natural gas power plants generate electricity. Therefore, it may be possible to repurpose much of a gas plant's equipment to save on costs.[53]

In the long term, a hybrid approach that combines CSP and PV might achieve record efficiencies without the drawback of the carbon emissions produced from burning natural gas. This approach would seek to put each part of the sun's spectrum to its most efficient use. The infrared part, which transmits heat, could be converted to electricity by a CSP system, and the higher-energy photons could be absorbed by PV panels and converted to electricity as well, resulting in a high overall efficiency for the hybrid plant.

The biggest barrier to such a hybrid system is a mismatch in optimal temperatures. Whereas CSP works better at higher temperatures, PV is better suited to lower ones. So more radical ideas might be called for, including a recent invention at Stanford University of a device in which solar photons and extreme heat cooperate to shake electrons free of a semiconductor, resulting in an electric current.[54]

The common theme uniting these exciting research directions is the need to reach higher temperatures. If the next generation of CSP plants can break through existing temperature barriers, the market could recover and start to grow rapidly alongside the breakneck expansion of the PV market. Because of CSP's built-in storage, CSP expansion could be crucial to enabling high penetration of solar energy into the power grid. Put more simply, if the CSP market heats up, the planet might not have to.

Planning for the Future

This chapter and the previous one introduced an array of technologies that share one important characteristic: The world's need for them will grow with the passage of time. Whereas silicon solar panels are presently the workhorse of a growing solar industry in a world where solar generates only 2 percent of global electricity, today's PV panels may not suffice in a world with higher solar penetration. To outrun value deflation, solar PV will need to get cheaper much faster, requiring new technologies—such as perovskite—that are as inexpensive to make as printing newspapers. And, to smooth out intermittent PV electricity production, CSP must grow rapidly to provide an alternative way to both harness sunlight and store the captured energy.

Finally, to enable solar energy to supply not only electricity to the power grid, but also fuel for other applications that resist electrification—such as for running cars, trucks, ships, planes, and industrial plants—the world will need massive solar fuel generators able to produce large quantities of hydrogen or even carbon-based liquid fuels. These technologies would be nice to have right now. But they will be essential in the decades to come if the world is to avoid the effects of catastrophic climate change and is to transition away from fossil fuels in all sectors of the economy.

Regrettably, scientists cannot snap their fingers once an urgent technology need arises and—poof—conjure up new contraptions. Rather, the process of converting small-scale research advances into large-scale commercial projects can span decades, and that timeline resists compression. For example, one study of CSP projects around the world concluded that the process of scaling up the technology from the first demonstrations took more than two decades—although much of the progress took place in the most recent decade.[55] One might make the aggressive assumption that the time lag between the first-of-its-kind demonstration plant and the industry's ability to repeatably deploy large-scale projects is a decade.

In that case, what would happen if countries and private firms were to barely fund CSP technology development over the next ten years, while it seemed as if PV would remain much more competitive economically? When the year 2030 rolled around, and solar PV had achieved significant penetration in several markets around the world, torpedoing its economics, countries might belatedly realize that CSP with built-in storage could alleviate the strain on their power grids. But, at that point, it could take until 2040 or beyond to push high-temperature, cost-effective CSP projects to commercial scale. Countries would rue the lost decade of investment in innovation that might have provided a viable option to mitigate solar's intermittency as soon as it started causing serious problems.

The situation is even more perilous for the other technologies discussed in this chapter because their commercial application requires scaling up innovations at the nanoscale to the scale of humanity's enormous energy demands. It will take at least several years to build the first real-world demonstration of a football field–sized tarp coated with perovskite photovoltaics to generate electricity or configured as a PEC to produce hydrogen. So far, scientists have barely managed to make fingernail-sized devices, which exhibit dubious durability. From there, it will take another decade to scale up from a demonstration facility to commercial-scale production and deployment. Failing to invest in preparing these technologies today will bring massive costs when those technologies are needed down the road.

Technology innovation, therefore, is a priority whose costs are incurred up front and whose rewards are reaped years or decades in the future. This priority will not be met by reacting to needs in real time. Rather, it will take long-term planning. Chapter 10, which makes recommendations to U.S. policymakers, will lay out a detailed blueprint for how the U.S. federal government can support innovation and lead a global push for research, development, and demonstration of new technologies. But the overarching thesis is simple—and Toyota nailed it in one word. It's that the *Mirai*—or "future"—is what the world urgently needs to prepare for.

PART IV PUTTING IT ALL TOGETHER

Highlights

- The final type of innovation that solar needs in order to achieve its potential is *systemic innovation*, which involves refashioning entire energy systems—including physical infrastructure, economic markets, and public policies—to enable a high penetration of solar energy.
- Solar photovoltaic (PV) panels—which produce electricity only when the sun shines—will likely remain the dominant means of harnessing sunlight. As solar PV's share of electricity supply rises, the electricity grid will need to tolerate massive amounts of intermittent power. Chapter 8, "Is Bigger Better?" contemplates whether it makes more sense to expand the grid to harness sunlight wherever the sun is shining or to make the grid smaller in a sense, by decentralizing the generation and consumption of energy through the use of smart-grid technology. Ultimately, the best solution might be a hybrid of both approaches to make the grid bigger, smaller, and smarter all at once.
- The most intuitive solution for the problem of intermittency is to bundle solar PV together with energy storage. Chapter 9, "No Silver Bullet," argues, however, that relying only on batteries, the most familiar storage technology, would be prohibitively expensive. Fortunately, there are many ways to re-create the same benefits as battery storage. A diverse mix of power plants can flexibly shift their output to offset variable solar power. And linking the electricity system with other sectors—such as transportation, heat, freshwater production, or agriculture—can provide flexible sources of demand to absorb surplus solar power.

- The United States has a crucial role to play in advancing the innovation that solar needs. Chapter 10, “A Solar City upon a Hill,” warns that the Trump administration’s policies threaten to dim the shining example that the United States has historically set as the world’s foremost funder of energy innovation. To seize the growing economic opportunity that solar presents and compete with the current market leader, China, U.S. policymakers must increase funding for research, development, and demonstration of new solar technologies, as well as other energy technologies that solar needs in order to thrive. In addition to supporting technological innovation, U.S. policymakers should set an example for the rest of the world by promoting financial and systemic innovations to pave the way for solar’s continued rise.

Chapter 8 Is Bigger Better?

The only thing more surprising than the partnership between a Japanese tycoon and a Chinese technocrat was the proposal they had joined forces to pitch. The "Global Energy Interconnection," as they called it, would cost $50 trillion, link every continent with undersea transmission lines, and power the globe with clean energy. Windmills on the North Pole and solar panels in the Sahara Desert would export their power to run the world's megacities. And oh, by the way, this supergrid would also secure world peace and harmony.

At least one half of the odd couple had made a habit of proposing audacious goals. For Masayoshi Son—the second-richest man in Japan, where as something of a celebrity, he is often called just "Masa"—the supergrid is his latest superlative. Masa has also set his sights on turning Softbank, the conglomerate he leads, into a business empire that will last 300 years, and in 2017, he launched a mammoth, $100 billion fund to invest in the tech sector. He has predicted that by midcentury, computers will surpass human intelligence, achieving an IQ of 10,000.[1] His bet on a supergrid fits right in with his other self-described "crazy ideas."[2]

Following the 2011 Fukushima disaster, Masa set out to harness renewable energy as an alternative to nuclear energy to power Japan. "I was a total layman in renewable energy at the time of the earthquake," he admits. Perhaps that inexperience explains a proposal that most experts would dismiss out of hand. But Masa's initial vision of Japan importing solar and wind power from the Gobi Desert resonated with utility executives in Russia, South Korea, and China. In 2016, the three utilities and Softbank signed a memorandum of understanding to collaborate on a pan-Asian supergrid.[3]

It was Masa's Chinese partner, Liu Zhenya—chairman of State Grid Corporation, the national utility and second-biggest company in the world—who masterminded the plan to ultimately go global once an Asian supergrid materialized. Unlike Masa, Liu was not known for articulating bold visions. In fact, he wasn't known for saying much of anything at all. An engineer by training, Liu had worked in the state power administration his whole career, quietly ascending to the top of State Grid's ranks.

But his work spoke for itself. Under Liu's tenure, China constructed a network of ultra-high-voltage-direct-current (UHVDC) transmission lines, a technology that has recently fallen in cost and can transmit power over long distances without excessive losses. China currently has seven of these gargantuan projects, which ship renewable energy from the remote western hinterlands of the country to the metropolitan east coast. It also has twice as many projects on the drawing board. By contrast, the United States is still trying to build its first UHVDC line, a $2.5 billion project to send wind power from Oklahoma to Tennessee.[4]

Capitalizing on its success at home, State Grid is now offering its expertise abroad. Brazil has hired it to build the longest transmission line in the world, measuring more than 1,500 miles, to deliver hydropower from the Amazon to Rio de Janeiro.[5] These efforts represent the first of three stages that Liu envisions to achieve a global supergrid. First, countries will build their own transmission grids—China plans to finish this stage by 2025. Next, countries will link up regionally, in line both with Masa's early vision of an Asian supergrid and other ambitious proposals, such as a grid to link sunny North Africa with windy Europe. Then, the grand third stage will bring together the regional supergrids to form a single global supergrid, linked by transoceanic undersea cables and electrical superstations where lines would converge (figure 8.1).

Now Liu is backing up his vision with action. In 2016, when he reached China's mandatory retirement age and stepped down as boss of State Grid, he immediately took up the chairmanship of an organization devoted to realizing his Global Energy Interconnection dream (Masa is a vice chairman). He has also written a dense textbook, *Global Energy Interconnection,* that provides a technical, step-by-step road map, including the specific technologies that will require further research and development (R&D) investment to become commercially viable.[6] He sums up by arguing that a global supergrid could "secure a safe, clean, efficient, and sustainable energy supply. With UHV [ultra-high-voltage] grids as its backbone, such a global energy interconnection transmits primarily clean energy."

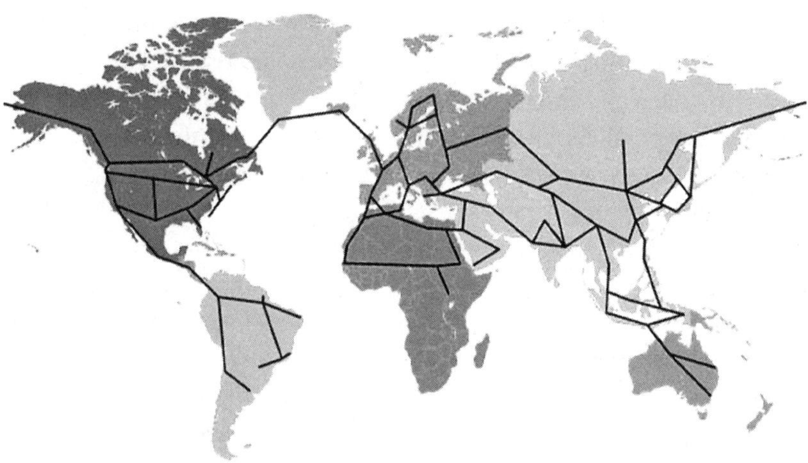

Figure 8.1
A global supergrid. This map combines various proposed regional supergrids (for example, in the Asia-Pacific region, Europe and the Middle East/North Africa, and North America). Black lines represent long-distance HVDC electricity transmission lines.
Source: Reprinted with permission from Gellings (2015).

Given China's prowess at building large infrastructure—from bullet trains to planned cities—the supergrid concept is understandably attractive and logical from Liu's perspective. Indeed, a supergrid is one way to solve the serious problem of renewable energy's intermittency, which existing, balkanized grids around the world are not equipped to handle well. Although the sun will not always shine over any given location, it will always be out somewhere in the world. A big grid can connect remote renewable resources with urban centers demanding energy. In general, the bigger the grid, the easier it is to match up supply and demand.

Yet a supergrid would create its own host of challenges, which Liu's tome addresses inadequately despite devoting more than 300 pages to engineering details. Liu appears to find his creative muse in the last chapter, entitled "Global Energy Interconnection Changes the World," where the previously staid textbook starts to veer off the rails with increasingly wishful subsections entitled "Creating a New Energy Scenario," "Infusing New Vigor into Economic Growth," "Creating a Wonderful New Social Life," and "Turning a New Chapter of Civilization."

In a similar vein, in a speech at the United Nations, Liu predicted that "the world will turn into a peaceful and harmonious global village with sufficient energy, green lands, and blue sky."[7] But Liu's predictions about international relations are at odds with how the world actually works. First, getting countries to pony up $50 trillion, as the plan requires, will be a tall order ("politically impossible," as Masa's advisors have warned him). Also, many countries might worry about importing power from abroad. Peter Littlewood, professor of physics at the University of Chicago, is skeptical of Liu's grand vision, invoking Europe's tumultuous experience depending on Russia for natural gas. In one of his characteristically British understatements, he has remarked, "My sense is that countries will be concerned about being reliant on partners that they may not always be friends with."[8]

Despite the political challenges, the practicalities of building a supergrid are worth considering, as are other out-of-the-box ideas for accommodating growing amounts of clean but intermittent sources into energy systems. In any case, the supergrid concept underscores the massive scale that might be needed to enable a global electricity system to rely heavily on fluctuating power sources like solar and wind. Even if technological innovation were to deliver endless rolls of almost-free, ultra-efficient solar photovoltaic (PV) coatings, today's power grids would still struggle to integrate the resulting gobs of unreliable electricity. Enabling continued expansion of solar PV will also require arresting its value deflation, so its electricity is worth more than the costs of generating it. To meet such demands, countries will have to rethink the entire architecture of their power grids, and do it in time for the world to reach the target of generating a third of its electricity from solar power by midcentury (and, overall, most of its electricity from zero-carbon sources).

Many believe that the key to accommodating solar's rise and addressing intermittency will be storing excess energy in batteries. But batteries remain expensive—at least for now. Grid expansion is an elegant alternative. Batteries would still have a place but would not be the only, or even the primary, solution (See chapter 9 for more details). If you build a big enough grid, the need to deploy massive amounts of expensive storage falls because the vagaries of weather and volatility of demand average out over large areas. Recognizing the advantage this feature offers, proposals for regional supergrids all over the world, notably in Asia, Europe, and North America, are gaining steam.

The quest to build ever-larger grids is not the only attempt under way to transform the power sector, though. In fact, the exact opposite idea has attracted excitement, particularly from New York, California, and some other U.S. states. Large, interconnected grids are vulnerable to massive failures, as Superstorm Sandy reminded people living in New York and New Jersey in 2012. But decentralized grids that rely more heavily on locally sited power resources—such as rooftop solar panels fuel cells, and batteries—could be more resilient in the face of disasters, natural or otherwise.

Moreover, a decentralized grid could, in theory, be cheaper than a centralized one. Scaling back investments in the sprawling infrastructure of the traditional grid, from power lines to substations, could slash customer bills. And those savings might not disappear if the cost gap between cheap power from large plants and traditionally expensive power from small-scale resources continues to narrow. Finally, if decentralized economic markets, where customers could trade energy services with their neighbors, took off, a decentralized grid could operate much more efficiently than today's overbuilt, clumsy, and centralized power system.

There are reasons to think that decentralized grids would have more difficulty incorporating solar power than larger grids would, yet counterarguments can also be made. A decentralized grid would rely more heavily on local power sources, such as rooftop solar, which is more expensive than utility-scale solar. And a decentralized grid would be hard-pressed to balance power supply and demand on the scale of individual communities, whereas a centralized grid can more easily average out supply-and-demand volatility over large areas. On the other hand, decentralized economic markets might increase the value of small-scale solar by compensating solar owners for helping to stabilize the grid. This increase in appeal could speed the deployment of distributed solar power installations, especially those of an intermediate size of a few megawatts that are both cost-effective and valuable to the grid. If a decentralized grid were also "smart"—that is, if the grid and the equipment that it powers could talk to each other—then the grid could adjust to customer demand on the fly. It could match demand with the fluctuating supply from intermittent solar power, whether from utility-scale solar plants or distributed installations.

Supergrids and decentralized grids may fall on opposite ends of the size spectrum, but both would require systemic innovation, or novel approaches to fitting all the puzzle pieces of an energy system together.

Systemic innovation can involve the use of new technologies; indeed, both new paradigms of the grid will require improved technologies to advance. But systemic innovation is distinct from technological innovation because it also encompasses getting fancy new widgets to work together seamlessly. For example, supergrids will require novel network topologies—that is, designs for laying out new power lines and tying them into existing grids. A decentralized smart grid would add two-way communication between utilities and customers and employ software algorithms to run the grid much more intelligently than today.

Which way is the world headed? And is bigger always better? There are no clear answers yet. The most promising way forward is probably to pursue a hybrid strategy of expanding the grid and localizing it at the same time, all the while making it much smarter than it is today. Such a hybrid grid might rely on a backbone of long-distance transmission lines to link faraway regions and deliver renewable energy from the most sun-drenched, windswept regions. Supplementing these clean energy highways would be decentralized microgrids serving, for example, neighborhoods, military bases, or schools, all networked together into a smart grid. Retiring much of the expensive, overbuilt infrastructure of today's grid could pay for both supergrids and asset-light microgrids. This hybrid grid model could weather the volatility of renewable energy both through the wide reach of its long-distance transmission backbone and the precise responsiveness of the decentralized smart grid.

Although the supergrid and decentralized grid models are each radical departures in opposite directions from today's power system, they might actually coexist in a truly advanced hybrid grid. Perhaps such a future is no more improbable than the partnership between Masa and Liu—two men with little in common except dreams of a future powered by clean energy.

Let's Get Together

A 2015 headline in *The Guardian* announced, "Wind Power Generates 140 Percent of Denmark's Electricity Demand."[9] Technically, that was true—it was so windy one summer day that Denmark's ubiquitous wind farms generated enough power to meet the entire country's demand, with surplus to sell to its neighbors. The bit about the neighbors might sound like an afterthought. But those neighbors are crucial to Denmark's ability to supply over a third of its annual electricity from highly variable wind energy.

Denmark's grid is part of the larger Nordic Synchronized Area, a grid that also encompasses Norway, Sweden, and Germany and delivers nearly thirty times as much power as Denmark alone uses. To that larger grid, Danish wind power is a drop in the bucket. A bucket is indeed an apt metaphor because the Nordic grid features vast hydro reservoirs in Sweden and Norway, which are adept at storing volatile renewable energy by pumping water uphill; the power can be recovered on demand by letting water flow back downhill to run a hydroelectric turbine. Across the whole Nordic grid, wind accounted for less than 15 percent of the electricity produced in 2015, despite the dramatic *Guardian* headline.[10]

Denmark's situation is an argument for designing large, cross-national grids. Such grids can be more efficient than isolated ones because they can draw in energy from whatever sources are cheapest and most available at the time, regardless of whether those sources are nearby. Larger grids can also make much more use of clean but intermittent sources, which reduces waste and increases incentives for expanding the penetration of renewable energy into the electricity sector. The question for planners of such grids is how best to link up the disparate parts.

In the case of the Nordic Grid, its existence enabled much more wind power to be deployed than would have been possible if the constituent countries were disconnected from one another. Indeed, one of the major reasons that Germany is a global leader in renewables, which supplied a third of its power in 2016, is its ability to export surplus power to its neighbors. And to use even more renewable energy, Germany is building new transmission lines to Sweden and Norway to access their extensive hydroelectric storage facilities.

Interconnecting their grids makes it easier for countries to increase their share of volatile renewable energy while still matching up power supply and demand. On the supply side, the territory covered by a larger grid can have more diverse weather patterns than an individual country would. The shared grid makes it possible to exploit these patterns to keep the power supply to customers steady. For example, a large enough grid will rarely experience overcast skies over its entire geographical span, so at least some solar panels will continue to produce power as production from others drops. Similarly, geographically diverse wind turbines will produce less volatile power than if they are regionally concentrated. The wind and the sun are also anticorrelated in many regions. That is, at night when the sun sets, the wind blows harder, so a large grid spanning windy and sunny areas can achieve relatively consistent levels of renewable output. It is true that there are limits to what grid expansion can achieve. Because the sun moves from east to west, grid expansion from north to south does not mitigate power fluctuations from the daily solar cycle. Long-distance east–west transmission lines, however, can help with this daily volatility. Grid expansion also will not help when a solar eclipse strikes—fortunately, those large-scale events are rare and predictable.[11]

On the demand side, the larger the grid, the easier it is to match up renewable supply with demand centers. Often, the best renewable energy resources are far from major urban areas—think about the sun-soaked Sahara Desert or the windswept Great Plains—but a large grid can link them. In addition, connecting different demand centers has a similar smoothing effect on overall demand as linking geographically diverse sources of various kinds of renewable energy supply. When some area needs a lot of energy, it can obtain it from locales that require less energy at the moment.[12]

The technology to link faraway regions with transmission lines has actually been around since the first half of the twentieth century. As early as the 1920s, power systems engineers realized that high-voltage direct current (HVDC) power lines were better suited than high-voltage alternating current (HVAC) counterparts for long-distance transmission. This is counterintuitive, given that chapter 5 explained that in the early twentieth century, AC became the global standard of choice for power grids because it was easy to transform the voltage of AC power (and nearly impossible to do so for DC power). At high voltages, less electricity is lost in transmission. AC power grids sprang up to serve burgeoning electricity demand because it made more sense to put power plants relatively far from where the power was consumed, rather than rely on a DC system, which would require colocated generation and consumption. Thomas Edison, who favored using DC, was on the losing side of this argument, even though he publicly electrocuted farm animals with AC to try and turn public opinion against HVAC. Nikola Tesla sealed AC's victory by powering New York City with an AC transmission line from Niagara Falls.

For transmission over really long distances (i.e., hundreds of miles or more), however, even HVAC just isn't up to the task. At the high voltages required for those distances (several hundred thousand to over a million volts), HVDC lines are considerably cheaper and lose less energy than their HVAC counterparts. In fact, DC power transmission is always more efficient (i.e., loses less energy) than AC power transmission, and DC power lines require less material than AC power lines, making them cheaper. But the prohibitive cost of converters to increase and decrease the voltage of DC electricity at the beginning and end of a transmission line has traditionally ruled out DC for most grid uses. By comparison, AC voltage transformers are relatively inexpensive.

Still, at the highest voltages and greatest distances, the savings from more efficient and cheaper HVDC power lines more than compensate for the expensive DC converters (figure 8.2). What's more, HVDC lines require less land when built above ground, and they can even be put underground, whereas long-distance AC lines cannot be put underground because of extremely high energy losses.

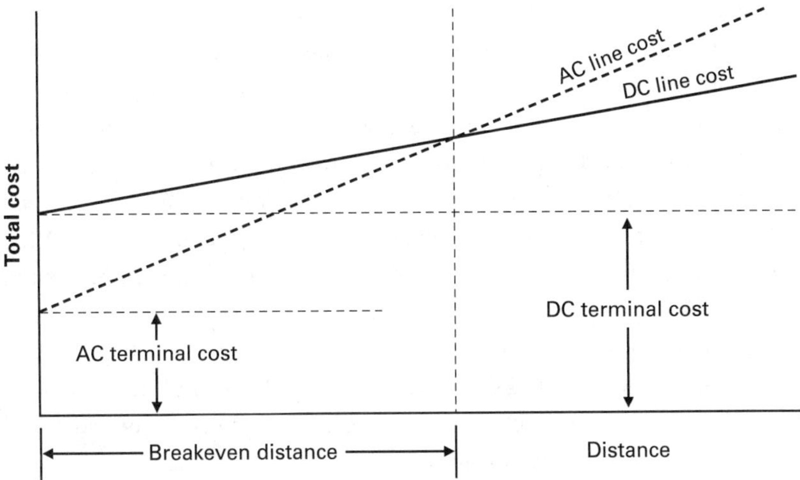

Figure 8.2
Schematic cost comparison of AC versus DC power lines. This schematic graph plots the total cost of AC and DC power lines as a function of their length. AC lines are cheaper over shorter distances because AC terminals, which transform the voltage to higher or lower levels, are cheaper than DC terminals, which convert the voltage to higher or lower levels. But over longer distances, AC lines quickly become more expensive because the cost of the power lines overwhelms the cost of the terminal. This is because long-distance AC lines have high losses and require substantially more material than equivalent-voltage DC lines. Therefore, beyond the breakeven distance, typically several hundred miles, high-voltage DC lines are the cheapest option, even taking into account the expensive terminals.

Recognizing that the voltage converters were the expensive bottleneck raising the cost of otherwise cheaper and superior HVDC technology, engineers in Europe and the United States worked throughout the twentieth century to develop less expensive converters. The first commercial HVDC project connected an island off Sweden with the mainland in 1954. In the 1970s, a better converter technology set off a flurry of new lines in Europe, Asia, and North America.[13] (One of these is the Pacific DC intertie, a nearly 1,000-mile HVDC line built in 1970 to connect the Pacific Northwest with Los Angeles. In 2013, when I was an advisor to Mayor Antonio Villaraigosa of Los Angeles, I recommended that the municipal utility invest over $100 million to upgrade the Sylmar converter station serving Los Angeles; those improvements are now ongoing).[14]

HVDC lines built in the twentieth century were limited to connecting just two faraway points. More recently, however, a new converter technology known as a "voltage source converter" has made it possible to tap into an HVDC line at many points along its journey. This capability raises the prospect of an interconnected, meshed grid of HVDC lines rather than single, one-off projects. Such a grid could allow many more sources of supply and demand to be connected while minimizing transmission losses over long distances. What's more, voltage source converters would enable this HVDC grid to link to existing AC grids, layering the former right on top of the latter.

For HVDC grids to be widely affordable and effective, more technologies are needed. These include DC circuit breakers that can shut down massive current flows within milliseconds to ensure grid reliability. Recent advances in materials known as "wide-bandgap semiconductors" might enable low-cost, high-performance circuit breakers, voltage converters, and other power electronics for HVDC grids.[15] Further on the horizon, replacing today's copper or aluminum power lines with superconducting cables could boost the power that an HVDC line could carry while plunging the energy losses to virtually zero. Such superconducting lines would need to be cooled to nearly –200°C, but the efficiency gains could outweigh the cooling costs.[16]

Although HVDC technologies are still under development, China is forging ahead, planning to develop everything that it needs along the way. Having already constructed the largest HVDC network in the world, it may spend $4 trillion through 2040 reducing emissions from its power sector and making an even bigger network of UHVDC (which is just HVDC at especially high voltages—around 1 million volts or higher) lines.[17] Some of this ambitious buildout might be excessive. Indeed, China has been known to build "white elephant" infrastructure projects, such as roads and railways to sparsely populated areas.[18] One study suggests that bolstering the good old AC grid could utilize surplus renewable energy better than building fancy, new long-distance UHVDC lines, which might backfire by providing distant markets for inefficient, inland coal plants.[19] Most experts agree, however, that China's transmission expansion will help reduce the amount of renewable energy that is thrown away because of being generated in remote areas cut off from demand centers.

Building on China's progress, Liu and Masa envision interconnecting China with other Asian countries to create a regional supergrid. Though expensive, the prospective benefits—such as the ability to send remote, cheap renewable energy to faraway cities—could outweigh the costs. Another advantage of interconnecting grids across national borders is that each country would no longer have to maintain backup generation capacity independently to ensure power reliability. Instead, the countries could pool their reserves, eliminate redundancies, and reduce the total capacity needed. Studies simulating different configurations have found that a Northeast Asian supergrid connecting China, Japan, South Korea, Mongolia, and Eastern Russia could be cost-effective, despite the high cost of building new transmission lines.[20] But linking Australia, via underwater cables and overland lines through Southeast Asia, might be a bridge too far for now.[21]

Another promising regional supergrid proposal would connect Europe with North Africa. This idea, however, has already faced obstacles. In 2009, a consortium of European investors founded DESERTEC, a scheme to supply Europe with solar energy from the sun-drenched deserts of North Africa. But by 2013, the investors backed out and the program collapsed. Still, in 2016, a CSP project in Ouarzazate, Morocco, came online (travel tip: this plant is less than an hour's drive from the popular tourist village of Ait-Benhaddou and is worth a visit just to gawk at the parabolic mirrors arrayed as far as the eye can see). The project was originally intended to export power to Europe and may help resuscitate the supergrid vision.[22]

A recent study confirmed the feasibility of connecting Europe's AC grid with North Africa via HVDC lines to dramatically reduce the carbon emissions of the combined supergrid, but the price tag is over $200 billion.[23] So in the near term, proposals to further interconnect Europe's grid—the largest in the world in terms of connected generation capacity—have the most realistic chance of completion. These include connecting the Nordic grid with Russia, delivering offshore wind power in the North Sea to various countries, and realizing a sixty-year-old plan to link Iceland to the rest of Europe through Scotland.

Across the Atlantic, North America is an excellent candidate for further interconnection, building on the well-integrated U.S.-Canada grid. One study focused on the United States found opportunities for more than 20,000 miles of new HVDC transmission lines to internally link up the entire country to enable a surge in renewable energy.[24] And there are further opportunities for continental grid integration. Canadian hydropower exports to the United States could rise tenfold if Canada fully developed its hydropower resources and the two countries built new HVDC connectors.[25] The biggest rewards, however, lie to the south. Cross-border electricity trade between the United States and Mexico has historically been limited. Now that Mexico has reformed its energy markets, though, the two countries have discussed integrating their grids with the addition of new transmission capacity.[26] This integration would offer the United States access to Mexico's enormous solar resources in sunny regions, such as Baja California. In 2016, the three North American heads of state agreed on a continental goal to reach 50 percent zero-carbon electricity by 2025.[27]

When it comes to hammering out the details of grid interconnection across borders, there are opportunities for cooperation (consistent with Liu's predictions of global harmony)—but also discord. Different countries have different rules and regulations governing their power markets, and harmonizing them across borders could prove tricky. Countries are also liable to squabble over how to allocate the costs of shared transmission projects.

And a whole host of international disagreements could color countries' willingness to jointly take the plunge and link up their power systems. For all the camaraderie between Masa and Liu, Japan and China are riven by serious political and military tensions, including maritime disputes in the East China Sea. Such tensions might prove the biggest obstacle to countries trusting one another enough to willingly increase their dependence on traded energy.

Therefore, Liu's eventual goal of going beyond regional supergrids to achieve a global one is pretty implausible, requiring more international trust, far more money, and further advances in such technologies as undersea cables. Nevertheless, that ultimate vision might function as an inspirational, if perhaps impossible, target toward which even partial progress—such as the establishment of regional supergrids—would constitute a big step forward for the world. Indeed, bigger grids will be essential for tapping the world's best solar and other renewable resources.

Still, the push to create ever-bigger grids has its critics, who contend instead that smaller, decentralized grids deliver a myriad of benefits in comparison with a centralized model. One of the most compelling of those benefits could be superior resilience in the face of natural or manmade disasters.

Bracing for the Next Superstorm

In meteorological terms, Hurricane Sandy in 2012 was a middling storm, a Category 2 runt compared with the Category 5 monsters that the Atlantic Ocean breeds every few years. But with precise aim and impeccable timing, Sandy plowed into New York City right at high tide and became a superstorm, inflicting tens of billions of dollars of damage, the second-highest total in U.S. history. The toll on the power grid was extreme. More than 2 million residents of New York City faced outages as Sandy knocked out a third of the generators serving the city, flooded five major transmission substations, and wrecked power poles and equipment on the distribution grid.[28]

Thanks to climate change, a higher proportion of future storms will be large. The flood of the century could soon become the flood of the decade.[29] At the same time as natural disasters are becoming more deadly, the U.S. electricity grid is aging and growing increasingly more vulnerable to being damaged by storms and other stresses. Even in the absence of aging, the interconnected nature of the grid makes it prone to large-scale disruptions. Being interconnected is great for delivering power across great distances, but it is calamitous when a problem in one section rapidly knocks out many other sections. In 2003, for example, an Ohio power line touched an overgrown tree branch, causing a cascading failure that blacked out vast swaths of the eastern United States and Canada, affecting 50 million people. Added to the mundane risks posed by vegetation are the malevolent threats of foreign adversaries who wish the United States harm and see the grid as a prime target.[30]

In the aftermath of Superstorm Sandy, New York governor Andrew Cuomo tasked the state's energy agencies to develop a comprehensive plan to prepare for future disasters. From that mandate evolved "Reforming the Energy Vision (REV)," the brainchild of Governor Cuomo's energy czar, Richard Kauffman.

REV sought to build resilience into New York's power grid from the ground up. By redesigning the grid to rely much more on distributed energy resources, the formerly centralized grid would not be vulnerable to failure in one fell swoop. For example, a hospital might be connected to the main grid but also generate and store power with solar panels, fuel cells, and batteries on site. If a disaster were to knock out the central grid, the hospital still would be able to run its critical equipment. Importantly, distributed energy resources would be installed in such a way that they themselves were resistant to failure. By contrast, many diesel generators powering New York City hospitals succumbed to flooding when Sandy struck, triggering evacuations of those hospitals.

Although a need for resilience inspired REV's decentralized architecture, many other benefits soon emerged. Foremost were the enormous potential economic savings from a power system that required only a skeleton of a central grid and could serve most demand with locally sited distributed energy resources. Richard Kauffman made the case to reform the traditional model of the grid by explaining, "We've spent $17 billion on the electric system in the past 10 years, and we're on track to spend $30 billion in the next 10 years. It doesn't make the system any smarter or more resilient just to replace what we have."[31]

What's more, REV could also make the power system cleaner, thanks to the emergence of low-cost, clean, and decentralized technologies such as rooftop solar panels, batteries, and energy-efficient appliances. These various benefit streams came together in late 2016 when Con Edison, New York City's power utility, successfully deferred the construction of a $1 billion substation in Brooklyn by soliciting bids for clean, distributed energy from rooftop solar, batteries, and energy-saving measures.[32]

I was fortunate to serve as an advisor to Richard and the Governor's Office during this time, where I helped design the regulations to transition New York from a twentieth-century power system to a modern one. I fondly remember one meeting in particular. The team was reviewing a sweeping new policy that would incentivize New York's power utilities to support distributed energy resources rather than pour money into expensive transmission lines and substations. Unremarkably titled "Track Two," this regulatory document was typeset in the stultifying, monospaced font that you would expect to see from a bureaucratic agency.[33] But Richard held the sheaf of paper tenderly and announced to the room that this document might be as important to the power industry as the Declaration of Independence had been to the United States.

Indeed, the regulatory reforms that document set in motion are declaring independence from the twentieth-century model of power systems. Under that model, which still characterizes the vast majority of power grids around the world, utilities operate a top-down grid. Centralized power plants produce electricity, which is then transmitted and distributed to customers much as the heart pumps blood through arteries and then capillaries to reach the body's extremities.

The problem with this power grid is that it is centrally planned, inefficient, and dumb. Utilities try to forecast demand patterns years in advance as they plan which segments of the grid to build out. These predictions are often fraught with errors, however. Utilities then oversize system components so that in the worst case—say, on a hot summer day with very high power demand from air conditioning—a substation or power line can deliver as much electricity as customers instantaneously need, even if that equipment is underutilized most of the year. Finally, most utilities have very little live information about how much power flows over the distribution grid. Until very recently, when some U.S. utilities began to roll out smart meters, they had no idea how much energy each customer consumed until a meter reader paid a monthly visit.

These features make the power grid more expensive than it needs to be, and its sprawling infrastructure has innumerable points of potential failure that threaten the whole system. Utilities, meanwhile, have no incentive to move away from this paradigm. Quite the opposite, in fact—the arcane way in which they make money is by collecting ever-higher customer payments to finance grid infrastructure projects and skimming some profit off the top to return to their investors; this paradigm gives utilities every incentive to continue building out the grid. Now, the industry certainly deserves credit for the miracle of delivering highly reliable power to the entire country. This feat led the National Academy of Engineering to proclaim the U.S. grid the most impressive engineering achievement of the twentieth century (figure 8.3).[34] But this century, a revamped grid can do much better.

In that spirit, REV aims to create a more decentralized, efficient, and smart grid. In a departure from existing regulations that compel utilities to support distributed energy resources as a matter of compliance, REV offers

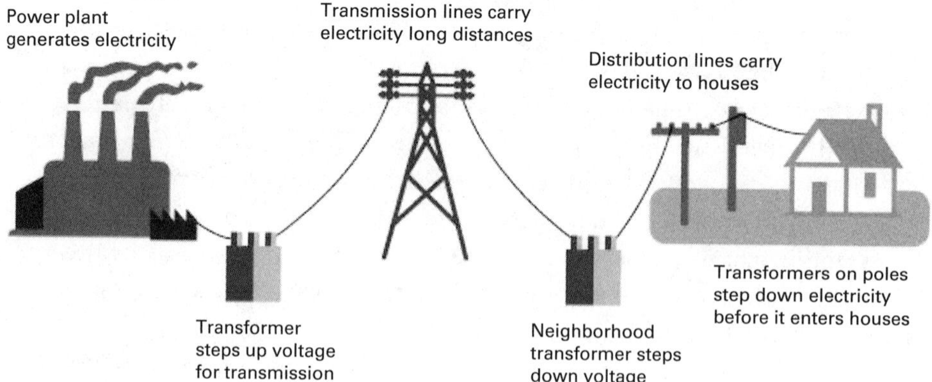

Figure 8.3
The twentieth-century paradigm of the electric grid.
Source: Energy Information Administration (EIA).

utilities new ways to make money. If they can persuade customers to cost-effectively meet local needs with on-site generation and to adopt energy-efficient appliances that can be programmed to reduce demand when the grid is under strain, they can avoid building out expensive new power lines and substations. To align their incentives with those of customers, they should be entitled to a cut of the cost savings to the power system.

Also, rather than a single, centralized wholesale power market that sets the price for power over a broad region, REV aims to set up distributed markets that would allow customers to trade energy services at the local level. It envisions dynamic prices for electricity services that change based on location, date, and time, so that customers receive finely tuned price signals based on the system costs that they incur. In a neighborhood with many rooftop solar panels, for instance, the household with a battery system could take advantage of an attractive price for storage capacity, stowing a noontime glut of solar power to prevent the energy from overloading the local circuitry and sending the stored energy back to the grid later on. And because most customers will not want to actively participate in these complex markets, third-party aggregators could step in to trade on behalf of their clients. This market-based approach would enable the most efficient use of distributed energy resources to meet customer needs.

New York's REV is not alone in its goals. On the West Coast, California is similarly exploring options to move toward a more decentralized model.[35] And, abroad, the United Kingdom has pioneered regulations that eliminated perverse incentives for utilities to invest only in major grid infrastructure projects, rather than meeting customer needs in the most efficient way possible.[36] Countless other utilities and regulatory bodies are closely watching what happens in such first-mover jurisdictions as New York to evaluate how they can modernize their power systems as well.

A crucial part of this effort will be using technology to create a smarter grid. Today's overbuilt grids exist because utilities have had little ability to see the real-time flow of power and the instantaneous demands of customers. But much less infrastructure would be required if an intelligent grid operator—or better, autonomous software programs—could reroute power flows and recruit distributed energy resources to meet local demand on the fly.

Achieving this scenario will require advanced equipment deployed across the distribution grid. Sensors on power lines and at substations could provide real-time intelligence about power flows. Power electronics could dynamically divert power to where it needs to go, rapidly shut down overloaded parts of the system, and restore service nearly immediately. Not only would the grid be less prone to massive outages (because it could section off problems before they spread elsewhere), but it would also be self-healing.[37]

What does this all have to do with solar? A transition toward a smarter, decentralized grid may well improve the grid's resilience, reduce power costs, and give customers more choices over their energy. But can it help cost-effectively deploy massive amounts of solar power and mitigate solar's volatility in the same way as grid expansion can?

At first blush, decentralizing the grid would appear to set back, rather than advance, efforts to integrate more solar power. Relying more heavily on local power sources would limit the size and location of solar installations. Instead of faraway utility-scale solar projects in the sunniest locations, a decentralized grid would recruit locally sited solar panels to power nearby communities. But the smaller a solar project, the more it costs (because bigger projects enjoy economies of scale). So, decentralizing the grid could reduce the economic competitiveness of solar power. And it would be challenging to balance intermittent solar power with local demand.

But distributed markets to facilitate local trade in energy services could increase the market value of distributed solar power. For the grid to maintain a highly reliable power supply, it needs to maintain certain attributes of that power, such as the frequency and voltage, at very precise levels. The equipment that connects distributed solar power to the grid—the inverter—could actually help the local distribution grid accomplish those goals.[38] Now that smart inverters have hit the market, they can perform these services and thus help to ensure high-quality power at local scales, earning distributed solar generators revenue in new distributed markets. And, if the value gap between utility-scale and distributed solar power narrows—because distributed solar would become more valuable and offset its high cost—deployment of distributed solar could start to catch up with that of utility-scale solar.

The way to cost-effectively deploy distributed solar power is to aim for the Goldilocks zone that sits between installations that are tiny and those that are massive. Rooftop solar installations are expensive because they are small and highly customized. Utility-scale installations are much cheaper, but they are remotely sited and require expensive transmission lines to deliver their power. In the middle are solar installations sized at just a few megawatts. These are small enough that they can be sited in the often empty surroundings of a grid substation, enabling them to plug right into the grid with limited additional expense. But they are large enough that they enjoy economies of scale that drive down their cost. In addition to being economically favorable, these installations—equipped with smart inverters—are an ideal size to help stabilize the grid.[39]

Finally, a smarter, market-driven decentralized grid also could make it easier to deal with the unreliability of solar PV installations—be they big, small, or Goldilocks-sized. Such a grid could modulate customer demand so that it matches up with fluctuating solar output. This demand-side solution to the problem of solar's intermittent supply is what we turn to next.

A Grid Hive Mind

Each January, while the world's most powerful business and political leaders hobnob at the World Economic Forum, leaders of the North American energy industry meet in Vail, Colorado, for the "Davos of Energy." Just as Davos has increasingly shined a spotlight on clean energy and climate change, so too has the Vail crowd expanded beyond just the oil and gas industry. On the final day of the 2017 summit, when participants took to the ski slopes, I found myself seated on a chair lift next to Microsoft's chief sustainability officer, Rob Bernard, with a long ride ahead of us.

We were on the first lift run of the day, at the crack of dawn, and the temperature was barely above zero Fahrenheit. But I forgot about the chill as Rob excitedly shared Microsoft's idea for how it might be possible to eliminate nearly all the carbon emissions from its data centers by running them only during periods of abundant renewable energy supply on the grid.[40] "The opportunity is huge," he gesticulated with his oversized gloves. One of Microsoft's data centers in the state of Washington alone uses as much energy as 40,000 homes.[41] Many of its operations—such as backing up or indexing its cloud customers' data—can be flexibly scheduled to increase or decrease the data center's instantaneous power consumption. And, by using a machine-learning algorithm to predict, based on past records and current weather data, when such renewable generators as solar panels will flood the grid with power, Microsoft can adjust its data centers' operations to consume that surplus solar power. Rob's idea was so captivating that I realized that my fingers were freezing only when the end of the lift interrupted our conversation. Graciously, he guided me down the quickest run to the lodge so I could warm up with some hot chocolate.

What Rob was proposing was an example of a general strategy called "demand response," in which customers adjust their power consumption to help the grid balance supply and demand. Demand response has actually been around for decades, although not in nearly as nimble a form as what Microsoft and others are pursuing today. Currently, utilities have various programs in which they pay customers to turn down the air conditioning on a hot summer day when high demand is straining the grid (to cite just one example). In some cases, utilities can directly control customer appliances to crank up the thermostat a few degrees.[42] And some large industrial power customers already regulate their demand at a greater scale. In most of the major U.S. electricity markets, they can sell negative megawatts ("negawatts") of power savings alongside the megawatts of power supplied by conventional power plants.[43]

But this is just the beginning for demand response. A wave of start-up companies has persuaded venture capital investors to fund demand-side innovations, early returns from which are much more promising than the flopped investments a decade ago in clean energy supply technologies.[44] As smarter grids gain the ability to harness a wide range of distributed energy resources and coordinate them, a much wider range of customer equipment—large and small—could act in concert to modulate demand in a way that matches up with intermittent renewable energy supply.

Many trends are on course to converge at enabling this reality. First, customers are increasingly buying appliances that connect to the Internet—be they smart thermostats, washing machines, lights, or refrigerators. Industrial power customers are also connecting their equipment to the Internet. By 2020, the overall number of devices composing the "Internet of Things" is on track to reach 50 billion—double the number in 2015.[45] These devices can be remotely controlled (for example, via a smartphone app), changing their instantaneous energy consumption. The same applies to the power-intensive equipment in large buildings, which increasingly is controlled through smart building energy management control systems.

Second, utilities are rolling out "smart meters" that measure household power consumption on a much more granular basis than every month—some measure it every hour, minute, or even second. These meters can communicate with the grid to help both grid operators and customers find out what the other needs. Over half of American households have smart meters now. Although the torrents of data pouring in from these meters have overwhelmed some utilities, others have started to manage power flows on the distribution grid intelligently to meet local customer needs.[46]

Third, two-way communications networks and software solutions are emerging that can be overlain on the new hardware to orchestrate effective demand response by managing distributed energy resources in concert. A utility can use these tools to act as the nerve center and centrally control everything on the grid, from power lines and substations to customer appliances.

But decentralized control algorithms are becoming available as well and should mirror the decentralization of the grid's hardware. In the future, the utility might coordinate only the macroscopic, or large-scale, operation of the grid, a virtual eye in the sky sending broad control signals via the cloud. But numerous local networks may also operate at the grid's edge, connecting individuals within a local community, such as a neighborhood or a university. Autonomous software algorithms at the local level could speedily coordinate the functioning of distributed energy resources to match up local supply and demand and respond to the coarse signals sent from the central utility. This might resemble an ant colony, in which decision-making is decentralized but manages to advance the goals of the entire collective.[47]

What could the grid's new hive mind mean for solar power? One exciting prospect is the emergence of virtual power plants. If distributed energy resources all over the grid could act in concert, their collective effect could be the ideal complement to solar's intermittency. For example, batteries might absorb energy as surplus solar power floods the grid. Or a combination of thermostats, water heaters, and electrical equipment might instantaneously scale back power demand to compensate for drooping solar output.[48] Already, countries around the world are experimenting with this strategy. To cope with worsening blackouts in southern Australia, for example, a utility switched on the world's largest virtual power plant in Adelaide in 2017, networking together 1,000 home batteries to better balance supply and demand.[49] (Tesla also has plans in the region to deploy the world's largest battery system to help improve the grid's reliability.)

Thus, a decentralized grid could make it easier to absorb large amounts of intermittent solar power. And combining the best features of centralized and distributed grids could integrate even more solar power. Expanding a centralized grid—possibly culminating in a supergrid—would smooth out solar output through geographical aggregation and also connect faraway solar supplies with the needs of power-hungry cities. Meanwhile, the demand response capability that could emerge from a decentralized grid's hive mind would complement the supergrid's activities, adjusting demand in response to variable solar supply.

Back at Microsoft, engineers are working to bridge the gap between the supergrid and distributed-grid strategies by combining virtual power plants with virtual transmission lines. Their idea is to swap out electrical HVDC transmission lines for much cheaper optical fibers that could create a different kind of supergrid. In their vision, a global network of interconnected data centers could shift energy-intensive computation around the world to wherever renewable energy output is strongest at that moment. So when the sun is shining over Europe, U.S. data centers would scale back their power consumption and transmit their data over to Europe to be processed and sent back.[50] Thus, demand response on a decentralized grid could give rise to an optical supergrid.

That idea is a little far-fetched—and possibly unworkable, given the latency, or delays, that would accumulate from trying to move data around the world to follow the sun. Also, data centers account for only a small (but rapidly growing) fraction of the world's power consumption. And yet, the core insight—a hybrid approach that would combine the demand response capability of a decentralized grid with the interconnections of a supergrid—is sound. An electrical, not optical, hybrid grid is not so far off, and it might represent the world's best shot at integrating massive amounts of solar power.

Best of Both Worlds

"Can you hear me now? Good!" That Verizon representative's pithy refrain from a memorable ad campaign sums up one of the remarkable successes of the twenty-first century: widespread cell-phone coverage networks. (If the ad instead conjures up frustrating experiences with cell phone carriers, at least remember that a couple of decades ago, there was no service to complain about.) Somehow, cell networks provide reasonably reliable 24/7 service to customers who collectively are forever starting and ending calls, surfing the Web, and moving around unpredictably. Embedded in that success is an important lesson for how to construct a hybrid power grid that copes well with unpredictability.

The way that cell phones access the network of cell towers is complex and dynamic. In the simplest case, a cell phone will access the nearest tower, which offers the strongest signal. If too many users saturate a single tower, your cellphone may be rerouted to a network of towers farther away. Sophisticated protocols hand off cellphone connections between towers when you are on the move.

In a similar way, in one expert's sketch of a hybrid grid, a honeycomb of micro-grids might connect to one another dynamically in a cellular fashion, rerouting power flows to adapt to congestion and instantaneous customer demand.[51] Recall from Chapter 5 that a microgrid networks together a community—perhaps a neighborhood, university, hospital, military base, or large office building—linking distributed energy resources that produce and consume energy. These microgrids would also be connected to a central grid but would each have locally sited control systems and the capability to operate autonomously.[52] And they would derive a large fraction of their electricity supply from megawatt-scale distributed solar installations located on site or nearby.

In the case of a disaster, microgrids designed with resilience in mind can disconnect from the main grid and continue to operate. Such independence can also stop a spreading blackout in its tracks. Microgrids can even make it harder for hackers to attack the overall grid by keeping localized intrusions from spreading.[53] To avoid having to overbuild power-generation sources and network capacity to ensure that the power supply can meet demand at the local community level even when the demand is unusually high, these modular microgrids could be networked together to connect dynamically with each other and trade energy services.

In this conception, long-distance transmission lines would then form a central grid backbone that connects neighboring regions (and even countries) to create a supergrid. Existing proposals for a supergrid call for adding HVDC interconnections to dramatically expand the grid's reach and access faraway renewable resources. But those proposals would largely leave the underlying grids interconnected by HVDC untouched. The hybrid grid, by contrast, would reengineer the underlying grids as well.

Much of the existing, overbuilt AC grid would become unnecessary—it would be replaced by bare-bones connections between microgrids. If the microgrids were to run on DC electricity (which is increasingly a good idea given advances in DC power electronics), then the entire hybrid grid would run on DC, from high-voltage, long-distance transmission lines to local, cellular microgrids.[54] This would minimize conversion losses from DC to AC, reduce energy consumption thanks to efficient DC appliances, and bring a myriad of other benefits, such as the prospect of underground, long-distance power lines. The grid would thus come full circle from the early days before Edison's DC technology was superseded by Tesla's AC grids.

Figure 8.4 portrays an illustrative schematic of what this hybrid grid might look like. It would combine microgrids that efficiently use distributed energy resources to regulate supply and demand at the local level with long-distance transmission links that can shuttle power between faraway regions and access remote but rich renewable resources. And it would replace much of today's existing, bloated grid that relies on expensive AC transmission and distribution infrastructure, relying on asset-light microgrids at the local scale and HVDC lines at the regional and global scales.

Achieving a hybrid grid would be the pinnacle of systemic innovation. But steep barriers stand in the way. Almost everywhere, clumsy regulations and conservative utilities are unwilling to move beyond the twentieth-century

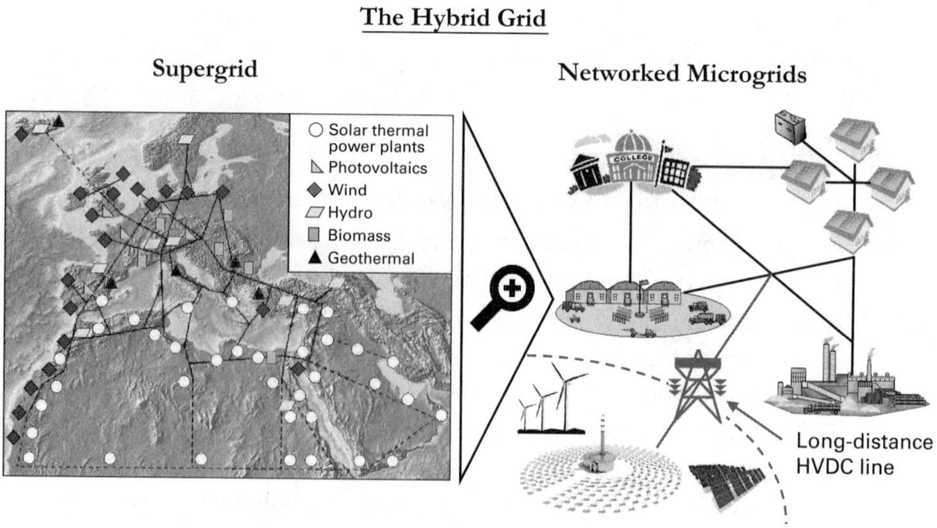

Figure 8.4

Schematic of what a hybrid grid might look like. The left panel represents a continent-sized supergrid (pictured: the regional supergrid connecting Europe and North Africa proposed by DESERTEC). The symbols represent renewable energy generators, and the lines represent long-distance, HVDC transmission lines. The right panel zooms in to reveal the decentralized microstructure of the hybrid grid. At this scale, the grid consists of networked microgrids with their own distributed energy resources (clockwise from top left are a college campus, a neighborhood, an industrial facility, and a military base). These networked microgrids connect to the superstructure of HVDC lines that connect disparate regions and enable access to faraway renewable resources.

Important note: This schematic is not exhaustive—that is, many other resources, like conventional power plants, can plug into this hybrid grid, though they are not shown owing to space constraints.

Source: DESERTEC map obtained from Wikimedia Commons.

paradigm of the power system—even in such pioneering states as New York and California, progress is slow. There are also considerable technical details to work out—including standards for how smart microgrids can talk to one another and effectively emulate a cellular network.[55] Cost is another issue. HVDC lines are expensive, and although a decentralized network of microgrids is a highly efficient setup that avoids the high capital costs of traditional grid equipment, utilities that have already financed the existing grid need to recoup their investments even as a new model of the grid emerges. And of course, there are geopolitical considerations, as the long-distance transmission parts of a hybrid grid might compel countries to depend on unsavory neighbors.

But as more solar power connects to the grid, overwhelming utilities, regulators may be forced to take rapid action. Cost will always obstruct change, but the compelling value proposition of the hybrid grid—saving money by greatly reducing today's bloated AC infrastructure and investing it instead in highly valuable, long-distance HVDC lines—could attract firms and governments to the new model.

And countries might just be willing to interconnect with their neighbors, friendly or not. Because the hybrid grid would both increase regional connectivity and decentralize control over power supply and demand, communities would become more self-reliant in the event of disruptions to long-distance power flows. Indeed, that is the point of the hybrid grid—to achieve the best of both worlds between decentralizing the grid and creating supergrids. And by dramatically improving the grid's versatility, the hybrid grid could be the best way to handle an influx of centralized and distributed solar power.

All of this means that perhaps Masa and Liu, the visionaries behind the global supergrid, actually weren't thinking big enough to envision going beyond even a supergrid to a hybrid grid. Or rather, they weren't thinking both big and small enough.

Chapter 9 No Silver Bullet

The pundits were united in their scorn—surely, this time, Elon Musk, the provocative CEO of Tesla Motors, had gone too far. On June 21, 2016, Tesla had announced plans to acquire SolarCity, the dominant player in the residential U.S. solar market but a company with no apparent connection to Tesla's electric car market. Tesla's shares plunged by as much as 10 percent as analysts panned the deal. One prominent investor even called the deal "shameful."[1]

The dominant narrative was that SolarCity, whose business model required fronting huge sums of capital to finance rooftop solar systems that homeowners would pay back over time, had been hemorrhaging cash and needed a bailout. Already, SpaceX—which Musk also helms—had lent hundreds of millions of dollars to SolarCity, which was run by Musk's cousins, Lyndon and Peter Rive. Now, analysts fumed, SolarCity's sale to Tesla would constitute a bailout within the family. On top of this, Tesla was facing production delays for its new Model 3 mass-market car, and an autonomously piloted Tesla Model S had just crashed, killing its driver. How could this be the right time to merge with an embattled firm from another industry?

Musk actually agreed with his critics that the timing wasn't ideal. But wryly, he quipped that the merger "may even be a little late."[2] As obviously disgraceful as the proposed sale was to the pundits, combining the two companies had been just as obviously a no-brainer for Musk for over a decade. In 2006, Musk published "The Secret Tesla Motors Master Plan" on his blog, promising to build an expensive electric vehicle (EV) for early adopters, use the proceeds to fund development of a cheaper EV for the masses, *and* in parallel produce cheap, zero-emission solar power.[3]

Now, the Tesla/SolarCity merger was a logical culmination of a single, overarching goal. What united both companies was Musk's drive to transform the way that the world produces and consumes energy. Solar power was a crucial component of that vision, but it was incomplete on its own. Only paired with energy storage—which Tesla Motors conveniently sold in the form of EVs and home batteries—could solar power actually meet most of a household's energy needs.

Confident in this logic, Musk shrugged off the opposition to his merger plans. He'd heard this type of criticism many times before. For a man who thinks decades and centuries ahead, Musk was never likely to be fazed by day-trader hysterics. In addition to plotting a transformation of the world's energy systems, he has set his sights on building reusable launch vehicles and spacecraft to colonize Mars. What sets him apart from other dreamers is an intimate familiarity with the details of his various ventures—from personally leading the investigation into faulty tanks of supercooled propellant that caused a SpaceX rocket to explode in 2016 to insisting on the specifications of retractable door handles on Tesla EVs to minimize their aerodynamic drag.[4]

This approach has led to astounding results. Among many other milestones, SpaceX won the race to land and relaunch a rocket, and Tesla cars have become so popular that over 300,000 eager buyers put down deposits within a week of the Tesla Model 3 announcement in 2016.

Still, Musk would need his investors to see the future in the way that he did—and it would help to restore the public hype over his companies and vision. So in October 2016, a couple of weeks before shareholders were due to vote on the proposed merger, Musk unveiled a stunning new product, hidden in plain sight.

At an event in Universal Studios, on the set of the television show *Desperate Housewives,* Musk interrupted his own speech to ask the audience if they noticed anything funny about the houses on the set. To the crowd's disbelief, it turned out that the houses—elegant but otherwise ordinary to the eye—actually had roof shingles and tiles that concealed silicon solar photovoltaic (PV) cells. What's more, these solar roofs would cost less than ordinary roofs (although that's a bit of hyperbole, given that Tesla's solar roofs aim to replace such materials as terra cotta and French slate, which can be more than twenty times as expensive as ordinary asphalt shingles). To underscore his thesis that SolarCity's products belonged under (or on) the same roof as those of Tesla Motors, Musk opened a garage door to reveal gleaming Tesla EVs and the company's Powerwall home battery. The tableau was a vivid depiction of Musk's vision of the future, in which solar panels and batteries work hand in hand to eliminate a household's carbon footprint—all in considerable style.

Predictably, aversion turned to adulation. Shareholders overwhelmingly approved Musk's proposed merger, and they were repaid handsomely. The combined firm promptly soared in value, and by April 2017, it reached a market cap of over $50 billion—more valuable than any U.S. car company.[5] On its website, Tesla Motors quietly changed its name to just "Tesla," signaling to the world that the ultimate energy company had arrived—it wasn't just a car company anymore.

Musk is betting the house—solar roof tiles and all—on his hypothesis that energy storage is crucial to enabling a solar-powered future. In particular, he is betting on a particular energy storage technology: lithium-ion batteries. Although these batteries were almost exclusively used in laptops and other consumer electronics a decade ago, Tesla is deploying them en masse not only to power its vehicles, but also as stand-alone battery packs, sized for individual households, or even as large-scale backup resources for the power grid.

Musk believes that he can re-create the dramatic cost declines achieved in solar by similarly scaling up the production of lithium-ion batteries. So out in the Nevada desert, Tesla has built its first Gigafactory, which aims to produce more lithium-ion batteries in 2018 than the entire world had produced just five years earlier. Word of the facility's size has sparked a lithium-ion arms race, as rivals from China (BYD) and South Korea (LG Chem and Samsung) have ratcheted up battery production in anticipation of the Gigafactory. All this activity assured that Musk's prediction of falling battery costs would be a self-fulfilling prophecy. Indeed, in 2016, the cost of a battery pack plunged, going from more than $400 per kilowatt-hour (kWh) of storage capacity to less than $200/kWh (figure 9.1).[6]

The logic of using battery storage to enable a high penetration of solar power is seductive. After all, combining the two technologies would yield a perfectly flexible power source, freed from the intermittency of sunlight. And if batteries were to get cheap enough, most, if not all, of solar's flaws would appear to vanish. Paired with batteries, solar PV would no longer be afflicted by economic value deflation because, instead of being worth nothing, any excess power output from solar panels at sunny times could be stored and sold to the grid during periods of peak demand. Power grids

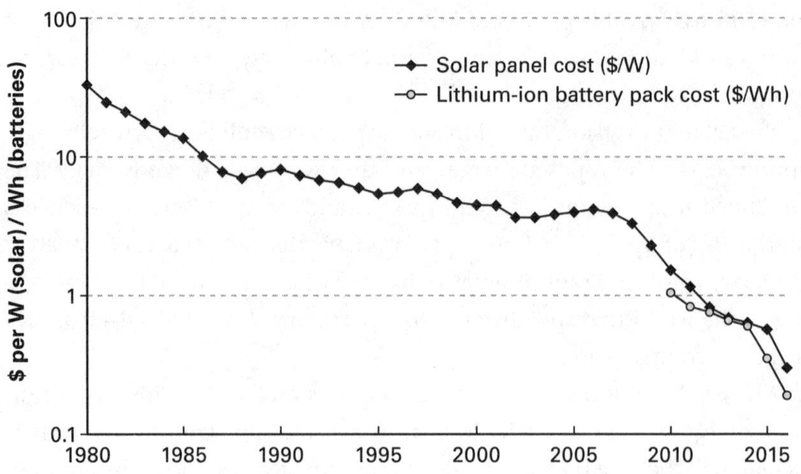

Figure 9.1

Comparison of lithium-ion battery and solar PV panel costs. This chart plots the falling cost of a solar PV panel, expressed in dollars per watt of power-generating capacity; and that of a lithium-ion battery pack, expressed in dollars per watt-hour of energy-storage capacity. (The cost of solar panels is just one component of the cost of a fully installed solar PV system; similarly, the cost of battery packs is just one component of a fully installed battery installation). The *y*-axis is logarithmic.
Source: Bloomberg New Energy Finance, industry reports.

would no longer strain to accommodate intermittent solar power and match supply and demand—the batteries would handle that. And if Musk succeeded in popularizing mass-market EVs, a grid powered by solar panels and buffered by batteries could loosen oil's viselike grip on transportation by charging up EVs.

Unfortunately, although pairing solar with grid-tied battery storage may be cognitively satisfying, it is no silver bullet. The combined cost of solar PV and lithium-ion batteries still exceeds that of a conventional power plant fueled by natural gas. Were that combined cost to plummet even faster than existing forecasts predict, lithium-ion batteries would still be ill-suited for storing large amounts of solar power for long durations—such as days, weeks, or even months. The need for such long-duration storage arises because of seasonal differences in how much solar energy strikes Earth, for example between winter and summer.

That lithium-ion batteries are ill-suited to long-term, mass storage shouldn't be surprising, given that they are great for powering your smartphone. Different applications demand different performance characteristics from a storage technology, such as how long it will live, how much energy it can store, and how fast that energy can be charged or discharged. A whole portfolio of storage technologies exists, including many different flavors of battery, pumped hydro storage, compressed air storage, and more. Each of these has different comparative advantages, whether powering an EV, balancing the power grid's instantaneous imbalances between supply and demand, or storing energy for the long haul. And brand new technologies at the lab bench hold promise to perform each of these functions better than existing products.

In addition, there are still more ways to store energy so as to add flexibility to otherwise inflexible, intermittent solar output. For example, if other power generators could adjust their output rapidly to compensate for fluctuating solar output, this ability would be equivalent to adding storage, at a fraction of the cost.

Indeed, a rich variety of academic studies has demonstrated that the cheapest way to zero out carbon emissions from the global electricity sector is to surround renewable energy with a mix of other resources, including storage, but also nuclear reactors and fossil-fueled power plants whose emissions are captured and stored. Some academics and environmentalists, however, prefer to rule out such a diverse power mix, recommending instead that countries rely solely on renewable energy and storage. That constraint would be foolhardy and disastrous. Jesse Jenkins at MIT points out that powering the United States with just renewable energy and battery storage would require "37.8 billion Tesla Powerwall 2.0 home energy storage systems."[7]

Rather, for solar to take center stage and achieve its midcentury target of powering a third of global electricity demand, it will need a truly diverse supporting cast. Unfortunately, power markets around the world are not set up to accommodate a diverse power mix. Because of how these markets work, solar and wind generators are pushing down wholesale power prices and driving more reliable generators like nuclear plants out of business. Reversing this trend will require markets to carefully value the different dimensions of flexibility that the grid will need so as to integrate large servings of solar. Reformed markets could induce investors to build reliable, flexible power plants to complement solar. They could also encourage developers of solar installations to upgrade the electronics that connect solar to the grid so solar can be part of the solution rather than just the problem.

Given the desirability of a diverse power mix, when Musk boasts that with Tesla battery packs backing up homes and power grids, "you can basically make all electricity generation in the world renewable and primarily solar," he is not describing an affordable, realistic future. But when he convinced his shareholders that merging an electric car company with a solar company made perfect sense, he was on to something more promising. That's because connecting the transportation and electric power sectors is an important step en route to reaching the long-term target of using the sun to power a majority of humanity's energy needs by century's end.

In the future, EVs could act as mobile batteries for the grid, intelligently charging and discharging to compensate for intermittent solar power on the grid without drivers even noticing. The next step beyond linking the transportation sector is to add the heat sector. Homes, commercial buildings, and industrial facilities all demand heat, but they can do so flexibly, thus providing effective storage of fluctuating solar energy output.

The linkages don't have to end there. Solar can meet pressing needs even outside the energy sector. For example, solar could power desalination facilities to provide fresh water, which will be increasingly scarce as climate change accelerates. Solar also could power a range of agricultural needs and make it possible to preserve food that otherwise would be wasted. In addition, these newly linked sectors could, in effect, provide storage of solar power by putting surplus output to valuable use.

The lesson here is that solar needs storage to thrive—but that storage can come in a myriad of different forms. Elon Musk has presented some of them to the world with his customary panache. Now it's time for other innovators to step up with equally bold ideas to complement Musk's vision.

A Class of Its Own

For all the hype over lithium-ion batteries, it might come as a surprise to many that virtually all the energy storage that exists today around the world does not actually take the form of electrochemical batteries. Rather, pumped hydro storage facilities—which pump water from a lower reservoir to an upper reservoir to store energy and release it by letting the water flow back downhill to run a turbine—account for 95 percent of global energy

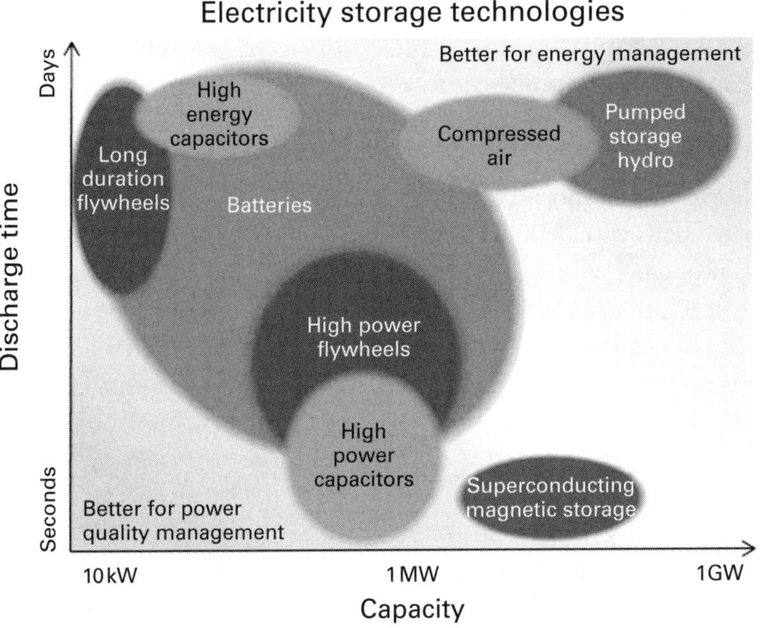

Figure 9.2

Overview of various electricity storage technologies and attributes. This illustrative chart assesses energy technologies by how much power they can instantaneously supply or store (*x*-axis) and for how long they can do so, a measure of energy-storage capacity (*y*-axis).

Source: Energy Information Administration (EIA).

storage capacity.[8] It is also not clear that lithium-ion batteries will, or should, ever dominate the energy storage landscape in the way that pumped hydro has to date. Rather, a whole class of various storage technologies exists that offers a range of solutions to the world's diverse storage needs.

Asking which storage technology is best, or even cheapest, is a meaningless question. There are too many different performance attributes of storage, each of which matters for different applications. Figure 9.2 lays out the landscape of different storage technology categories, plotted according to two of the most important performance characteristics: power capacity and discharge time. Technologies with high power capacity can provide a surge of instantaneous power. And technologies with long discharge times store a lot of energy and can thus provide a constant supply of power for hours, days, or longer. Pumped hydro storage is in the upper-right portion of the graph in figure 9.2, indicating that it can deliver a lot of instantaneous power and sustain that output for long periods of time, which is why it provides almost all the energy storage for power grids around the world, backing up massive power plants and compensating for swings in demand from megacities.

Not every application of energy storage requires high power capacity and discharge time, though. In fact, storage can help stabilize the power grid at a variety of power and time scales. For example, to guarantee that alternating current (AC) electricity is of high quality—that is, has desired and stable voltage and frequency—a grid operator might turn to storage resources that react within milliseconds to charge or discharge small amounts of power for just a few seconds. That need falls in the lower-left corner of figure 9.2. Other needs include filling the gap between supply and demand while a slower generator, perhaps fueled by natural gas, ramps up. This kind of use might require megawatts of power capacity over a few minutes. Still another need, which falls in the upper-right corner of figure 9.2, is to shift generated power from one period of the day, when demand is low, to another period, when it is high—requiring a high power capacity and hours of discharge time.[9]

Just as the grid's needs are all over the map of figure 9.2, so too are the sweet spots of various different storage technologies. Some of them are great at producing bursts of high power. These include good old flywheels, which are just spinning masses that store energy in the form of mechanical rotation (one is on the front of your bike in spin class). Newer technologies include supercapacitors, which look similar to batteries and store electrical charge along a highly corrugated surface, and superconducting magnetic energy storage (SMES), which stores energy in the magnetic field created by the current in an ultracold, superconducting coil of wire.

Electrochemical batteries—which store energy in the form of chemical bonds—take up a big swath of figure 9.2. Their output ranges from small to medium-sized power flows that can last anywhere from seconds to hours. But that big, blue region obscures the diversity of battery types. In addition to familiar lead-acid (car) batteries and increasingly popular lithium-ion batteries, others like sodium-sulfur and flow batteries have their own advantages, like the ability to store substantial amounts of energy to discharge over several hours.

Lithium-ion batteries have become the fastest-growing, most-hyped storage technology for several reasons. Compared with other commercially available technologies, lithium-ion has a reasonably high energy density—that is, it packs a lot of energy per unit of mass—which is why it has come to dominate consumer electronics and then EVs. Lithium-ion batteries are also quite reliable in charging and discharging. On the other hand, they can be flammable—witness Samsung phones catching fire on flights in 2016—and their performance can degrade over several hundred discharge cycles.

Researchers are also pushing the performance limits of lithium-ion batteries. The label "lithium-ion" encompasses a whole class of battery chemistries that all charge and discharge by shuttling lithium ions from one side of the battery to the other but can vary in their exact constituents. Elon Musk and Tesla use one of the oldest designs, fashioning one end of the battery (the "cathode") out of nickel, cobalt, and aluminum (NCA). A more recent version, the nickel-manganese-cobalt (NMC) battery, found its way into the Chevy Bolt, the 238-mile range, mass-market EV that beat Tesla's Model 3 to market in 2017.

Whether lithium-ion batteries will ultimately prove to be the best solution to power EVs is still up in the air (although studies suggesting that they are close to their energy density ceiling are discouraging because longer-range, affordable EVs will require more energy-dense batteries).[10] Certainly, though, they cannot meet the full range of the power grid's needs. For one thing, they suffer from their own form of value deflation. These batteries are best suited to providing short bursts of stored energy to meet brief spikes in energy demand. But the more batteries that are connected to the grid, the fewer spiky demand peaks there will be to shave, degrading the value of the marginal battery addition.[11]

As solar penetration increases, the grid will need much more than just smoothing brief spikes in demand. But lithium-ion batteries are unsuited for many of those needs because installations of them tend to be able to provide only up to four hours of storage—less than the duration needed to buffer the variation in solar output between day and night or on longer timescales.

The reason for the time limit may not be obvious to a casual observer. After all, lithium-ion batteries come in modular units that look just like the cylindrical batteries in your television's remote. It may seem logical, therefore, to assume that stacking enough of the batteries together could shift the output of a large, utility-scale solar farm's output by, say, six hours to match an evening spike in customer demand. Such a move might, in fact, be physically feasible but is economically unviable. Lithium-ion batteries have a fixed ratio of energy and power density—the bigger the stack of batteries, the more power that they can instantaneously discharge *and* the longer they can do it. A battery installation sized to discharge for over four hours will end up underutilizing its power capacity, and underutilization prevents the project developer from paying off the high up-front capital cost of the batteries.

A completely different kind of battery—the flow battery—might be a better solution for storing solar power for several hours, or even days. Flow batteries stow energy in the form of liquids that charge and discharge by exchanging ions across a membrane. In a big advantage over lithium-ion batteries, the amount of energy stored in a flow battery can be increased almost without limit just by adding more tanks of liquid, without changing the power capacity. Because its power capacity is decoupled from the discharge time, a flow battery can be sized to cost-effectively store intermittent renewable energy for long durations to help the grid balance supply and demand. Moreover, flow batteries have much longer lifetimes than lithium-ion batteries.

At the moment, flow batteries are a less mature—and hence more expensive—technology than lithium-ion batteries, and they rely on rare elements (like vanadium).[12] Reliance on scarce materials should be a red flag for a storage technology with any hope of backing up massive amounts of solar power around the world. (Lithium-ion batteries likewise face issues with scarcity of materials because of their reliance on cobalt, which is one of the world's most expensive metals and is found primarily in war-torn Congo.)[13]

To sidestep the high cost and messy risks of resource scarcity, researchers are trying to make inexpensive flow batteries out of Earth-abundant materials, although they are a long way from commercializing a product.[14] Others have opted against both the flow battery and lithium-ion battery designs but ensured that their alternatives use Earth-abundant materials. For example, the MIT spin-out Ambri manufactures a liquid-metal battery that could cost-effectively provide several hours of energy storage and has a much longer lifetime than lithium-ion batteries.[15]

These developments are steps in the right direction toward cost-effective storage that can buffer the daily fluctuations of solar energy. But a whole portfolio of existing and new technologies will likely be required to achieve this at scale. Lithium-ion batteries, complemented by such high-power-capacity technologies as supercapacitors, might be able to smooth solar volatility over seconds or minutes (such as when clouds pass overhead, briefly blocking the sun). They might also shift solar's output within a couple of hours to better line up with demand. But innovative products made of Earth-abundant materials will probably be needed to shift solar's output over longer time scales.

Unfortunately, the inexorable rise in manufacturing scale of lithium-ion batteries threatens to lock out new, contender technologies, just as silicon solar panels have locked out subsequent generations of solar materials.[16] In a repeat of the solar manufacturing glut a decade ago, the production arms race among lithium-ion battery producers is on track to reduce costs through enormous scale and oversupply, while creating a moat around the industry that emerging technologies cannot cross. And just as it is dangerous to bet on a single solar horse, so too is it suboptimal to bet only on lithium-ion batteries and risk shutting out other technologies that could enable greater solar penetration.

More broadly, it is dangerous to bet even on the entire class of storage technologies to do all the heavy lifting of integrating solar power. Certainly storage has an important role to play—but not the only role. This limitation is clearest when examining the seasonal variation in solar output, which any form of storage would struggle to cost-effectively smooth out. In several parts of the United States, for example, the average solar radiation in the winter is less than half of that in the summer. Because seasonal customer demand may offset only some—or none—of that variation, massive amounts of solar power would need to be stored in the summer months and discharged in the winter months in a scenario with high solar penetration and no other options to balance supply and demand. The cost of seasonal storage would be prohibitive—possibly several times more than the entire existing power system.[17]

Today, there is really only one commercially available technology capable of providing seasonal storage: pumped hydro storage. But in many parts of the world, including the United States, it is exceedingly difficult to site new, cost-effective hydro facilities in an environmentally friendly way, so a massive buildout is unlikely. Moreover, seasonal storage is an extremely uneconomical way to run a storage resource. Storing energy in the summer and discharging it in the winter cycles the storage resource only once a year, making it virtually impossible to earn enough revenue to defray its capital costs.

Large-scale compressed air storage—in which electricity is used to compress ambient air for storage in an underground cavern and is recovered by expanding the air to run a turbine—is another example of a technology that might provide seasonal energy storage. Yet its viability is hampered by the limited availability of appropriate geological storage caverns. Some researchers and firms have proposed surprisingly low-tech but intriguing ideas, such as having a train lug concrete slabs uphill to store potential energy. It remains to be seen, however, whether those ideas will successfully leave the station.[18]

All of this means that grid-scale energy storage technologies cannot be the only solution for coping with the intermittency of solar energy. Successful energy systems will require both storage and other ways to adjust electricity flows flexibly. Chapter 8 proposed extending the geographical reach of the grid and creating a smart, decentralized grid to enable responsive demand—both of which are important tools to ease the integration of solar power. But there are many more puzzle pieces that could add further flexibility. Truly transforming the world's energy systems this century will require taking advantage of all of them.

Getting to Deep Decarbonization

I recently learned that such a logical conclusion can run afoul of politics and preferences. *Proceedings of the National Academy of Sciences of the United States of America* (*PNAS*) is one of the world's most highly respected scientific journals. Each year, it honors six exemplary articles from disparate fields. In 2015, one of the awards went to an article whose lead author was a Stanford professor of atmospheric science, Dr. Mark Jacobson. Entitled, "Low-Cost Solution to the Grid Reliability Problem with 100% Penetration of Intermittent Wind, Water, and Solar for All Purposes," the paper claimed to lay out a way to power the entire United States only with existing technologies.[19] The best part was that this system would be cheaper than using fossil fuels—and just as reliable.

This proposal caused a stir in the popular media, thanks to the enthusiastic stamp of approval from a prestigious journal. It all sounded like a dream scenario—power from all-natural sunshine, wind, and water, without any need for dangerous nuclear reactors or complicated capturing and storage of carbon emissions from fossil-fueled plants.

Unfortunately, this dream scenario was just that: a fantastical dream. As it turned out, the paper was filled with implausible assumptions, and its headline conclusion was almost certainly erroneous. Instead of a "low-cost solution," the paper's proposal would be astronomically expensive and complicated. It would require adding hydroelectric generation capacity equivalent to 600 Hoover Dams. It would take trillions of dollars of investment in new electricity transmission lines and infrastructure to produce, transport, and store hydrogen. It would demand an expansion of solar and wind power capacity well in excess of any buildout of power plants that the world has ever seen.[20] And it would require underground thermal energy storage—a technology to store heat in groundwater or bedrock underground that is unproven at any meaningful scale—beneath "nearly every home, business, office building, hospital, school, and factory in the United States."[21]

That last line is a quote from a rebuttal in the same journal, which I wrote with twenty of the scholars I respect most in the fields of energy science, economics, and policy. We thought that the Jacobson paper created a dangerous illusion that today's renewable energy and energy storage technologies could cost-effectively decarbonize the world's energy systems. On top of this, the paper excluded viable options like nuclear power—effectively tying one arm behind the back.

The day after we published our rejoinder, the front page of the *New York Times* business section reported "Fisticuffs over the Route to a Clean-Energy Future." Other media outlets declared a "Battle Royale," a "Bitter Scientific Debate," and "One of the Most Vitriolic Fights in Science Publishing."[22] And my coauthors and I were accused of being fossil-fuel shills by no less an expert than Mark Ruffalo (the actor who plays the Incredible Hulk). The episode underscored that the topic of how the world slashes its carbon emissions is politically fraught, even in the supposedly apolitical realm of academia.

Politics aside, getting to near-zero emissions—or as insiders call it, "deep decarbonization"—in the power sector is a crucial prerequisite to limiting climate change, and it will be an uphill battle even with all options on the table. A survey of eighteen different models of the global economy concluded that to halt runaway carbon emissions in the atmosphere, emissions from electricity would need to fall by between 80 and 100 percent by 2050, and emissions from all other sources would need to vanish by 2100.[23,24] The urgency behind cleaning up the power sector is that many other uses of energy—including aviation, shipping, heavy-duty trucking, and fertilizer production—are tougher or impossible to decarbonize.[25] So it is crucial to apply existing and emerging technologies to slash emissions in the power sector, while electrifying as many other uses of energy—among them, passenger vehicle transportation—as possible. Down the road, it will also be important to find clean fuels to replace oil to zero out emissions from more stubbornly dirty sectors. It may even be necessary to figure out how to suck carbon out of the air. Decarbonizing power is the least difficult of these monumental tasks, so it makes sense to start there.

Complicating the path to deep decarbonization of the power sector is the pesky fact that eliminating the first 10 percent tranche of emissions is much easier than eliminating the last one. For example, thanks to the favorable economics of switching from coal to natural gas–fired power (whose emissions are only half those of coal), U.S. emissions fell by several percentage points from their peak in 2007.[26] But reducing emissions from natural gas plants, for example by capturing and storing them, is hugely expensive at present. Similarly, the first solar panel on a grid can displace some fossil-generated power without disrupting the balance between supply and demand. But a high penetration of solar power leads to skyrocketing costs to accommodate its intermittency.

Hence, a power system can easily get stuck in a cul-de-sac off the highway to deep decarbonization. For example, a review of decarbonization studies concluded that steadily increasing renewable energy, switching from coal to natural gas, and just maintaining existing nuclear and hydropower capacity could reduce power-sector emissions by over 50 percent.[27] But reducing emissions by 80–100 percent would require a surge in new nuclear reactors, carbon capture and storage setups for almost all fossil plants, and an explosion of new solar and wind capacity.[28] It is crucial, then, to start planning and investing today in a power system with all the right elements to reach deep decarbonization decades later.

In such a system, three broad classes of power supply are needed. The first is renewable energy, mostly from wind and solar power. But because these sources are intermittent, much more reliable power is needed, from what Jesse Jenkins at MIT calls "flexible-base" resources. These include nuclear reactors and a type of natural gas power plant known as a "combined-cycle gas turbine," which is the most efficient type of gas plant. (For natural gas plants to contribute to a decarbonized power system, they would need to be equipped with carbon capture and storage). The flexible-base plants would consistently pump out power but would be capable of cranking their output up or down to compensate for fluctuating renewable energy. Still, because these plants might not be able to immediately adjust their output in response to capricious solar and wind generators, a third class of fast-acting resources would fill the gaps and provide surges of power during rare spikes in customer demand. This third class might include another type of natural gas plant—an "open-cycle gas turbine"—that is less efficient than a combined-cycle gas turbine but can change its power output more quickly. Other fast-acting resources include batteries and demand response systems (possibly controlled by a grid hive mind as discussed in chapter 8).

No two of these classes can cost-effectively meet customer demand without the third. Figure 9.3 illustrates the challenge of trying to cut out flexible-base resources and power the United States using only renewable energy and energy storage resources. Doing so would require enough batteries or other storage capacity to hold between eight and sixteen weeks worth of *all* U.S. electricity consumption—an absolutely massive quantity. For some perspective, the United States currently has storage equivalent to about forty-three minutes of its power consumption, and nearly all that storage is in the form of pumped hydropower.

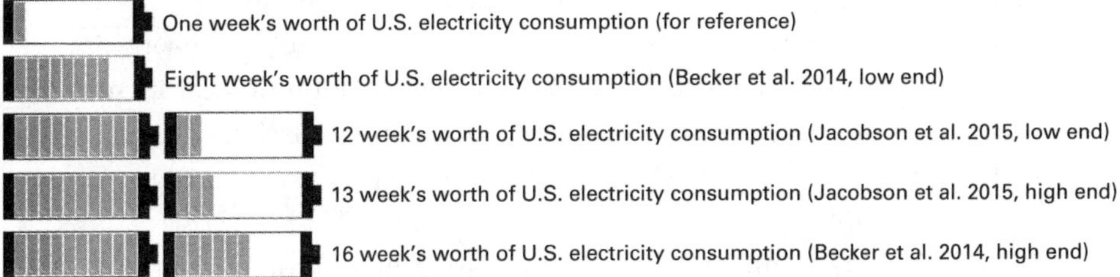

Figure 9.3
Estimates of battery storage capacity needed to power the United States with 100 percent renewable energy. The top row represents the amount of stored electricity that would be needed to supply one week of national electricity demand if no other supply sources were available. The remaining four rows display the estimates from each of four academic studies of the amount of energy-storage capacity that would be needed to ensure that U.S. electricity demand were reliably met in the event that all electricity supply came from renewable sources.
Source: Jenkins and Thernstrom (2017).

Adding flexible-base resources is the much saner route, and this lesson applies around the world. For example, a study of China's power system concluded that the cheapest route to reducing emissions by 80 percent by 2050 entails an even mix of renewable energy and flexible base, comprising nuclear reactors and coal plants equipped with carbon capture and storage.[29] Although some studies—including careful ones by the National Renewable Energy Laboratory (NREL) and the Climate Policy Initiative—suggest that the share of renewable electricity could get all the way to 80 percent, they also maintain that flexible base would still play an essential role.[30,31] Other studies that purport to demonstrate the feasibility of relying on 100 percent renewable power sources would find far lower power system costs if they removed their artificial constraints on which zero-carbon power sources are allowed.

My collaborators at MIT and GTM Research and I have done just that: We simulated the Texas power grid without arbitrarily excluding any source of power. Predictably, we found that the most economical penetration of solar PV rose as it got cheaper (figure 9.4). But no matter how cheap solar got, flexible-base resources—not solar—provided a majority of the system's electricity. Then, we really stacked the deck in solar's favor, imagining a dream scenario in which batteries were four times cheaper than they were in 2016 (we assumed a cost of $150/kWh for a fully installed battery system, even though such a system is projected to only fall in cost to $280/kWh by 2040).[32] Yet, even with the option to store energy in extremely low-cost batteries, the economical penetration of solar inched up by only around 5 percent—flexible base was still indispensable. Thus, batteries have a limited—albeit important—role to play in enabling greater solar penetration.

Still, it will take innovation to deliver zero-carbon, flexible-base plants, such as advanced nuclear reactors. Importantly, this is not because today's nuclear plants are technically incapable of operating flexibly (a common misconception). Actually, nuclear plants can ramp their output up and down to help the grid balance supply and demand, as they have done in France for decades.[33] Rather, the trouble with today's nuclear plants, known as light-water reactors, is that they are expensive and—in extremely rare circumstances—vulnerable to meltdowns or other accidents.

The 2017 bankruptcy of Westinghouse, a nuclear pioneer that faced mounting costs and delays to construct its plants, has dimmed the prospects

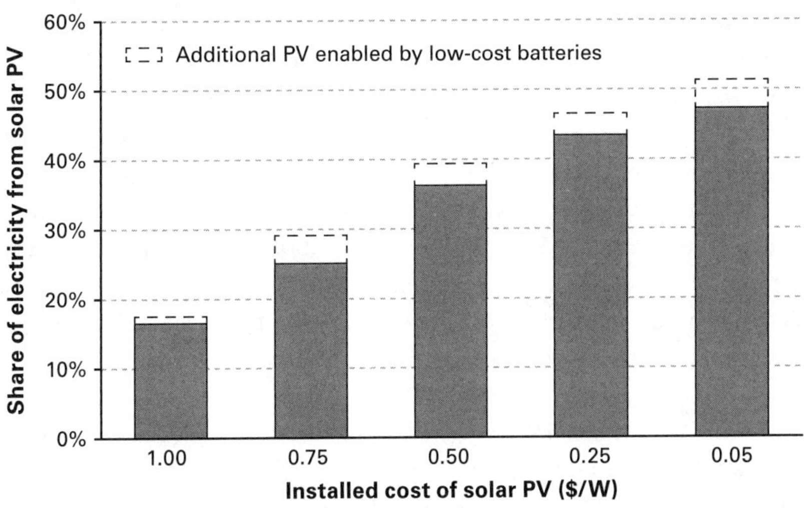

Figure 9.4

Grid penetration of solar PV as a function of PV and storage costs. For each of the assumptions of the installed cost of solar PV along the *x*-axis, the filled bars represent the proportion of total electric energy, measured in kilowatt-hours (kWh), that solar PV would generate. The dotted extensions above the bars illustrate the additional amount of electricity that would be economical to generate with solar PV if a fully installed battery system cost only $150/kWh. These results were obtained by simulating a region with similar weather, grid transmission capacity, and electricity demand to Texas and then determining the cheapest set of power-generating resources to reliably meet demand.

Source: Brown, Jenkins, Sepulveda, and Sivaram (2017).

for new nuclear reactors in the United States. But newer designs (actually based on ideas shelved decades ago), known as "Generation IV" nuclear reactors, could be both cheaper and safer. Unfortunately for the United States, China and Russia are leading the race to commercialize advanced nuclear reactors, while America lags mostly because of limited government research and development (R&D) investment and outdated regulations that discourage new plant designs.[34]

Similarly, carbon capture and storage technologies need to become vastly cheaper to enable fossil-fueled plants to provide zero-carbon, flexible-base power. The historical trend of carbon capture and storage demonstration projects ballooning in cost is not encouraging. Some cite this pattern as evidence for the superiority of an all-renewable solution, and they argue that betting on carbon capture and storage might open the door for the continued burning of fossil fuels. Then, if cost-effective carbon capture and storage technology does not materialize, the world will be locked in to fossil fuel infrastructure.

Two developments in Texas suggest that carbon capture and storage does not have to be impossibly expensive. First, through the Petro Nova project, the power producer NRG has retrofitted one of the largest coal plants in the United States—the WA Parish Generating Station outside Houston—with equipment to capture its carbon dioxide emissions. The project was completed on time and on budget, and by pumping the carbon dioxide into the ground to bring lucrative oil back to the surface, the project generates revenue to defray its capital costs. Nearby, the start-up NET Power has built an even more advanced pilot plant in which supercritical carbon dioxide derived from burning natural gas drives a turbine, making it simple to capture the resulting carbon emissions. Still, much more progress needs to be made, both on the technology to capture carbon as well as to invent valuable uses for it. If plants can make money by selling carbon dioxide to make cement for buildings or carbon fiber for planes and cars, for example, then the attractiveness of zero-carbon fossil electricity could skyrocket.[35]

With a strong foundation of flexible-base power in place, the quantities of solar power and energy storage required to achieve deep decarbonization become much more tractable. Continued cost declines for both solar and storage will nonetheless be important to make their deployment cost-effective. Storage can improve the economics of solar power.[36] Therefore, it makes the most sense to talk about solar generation and storage costs in the same breath rather than separately. One study found that if the costs of both solar and storage were to plunge together, the share of solar in the American West could triple. This intuitively makes sense—solar paired with storage looks to the grid like a really flexible power plant, so their combined cost would drive the optimal level of deployment. Don't forget about flexible base, though; the same study found that even with rock-bottom solar and storage prices, the most cost-effective power mix included a 43 percent share of supply from flexible base.[37]

The lesson here is that deep decarbonization of the power sector—a prerequisite for limiting climate change—will require a diverse cast of characters. Both flexible-base power and fast-acting resources, including those that store energy, are jointly needed to enable solar power to shine. Alas, deep decarbonization is not one of the goals of the free market. As a result, it has become increasingly difficult for all three categories of zero-carbon power resources to coexist in the rough-and-tumble of power markets.

From Capacity to Capability

Another aspect of systemic innovation, in addition to designing the power mix of the future, is conceiving the markets that will enable that mix to emerge. Chapter 3 recounted the ways that the rise of solar has wrought havoc on power markets around the world, from Chile to Germany. Surplus solar power is forcing the price commanded for the resulting electricity below zero and driving other kinds of power plants out of the market. In particular, flexible-base power plants are struggling to stay in business, even though they are crucial to enabling high penetration of the renewable energy that is slashing their bottom lines right now.

For example, nuclear power plants from Germany to the United States are shutting down, largely because they can no longer cover their costs. The U.S. nuclear reactor fleet—which generates a fifth of the country's electricity and most of its zero-carbon power—is in danger of losing half its reactors to early shutdowns by 2030.[38] Nuclear's economic woes stem from two main causes (other than project mismanagement): cheap natural gas and a surge in solar and wind power. Both trends have upended the way that electricity markets have historically kept nuclear plants in business.

In the old paradigm of a power market, every power plant would provide a bid for how much power it could produce and the price at which it was willing to sell it to the grid. Nuclear plants would offer to sell power at a low cost because once a plant is up and running, spitting out the next kilowatt-hour of energy does not cost much. Fortunately for those plants, the market would accept bids in ascending order to meet all the customer demand. So, once bids from the low-cost plants, such as nuclear reactors, were accepted, the market would have to accept higher-cost bids, such as from natural gas turbines that would charge an arm and a leg to burn expensive fuel and boost output quickly when demand surged. Markets also paid every power plant the same, "market-clearing" price—that is, the price charged for the last bid accepted (that of the expensive natural gas turbine). This practice was a relief for the nuclear reactors because, despite the low cost of producing power, the plants relied on high ongoing revenues to pay off the hugely expensive construction costs of the plant.

Together, cheap renewable energy and natural gas have turned that old market paradigm on its head. As the penetration of solar and wind power rises, these generators are happy to offer to sell their power at zero cost to the grid because they have zero fuel costs. Their influence, along with that of cheap natural gas, drags down the market-clearing price. In other words, solar and wind generators compete with nuclear power to have their low-cost bids accepted by the market. Whoever wins ends up getting paid only a pittance. And nuclear plants that can no longer pay off their capital costs go bust.

The same thing would happen to the economics of solar and wind generators, except that they are protected by policy or contract structures. Public incentives, such as the German feed-in tariff, supplement the income that renewables ordinarily would make from depressed market prices. And because most solar power is contracted through long-term power purchase agreements (PPAs) with a locked-in price, solar owners are guaranteed that their costs will be covered even as the market price craters. Some places, such as the state of New York, have opted to provide incentive payments to nuclear plants to similarly insulate them from an imploding market.[39] But in most other U.S. markets, nuclear is left out in the cold as renewables thrive.

Today's markets thus have a "missing money" problem: they fail to pay enough to flexible-base plants, such as nuclear reactors and fossil-fueled plants (whose emissions, ultimately, need to be captured and stored), for investors to want to build more. This state of affairs is untenable if deep decarbonization is to be achieved.

Some jurisdictions have tried to fill the missing money gap; their efforts fall into three categories. First, California (among others) obligates the utilities that transmit and distribute power to sign long-term contracts with reliable generators to guarantee that they will have enough power for forecast customer demand—plus a 15 percent safety margin. This way, investors in power plants have some long-term security that the rug won't be pulled out from under them as rising solar output reduces market prices. Second, most of the states on the U.S. East Coast, as well as several European countries like the United Kingdom, have created separate "capacity" markets, which pay reliable generators to sit around until the grid calls on them urgently for support.

The third category is exemplified by Texas, which is known for going it alone. A paragon of free-market economic purity, Texas has preserved an "energy-only" wholesale market that works just as in the past, except with an extremely high cap on the instantaneous price for a kilowatt-hour of electricity. Under this approach, if power supplies are really scarce, a power plant can save the day by selling its wares for $9,000/kWh. That mouth-watering possibility, even if it happens only once every year or even less frequently, is a strong incentive for investors to build flexible power plants. But, in most places, the prospect of astronomical power prices is a political nonstarter—and some scholars argue that the missing money problem would still persist.[40]

Each of these approaches has its own die-hard adherents. In Europe, an ongoing effort to create a unified, continentwide power market faces hurdles owing to the twenty-eight different capacity market schemes created by the member-states of the European Union.[41] Some members, including Germany, want to abolish capacity markets altogether. Others, including France, which does not share Germany's obsession with shutting down nuclear plants, are not so sure. Many argue that, by paying reliable plants to sit around rather than actually producing power, capacity markets raise customer prices. Just as many others counter that this approach is a sort of insurance that is well worth the investment, lest rolling blackouts and surging prices cost customers even more dearly.

Setting this stale debate aside, other, innovative options could modernize power markets, accommodate a rising share of renewable energy, and fund a strong foundation of flexible-base power. The first priority is minimizing the amount of expensive reserves needed to accommodate renewable energy unpredictability. Better weather forecasting technology is emerging that can help by enabling grid operators to predict more accurately what solar and wind output will be like hours or days in advance and calling in compensating resources accordingly.[42] The advent of "deep learning"—the artificial intelligence algorithms that run your Alexa device at home and learn from past experience— could make forecasts of solar production even more accurate and precise.[43]

In addition, markets should operate on a quicker cadence, reducing from an hour to five minutes or less the time interval between successive decisions on which generators to dispatch and how much to pay them. More powerful computers and smarter grids make this overdue change possible.[44]

This would enable grid operators to dispatch other generators to react to renewable energy volatility most efficiently, rather than relying on the crutch of overbuilt reserve capacity.[45]

Another important step is to retool power markets so that they value the capability to meet the grid's needs, not just the nameplate capacity of how much power a generator can provide. An essential capability is the provision of inertia. Recall from chapter 3 that conventional power generators give the grid inertia, so if one plant goes down, the synchronized rotation of other generators prevents the grid's frequency from plunging for long enough to allow alternative supply sources to ramp up. But solar panels do not produce electricity through physical rotational motion, and thus do not provide any inertia to the grid. Inverters that connect solar to the grid can be programmed to provide synthetic inertia, however, that recreates the effect of the real thing. A study of the western United States found solar power would achieve much higher penetration if all utility-scale solar plants had smart inverters that provided synthetic inertia.[46]

In fact, solar plants can do even better than conventional power plants when it comes to supporting the grid and ensuring that the power system operates within narrow frequency and voltage bands.[47] By delivering such ancillary services, solar power could be part of the solution rather than the problem. In 2017, First Solar demonstrated just how useful a utility-scale solar plant could be to the grid. In collaboration with California's grid operator, a 300-megawatt (MW) First Solar plant proved that it could beat conventional natural gas plants at rapidly boosting the grid's frequency level.[48] Another plant in Arizona was even able to support the grid in the middle of the night, when its solar panels produced no power but its sophisticated power electronics propped up the voltage on a transmission line after an unplanned shutdown of an upstream nuclear reactor.[49] California is already starting to compensate solar plants for the advanced capabilities that they offer. If other states and countries do the same, developers might follow suit and build advanced solar plants that can stabilize the grid.

In addition to the market tweaks described above, even more fundamental changes to the design of electricity markets could help the power system accommodate expanding use of intermittent renewable energy. For example, some scholars have suggested splitting wholesale energy markets into two in order to insulate flexible-base and renewable resources from destructive competition. The first market would be for on-demand, or firm, power from plants whose output can be reliably controlled. The other market would be for variable power from unpredictable generators, such as solar and wind, which cannot guarantee their output.[50] Prominent energy analyst Michael Liebreich argues that the difference in prices between the two markets, which he dubs the "Firm Spread," will rise as value deflation accompanies the rise of variable solar and wind power. And that spread will attract reliable sources of firm generation capacity, as well as innovation to develop such new, flexible resources as virtual power plants or storage technologies.[51]

Ideas like that one are still very much on the drawing board. But that is the sort of innovative market design that might be required to ensure that a diverse mix of zero-carbon power resources coexists. Indeed, the power sector is supposed to be the easy one to decarbonize. The rest of the economy, starting with transportation, presents even thornier challenges.

Batteries on the Go

The most obvious way to extend decarbonization from the power sector to the transportation sector is through vehicle electrification. Seduced by Elon Musk's sleek creations, masses of customers would buy EVs, plug them into their garage outlet, and replace oil with electricity produced by zero-carbon sources. Simple, right?

Probably not. Even if customers were to flock to EVs—which is still very uncertain—it is unclear whether the grid would be able to cope with them. Level II chargers, which can recharge an EV in a few hours, add the equivalent of an entire household's power demand to a neighborhood distribution circuit. These circuits are not sized to handle many EVs, since they normally serve only five to ten homes. Even worse, charging a Tesla at one of the company's Supercharger stations suddenly sucks as much power from the grid as two hundred window air-conditioning units running all at once. So, utilities are anxiously eyeing massively expensive upgrades across the distribution grid if EV adoption really takes off.[52]

The story would be different if EVs could support, rather than strain, the grid. After all, from the grid's point of view, an EV is just a battery on the go. If EV batteries could double as an energy storage resource for the power grid, the 50 million EVs that Bloomberg projects will be sold globally in 2040 could be put to work smoothing the volatile output from solar power.[53]

Indeed, linking the transportation and power sectors could add even more flexibility to integrate a high penetration of solar power, although doing so won't be easy. In the near term, as smart grids learn how to talk to EVs, they might orchestrate small changes in how fast an EV charges up while plugged in. This cooperation could provide ancillary services for maintaining the grid's voltage and frequency levels without an EV driver ever noticing the difference. In the longer term, as more EVs hit the roads and grid operators become more sophisticated, the grid could actually harness the full capability of EV batteries to absorb or supply energy as needed. EVs, acting in concert with other grid resources, such as stationary batteries and power plants, could store solar power and discharge it when customer demand peaks.[54]

Transportation is not the only energy sector that could be linked to the power sector to provide flexibility. Linking the heat and power sectors could be an equally important way to enable a high penetration of solar power. Such a link would not be new. Existing cogeneration plants, which produce both power and heat, can serve densely populated communities, as well as such industrial facilities as chemical plants, refineries, and paper mills that require both electricity and heat. Expanding cogeneration is one way to harness sunlight to meet demand for heat. Although most cogeneration today relies on burning fossil fuels, it could be powered by solar thermal collectors. Indeed, pilot projects from Denmark to Saudi Arabia have demonstrated the viability of using solar thermal to drive the cogeneration of both power and heat. In those projects, heat from the cogeneration facilities was piped into district-heating networks, which connect a community's homes and buildings and can more efficiently provide heat than individual boilers.[55]

In addition to combining the production of heat and power through cogeneration, it is possible to manage the demand for heat in ways that would smooth out the amount of electricity that utilities deliver to customers in the course of a day. New electric heat pumps and electric water heaters are highly efficient at space and water heating, either for individual homes or for district heating networks. A smart grid connected to such devices could switch on heaters when the electricity supply is high, essentially pre-heating a room or hot-water tank in anticipation of need, rather than waiting for customers to call for heat only later, when solar energy is no longer available.[56]

In effect, just as was the case with linking the transportation and power sectors, linking the heat and power sectors could provide another big battery to store intermittent solar power in the form of hot air and water. Indeed, integrating all three of these sectors would maximize the flexibility of the combined power-heat-transportation system.[57] Electrification—of both vehicles and heating appliances—is one way to accomplish this. And if solar-driven water splitting technology, discussed in chapter 7, were to become commercially viable, then solar could drive a hydrogen economy that would also link the transportation and heating sectors.

Aware of such possibilities, just before President Barack Obama left office, his administration released an ambitious "United States Mid-Century Strategy for Deep Decarbonization" road map. It projects that for the United States to reduce its economywide carbon emissions by 80 percent by 2050, 60 percent of the miles driven by vehicles will need to be fueled by either electricity or hydrogen, and electricity must supply the majority of space and water heating.[58]

Chapter 8 introduced the concept of how linkages between the electricity grids of different regions to form a supergrid could raise the potential penetration of solar power. This chapter added others, between the power, transportation, and heating sectors. These linkages all add flexibility to the overall energy system, making it possible to run an economy off volatile solar energy. But the potential benefits of interconnectivity don't end there; interactions with processes outside of today's energy sector offer additional ways for the electricity sector to accommodate intermittency.

Beyond Energy

On July 31, 2012, an unseasonably dry summer day, the biggest blackout in human history hit India. Altogether, 700 million people lost access to power (adding that figure to the numbers of people without any access to begin with meant that more than 1 billion Indians went without electricity that day). The culprit? Grid-connected irrigation pumps.

Delayed monsoon rains had driven millions of farmers to set their pumps on overdrive to suck up groundwater from deep underground to irrigate their crops. The combination of the spike in electricity demand and the dilapidated Indian electricity grid was too much for the system to handle. This episode was a stark reminder that energy, water, and food systems are inextricably intertwined, and the needs of the food and water sectors could increase demands on the energy sector. Intelligent management of those connections, however, can increase the flexible operation of each sector and ease the strains they put on one another. Indeed, done right, increasing the links between energy, water, and food offers yet another way to accommodate a rising share of volatile solar energy and put that energy to good use.

Start with water. Countries around the world will increasingly face water scarcity as populations grow and the climate changes. Already, the production and transportation of freshwater require massive energy consumption. Nowhere is this more true than the parched Middle East. Much of the region's freshwater supply comes from desalination of seawater—a technology so energy-intensive that it consumes between one-tenth and one-third of the electricity produced in countries in the Persian Gulf.[59]

Those desalination plants could provide flexibility for the grid to accommodate a high share of solar power. By adjusting their output, desalination plants can modulate their demand for electricity, operating more when the sun is shining and less when it is not, and therefore making use of excess daytime solar capacity. There are economic limits to how flexibly they can run—if they operate below full output for too long, they will struggle to earn enough revenue from water sales to cover their capital costs. But, they could certainly be an additional puzzle piece in constructing a flexible, solar-powered grid.[60] The biggest benefit could be cheap water. Recognizing this, Saudi Arabia wants to slash the cost of its water by over 80 percent by investing heavily in solar-powered desalination.[61]

New desalination technologies are on the horizon that could also take advantage of the waste heat from a concentrated solar power (CSP) plant, improving its economics compared with a CSP plant producing only electricity. The most popular desalination technology today—reverse osmosis, which forces salty water through filtration membranes—runs on electricity. But multiple-effect distillation desalination, in which heat is used to vaporize water in multiple stages and leave behind the salt, could become cost-competitive if the technology advances. Combining this technology with CSP could make fresh water even cheaper in the thirsty Middle East.[62]

What about food? The 2012 blackout that occurred in India when the agricultural sector's pumping of water overwhelmed the grid highlights the way a poorly managed linkage between the power and agricultural sectors can lead to disaster. In this case, it might actually make more sense to delink agricultural demand for irrigation from India's overstretched power grid.

Irrigation pumping is an ideal application for distributed solar power because it does not require a highly reliable and constant power supply and can instead tolerate volatile solar output. If their irrigation pumps were powered by solar panels, farmers would not need to connect them to the grid.

The use of solar would have a couple of major benefits. First, fewer connected pumps would lower demand on the strained power grid. Second, solar-powered irrigation pumps could limit wasteful pumping practices. Farmers in India receive subsidized electricity from the grid, perversely incentivizing them to run their pumps more often and deplete groundwater supplies. Indeed, India is the largest user of groundwater for agricultural purposes in the world. If a solar irrigation pump were designed to pump only a sustainable amount of water, it could better preserve groundwater supplies. (If solar costs continue to fall, however, oversized solar irrigation systems might also enable wasteful pumping.) The Indian government has embarked on an ambitious program to replace 26 million groundwater irrigation pumps with solar pumps.[63]

A pilot project planned in Karnataka, in the south of India, aims to harness sunlight to provide electricity, food, and water to nearby communities. The first step will be to concentrate solar radiation with mirrors to generate steam. That steam will then drive a turbine to generate electricity, and the waste heat will be used to distill water and provide refrigeration to preserve food.[64] In a sense, the distilled water and preserved food are storage technologies, converting ephemeral sunlight into a more permanent form that can be consumed when needed.

Neither of those storage technologies is anywhere near as flashy as the battery packs on the *Desperate Housewives* set under Elon Musk's solar roofs. But they are nonetheless important pieces for solving the puzzle of how the world can harness sunlight to meet not only its energy needs, but also other basic needs, such as food and water.

Chapter 10 A Solar City upon a Hill

My favorite conference happens every February in National Harbor, Maryland. The setting—a gorgeous convention center with an expansive, nineteen-story glass atrium that looks out onto the Potomac—evokes an ambience of sweeping possibilities. This is the ARPA-E Summit, the flagship event of a futuristic government agency tasked with finding and funding the most innovative energy technologies. Hundreds of scientists and entrepreneurs showcase their research at endless rows of booths brimming with posters, prototypes, and pitch decks. Like kids in a candy store, college students from all over the country furiously take notes as they chart careers in energy innovation.

I remember my first summit vividly. The year was 2012. I was still a graduate student, working on perovskite photovoltaic (PV) cells and eager to peer out of my technology silo to survey other technologies, from next-generation batteries to software that could manage the smart grid. But my top priority was to meet Dr. Arun Majumdar, the founding director of the Advanced Research Projects Agency-Energy (ARPA-E).

An acclaimed scientist from Berkeley in his previous life, Arun had deftly transitioned to the role of D.C. dealmaker in 2009, when President Barack Obama tapped him to run the new agency. He quickly drummed up strongly bipartisan support for the Advanced Research Projects Agency-Energy (ARPA-E), which was modeled after the Defense Department's early-stage innovation arm, the Defense Advanced Research Projects Agency (DARPA), which, among many other successes, helped create the Internet. Energy and climate issues provoked deep disagreements between Democrats and Republicans at the time, and still do. Yet both sides of the aisle—from Senator Chris Coons (D-DE) to Senator Lamar Alexander (R-TN)—heaped praise on Arun and his new agency.[1]

I ended up cornering Arun at a bar at the end of a long day of sessions. I peppered him with questions about science, policy, and the future of energy, which he casually fielded while waving to old friends and cracking jokes. Looking back, I'm a little embarrassed for harassing the poor man, who probably just wanted to sip his beer and reflect on a successful summit. More broadly, ARPA-E's model has enjoyed early success. Through 2016, less than a decade after its founding, the agency's grants to researchers developing early-stage energy technologies had already stimulated even more investment—nearly $2 billion—in those projects from the private sector.

When I returned in February 2017 for the annual summit, the mood was different. The technology showcase was still impressive, and the speakers still presented optimistic visions of roads filled with autonomous electric vehicles (EVs) or a grid run by sophisticated artificial intelligence. But Donald Trump was now president, and the elephant in the room was the unanswered question of whether his administration would continue to prioritize energy innovation.

The answer emerged a month later: an emphatic "no." The Trump administration's budget proposal to Congress set out to slash funding for research and development (R&D) into renewable energy by 70 percent. Similarly, it aimed to eviscerate R&D related to the power grid and nuclear energy. And one proposal in particular was particularly concerning: ARPA-E would be completely defunded. The curt rationale in the president's so-called skinny budget was that "the private sector is better positioned to finance disruptive energy R&D and to commercialize innovative technologies."[2]

This is a statement of pure ideology. In fact, America's history of sporadic support for energy innovation has demonstrated exactly the opposite. Whenever public support for energy innovation has waned, so too has private-sector investment, promptly stalling progress on developing and commercializing new technologies. Fortunately, the president's proposal was sharply rebuked by lawmakers in his own party—a Senate subcommittee chaired by Sen. Alexander reported that it "definitely rejects this short-sighted proposal" to defund ARPA-E.[3]

American politicians are fond of calling the United States a shining "city upon a hill," and when it comes to energy innovation, America has historically lived up to this billing. As I write this in 2017, the United States still outspends every other country on energy R&D, its researchers lead their global peers in securing patents for energy inventions, and its firms,

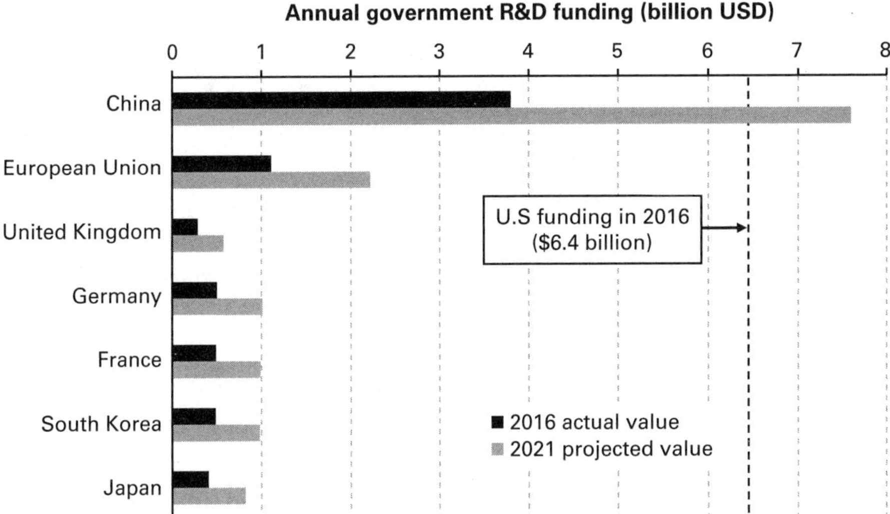

Figure 10.1

Historical and projected government funding for energy innovation in top countries. The black bars display current public funding for R&D and demonstration of energy technologies. The gray bars correspond to countries' commitments under Mission Innovation to double their funding levels.

Source: Mission Innovation.

such as General Electric, continue a proud tradition of investing in new technologies. But that primacy is not guaranteed. For nearly two decades, federal investment in R&D across all fields has flatlined, after half a century of brisk growth. Projections indicate that if public funding for energy innovation in particular stagnates in the coming years, China will surpass the United States (figure 10.1).

Stagnant U.S. funding would be disastrous on many levels. First, it could preclude the technological innovation that solar energy needs to realize its potential. Even if China and other countries step up their funding for energy R&D, the United States has by far the most well-developed innovation institutions and top-flight talent; therefore, without U.S. leadership, the global pace of energy innovation will slow. Then, such breakthrough technologies as perovskite PV, solar fuel generators, and high-temperature concentrated solar power (CSP) plants may languish on the drawing board, falling short of commercialization. Similarly, the constellation of enabling technologies for a flexible system that can accommodate volatile solar PV output—from flow batteries to advanced nuclear reactors—might also progress more slowly. Limited to existing silicon solar PV and a mediocre supporting cast, solar energy is likely to fall short of supplying a third of global power demand by midcentury or a majority of humanity's energy needs by century's end.

Canceling funding for energy innovation also would directly harm U.S. economic prosperity and competitiveness. That's because even if solar energy does not achieve its full potential, solar PV is still on track to grow significantly, and the United States will fail to capture a significant piece of this growing pie if it does not invest in innovation. Bloomberg forecasts that even with no major technological shift away from silicon solar PV, fifteen times more solar power than the amount installed through 2016 will be added globally through 2040.[4] More broadly, today's global clean energy market is worth $300 billion, and it is set to grow rapidly. China has raced ahead to a daunting lead, not only dominating the production of solar panels, but also leading in the manufacture of batteries and wind turbines. Its dominance will only grow if unchallenged by innovative products from the United States. Not only would that constitute a missed economic opportunity, but the United States might even rely to an unhealthy level on imports of Chinese clean-energy products, reminiscent of U.S. dependence on foreign oil in decades past.

Skeptics of the need for U.S. leadership might counter that the United States has already lost the race to manufacture such clean energy products as solar panels, which China's economy is structurally better adapted to produce. Moreover, solar panels are low-margin commodities, a business that the United States should want no part of. These arguments are certainly true, and the United States should not be competing to manufacture commodities. Rather, the U.S. economy shines when it invents new technologies, applies advanced manufacturing techniques, and constantly improves the performance of its products faster than the competition can keep up. Today's solar industry—reliant, as it is, on silicon photovoltaic panels—may appear unsuited to U.S. strengths, but by investing in technological innovation, the United States has the ability to reshape the industry to better harness its core competencies.

To do so, U.S. policymakers' first priority should be to boost R&D funding for next-generation solar technologies, as well as for the raft of other technologies that will be needed to support a solar-powered energy system. But federal dollars alone are insufficient—the private sector ultimately must provide the bulk of the investment to bring promising technologies to market. To adapt to this reality, the federal government will need to modernize the way it provides support for innovation, taking care to do so in a way that also attracts private sector investment. ARPA-E is a good start and should be expanded, not eliminated. In addition, the government will need to fill the gaping funding hole for demonstrating first-of-a-kind, commercial-scale energy projects, so the private sector knows when a technology is ready for prime time.

Technological innovation presents a tantalizing opportunity for the United States to develop new solar technologies to be used around the world. In addition, America can set an example for how to promote the other forms of innovation that solar needs to achieve its potential. For example, tweaking the U.S. tax code could accelerate financial innovation, opening the spigots of capital flow to deploy more solar. And to advance systemic innovation, federal and state governments could work together on improving the power grid's ability to flexibly accommodate a high penetration of solar power—for example, by building long-distance transmission lines, modernizing markets, and encouraging a diverse, zero-carbon power mix. These proposals tend to get less airtime than others, such as putting a price on carbon emissions to create a level playing field between dirty and clean energy sources. But a carbon price is no panacea—just a sensible policy that should be accompanied by others that advance innovation.

Unfortunately, today's solar policies mostly fail to advance any of the three types of innovation. Costly federal tax credits and state renewable energy mandates encourage more deployment of existing solar PV technology (and can even discourage the commercialization of emerging solar technologies) without preparing for a future in which the value of solar PV plunges below its cost. Today's policies are at best an expensive effort to trim U.S. carbon emissions and create jobs involved in the installation of solar projects. Instead, by investing in the three types of innovation needed to continue solar's rise, the United States can reap the economic rewards of an advanced solar industry and serve as a solar city upon a hill—an example for the rest of the world to follow to substantially displace fossil fuels with solar energy.

Still, it will take more than just domestic policies to enable solar to reach its global potential. In particular, commercializing a suite of new solar technologies could require public funding from countries around the world and a newly transformed solar industry willing to invest in innovation. U.S. leadership can make that happen. Through Mission Innovation, an international initiative to advance energy innovation, the United States should urge other countries to invest more in R&D and help them set up their own institutions like ARPA-E. (Before making recommendations abroad, however, the United States must invest in innovation at home, and President Trump should walk back his pledge to pull out of the Paris Agreement on Climate Change in 2020, a move that would destroy U.S. credibility with international partners.) And the United States should reduce trade barriers, opting instead to foster a globalized solar industry. These steps might appear to help the competition. But this is a competition that plays to U.S. strengths. Indeed, in other innovation-led industries, such as semiconductor manufacturing, U.S. firms command global supply chains and invest liberally in the next technology generation.

The United States is fully capable of transforming solar—from how it is financed, to what it looks like, to how flexible the system that it plugs into is—and enjoying the benefits of doing so. President Trump should rethink his administration's priorities. Energy innovation remains a goal that is just as rational and bipartisan today as it was when both sides of the aisle resoundingly applauded the creation of ARPA-E.

Third Time's the Charm?

The assertion in President Trump's budget statement that the private sector is best positioned to finance applied energy R&D and commercialize technologies is not new. The roots of that sentiment stretch back more than half a century, to the final years of World War II. In late 1944, President Franklin Delano Roosevelt wrote a letter to Vannevar Bush, who had run the wartime Office of Scientific Research and Development, which honed radar, mass-produced antibiotics, and launched the Manhattan Project. In the letter, President Roosevelt wondered if the scientific innovation that had given the Allies the advantage—and would ultimately win them the war—might also "be used in the days of peace ahead for the improvement of the national health, the creation of new enterprises bringing new jobs, and the betterment of the national standard of living."[5]

Absolutely, responded Bush. In a report entitled *Science: The Endless Frontier,* he argued that the government should fund "research in the purest realms of science," which would generate "a stream of new scientific knowledge to turn the wheels of private and public enterprise." He cautioned, though, that federal support must come with "complete independence and freedom for the nature, scope, and methodology of research."[6] A prolific scientist and inventor himself, Bush was no doubt aiming to secure a healthy funding stream for his fellow scientists that came with no strings attached, so that they could freely pursue interesting research. He would succeed wildly. From 1953 to 2012, federal funding for basic scientific research would increase from $265 million to $38 billion.[7] (Although there is no hard-and-fast distinction, a rule of thumb is that basic research aims to fill gaps in the body of scientific knowledge, whereas applied research aims to solve practical problems in the real world.)

But the model of innovation that Bush proposed was seriously flawed. In the more than seventy years since the publication of his landmark report, it has become clear that just funding basic scientific research is not enough to guarantee new commercial technologies, especially in energy. Yet along the way, Bush's philosophy has entered the conservative canon. President Ronald Reagan and his advisers fused Bush's support for basic research with their free-market principles, concluding that federal support for applied R&D would encroach on the private sector's territory. The Trump administration, focused on paring back what it perceives as a bloated government, is channeling Reagan's aversion to applied R&D to hack off any government program that advances technology development with an application in mind.

The available evidence, however, does not bear out the thesis that government support for applied R&D cramps private investment. In fact, two short-lived waves of investment in applied energy R&D over the last half-century suggest exactly the opposite conclusion. The first wave, both initiated and abruptly ended by the federal government, demonstrated that unpredictable federal funding for applied R&D can chill the private investment climate in energy innovation. The second, led by private investors who ran out of money, demonstrated that emerging technologies face a gap in funding that the private sector is unwilling or unable to fill. Still, learning the lessons of these two failed waves of investment in innovation can inform a policy strategy to induce a third, sustained wave.

The first wave came in the 1970s in response to the oil crisis. Under President Jimmy Carter, the United States steeply ramped up funding for R&D into both solar PV and CSP (figure 10.2). These funds focused on applied activities to improve solar technology, spanning efforts to boost

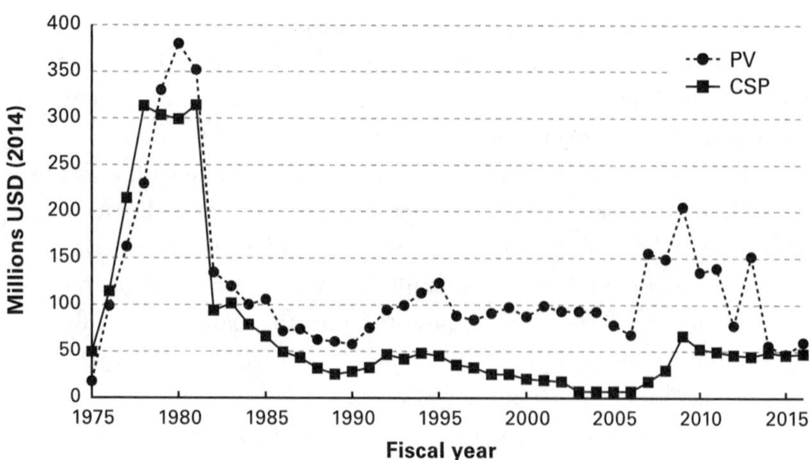

Figure 10.2

Historical U.S. DOE funding for applied R&D in solar technologies. Record of funding levels for DOE-sponsored applied R&D in solar PV and CSP. Note that DOE also funds basic science research that is relevant to solar technologies; and other U.S. federal agencies, like the National Science Foundation, also fund solar R&D. DOE funding, however, represents the bulk of funding dedicated to the development of new solar technologies.

Source: Schmalensee et al. (2015).

efficiencies in the lab and demonstrate solar technologies on a large scale. But as steeply as federal support rose, it plunged even more quickly. Spared an energy crisis by cratering oil prices in the 1980s, President Reagan had a free hand to slash applied R&D activities that did not comport with his vision of small government and free markets.

This move crippled solar innovation in the United States. It stranded federally funded research projects midstream, and it halted the $2 billion demonstration program before it could fully show the commercial potential of solar technologies.[8] Rather than create space for the private sector to take over and invest in innovation, it led to a 50 percent decline in private investment in solar R&D from 1985 to 1995, when federal funding for applied R&D remained low.[9]

The salient lessons here are first, that unpredictable government funding for applied R&D can chill the private-sector investment climate; and second, that sustained low funding levels can keep the private sector away rather than creating space for it to invest in innovation. Notably, Reagan did largely spare basic scientific research, and his budgets would serve as a template for decades; basic science would account for 60 percent of all energy R&D into the late 1990s.

In the second wave of investment in solar innovation, driven by the private sector, Silicon Valley venture capitalists invested $25 billion in start-ups (many of them solar companies), from 2006 to 2011, and lost over half their money.[10] These venture-backed start-ups failed in large part because of the terrible timing of China's surge in silicon solar panel production, which produced a flood of cheap supply that washed away upstart technologies before they could reach commercial scale. The start-ups themselves weren't blameless, and many made poor business decisions (for instance, to prematurely scale up production of products that weren't yet ready for commercial prime time).

The start-up bust also stemmed in great measure from the inadequacy of private-sector support. My collaborator Ben Gaddy and I have looked at hundreds of clean energy technology start-ups that received funding from 2006 to 2011 and concluded that the venture capital model was a particularly bad fit for solar companies. Venture capital is great for getting software companies off the ground because they need limited capital and can return eye-popping sums to their investors if they succeed. The model also can work for more capital-intensive medical technology start-ups because large firms, like pharmaceutical companies, are often willing to coinvest or acquire start-ups.

But when it came to start-ups developing new solar materials—or battery chemistries, or biofuel syntheses—venture capitalists found themselves all alone. The major oil companies were exiting, rather than entering, the solar space. And government funding for applied R&D peaked in 2009, thanks to one-time stimulus funding, but then it dropped away (figure 10.2). Left to fund solar companies with capital needs in the hundreds of millions of dollars to set up production facilities and with commercialization timelines that might stretch a decade or more, venture investors often insisted that companies race to scale up and abandoned their bets once the companies ran out of money. The lion's share of their losses on clean energy technologies came from start-ups developing new materials, chemicals, and processes. Their clean energy software bets, by contrast, paid off handsomely (figure 10.3).

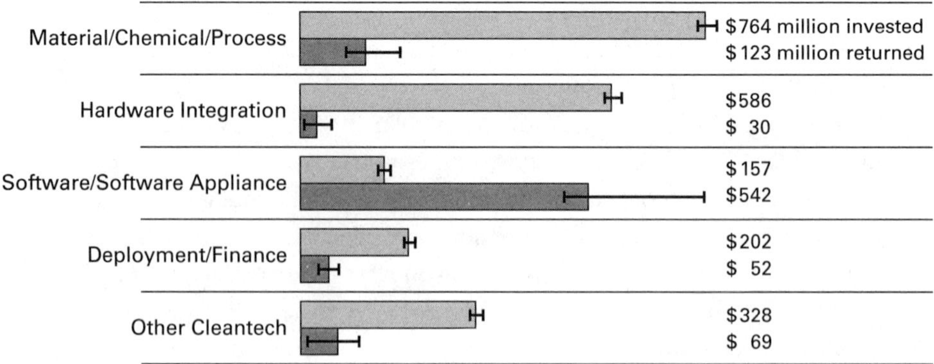

Figure 10.3
Venture capital investments and returns by clean energy technology subsector. These figures were calculated from a database of all known clean energy technology start-ups receiving their first substantial ("A-round") investments from venture capital firms between 2006 and 2011. For each subsector, the bars compare the total quantity of A-round investment in that subsector's start-ups with the returns that those A-round investors realized when any of those companies were either acquired or taken public on the stock market. Each bar has an associated uncertainty range that arises from gaps in publicly available data.
Source: Gaddy, Sivaram, Jones, and Wayman (2017).

Some might say that this episode proved that the federal government has no business intervening in applied technology development. After all, the U.S. government lost a half-billion dollars on an infamous loan guarantee to Solyndra. But the overall federal loan program for energy projects actually ended up in the black, not the red (it also had notable successes, such as funding Tesla).[11]

On that count, the federal government might be faulted for actually not taking enough risk, rather than too much. Apart from a few risky bets, the loan program focused on funding large-scale demonstrations of well-understood technologies, such as solar PV farms. That money might have been better spent in smaller chunks than a half-billion dollars, and on demonstrating emerging technologies at a moderate scale to intrigue private investors. Because venture capitalists were unable or unwilling to foot the bill for such technology demonstrations, promising energy start-ups perished in the so-called Valley of Death, unable to reach the scale needed to attract more conservative, deep-pocketed investors.

The lesson from this discussion is not that all government funding for applied R&D and demonstration is effective. Rather, it is evident in hindsight that the Department of Energy (DOE) loan program should have targeted demonstration of earlier-stage technologies and spread out its funds among more projects. The surge in energy R&D funding in the 1970s produced boondoggles such as the $4.5 billion Synfuels program, which failed to produce any alternative to oil (though Laura Anadon and Greg Nemet argue in a recent retrospective that the program generated valuable technologies for other energy applications).[12] Certainly, it is important to improve on past attempts to design more effective government schemes to support applied R&D and technology demonstration. But, without any government support at all, there is little chance that the private sector alone will carry new solar technologies through the Valley of Death.

Taking a step back from energy, the thesis that funding only basic science (with no intended application) is the best way to support innovation is out of touch with the reality across many fields. In fact, in the postwar period, the most prolific supporter of innovation has been the U.S. Department of Defense, which bets on technologies with clear national security aims in mind. The military's goal-oriented approach to funding technology bets at the early stage (through DARPA) and continuing to support the development of those that show promise has resulted in many successes, including the deployment of precision missiles, stealth fighters, and drones.[13] Some efforts have been plagued by cost and schedule overruns—notably, the ongoing development of a joint strike fighter—but the military can still boast that it played a principal role in enabling America's technological primacy today.

Sometimes, as a welcome side benefit, the military's targeted investments have ended up having broader application that was anticipated. For example, the military was the only buyer of integrated circuits back in the 1950s; it planned to use them in missile guidance systems but ended up spawning the entire semiconductor industry, whose chips are now in your iPhone.[14] Similarly, the military's objective in creating ARPANET—the precursor to the Internet—was to make it easier to share results from the few, spread-out research computers around the country. Obviously, that mission has now expanded to include sharing cat memes.

The Department of Defense's successes are a powerful argument in favor of including applied R&D alongside basic science in the government's portfolio of support for innovation. In fact, Venky Narayanamurti, former dean of engineering at Harvard, argues in his 2016 book that the distinction between basic and applied R&D is artificial.[15] In 1945, Vannevar Bush's model—that public support for basic science would lead linearly to private funding of technology development—might have been believable. Since then, too many examples of innovation's twisted, nonlinear path have emerged to continue to separate basic and applied R&D. Venky's book looks back at Bell Labs, a hotbed of innovation in the postwar period, and concludes that cross-fertilization of researchers thinking about theoretical, "pure science" problems with those turning these insights into real products, such as transistors, is the most effective way to develop technologies that improve society. Similarly, the best research labs today, such as the Howard Hughes Medical Institute, ignore the distinction between basic and applied R&D.

The right question to ask, then, is not *if* the federal government should support applied innovation. The case for doing so is open and shut. Much more important in the twenty-first century is figuring out *how* to do so most effectively.

How to Fund Energy Innovation

In 2016, I served on a review committee to evaluate postdoctoral researchers who had applied for grants from the DOE's "SunShot" program. The goals were to pick dynamic, talented researchers who were studying innovative solar PV technologies, such as perovskite or quantum dot cells, and to prepare a new generation of leaders in this field.

The applicants rose to the challenge. Some projects had the potential to shatter existing efficiency records. Others focused on bread-and-butter studies of repeatable manufacturing processes. Some researchers had many years of experience, whereas others were fresh out of PhD programs, though with multiple top-tier journal articles to their names. I couldn't help but think, "We should be funding every single one of these applicants."

Reality set in when the committee convened to compare applicants. It soon became clear that only a handful of the researchers would actually receive funding, given the program's strict budgetary limits. Most would be turned away. Although they might receive support from other U.S. funding sources, such as the National Science Foundation, those streams are also limited. Outside the United States, by contrast, they would be highly prized targets to be snapped up by other countries in Europe or Asia that would eagerly fund their cutting-edge research. Letting them go elsewhere would amount to the United States shooting itself in the foot—the economic returns that they were capable of generating would far outstrip the up-front investment in their research.

To accelerate solar innovation, the U.S. government's first priority should be to dramatically boost funding for applied R&D into breakthrough solar technologies. Researchers at the Massachusetts Institute of Technology (MIT) point out that one way to do this is to reallocate funds that currently go to supporting less cutting-edge activities, such as research into reducing the soft costs of rooftop solar installations or making existing silicon solar panels live a little longer. That shift would be sensible. Out of the DOE's more than $200 million budget for applied solar energy R&D, less than half goes toward new solar PV and CSP technologies.[16] Although some R&D into incrementally improving existing technology might fill a gap that the private sector is failing to address, the government would be far more effective if it funded the next generation of technology development.

It would be a mistake, though, to fixate on shifting around nickels and dimes within the tiny budget that the federal government assigns to solar R&D. A generous accounting across all government agencies, lumping together everything from fundamental scientific research on semiconductor physics to economic analyses of solar manufacturing costs, yields an estimate for solar R&D of less than $400 million in 2015.[17] By comparison, the federal government spends over ten times as much on tax breaks for the oil and gas industry.

U.S. policymakers should recognize that its paltry funding pales in comparison with the importance of solar innovation. This mismatch afflicts the broader state of support for energy innovation. As figure 10.4 illustrates, U.S. federal funding for energy innovation is several times lower than for health and space R&D. Left off the chart is funding for defense R&D, which is greater than that for all nondefense R&D combined.

And neglect for energy R&D has been growing. From 1979 to 2017, energy R&D dropped from 13 percent to 2 percent of all federal R&D. Gravely concerned about the "economic, security, and environmental consequences"

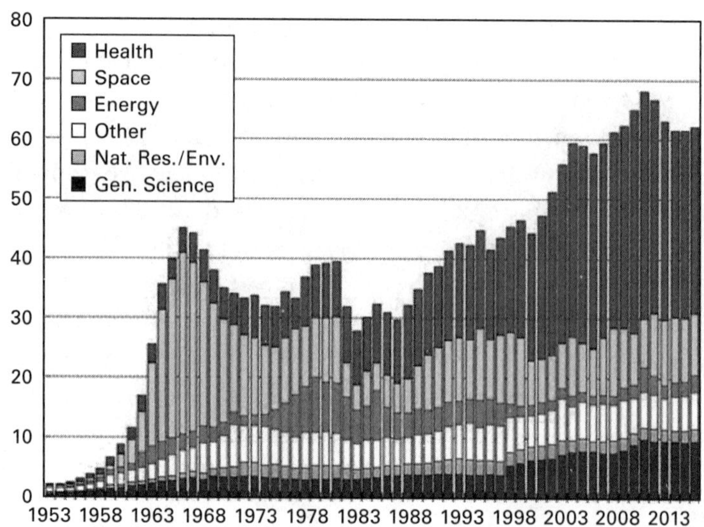

Figure 10.4

U.S. federal investment in nondefense R&D, by function. Each bar breaks down the federal government's budget for nondefense R&D, measured in billions of 2016 dollars. Note that "Nat. Res./Env" refers to "Natural Resources" or "Environment." Source: American Association for the Advancement of Science.

of underinvestment, several business leaders including Bill Gates called in April 2017 for the federal government to more than double funding for energy innovation to $16 billion annually.[18]

Still, just boosting funding for R&D is not enough. The federal government also needs to invest those dollars more intelligently. To do so, it should adopt many of the techniques used by ARPA-E, which takes a highly goal-oriented approach to funding "game-changing" technologies early in their development, with an eye toward their ultimate application.[19] For example, recognizing that existing PV or CSP technologies harness only a fraction of incoming sunlight, ARPA-E has invested in a portfolio of "hybrid technologies" that generate both power and heat and use thermal energy storage to smooth out intermittency.[20] Each ARPA-E portfolio of investments is linked by a pressing problem rather than siloed into a particular scientific discipline. And unlike most federal R&D funding streams, which are difficult to discontinue, ARPA-E is ruthless about cutting off funding to projects that are clearly missing their milestones.

Although ARPA-E is still less than a decade old, early analyses suggest its approach is effective. Anna Goldstein, a researcher at Harvard, was kind enough to share some of her preliminary findings with me.[21] On average, researchers funded by ARPA-E are five times more likely to produce patents and publications, compared with those funded by other DOE arms that fund energy R&D. And when ARPA-E funds start-ups, they tend to receive more follow-on funding from the private sector than do energy start-ups funded by other parts of the government. Anna isn't alone in lauding ARPA-E—in 2017, the National Academy of Sciences released a major report endorsing the agency's early performance.[22] Recognizing the early success of the model, President Obama's administration urged Congress to increase ARPA-E's budget from $300 million to $1 billion.[23]

Even so, the federal government cannot bootstrap the commercialization of new energy technologies all by itself. Rather, the private sector ultimately must provide the lion's share of investment—the point of government funding is to encourage private entrepreneurs, investors, and firms to make bets on promising technologies. In addition to ARPA-E, which has succeeded in attracting private follow-on investments for the technologies it selects, the Obama administration devised several other institutions to encourage collaboration between the public and private sectors. These deserve to be expanded.

The first new set of institutions, called "Energy Frontier Research Centers (EFRCs)," aims to connect fundamental scientific research with urgent technology needs. Several of the thirty-six existing EFRCs are directly relevant to solar energy conversion, including the Center for Advanced Solar Photo-Physics at Los Alamos National Laboratory. EFRCs are located in universities or national laboratories, where private firms can fund or collaborate with academic researchers.[24]

Another set of institutions that convene researchers from industry, academia, and federally funded laboratories is the network of Energy Innovation Hubs.[25] These hubs are housed in U.S. National Laboratories, a network of seventeen crown jewels of American innovation whose origins date back to the Manhattan Project but which today are leaders in conducting energy R&D. Four hubs exist as of 2017, including the Fuels from Sunlight hub at Lawrence Berkeley National Laboratory and the Batteries and Energy Storage hub at Argonne National Laboratory.

Although these hubs can anchor a regional innovation ecosystem and convene the public and private sectors to intensely push toward solving major technology challenges, hubs received a total of less than $100 million in 2016—less than 2 percent of federal funding for energy innovation. It would be eminently sensible to expand the hubs and add new ones. These additional hubs might advance PV and CSP technology, as well as help develop flexible power grids to integrate high levels of intermittent renewable energy.

To make investment in energy innovation more palatable to the private sector, the federal government should provide shared facilities for private use in order to reduce the steep and redundant capital costs of each firm building its own facilities. The National Laboratories make their labs and equipment available for a fee, and they have recently rolled out innovative programs, such as Cyclotron Road, to fund and house entrepreneurs who can develop their technologies using the extensive resources on campus.[26] This arrangement can fill the gap left by venture capital investors skittish about funding research into, for example, new solar materials.

Further down the line of technology development, the national network of federally funded manufacturing institutes (Manufacturing USA) offers facilities for firms to develop the processes to make new products.[27] So, for example, a company might be emboldened to invest in developing a high-temperature CSP collector if it can experiment with the advanced equipment at a federal facility to figure out how to manufacture such a product at scale.

Finally, the biggest gap that the private sector alone has not filled is for demonstrating new technologies at commercial scale. Achieving successful demonstrations is absolutely crucial to bring down the risks perceived by private investors and firms weighing whether to undertake the time and expense to bring a technology to market. Unfortunately, the DOE's Loan Programs Office, which made the infamous Solyndra bet, is politically embattled and unlikely to be the vehicle to fund demonstrations in the future.

There is no shortage of good ideas about what could replace it. The group of business leaders that recommended boosting funds for energy innovation to $16 billion annually also recommended the creation of a private corporation, funded by a single congressional appropriation of $20 billion over a decade, to invest in technology demonstrations.[28] Because this corporation would be held at arm's length from the government, it would be insulated from political meddling. And, it would take equity stakes in companies and projects rather than just insuring loans, so that the company could actually make money off its bets. To allay concerns that such a corporation would crowd out the private sector, it might be required to make each of its investments alongside private partners, which would attract rather than repel private investment.

Others have suggested recruiting state governments to guide the funding of demonstration projects that make the most sense from a regional context. And still others have proposed using prizes to attract private investment in demonstration projects. The National Aeronautics and Space Administration (NASA) has used such a strategy effectively (for example inducing Elon Musk's SpaceX to meet a series of performance milestones).[29] An energy prize might foster competition among firms and entrepreneurs to, for example, demonstrate a large-area installation of flexible, highly efficient PV coatings or generate substantial quantities of hydrogen from a solar fuel generator. Given the scale of the funding gap, all these different avenues for the government to support technology demonstrations are worth pursuing.

A likely objection, however, is that doing so would encroach on the free market and "pick winners and losers." But this approach of providing government support—not just for fundamental science in the lab, but also for applied research, manufacturing scale-up, and commercial demonstrations—is exactly what the military has done, with striking results.

Its process starts with DARPA making numerous bets on high-risk, unproven technologies. Then the military can fund the most promising projects, and it has provided support for manufacturing and for demonstrating at scale for decades—from transistor factories in the 1950s to a planned refinery, announced in 2017, to produce biofuels for the U.S. navy.[30] And the various service branches will often purchase the end product of a technology that the military has supported, giving firms the confidence that their products will ultimately find a buyer if they perform as desired.

In fact, the military could become the most effective supporter of clean energy innovation. New solar technologies in particular could provide direct security benefits for the military. For example, lightweight, flexible solar coatings could improve the operational versatility of U.S. troops and reduce the need for costly and vulnerable fuel convoys. Indeed, some scholars have argued:

The [Department of Defense (DOD)] is better placed for catalyzing rapid innovation in energy technologies than the DOE because the DOD is a major customer for energy-consuming systems and equipment for its roughly 500 permanent installations, as well as for operational equipment (spending $10 billion a year on liquid fuels alone). The scale of the resources that the DOD brings to technology development is impressive. It employs more than 30,000 engineers and scientists in R&D and procurement, and its annual R&D spending comes to about $80 billion, with procurement spending in excess of $100 billion. The DOD thus has the incentives and capacity to be a smart and demanding customer for new energy technologies.[31]

This two-pronged model of inducing innovation—funding technology development and creating a market for the products that emerge—has worked for the military and could accelerate innovation in solar technology, as well as for a range of other energy technologies needed for a solar-powered future. Clearly, the federal government currently underfunds R&D and demonstration of new technologies and should boost its support.

One might be forgiven for assuming that the government is doing well on the other prong, given that its subsidies to deploy solar power vastly outweigh its expenditures in research, development, and demonstration. Unfortunately, it turns out that U.S. policies to create the right market conditions for solar to thrive are also in need of reform.

No Taxation without Innovation

The problem with U.S. public policies that seek to encourage market adoption of solar power is not how much money is spent, but what that money is spent on. The goal of solar policy should be to encourage financial, technological, and systemic innovation that enables a sharply rising share of solar energy to decrease customer costs and carbon emissions at home, while providing an example of what works to the rest of the world. Today's policies do not accomplish this. And even widely endorsed proposals to tax carbon emissions are not policy silver bullets; a carbon tax would need to be paired with support for new technologies to stimulate innovation most effectively.

At present, the largest federal subsidy for solar power is the investment tax credit, worth 30 percent of the up-front cost of a solar installation. In 2015, the federal government extended this credit through 2020, at which point the tax credit steps down to 10 percent over the next two years. As a result, the U.S. Treasury forecasts that the federal government will spend over $2 billion per year subsidizing solar power. Another federal tax incentive, which allows solar project owners to apply an accelerated depreciation schedule, could cost another $200 million annually.[32]

These tax incentives promote the wrong things, however. They almost exclusively benefit mature technologies—mostly silicon solar PV panels. Given the choice between an emerging, innovative technology and a commercially established one, both of which are equally eligible for the same tax credit, an investor will prudently choose the established one, even if the emerging technology might be cheaper and more efficient when produced at scale.[33]

A better approach would be to design incentives that fell in value as a technology got cheaper, weaning it off subsidies that it would not need and focusing support on the deployment of newer technologies that need an early boost. A rational policy would also cut support for technologies that failed to improve their cost or performance over time. Finally, none of these incentives should be disbursed through tax breaks, which can be hard to monetize in the first place; instead, direct cash incentives could be twice as effective at stimulating deployment without raising the fiscal burden on the federal government.[34] These are all promising policy directions for Congress to pursue rather than choosing to extend the current investment tax credit beyond 2020, when the phase-out begins.

Critics of eliminating tax credits might contend that the credits have been crucial to establishing a thriving U.S. solar market. Indeed, through 2016, the United States had installed over 40 gigawatts (GW) of solar and was second only to China as the largest annual market in the world. Domestic subsidies played a large role in these achievements. Yet, I would counter that, from here on out, subsidizing existing solar technology will do little to reduce the U.S. carbon footprint, let alone the world's. It will speed arrival of the day when existing solar technology penetrates as much of the market as it ever will, but solar will never go further if various forms of innovation do not materialize.

From an economic point of view, the solar industry is fond of trumpeting that it has created over a quarter of a million jobs in the United States.[35] But most of those jobs are in the installation of projects using imported solar panels; government support for those jobs provides limited knock-on economic benefits. By contrast, investments in innovation could deliver a much higher return on public spending, generating nearly five additional jobs for the economy from stimulating a single new job in advanced manufacturing.[36] Therefore, from both environmental and economic perspectives, any subsidies would be more effective if they were pointed toward innovation.

Critics might also argue that if fossil fuels receive billions in tax breaks, it is only fair for solar power to receive similar handouts. This observation raises an important point. The U.S. government should eliminate the $4 billion in tax breaks for oil and gas companies, which—as research I commissioned at the Council on Foreign Relations demonstrated—does not actually improve U.S. energy security or reduce prices at the pump.[37] Still, even if those fossil fuel subsidies persist, it will still make sense to reform solar subsidies to encourage innovative new technologies that will be even more competitive with fossil fuels.

In addition to the federal solar investment tax credit, many states have supported solar deployment. One way they do that is through a mandate known as a "renewable portfolio standard," which sets a quota for the share of electricity the state must procure from renewable sources such as wind and solar. Again, these policies can justifiably claim important achievements in deploying solar power, most notably in California. But, as with the investment tax credit, they do little to support technological innovation, mostly supporting the deployment of existing silicon solar panels instead.

Moreover, renewable portfolio standards obstruct systemic innovation by discriminating against nonrenewable, zero-carbon sources, such as nuclear power or fossil plants with carbon capture and storage. This discrimination runs counter to the goal of building a diverse mix of power resources to enable deep decarbonization. So, in California, although the share of wind and solar is rocketing upward, the last remaining nuclear plant is slated to close, in a state where nuclear contributed 15 percent of its power as recently as 2011.[38]

By contrast, in 2016, New York enacted policies to encourage both renewable energy and nuclear power, aiming to get most of the state's electricity from clean sources by 2030.[39] Policies like these, which do not discriminate against nuclear and other nonrenewable clean energy resources, are far more sensible than renewable portfolio standards. More states should enact them to ensure that a high penetration of solar power is made possible by the continued existence of flexible base resources, which, as chapter 9 noted, are plants that can be ramped up and down to compensate for fluctuating renewable energy output.

Mandates may not even be necessary to encourage renewable energy deployment. Texas provides an instructive case study. Although the state had mandated 10 GW of renewable capacity by 2025, the energy industry paid little attention to the mandate, and Texas blew through the target in 2012, over a decade early (although most of the installed capacity was wind rather than solar). The actual driver of renewable energy growth, rather than the renewable portfolio standard, was Texas's buildout of transmission lines that linked faraway, windy regions like the Texas Panhandle—known as a "Competitive Renewable Energy Zone (CREZ)"—to demand centers in major cities. Emboldened by the CREZ transmission lines, developers eagerly added generation capacity, and Texas is now the biggest wind powerhouse in the country.[40] Texas's growth was motivated by the favorable economics of renewable energy once sufficient transmission capacity was in place, rather than by the government mandate.

Investments in expanding the electricity grid exemplify policies that advance systemic innovation to lay the groundwork for much higher penetrations of solar power in the future. Therefore, the federal government and states should work together to install a network of long-distance, high-voltage direct current (HVDC) transmission lines across the country to expand access to remote but rich renewable energy resources. The Trump administration has already expressed its eagerness to put new infrastructure projects in the ground. It could do so by exerting federal regulatory authority to speed up the siting and permitting process for new transmission lines.[41]

In tandem with this kind of initiative, state governments should work together to link their power markets, so renewable energy generated in one state can travel via long-distance transmission to demand centers in other states. For example, if California moves forward with its embattled plan to link its power market with those of its neighbors in the West, it may not have to throw away thousands of megawatts of surplus renewable power that exceed in-state demand. Transmission expansion and power market reforms are steps that, in the near term, may support only the expansion of existing technologies. But by promoting systemic innovation that enables a flexible grid capable of hosting more solar power, these policy steps would set the stage for emerging technologies to ultimately succeed existing ones.

Similarly, U.S. policymakers should undertake policies that spur financial innovation as well. Again, although this approach may benefit only existing technologies in the near term, financial innovation that unlocks vast pools of capital could make it possible to scale up advanced technologies rapidly in the future. A step that lawmakers could take in this direction would be to pass the MLP Parity Act. Recall from chapter 4 that Master Limited Partnerships (MLPs) are financial vehicles used extensively to finance oil and gas infrastructure such as pipelines and pay no corporate income tax. Renewable energy firms attempted to recreate the MLP with the growth-oriented YieldCo model (bundling together a portfolio of renewable energy projects to be traded on the stock market), which blew up in their faces. But the bipartisan MLP Parity Act, first introduced in 2012 by Senator Chris Coons (D-DE) and Senator Jerry Moran (R-KS), would enable institutional investors to invest in listed MLPs comprising solar power assets. Safe, tried-and-true vehicles, these MLPs could speed the flow of capital into solar.[42] And down the road, if newer technologies can achieve commercial scale, they would benefit from the availability of this financing structure to tap into institutional investors' deep pockets.

Finally, no discussion of clean energy policy would be complete without mention of pricing carbon. A carbon tax, a trading system for carbon pollution with an overall cap, or some other system to create economic pain for those entities that cause greenhouse gas emissions would indeed be a welcome correction to existing markets, which do not penalize polluters.[43] In addition to a steady chorus of just about every economist singing its praises, prominent politicians on both sides of the aisle support a price on carbon. In the first year of the Obama administration, the U.S. House of Representatives passed the Waxman-Markey Bill to create a carbon cap-and-trade scheme, enticing eight Republicans to cross the aisle (the bill, however, was never taken up by the Senate). More recently, an all-star delegation of senior Republican statesmen paid a visit to the White House in 2017 to convince President Trump of the merit of a revenue-neutral carbon tax. Their plan would apply a price on carbon emissions across the U.S. economy, scrap the entire patchwork of clean energy deployment subsidies and mandates that drive conservatives crazy, and deliver a politically attractive tax break to working-class families.[44] This solution would seem to be elegant and efficient, right?

Probably not on its own. As the MIT economist Daron Acemoglu and colleagues argue, a carbon tax solves one important market failure but leaves another unaddressed. It corrects the market's failure to put a value on the damage from carbon emissions, which levels the playing field between clean and dirty sources of energy. That adjustment sets up the market to cost-effectively match energy supply and demand while limiting pollution.

Whereas this policy is ideal for efficiently dispatching existing technologies, however, it is not ideal for accelerating innovation.[45] Absent government support for R&D—which creates scientific knowledge and intellectual property for the good of all, but which the market does not fully value—technological innovation proceeds more slowly than it would with government support. Acemoglu and colleagues find that even with a price on carbon, delaying investment in technological innovation can set back a clean energy transition and steeply raise its cost.[46]

Pricing carbon is an elegant, important policy, but it is by no means a panacea. Rather, an ideal policy portfolio for smartly promoting clean energy in the United States would direct a substantial fraction of the proceeds from a nationwide carbon tax to boost funding for technological innovation. This policy would be a grand bargain that would exchange ineffective mandates and clean-energy subsidies with a single carbon tax. (Importantly, environmental regulations, such as pollution controls on coal power plants—which are justified by health concerns—should remain.) This new approach could still be politically palatable, with substantial funds left over to compensate those who might be hardest hit by a carbon tax. It is crucial that support for energy innovation is prioritized in such a grand bargain. Otherwise, the United States might forego the game-changing technologies that it and the world need.

Executing Mission Innovation

I will never forget the Paris Climate Change Conference of 2015. For two weeks, the world's attention fixated on the diplomats hammering away at a historic agreement. I caught glimpses of U.S. secretary of state John Kerry emerging from the negotiating room in the middle of the night, somehow energized, even as his staff trailed sleepily behind him. A brightly lit Eiffel Tower bore the ominous message: "No Plan B." At last, on the final day, weary ministers joined hands and raised them in triumph, having signed a nonbinding agreement to limit global warming to 2°C. That agreement set up a framework for the countries of the world to curb their emissions, hold one another accountable, and ratchet up the ambition of their targets over time.

But for all the drama, the most important element of the Paris summit was decided on Day 1, on the sidelines of the formal negotiations. That day, the triumvirate of Bill Gates, President Obama, and Prime Minister Narendra Modi of India led the unveiling of an initiative to boost global energy innovation: Mission Innovation. All told, twenty world leaders signed up to double their countries' public funding for energy R&D within five years. And twenty-eight billionaires, led by Gates, pledged to invest billions to bring breakthrough energy technologies to market.

This was the crucial breakthrough that happened in Paris, for the development of radically superior technologies is what will enable countries to make increasingly ambitious emissions pledges. And both the public and private sectors will need to come together to fulfill the promise of accelerating innovation.

Unfortunately, early actions by the Trump administration threaten to undo recent progress. In June 2017, the president announced his intention to withdraw the United States from the Paris Agreement in 2020. Following through on that pledge would wipe out the international goodwill President Obama and Secretary Kerry earned from negotiating the accord, damaging U.S. credibility on global energy and climate issues (and destroying diplomatic capital America needs to advance other foreign-policy priorities). In addition, President Trump's determination to renege on the U.S. commitment to double its R&D spending threatens to further erode U.S. credibility as a leader on energy innovation. Other countries, including China, are eager to advance innovation in America's stead, though, both increasing R&D funding at home and coordinating the direction of energy innovation abroad.[47]

Trump is misguided; if he continues to exclude energy innovation from his "America First" agenda, America could well end up last. The United States has compelling reasons to lead internationally on energy innovation. In particular, reshaping solar into a global, technology-driven industry would make use of and enhance U.S. strengths. Today, both the production and deployment of solar energy are concentrated in Asia. The combination of Chinese scale and tried-and-true silicon solar technology has proved unbeatable so far. The United States should not attempt to try and beat China at its own game.

Rather, the United States should spearhead a global push to commercialize new solar technologies. My colleague Dan Sanchez at Stanford and I have urged the United States to share lessons with other countries from its experience setting up ARPA-E to support innovative technologies.[48] And researchers at Columbia University have proposed an initiative for some of the top funders of solar R&D—the United States, South Korea, Japan, and Germany—to freely share information and coordinate their funding priorities to advance new solar technologies rapidly. Importantly, such a collaboration would intimately involve private-sector firms, encouraging them to invest corporate dollars in R&D and seeking to bring new technologies to market.[49]

Precompetitive, international research collaborations play to U.S. strengths, because of the surfeit of talented scientists and engineers and boldly innovative firms in the United States. In the semiconductor industry, U.S. firms collaborate with international competitors all the time, often sharing the capital cost of R&D and factories so that they can afford to invest proportionally more of their revenue in advancing innovation. By spearheading a major solar research collaboration effort, the United States could inculcate norms currently lacking in the global solar PV industry. For example, the average Chinese solar company invests just 1 percent of its revenues in R&D, whereas the average American semiconductor firm invests more than ten times as much.[50]

Naysayers might contend that an energy industry will never resemble a high-tech sector. Energy is dominated by lumbering utilities and state-owned behemoths, it is politically bedeviled, and its core products—kilowatt-hours of electricity or gallons of gasoline—are low-margin commodities. Tech companies, by contrast, are nimble, write the rules as they go along, and use the high margins from computer chips, iPhones, and the like to fund ongoing R&D.

It would be better instead, the critics might continue, to employ aggressive trade policies to protect domestic solar manufacturers beleaguered by cheap Chinese imports. And indeed, the United States has rightfully imposed tariffs to retaliate against Chinese solar dumping that wiped out innovative Silicon Valley start-ups. At the time of writing, the Trump administration was preparing to erect additional, sweeping trade barriers to imported silicon solar cells and panels from around the world, relying on the rarely invoked Section 201 of the 1974 Trade Act. But trade barriers are blunt, destructive tools that should be only a small component of America's innovation strategy. Deployed recklessly, they can provoke trade wars that might stymie U.S. chances of taking the helm of an innovative industry with a global supply chain along which goods, services, and capital can flow efficiently across borders.[51]

Rather than retreating within its borders, America should embrace the chance to reshape the global solar industry in its innovative image. There are important differences between solar panels and semiconductors, and the business model of the latter may not translate exactly to the former. But that is no excuse to accept the current industry's culture of painfully slow technology progress, especially given the exciting advances emerging from top labs around the world.

Remember, the great solar game is not over; it is just beginning. To meet the goals set out by this book, solar power will have to grow over thirtyfold by midcentury, and much more beyond that horizon. Although the United States finds itself at a daunting disadvantage to China's early lead, America can win back market share and deliver planet-saving technologies by leading a global push for innovation.

I've spent a decade studying solar. Today's industry is barely recognizable from the one I started in. But for humanity to finally tame the sun, solar technology and the solar industry must become even more unrecognizable in the decades to come. Now, *that* is a future I look forward to.

Acknowledgments

I am grateful first for the invaluable support I received from the Council on Foreign Relations (CFR). Richard Haass and James Lindsay have given me a professional home, along with the opportunity to convene diverse experts, the resources to understand solar markets around the world, and the time to write and revise this book. I owe an enormous debt to Michael Levi, who recruited me to CFR and took me under his wing—this book exists because of his mentorship and the example he set. I was lucky to have as a research associate the talented Sagatom Saha, who dove into financial securitization and solar cell efficiency tables with equal gusto; Madison Freeman succeeded him, rapidly became a clean-energy expert, and planned the book's roll-out. I am also thankful to Quinn Marschik, Ellie Valencia, Jacob Kincer, Jules Ross, and Maximilian Fiege, who all spent long hours researching, editing, and sourcing the book. Finally, at CFR I also thank Patricia Dorff, Sumit Poudyal, and Dustin Kingsmill for their guidance throughout the process, as well as Anya Schmemann and the communications team, Irina Faskianos and the National Program team, Lisa Ortiz and the digital team, and Amy Baker and the studies team.

This book has benefited from comments from nearly 100 reviewers (any errors, though, are mine alone, and probably the result of ignoring excellent advice). I am especially grateful to Michael Levi, Lidija Sekarjic, and Arun Majumdar, for chairing study group sessions in New York, Washington, D.C., and Silicon Valley, and to those who participated in the sessions and, in many cases, provided extensive written feedback: (NYC): Riju Agrawal, Ed Crooks, Sarah Davidson, Mark Gallogly, Jesse Gerstin, Justin Gillis, Jamil Khan, Kenneth Kramer, Varun Mehra, Tyler Norris, John O'Leary, Sumit Poudyal, John Rhodes, and David Sandalow; (DC): Doug Arent, Alexandra Britton, Claire Casey, Mitchell Craft, Mike Derzko, Bennett Duval, Jorge

Kamine, Sarah Ladislaw, Robert Margolis, Colin McCormick, Sean Mirski, Nakita Noel, Dana Olson, Dylan Rebois, Ian Rinehart, Jonathan Silver, Gregory Stamas, and Ethan Zindler; (Silicon Valley): Matt Baker, Sally Benson, Stacey Bent, Madhur Boloor, Bruce Clemens, Stephen Comello, Raffi Garabedian, Ilan Gur, Leigh Johnson, Rahul Kini, Sydney Larson, Tomas Leijtens, Nathan Lewis, Arnav Mariwala, Laxmi Parthasarathy, Lara Pierpoint, Daniel Sanchez, Ranjana Sivaram, Saya Sivaram, Srinivasan Sivaram, Uttara Sivaram, Dick Swanson, Alex Trembath, Seth Winger, Ward Woods, and Minjia Zhong. (Minjia, Arnav, Emily Davis, and Erin Pang wrote me an excellent research paper to inform the chapter on the electricity grid.) I also appreciate receiving manuscript feedback and research guidance from: Jonathan Bass, Manish Bhatia, Jenny Chase, Nicky Dean, Daniel Kammen, Andy Karsner, Richard Kauffman, Erica Mackey, Bill Martin, Nancy Pfund, Catherine and Wayne Reynolds, Jackson Salovaara, Graham Smith, Henry Snaith, Sam Stranks, David Victor, and Justin Vogt. I thank Fareed Zakaria for guiding me to rewrite the book's opening to broaden its appeal.

I am grateful to Beth Clevenger at MIT Press for believing in this project, overseeing a timely and constructive peer review process, and advising me throughout the publication journey. Anthony Zannino facilitated the delivery of the final manuscript and art package; Marcy Ross and the MIT editorial staff carefully edited the manuscript; Susan Clark and Katie Hope developed a promotional strategy; Molly Seamans designed the cover; and Jim Mitchell kept the production schedule on track. I am also deeply thankful to Ricki Rusting for ensuring that my prose was clear, correct, and compelling—as only a *Scientific American* managing editor could have done.

Throughout my time at CFR, I have been grateful for the generosity of the Sloan Foundation. Evan Michelson not only supported this project, he was also a partner, suggesting strategies to increase the book's impact.

I've been fortunate to work with terrific collaborators, and I cite our joint research studies throughout this book. They include: Christopher Clack, Ben Gaddy, David Hart, Jesse Jenkins, Shayle Kann, Colin McCormick, Tyler Norris, Frank O'Sullivan, Varun Rai, Dan Reicher, Dan Sanchez, Gireesh Shrimali, Henry Snaith, and Sam Stranks.

I am also blessed to count so many people close to me who were deeply invested in this project. Yashraj Narang, Aroon Vijaykar, David Livingston, Ellen Huet, Stephanie Wright, Adam Creasman, Cyrus Navabi, Devin Banerjee, Arjun Aggarwal, and Andy Brody came to the rescue on short notice to triage the manuscript's opening chapters. Monica Varman shared her time and expertise to guide my research on the off-grid solar market. Tomas Leijtens, Nakita Noel, and Fadl Saadi kept me up to date on the literature and edited the solar technology chapters. Sean Mirski applied his keen legal eye to the book's every adverb—whenever I made a major organizational or thematic decision, I looked for Sean's affirmation. And I'm truly grateful to Laxmi Parthasarathy, my rock through a tumultuous year of writing, who edited every single draft from the initial proposal through the final proofs.

I've had the opportunity over the last decade to learn from pioneers who advanced the frontiers of solar energy and inspired me to write this book. Martin Roscheisen gave me a shot as a module engineer at Nanosolar before I knew what a module was. Bruce Clemens at Stanford supervised my "Four-year transform" into a scientist. Henry Snaith, at Oxford, welcomed me into his solar lab and showed me what world-class research looks like. Mayor Antonio Villaraigosa shared with me his vision for a greener Los Angeles and trusted me to execute it. Ron Nichols at the LADWP instructed me on the nitty-gritty of deploying renewable energy while keeping the lights on. Matt Rogers at McKinsey trained me to reimagine the energy industry's future. And Richard Kauffman invited me to work on the regulatory overhaul of New York state's electric power sector.

But the visionary I've learned the most from is my father, Srinivasan (Siva), whose career in science and technology has inspired me to argue in this book that the solar industry should not settle for technological mediocrity. He is my harshest critic but also my biggest fan, and neither of us would have it any other way. Speaking of critics, my two sisters didn't pull any punches when editing the manuscript. But I was fortunate to learn from Uttara's expertise—from electric utility trends to smart energy management—and grateful that she spent late nights after work redlining my drafts and coaching me on integrating the flood of feedback from reviewers. Not to be outdone, Saya even took time out of her first week of college at Berkeley to help me craft the opening chapter; she also shared her literary flair to help me replace repetition with variety throughout the text. Finally, my mother, Ranjana, to whom this book is dedicated, has been a sounding board for titles and themes as well as a constant source of support. Even while shuttling back and forth to India to care for my grandparents (whose blessings I've been lucky to receive), she never let me forget that she believed I could pull off this book and that there was a village cheering me on.

Glossary

Scientific Terms

Alternating current (AC) An electric current that reverses its direction many times a second and is almost universally used in modern electricity grids. Solar photovoltaic (PV) panels are often connected to a grid through an inverter that converts direct current (DC) to AC electricity.

Bandgap A property of a semiconductor that determines how much energy an electron must gain, for example from sunlight, to break free of its host atom and contribute to an electric current. The most efficient solar cell designs use multiple semiconductor layers, each with a bandgap optimized for harnessing the energy of a portion of the sun's spectrum of colors.

Current A flow of electric charge. The current of a solar photovoltaic (PV) cell is related to how many electrons flow out of the cell.

Direct current (DC) An electric current that runs in a single direction. DC electricity is more efficient to transmit than alternating current (AC) electricity, but it is currently only economical to transmit DC over very long distances (hundreds of miles or more). Solar photovoltaic (PV) panels produce DC electricity.

Electron A subatomic, elementary particle that is negatively charged, typically bound to the positively charged nucleus of an atom, and the source of an electric current when moving freely.

Energy The capability of doing work. Energy comes in many interconvertible forms, including kinetic, chemical, potential, thermal, electric, and radiant (from light) energy. Electric energy is measured in kilowatt-hours (kWh).

Energy density The amount of energy stored per unit volume (in colloquial usage this term is often used to refer to the amount of energy stored per unit mass, for example, in a battery).

Kilowatt-hour (kWh) The amount of electric energy delivered by 1,000 watts (W) sustained over one hour. For reference, a typical U.S. household consumes roughly 900 kWh of electricity per month.

Photon An elementary particle that is the fundamental constituent of light (otherwise known as electromagnetic radiation) and carries an amount of energy proportional to its frequency.

Power The amount of energy produced or consumed per unit time. The power output of a solar photovoltaic (PV) cell is the instantaneous product of its electric current and voltage. Electric power is measured in watts (W).

Semiconductor A material that can switch between an insulator and conductor of electricity. In a solar photovoltaic (PV) cell, sunlight transfers energy to a semiconductor's electrons, which then flow out of the cell as electric current. Silicon is the most commonly used semiconductor for solar cells as well as for other electronic devices such as computer chips.

Voltage The amount of energy, per unit of electric charge, that is driving an electric current in a circuit. The voltage of a solar photovoltaic (PV) cell is related to how much energy is in each electron that flows out of the cell.

Watt (W) A unit of electric power. For reference, a conventional incandescent lightbulb continuously consumes 60 W of power when turned on, and a typical solar panel produces up to 300 W at midday. Other commonly used units of power include kilowatt (kW; 1,000 watts), megawatt (MW; 1 million watts), and gigawatt (GW; 1 billion watts). The largest solar farms can produce hundreds of megawatts of power.

Solar Industry and Technology Terms

Amorphous silicon A solar photovoltaic (PV) material that can be used to make flexible, thin, and cheap solar cells, though these cells are less efficient than crystalline silicon solar cells.

Cadmium telluride (CdTe) A solar photovoltaic (PV) material that is deposited as a thin film. Although over 90 percent of all solar panels are based on silicon technology, most of the rest are made from CdTe. The U.S. firm First Solar is the largest manufacturer of CdTe solar panels.

Commercial and industrial (C&I) One of the market segments for the deployment of solar photovoltaic (PV) systems. C&I systems are typically smaller than 2 megawatts (MW) and can be installed on large rooftops of businesses or warehouses or mounted on the ground.

Community solar Projects in which consumers can band together to collectively own or lease a solar installation, often on the scale of several megawatts (MW), and use the generated power to offset their power purchases from the grid.

Concentrated solar power (CSP) A solar technology that uses mirrors to concentrate sunlight to generate heat that can then be used to drive a turbine and produce electricity. Although many CSP configurations exist, the power tower design—in which a field of mirrors (heliostats) concentrate sunlight on the top of a central tower—is gaining popularity. This design is compatible with thermal energy storage, which enables a CSP plant to produce electricity during the night.

Copper indium gallium (di)selenide (CIGS) A solar photovoltaic (PV) material that is deposited as a thin film. Many Silicon Valley start-up companies, including Solyndra, tried and failed to commercialize this technology.

Distributed solar The use of solar photovoltaic (PV) panels on rooftops or in a ground-mounted arrangement smaller than a utility-scale project. Distributed solar projects can be sited close to where the power they generate will be used.

Efficiency For a solar photovoltaic (PV) cell, the efficiency is the percentage of the energy embodied in sunlight that the cell converts into electricity—as of 2017, the record efficiency for a silicon solar cell is 26 percent, and the record for a multijunction cell comprising several layers is 46 percent. The record efficiency for a concentrated solar power (CSP) plant is 31 percent conversion of solar radiation into electricity. For a photoelectrochemical cell (PEC), the efficiency is the percentage of energy in sunlight that is converted into hydrogen fuel, the record for which is 22 percent.

Feed-in tariff A policy mechanism designed to attract investment in renewable energy technologies by offering long-term contracts to buy power at a fixed price from renewable energy projects; the price is typically based on the cost of that technology rather than on the prevailing market price of electricity. Germany's feed-in tariff scheme played an important role in driving the growth of the solar industry in the 2000s.

Gallium arsenide (GaAs) A solar photovoltaic (PV) material from which solar cells even more efficient than silicon cells can be made. Although solar panels made out of GaAs and other semiconductors are more popular than silicon panels for space applications, they are too expensive for economical deployment on Earth.

Inverter An electronic device that converts direct current (DC) electricity to alternating current (AC) electricity. Solar photovoltaic (PV) panels are connected to the grid through inverters.

Investment tax credit (ITC) A subsidy from the U.S. federal government for the installation of some renewable energy projects, including solar power projects. The subsidy is a tax credit worth 30 percent of the upfront cost of a solar installation, and it is scheduled to decline to 10 percent by 2022.

Net metering A policy under which electricity customers who generate their own electricity send it to the grid—for example, during the daytime when rooftop solar panels generate power—and offset the expense of consuming electricity from the grid at other times, such as nighttime.

Off-grid The smallest of the market segments for the deployment of solar photovoltaic (PV) systems. Off-grid solar systems, which can be as small as a single solar panel, are typically installed in regions of the developing world with limited or no connectivity to a main grid.

Organic solar cell A photovoltaic (PV) technology based on organic polymers, which could one day enable nontoxic, flexible, colorful, and semitransparent solar cells. As of 2017, the record efficiency for organic solar cells is 12 percent.

Pay-as-you-go (PAYG) A system for customers to pay for power from off-grid solar systems on an ongoing basis, rather than paying for the cost of the system upfront. Startup companies are increasingly using PAYG offerings to market solar home systems (SHS) to rural customers in sub-Saharan Africa and South Asia. This requires the startups to find sources of capital to finance the upfront cost of the solar systems.

Perovskite A solar photovoltaic (PV) material from which solar cells of 22 percent efficiency have been made as of 2017. This technology could enable low-cost, flexible, and highly efficient solar cells, but the most likely near-term route to commercialization is to layer perovskite on top of existing silicon solar cells to boost their efficiencies.

Photoelectrochemical cell (PEC) A device that harnesses the energy embodied in sunlight to split water and produce hydrogen fuel. A PEC consists of two stacked photoelectrodes, each of which is coated with a catalyst that speeds up the production of either hydrogen or oxygen, and a membrane that separates the reaction products.

Photovoltaics (PV) Technology to convert the energy in sunlight into electricity using solar PV cells made out of semiconductors that exhibit an electric voltage and current upon exposure to light. Many solar PV cells connected together form a solar PV panel, which is the building block of a solar PV system.

Power-purchase agreement (PPA) A contract for the sale of electricity. Most utility-scale solar projects are contracted through PPAs to sell power to a utility for fifteen or more years, providing certainty of future revenues to a developer that undertakes the risk of financing and constructing a solar project.

Quantum dot solar cell A solar photovoltaic (PV) device consisting of semiconductor particles that are only a few nanometers in diameter. As of 2017, the record efficiency of a quantum dot solar cell is 13 percent.

Residential One of the market segments for the deployment of solar photovoltaic (PV) systems. Residential systems are typically installed on top of a household's roof and are smaller than 50 kilowatts (kW).

Silicon A semiconductor out of which nearly all solar photovoltaic (PV) cells are made, as well as electronic devices like microchips. After it is mined, silicon is purified into polysilicon, cast into cylindrical ingots, sliced into thin wafers, and then processed to make solar cells.

Soft costs Non-hardware costs associated with deploying solar power. These costs include permitting, financing, and installation as well as acquiring new customers and paying suppliers. These costs can represent over half of the cost of a residential solar installation.

Solar home system (SHS) Typically used in the developing world to power rural homes unconnected to a main grid. An SHS combines solar panels of up to 300 watts (W) of power-generating capacity with batteries, electronics, and energy-efficient appliances.

Solar panel Also known as a module, a solar photovoltaic (PV) panel is the basic building block of a solar system and consists of many solar cells connected together.

Solar power satellite A technology under consideration to harness solar energy outside the Earth's atmosphere and beam it down to the planet's surface, in the form of microwaves, for terrestrial electricity use.

Tandem solar cell A photovoltaic (PV) cell consisting of two semiconducting layers—one optimized to absorb high-frequency light and the other to absorb low-frequency light. More generally, a multijunction solar cell can employ two or more layers to more efficiently convert sunlight into electricity than a single semiconductor layer can.

Thin film A category of solar photovoltaic (PV) technologies—including copper indium gallium (di)selenide (CIGS), cadmium telluride (CdTe), and amorphous silicon—based on the deposition of materials only a few micrometers thick.

Utility-scale The largest of the market segments for the deployment of solar photovoltaic (PV) systems. Utility-scale projects range from several to several hundred megawatts (MW) of power-generating capacity, and their owners typically contract to sell solar power to a utility for a fixed price and duration.

Value deflation The reduction in the value of the electricity generated by solar photovoltaic (PV) panels as more of them connect to the grid and supply electricity in excess of demand in the middle of the day.

General Energy Terms

Battery Electrochemical devices that store and release electric energy by using chemical reactions. Lithium-ion batteries, which operate by shuttling lithium ions between two electrodes, are increasingly popular for powering electric vehicles as well as for stationary uses such as stabilizing the electricity grid. Many other battery designs exist or are under development—from well-established lead-acid batteries to promising flow batteries.

Capacity The amount of electric power that can be generated by a power plant, typically measured in megawatts (MW). Conventional power plants, such as those that use fossil fuels, can consistently produce an amount of power close to their capacity, whereas intermittent sources, like solar and wind power, only produce at their rated capacity when the weather permits.

Capacity markets Economic markets created to ensure the reliability of the electricity grid by requiring electricity customers to pay to reserve power-generating capacity from power plants in future years.

Carbon capture, utilization, and storage A process that captures carbon dioxide emissions from sources like coal-fired power plants and either stores or reuses it so it will not enter the atmosphere. Carbon dioxide can be used to generate economic value—for example, by improving the extraction of oil or serving as a raw material input for the production of plastics or cement—and it can be permanently stored in geological formations.

Decarbonization The elimination of emissions of greenhouse gases (of which carbon dioxide is the most prevalent) from the global economy.

Demand response The modification of customer demand for electricity to reduce strain on the grid and better match up electric demand with supply, for example from intermittent sources such as solar power. Strategies include financial incentives and behavioral programs to encourage demand shifts as well as direct utility control of a customer's appliances.

Desalination An energy-intensive technology that removes salt from saline water to produce potable water.

Distributed energy resources Decentralized, locally sited equipment to generate, store, or use electricity, including diesel generators, rooftop solar panels, fuel cells, batteries, and smart appliances.

Distribution The final stage in the delivery of electric power, which carries electricity from the transmission system to individual customers. The distribution system comprises substations that lower the voltage and distribution lines that deliver power to customers.

Electric vehicle (EV) A vehicle that relies on one or more electric motors for propulsion, rather than an internal combustion engine. Most EVs are powered by charged lithium-ion batteries, though fuel-cell EVs consume hydrogen fuel to produce electricity that then runs the car's motors.

Electrolysis The use of electricity to split a substance. In the electrolysis of water, a device called an electrolyzer runs an electric current through water to split it into oxygen and hydrogen fuel.

Energy storage The process of storing energy, or converting it from one form to another, for later use. Energy storage technologies used—or under development for future use—in the electric power sector include pumped hydro storage, electrochemical batteries, superconducting magnetic energy storage, supercapacitors, flywheels, compressed air, and underground thermal energy storage.

Flexible base Power plants that can consistently generate electricity but can also modulate their power output to compensate for fluctuating renewable energy. These resources include nuclear reactors, hydropower plants with reservoir storage, and fossil-fueled power plants.

Fossil fuel A fuel consisting of ancient, decomposed organisms that contains a large proportion of the element carbon. Fossil fuels—which include coal, natural gas, and petroleum—account for the large majority of human energy use, and the greenhouse gas emissions resulting from their combustion by humans is the largest contributor to global climate change.

Fuel cell A device that converts the chemical energy from a fuel, such as hydrogen, into electricity, using an electrochemical reaction (in contrast to a combustion engine, which burns fuel). Applications of fuel cells include powering electric vehicles as well as supplying electricity to the grid or directly to end-users.

High-voltage direct current (HVDC) A technology to transmit electricity over long distances (hundreds of miles or more) to minimize power losses in transit and reduce costs. The term *ultra-high voltage direct current* (UHVDC) is applied to lines operating at voltages of 1 million volts or more.

Hydrogen A colorless, gaseous fuel that releases energy when combined with oxygen to form water, either electrochemically in a fuel cell or through combustion. Most production of hydrogen fuel today relies on fossil fuels such as natural gas, but solar energy could be harnessed to split water and produce hydrogen. If produced in this way, hydrogen fuel could be used without causing the release of any harmful emissions.

Hydropower (or hydroelectric power) The world's largest source of renewable electricity, which uses the downhill flow of water to drive a turbine and generate electricity. Hydropower plants can often vary their power output, for example if a dam regulates the level of a reservoir. In addition, pumped hydro storage can store excess electric energy by pumping water uphill from a lower reservoir to a higher one and then running a turbine later on when there is a need for electricity.

Inertia A property of conventional power generators connected to the electricity grid that aids reliability by resisting changes to the operating frequency of the grid.

Because conventional, synchronous generators contain large masses rotating at the same frequency, an imbalance between the grid's electric supply and demand that raises or lowers the grid's operating frequency is countered by the system's inertia, affording grid operators time to fix the imbalance. Some generators, like solar photovoltaic (PV) panels, do not contribute inertia (although inverters can be programmed to simulate it, through synthetic inertia).

Light-emitting diode (LED) A more efficient lighting technology than conventional incandescent bulbs. Like solar photovoltaic (PV) cells, LEDs are made out of semiconductors. LEDs fell in cost by a factor of ten between 2009 and 2015.

Microgrid A small network of interconnected equipment to generate and use electrical power. Typically, microgrids have the capacity to generate less than 15 megawatts (MW) of power. They are often connected to the main grid, but they can also be standalone, off-grid systems, for example in rural areas. Some grid-connected microgrids can continue to operate as autonomous islands even when there is a blackout on the main grid.

Nuclear power The use of the energy contained within atomic nuclei to produce electricity. A nuclear reactor harnesses the heat released from the splitting, or fission, of atomic nuclei to generate steam, drive a steam turbine, and generate electricity. Most nuclear reactors are light-water reactors, which use water to cool and moderate the nuclear reaction.

Renewable energy Energy from sources that are not depleted when used. These include solar, wind, geothermal, wave, tidal, and hydropower. Some sources, such as solar and wind power, are intermittent, whereas others, such as geothermal, are more constant. Biomass is also a renewable source of energy, but unlike other renewable sources, it can generate significant net emissions of greenhouse gases and other pollutants depending on how biomass is grown, harvested, used, and replaced.

Renewable portfolio standard (RPS) A regulation that requires companies that supply electricity to customers to produce or procure a specified fraction of their electricity from renewable energy sources. For example, California's RPS requires that by 2030, retailers and public utilities procure half of their electricity from eligible renewable energy sources, which include power from solar, wind, geothermal, biomass, and small hydropower facilities but exclude large hydropower facilities as well as zero-carbon sources such as nuclear energy.

Smart grid An electricity grid equipped with digital technologies enabling two-way communication between a utility and its customers, sensors, responsive transmission and distribution grid components, and software and protocols able to dynamically manage the grid.

Smart meter An electronic device that records a customer's electric consumption in intervals of one hour or less and communicates that information to the utility for monitoring and billing.

Substation A collection of electrical equipment that transforms the voltage of electricity. High voltages are best for long-distance transmission, whereas low-voltages are best for safe electricity use. Substations can raise the voltage to send power from a generator along a transmission line, connect multiple transmission lines, or reduce the voltage to transfer power between the transmission and distribution system.

Transmission The bulk movement of electricity at high voltages over long distances, starting from power generators and ending at electrical substations that reduce the voltage of electricity for transfer to the distribution system.

Utility In the electric power industry, an electric utility delivers electric energy for use primarily by the public. Utilities can be publicly or privately owned. In many parts of the United States known as regulated markets, a utility is guaranteed a monopoly over a defined service territory to generate, transmit, distribute, and sell electricity to customers, and government regulators oversee customer rates. Elsewhere, regulated utilities only own the transmission and distribution grid, whereas private companies generate electricity to sell to utilities and, in some cases, retail electricity to customers. Often, such private companies are unregulated arms of holding companies that also own regulated utilities.

Wholesale electricity market A market for competing generators of electricity to sell their output to retailers, who then sell it on to customers. In the United States, wholesale electricity markets often span multiple states and follow an auction process in which bids to sell electricity are accepted in ascending order until all electric demand is met, and the highest accepted bid sets the market-clearing price.

Wind power A form of renewable energy that uses air flow through wind turbines to produce electricity. Like solar power, wind power is intermittent and depends on wind speeds. Wind turbines can be sited on land or at sea; offshore wind turbines are becoming increasingly economical.

Business and Finance Terms

Asset-backed security A tradable financial asset with income flows that are derived from a pool of underlying assets.

Capital Wealth in the form of money or other assets. Investors provide equity capital to fund a business venture in exchange for an ownership stake in that venture. Debt capital is provided by investors with the expectation they will be paid back with interest.

Cost of capital The rate of return demanded by investors who provide debt and/or equity capital to a business venture. A solar project will require more expensive capital if it is perceived to be a riskier investment.

Economies of scale Cost advantages obtained as a result of increasing the size of a business operation. For example, by increasing its production of solar panels, a factory can spread its fixed costs over more units, thereby decreasing the cost per solar panel. Economies of scale also apply to the downstream deployment of solar projects; a larger solar project can spread overhead costs over a larger power-generating capacity, reducing the cost per watt of the project.

Green bond (or climate bond) Fixed-income financial instrument comprising assets, such as renewable energy projects, that are helpful for reducing greenhouse gas emissions or adapting to climate change.

Institutional investor An entity that pools money to purchase assets. Institutional investors include banks, insurance companies, pension funds, hedge funds, sovereign wealth funds, and endowments. Collectively, they manage over $100 trillion and will be important to scaling up solar power.

Lease A contractual arrangement in which a user pays the owner of an asset to use it. In the United States, firms such as SolarCity (now part of Tesla) marketed solar leases to drive growth in the market for rooftop solar panels, from which homeowners could purchase power on an ongoing basis rather than paying the high, upfront cost of the solar system.

Master limited partnership (MLP) A publicly traded entity that pools a portfolio of income-producing assets. To qualify for exemption from corporate taxation, 90 percent of an MLP's income must come from qualifying sources, which include activities such as the production and transportation of depletable natural resources. Most MLPs own and operate fossil fuel pipelines and similar assets.

Real estate investment trust (REIT) A company that owns income-producing real estate, can be publicly traded, and is not subject to corporate taxes so long as it distributes 95 percent of its income to shareholders.

Securitization The financial practice of pooling various types of debt, such as residential mortgages, auto loans, or credit card debt, and selling the portfolio's cash flows as tradable securities to third-party investors. Securitization is an increasingly popular way to raise debt capital for distributed solar projects.

Venture capital (VC) A form of financing provided by firms or funds to small companies in exchange for an ownership stake. Such investments are based on the perception that the ventures could grow substantially in value, often through the development of new technologies and products.

Innovation Terms

Business model innovation Introduction of product offerings, revenue models, or operational practices that are new to a particular sector.

Demonstration The first use of a technology at scale and in real-world conditions with the aim of demonstrating the technology's feasibility and commercial potential. New energy technologies are likely to require successful demonstrations to persuade private investors to take them to market. Demonstration typically follows research and development (R&D) and requires a larger scale of funding; recognizing that demonstration is an important aspect of the technology development process, the U.S. Department of Energy's strategy for energy innovation involves the promotion of research, development, and demonstration (RD&D).

Experience curve A graphical illustration of the industrial principle that increased production of a product or delivery of a service leads to lower unit costs of the product or service. This relationship exists for several reasons, including learning—the improvement in production efficiency and cost that accompanies repeated performance of tasks—as well as economies of scale.

Financial innovation Popularization of financial instruments, institutions, or markets that are new to a particular sector.

Innovation The introduction of something that is adopted in a real-world context for the first time. (Alternatively, an innovation can refer to the technology, business model, etc., that has been introduced and adopted.)

Lock-in (technological) A form of economic path dependence in which the next technological generation cannot replace the current one. Technological lock-in can occur if an incumbent technology gets an advantage against emerging technology upstarts; even if the upstarts might have the potential to cost less and perform better upon further development and scale production, they may flounder in a free market that favors first movers. A well-documented case of lock-in is the global dominance of nuclear light-water reactors over alternative designs; in addition, the current dominance of silicon solar photovoltaic (PV) panels may in the future prevent technological succession.

Research and development (R&D) The first stage of development of a potential new service or product, encompassing scientific research and applied technology development, often with an aim to solve a real-world problem. Companies, nonprofits, and governments engage in R&D, and economic theory predicts that the private sector has insufficient incentives to invest in the socially optimal level of R&D, both in general and specifically for new energy technologies.

Systemic innovation Implementation of novel approaches to designing a particular system. An energy system includes physical infrastructure (e.g., the power grid), economic markets (e.g., wholesale power markets), and public policies (e.g., regulations that govern power utilities).

Technological innovation A technological product or process that has been commercialized, or brought to market, for the first time. Even if a firm does not invent a technology, it can *innovate* by successfully introducing that technology into the marketplace.

Organizations

Advanced Research Projects Agency-Energy (ARPA-E) A U.S. government agency, housed within the Department of Energy, that is tasked with promoting and funding research and development (R&D) of advanced energy technologies. It is modeled after the Defense Advanced Research Projects Agency (DARPA).

Department of Energy (DOE) A U.S. federal department with oversight over energy, nuclear weapons, and radioactive waste disposal. The DOE sponsors substantial research, development, and demonstration of solar energy technologies, notably through its SunShot program.

California Independent System Operator (CAISO) An independent, nonprofit entity that oversees the operation of California's electric power transmission grid and wholesale electricity market.

Green bank A financial institution, typically supported by a local or national government, that uses innovative financing techniques to stimulate private investment in clean energy technologies. In the United States, the states of Connecticut and New York founded the first green banks.

International Energy Agency (IEA) An intergovernmental organization, comprising twenty-nine member states in the developed world, that promotes energy security, economic development, and environmental protection and publishes research on energy markets and technologies.

International Renewable Energy Agency (IRENA) An intergovernmental organization that promotes the adoption and sustainable use of renewable energy.

Joint Center for Artificial Photosynthesis (JCAP) A U.S. Department of Energy Innovation Hub, with two main centers at the California Institute of Technology and Lawrence Berkeley National Laboratory, the primary mission of which is to find a cost-effective method to produce fuels using only sunlight, water, and carbon dioxide.

Multilateral development bank (MDB) An institution created by a group of countries that provides financing and professional advising to promote economic development. Examples include the World Bank, Inter-American Development Bank, and the Asian Development Bank.

Notes

Preface

1. Mayor Antonio R. Villaraigosa, Varun Sivaram, and Ron Nichols, "Powering Los Angeles with renewable energy," *Nature Climate Change* 3 (2013).

2. Lucas Mearian, "Data Storage Goes from $1M to 2 Cents per Gigabyte." *Computerworld*. April 10, 2017, http://core0.staticworld.net/assets/2017/04/10/cw-50th-anniversary-storage-trends.pdf.

Chapter 1

1. Tom Randall, "World Energy Hits a Turning Point: Solar That's Cheaper Than Wind," *Bloomberg*, December 14, 2016, https://www.bloomberg.com/news/articles/2016-12-15/world-energy-hits-a-turning-point-solar-that-s-cheaper-than-wind.

2. For an accessible discussion of the challenges that India's aging grid infrastructure poses to the continued rise of solar power, see Urmi Goswami, "Realizing India's Renewable Ambition," *The Economic Times*, July 2, 2016, http://economictimes.indiatimes.com/industry/energy/power/realising-indias-renewable-ambition/articleshow/53016854.cms.

3. Myriam Alexander-Kearns et al., "The Impact of Vehicle Automation of Carbon Emissions," Center for American Progress, November 18, 2016, https://www.americanprogress.org/issues/green/reports/2016/11/18/292588/the-impact-of-vehicle-automation-on-carbon-emissions-where-uncertainty-lies.

4. "The Emissions Gap Report 2016: A UNEP Synthesis Report," United Nations Environment Programme, 2016, http://wedocs.unep.org/bitstream/handle/20.500.11822/10016/emission_gap_report_2016.pdf.

5. For an overview of the projected impacts of climate change, see Working Group II, "Fifth Assessment Report. Climate Change 2014: Impacts, Adaptation, and

Vulnerability," United Nations Intergovernmental Panel on Climate Change, 2014, https://www.ipcc.ch/report/ar5/wg2.

6. David Wallace-Wells, "The Uninhabitable Earth," *New York Magazine*, July 9, 2017, http://nymag.com/daily/intelligencer/2017/07/climate-change-earth-too-hot-for-humans.html.

7. Peter U. Clark et al., "Consequences of Twenty-First-Century Policy for Multi-Millennial Climate and Sea-Level Change," *Nature Climate Change* 6 (February 8, 2016), http://www.nature.com/nclimate/journal/v6/n4/abs/nclimate2923.html.

8. "Climate Change and Migration Issues in the Pacific," United Nations Economic and Social Commission for Asia and the Pacific, 2015, http://www.ilo.org/dyn/migpractice/docs/261/Pacific.pdf.

9. Varun Sivaram et al., "Energy Innovation Policy: Priorities for the Trump Administration and Congress," Information Technology and Innovation Foundation, December 2016, http://www2.itif.org/2016-energy-innovation-policy.pdf?_ga=2.100848641.127748496.1496762242-636560486.1494874808.

10. Bradley E. Layton, "A Comparison of Energy Densities of Prevalent Energy Sources in Units of Joules per Cubic Meter," *International Journal of Green Energy* 6 (2006), http://www.usclcorp.com/news/energy-docs/A%20Comparison%20of%20Energy%20Densities.pdf.

11. "Tracking Clean Energy Progress 2017," International Energy Agency (IEA), 2017, https://www.iea.org/publications/freepublications/publication/TrackingCleanEnergyProgress2017.pdf.

12. Samuel D. Stranks and Henry J. Snaith, "Perovskite Solar Cells," in *Photovoltaic Solar Energy: From Fundamentals to Applications*, ed. Angèle Reinders, Pierre Verlinden, Wilfried van Sark, and Alexandre Freundlich (John Wiley & Sons, 2017), 277–289.

13. Joshua Christian and Clifford Ho, "Design Requirements, Challenges, and Solutions for High-Temperature Falling Particle Receivers," Albuquerque: Concentrating Solar Technologies Department, Sandia National Lab (2016): doi:10.1063/1.4949060.

14. Katherine Bourzac, "News Feature: Liquid Sunlight," *Proceedings of the National Academy of Sciences* 113, no. 17 (2016): 4545–4548, doi:10.1073/pnas.1604811113.

15. Bill Gates, "Energy Innovation: Why We Need It and How to Get It," *Gates Notes*, November 30, 2015, https://www.gatesnotes.com/~/media/Files/Energy/Energy_Innovation_Nov_30_2015.pdf.

16. Madhvi Sally and Shreya Jai, "Agri Companies Now Prefer Solar Powered Products in Rural India," *The Economic Times*, December 25, 2013, http://articles.economictimes.indiatimes.com/2013-12-25/news/45561591_1_mahindra-partners-karan-dangayach-shashwat-green-fuels.

17. M. Soundariya Preetha, "Textile Mills Go in for Solar Energy Projects," *Hindu*, May 25, 2014, http://www.thehindu.com/news/cities/Coimbatore/textile-mills-go-in-for-solar-energy-projects/article6045981.ece.

18. Anindya Upadhyay, "Softbank Eyes Indian Solar Manufacturing in Boost to Modi's Goal," *Bloomberg*, September 19, 2016, http://www.bloomberg.com/news/articles/2016-09-20/softbank-eyes-indian-solar-manufacturing-in-boost-to-modi-s-goal.

19. "Renewables 2016: Global Status Report," Renewable Energy Network for the 21st Century, 2016, 65, http://www.ren21.net/wp-content/uploads/2016/06/GSR_2016_Full_Report.pdf.

20. Varun Sivaram, Gireesh Shrimali, and Dan Reicher, "Reach for the Sun: How India's Audacious Solar Ambitions Could Make or Break Its Climate Commitments," Stanford Steyer-Taylor Center for Energy Policy and Finance, December 8, 2015, https://law.stanford.edu/reach-for-the-sun-how-indias-audacious-solar-ambitions-could-make-or-break-its-climate-commitments.

21. Varun Sivaram, "Can India Save the Warming Planet?" *Scientific American* (May 2017), https://www.scientificamerican.com/article/can-india-save-the-warming-planet.

22. "Financing India's Energy Transition," Bloomberg New Energy Finance, November 1, 2016, https://about.bnef.com/blog/financing-indias-clean-energy-transition.

23. Rajesh Kumar Singh and Saket Sundria, "Living in the Dark: 240 Million Indians Have No Electricity," *Bloomberg*, January 24, 2017, https://www.bloomberg.com/news/features/2017-01-24/living-in-the-dark-240-million-indians-have-no-electricity.

24. Rajesh Kumar Singh and Anindya Upadhyay, "Modi's Plan to Clean up World's Worst Air Resisted by Indian Power Generators," *Bloomberg*, March 30, 2016, https://www.bloomberg.com/news/articles/2016-03-30/modi-s-picnic-spot-plan-resisted-by-indian-power-generators.

25. Charles K. Ebinger, "India's Energy and Climate Policy: Can India Meet the Challenge of Industrialization and Climate Change?" The Brookings Institution, June 2016, https://www.brookings.edu/wp-content/uploads/2016/07/india_energy_climate_policy_ebinger.pdf.

26. Vlado Vivoda, *Energy Security in Japan: Challenges After Fukushima* (New York: Routledge, 2016), 36–37.

27. Toko Sekiguchi, "Returning Home: Japan Nuclear Disaster Forced Thousands to Flee; Many Are Now Divided over Whether to Come Back," *Wall Street Journal*, October 23, 2014, http://www.wsj.com/articles/fukushima-refugees-wary-of-returning-home-1414099802.

28. "Japan's Strategic Energy Plan," Ministry of Economy, Trade, and Industry of Japan, 2012, http://energypolicy.columbia.edu/sites/default/files/energy/Japan's%20 Strategic%20Energy%20Plan_vF.pdf.

29. "Japan Nuclear Update," Nuclear Energy Institute, April 20, 2017, http://www .nei.org/News-Media/News/Japan-Nuclear-Update.

30. Jason Deign, "Subsidy Cuts Will Cause a 'Sharp Negative Turn' in Japan's Solar Market Through 2020," Greentech Media, June 1, 2016, http://www.greentechmedia .com/articles/read/japan-plans-to-curb-solar-growth.

31. Tim Buckley and Simon Nicholas, "Japan: Greater Energy Security Through Renewables," Institute for Energy Economics and Financial Analysis, March 2017, http://ieefa.org/wp-content/uploads/2017/03/Japan_-Greater-Energy-Security -Through-Renewables-_March-2017.pdf.

32. Aaron Sheldrick, "Japan to Cut Emphasis on Nuclear in Next Energy Plan: Sources," *Reuters*, May 26, 2016, http://www.reuters.com/article/us-japan-nuclear -idUSKCN0YI06Z.

33. Mike Stone, "Japanese Utilities Invest in Big Batteries to Help Bring More Renewables On-Line," Greentech Media, May 19, 2015, http://www.greentechmedia.com /articles/read/japanese-utilities-invest-in-big-batteries.

34. "The Photovoltaic Power Systems Programme Annual Report 2015," International Energy Agency (IEA), August 2016, http://www.iea-pvps.org/index.php?id=6.

35. Jessica Belt, "How Will Latin America Deal with Its Hydropower Problem," *GreenBiz*, May 20, 2015, https://www.greenbiz.com/article/how-will-latin-america-deal-its -hydropower-problem.

36. Sushma Udipi Nagendran, "4 Charts Explaining Latin America's Impending Solar Boom," Greentech Media, March 10, 2017, https://www.greentechmedia.com /articles/read/explaining-latin-americas-impending-solar-boom1.

37. Vanessa Dezem and Javiera Quiroga, "Chile Has So Much Solar Energy It's Giving It Away for Free," *Bloomberg*, June 1, 2016, https://www.bloomberg.com/news/articles /2016-06-01/chile-has-so-much-solar-energy-it-s-giving-it-away-for-free.

38. Wael Mahdi and Vivian Nereim, "Saudis Target 30 Solar, Wind Projects in $50 Billion Pledge," *Bloomberg*, April 17, 2017, https://www.bloomberg.com/news/articles /2017-04-17/saudis-seek-30-solar-wind-projects-in-50-billion-pledge.

39. Glada Lahn and Paul Stevens, "Burning Oil to Keep Cool: The Hidden Energy Crisis in Saudi Arabia," December 2011, https://www.chathamhouse.org/sites/files/chatham house/public/Research/Energy,%20Environment%20and%20Development/1211pr _lahn_stevens.pdf.

40. Thomas Wellock, "'Too Cheap to Meter:' A History of the Phrase," U.S. Nuclear Regulatory Commission, June 3, 2016, https://public-blog.nrc-gateway.gov/2016/06/03/too-cheap-to-meter-a-history-of-the-phrase.

41. Derek Gill, "I Only Wish I Could Have Been Born Into the Age My Six Children Will See," *Chicago Tribune*, June 22, 1969, http://archives.chicagotribune.com/1969/06/22/page/256/article/i-only-wish-i-could-have-been-born-into-the-age-my-six-children-will-see.

42. Varun Sivaram, "Unlocking Energy," *Issues in Science and Technology* 33, no. 2 (Winter 2017), http://issues.org/33-2/unlocking-clean-energy.

43. Angus McCrone et al., "Global Trends in Renewable Energy Investment," Frankfurt School-United Nations Environment Programme Collaborating Centre for Climate and Sustainable Energy Finance, 2016, http://fs-unep-centre.org/publications/global-trends-renewable-energy-investment-2016.

44. Nancy M. Haegel et al., "Terrawatt-Scale Photovoltaics: Trajectories and Challenges," *Science*, April 14, 2017, http://science.sciencemag.org/content/356/6334/141.

45. Vaclav Smil. *Energy and Civilization: A History* (Cambridge, MA: MIT Press, 2017).

46. "Climate Change 2014 Synthesis Report: Summary for Policymakers," Intergovernmental Panel on Climate Change, 2014, http://www.ipcc.ch/pdf/assessment-report/ar5/syr/AR5_SYR_FINAL_SPM.pdf.

47. Benjamin K. Sovacool, "How Long Will It Take? Conceptualizing the Temporal Dynamics of Energy Transitions," *Energy Research & Social Science* 13 (March 2016), http://www.sciencedirect.com/science/article/pii/S2214629615300827.

48. Jessica F. Green, "Don't Link Carbon Markets," *Nature* 543, no. 7646, (March 21, 2017), http://www.nature.com/news/don-t-link-carbon-markets-1.21663.

Chapter 2

1. Kevin Bullis, "A Price Drop for Solar Panels," *MIT Technology Review*, October 22, 2012, https://www.technologyreview.com/s/410064/a-price-drop-for-solar-panels.

2. DealBook, "Nanosolar Raises $300 Million," *New York Times*, August 28, 2008, http://dealbook.nytimes.com/2008/08/28/nanosolar-announces-300-million-financing-round.

3. Christian Roselund, "BNEF: Global Solar Investment Fell 32% in 2016," *PV Magazine International*, January 12, 2017, https://www.pv-magazine.com/2017/01/12/bnef-global-solar-investment-fell-32-in-2016/.

4. John Perlin, *Let It Shine: The 6,000-Year Story of Solar Energy* (Novato, CA: New World Library, 2013), 115–117.

5. Geoffrey Jones and Loubna Bouamane, "'Power from Sunshine': A Business History of Solar Energy," Harvard Business School Working Paper, May 2012, 9.

6. Perlin, *Let It Shine*, 115–117.

7. Travis Bradford, *Solar Revolution: The Economic Transformation of the Global Energy Industry* (Cambridge, MA: MIT Press, 2006), 98.

8. Werner Weiss and Franz Mauthner, *Solar Heat Worldwide: Markets and Contribution to the Energy Supply 2010,* Gleisdorf, Austria: AEE–Institute for Sustainable Technologies, 2012, 12.

9. Perlin, *Let It Shine*, 362.

10. Catherine Wu, "Global CSP Installed Capacity Increased to 5017 MW by the End of 2016," CSP Plaza, January 17, 2017, http://en.cspplaza.com/global-csp-installed-capacity-increased-to-5017-mw-by-the-end-of-2016.html.

11. "Photovoltaic Milestone: 300 Gigawatts of Global Installed PV Capacity," German Solar Association, January 26, 2017, https://www.solarwirtschaft.de/en/media/single-view/news/photovoltaic-milestone-300-gigawatts-of-global-installed-pv-capacity.html.

12. Perlin, *Let It Shine*, 362.

13. Albert Einstein, "Concerning an Heuristic Point of View Toward the Emission and Transformation of Light," *Annals of Physics* 17, no. 132: 1905.

14. E. D. Wilson, "Power from the Sun," *Power* 28 (October 1935): 517.

15. Jon Gertner, *The Idea Factory* (New York: Penguin Press, 2012).

16. "Vast Power of the Sun Is Tapped by Battery Using Sand Ingredient," *The New York Times*, April 26, 1954, http://www.nytimes.com/packages/pdf/science/TOPICS_SOLAR_TIMELINE/solar1954.pdf.

17. Dwight D. Eisenhower, "Atoms for Peace," speech delivered at the 470th Plenary Meeting of the United Nations General Assembly, December 8, 1953, https://www.iaea.org/about/history/atoms-for-peace-speech.

18. Ubaid Asad, Zulfiqar, Sajid Riaz, and Muhammad Imran., "Role of Solar Energy in Atmospheric Pollution Reduction—A Review." *International Journal of Science, Engineering and Innovation Research* 1 (July 2015), 2.

19. Harvey Strum, "Eisenhower's Solar Energy Policy," *The Public Historian* 6, no. 2 (Spring 1984), 37–50.

20. National Research Council et al., *Solar Cells: Outlook for Improved Efficiency* (Washington, DC: The National Academies Press, 1972).

21. N. K. Thuan, "Telecommunications Power in Australia," presentation at the International Telecommunications Energy Conference, Washington, DC, 1982, 395–401.

22. B. McNelis, "The Photovoltaic Business: Manufacturers and Markets," in *Clean Electricity from Photovoltaics*, ed. Mary D. Archer and Robert Hill (London: Imperial College Press, 2001), 713–740.

23. Jones and Bouamane, "Power from Sunshine."

24. Jimmy Carter, "Solar Photovoltaic Energy Research, Development, and Demonstration Act of 1978 Statement on Signing H.R. 12874 into Law," The American Presidency Project, November 4, 1978, http://www.presidency.ucsb.edu/ws/?pid=30122.

25. "A Shakedown Shapes up in Photovoltaics," *Chemical Week*, February 3, 1982, 33.

26. Peter Z. Grossman, *U.S. Energy Policy and the Pursuit of Failure* (New York: Cambridge University Press, 2013).

27. John Abbots, "All the King's Horses and All the King's Men," *Bulletin of the Atomic Scientists* (January/February 1989), 49.

28. Bob Johnstone, *Switching to Solar* (New York: Prometheus Books, 2011), 129–130.

29. "Solar Energy Support in Germany: A Closer Look," Solar Energy Industries Association, July 2014.

30. Kristen Ardani, Robert Margolis, Galen Barbose, et al. "2010 Solar Market Trends Report," National Renewable Energy Laboratory (NREL), November 2011, xiii–1.

31. R. C. Chittick and H. F. Sterling, "Glow Discharge Disposition of Amorphous Semiconductors: The Early Years," in *Tetrahedrally-Bonded Amorphous Semiconductors*, ed. David A. Adler and Helmut Fritzsche (New York: Springer Science & Business Media, 1985), 6.

32. Matthew L. Wald, "Slicing Silicon Thinner to Cut the Price of Solar Cells," *New York Times*, March 13, 2017, https://green.blogs.nytimes.com/2012/03/13/slicing-silicon-thinner-to-cut-the-price-of-solar-cells.

33. Steven Mufson, "Chinese Tariffs May Hurt U.S. Makers of Solar Cells' Raw Material," *Washington Post*, July 23, 2013, https://www.washingtonpost.com/business/economy/chinese-tariffs-may-hurt-us-makers-of-solar-cells-raw-material/2013/07/23/01ac60a4-f3d9-11e2-aa2e-4088616498b4_story.html.

34. Tim Worstall, "Solyndra: Yes, It Was Possible to See This Failure Coming," *Forbes*, September 17, 2011, http://www.forbes.com/sites/timworstall/2011/09/17/solyndra-yes-it-was-possible-to-see-this-failure-coming.

35. Ashley Parker, "Romney Campaigns at Failed Solyndra Factory," *The New York Times*, May 21, 2012, http://thecaucus.blogs.nytimes.com/2012/05/31/romney-to-campaign-at-failed-solyndra-factory.

36. Benjamin Gaddy, Varun Sivaram, and Francis O'Sullivan, "Venture Capital and Cleantech: The Wrong Model for Clean Energy Innovation," July 2016, https://energy.mit.edu/wp-content/uploads/2016/07/MITEI-WP-2016-06.pdf.

37. Kevin Desmond, *Innovators in Battery Technology Profiles of 95 Influential Electrochemists* (Jefferson, NC: McFarland & Company, Inc., 2016).

38. Martin A. Green, "Silicon Solar Cells: The Ultimate Photovoltaic Solution?" *Progress in Photovoltaics* 2, no. 2 (April 1994): 87–94.

39. Chetan Singh Solanki, "Solar Photovoltaics: Fundamentals, Technologies, and Applications," New Delhi, India: Prentice-Hall of India, 2015.

40. Jianhua Zhao, Aihua Wang, and Martin A. Green, "24.5% Efficiency Silicon PERT Cells on MCZ Substrates and 24.7% Efficiency PERL Cells on FZ Substrates," *Progress in Photovoltaics* 7, no. 6 (1999): doi: 10.1002/(SICI)1099-159X(199911/12)7:6<471::AID-PIP298>3.0.CO;2-7

41. Mohamed Bououdina and J. Paulo Davim, *Handbook of Research on Nanoscience, Nanotechnology, and Advanced Materials* (Hershey, PA: Engineering Science Reference, 2014).

42. "International Technology Roadmap for Photovoltaics: Seventh Edition," 2016, http://www.itrpv.net/.cm4all/iproc.php/ITRPV%20Seventh%20Edition%20including%20maturity%20report%2020161026.pdf.

43. Martin Green, "Silicon Photovoltaic Modules: A Brief History of the First 50 Years," *Progress in Photovoltaic Research and Applications*, August 2005, 449–451.

44. Yu Zhou, eds., *China as an Innovation Nation* (Oxford, U.K.: Oxford University Press, 2016).

45. Ping Huang, Simona O. Negro, Marko P. Hekkert, and Kexin Bi, "How China became a Leader in Solar PV: An Innovation System Analysis," *Renewable and Sustainable Energy Reviews* 64, (2016): 777-789.

46. Arnaud De La Tour, Matthieu Glachant, and Yann Ménière, "Innovation and International Technology Transfer: The Case of the Chinese Photovoltaic Industry," *Energy Policy* 39, no. 2 (2011): 761–770.

47. Gang Chen, "From Mercantile Strategy to Domestic Demand Stimulation: Changes in China's Solar PV Subsidies," *Asia Pacific Business Review* 21, no. 1, (2015): 96–112.

48. Usha C. V. Haley and George T. Haley, "How Chinese Subsidies Changed the World," *Harvard Business Review*, April 25, 2013, https://hbr.org/2013/04/how-chinese-subsidies-changed.

49. Nagalakshmi Puttaswamy and Mohd. Sahil Ali, "How Did China Become the Largest Solar PV Manufacturing Country?" Center for the Study of Science Technology and Policy, February 2015, 2. http://www.cstep.in/uploads/default/files/publications/stuff/CSTEP_Solar_PV_Working_Series_2015.pdf.

50. John Deutch and Edward Steinfeld, "A Duel in the Sun: The Solar Photovoltaics Technology Conflict Between China and the United States." MIT Future of Solar Energy Study Working Paper, 2013. https://energy.mit.edu/wp-content/uploads/2013/05/MITEI-WP-2013-01.pdf.

51. Xin-gang Zhao, Guan Wan, and Yahui Yang, "The Turning Point of Solar Photovoltaic Industry in China: Will It Come?" *Renewable and Sustainable Energy Reviews* 41 (January 2015): 178–188.

52. James Murray, "Spain Proposes Deep Cuts to Solar PV Support," *The Guardian*, August 3, 2010, https://www.theguardian.com/environment/2010/aug/03/spain-cuts-solar-pv.

53. Edgar Meza, "IRENA: PV Prices Have Declined 80% Since 2008," *PV Magazine: Photovolaic Markets & Technology*, September 11, 2014, http://www.pv-magazine.com/news/details/beitrag/irena--pv-prices-have-declined-80-since-2008_100016383/.

54. Beata Śliż-Szkliniarz, *Energy Planning in Selected European Regions: Methods for Evaluating the Potential of Renewable Energy Sources* (Karlsruhe, Germany: Karlsruhe Institute for Technology Scientific Publishing, 2013), 17.

55. Yuanyuan Liu, "Developing Trends in China's Solar PV Industry for 2016," *Renewable Energy World*, March 10, 2016, http://www.renewableenergyworld.com/articles/2016/03/developing-trends-in-china-s-pv-industry-for-2016.html.

56. Fraunhofer Institute for Solar Energy Systems and PSE AG, "Photovoltaics Report," November 17, 2016.

57. S. Blakewell, "Chinese Renewable Companies Slow to Tap $47 Billion Credit," *Bloomberg*, November 16, 2011, http://www.bloomberg.com/news/articles/2011-11-16/chinese-renewable-companies-slow-to-tap-47-billion-credit-line.

58. Keith Bradsher, "Suntech Unit Declares Bankruptcy," *The New York Times*, March 20, 2013, http://www.nytimes.com/2013/03/21/business/energy-environment/suntech-declares-bankruptcy-china-says.html.

59. Eric Wesoff and Stephen Lacey, "Solar Costs Are Hitting Jaw-Dropping Lows in Every Region of the World," *Greentech Media*, June 27, 2017, https://www

.greentechmedia.com/articles/read/solar-costs-are-hitting-jaw-dropping-lows-in-every-region-of-the-world.

60. Lazard, "Lazard's Levelized Cost of Energy Analysis—Version 10.0," December 2016, https://www.lazard.com/media/438038/levelized-cost-of-energy-v100.pdf.

61. Dolf Gielen et al., "Letting in the Light," International Renewable Energy Agency, 2016, http://www.irena.org/DocumentDownloads/Publications/IRENA_Letting_in_the_Light_2016.pdf.

62. Goksin Kavlak, James McNerney, and Jessika Trancik, "Evaluating the Changing Causes of Photovoltaics Cost Reduction," Working Paper, 2017, https://papers.ssrn.com/sol3/papers.cfm?abstract_id=2891516.

63. Jones and Bouamane, "'Power from Sunshine'."

64. Renewable Energy Policy Network, "Renewables 2016: Global Status Report," http://www.ren21.net/wp-content/uploads/2016/06/GSR_2016_Full_Report.pdf.

65. Institute for Energy Economics and Financial Analysis, "2016: Year in Review," http://ieefa.org/wp-content/uploads/2016/11/2016-Year-in-Review.pdf.

66. Stephen Lacey, "Jinko and Marubeni Bid 2.4 Cents to Supply Solar in Abu Dhabi. How Low Can Solar Prices Go?" *Greentech Media,* September 20, 2016, https://www.greentechmedia.com/articles/read/jinko-solar-and-marubeni-bid-2.4-cents-for-solar-power-plant-in-abu-dhabi.

67. Bloomberg New Energy Finance (BNEF), "New Energy Outlook 2017," June 2017, https://www.bloomberg.com/company/new-energy-outlook/.

68. "International Technology Roadmap for Photovoltaics."

69. Jeffrey Ball, Dan Reicher, Xiaojing Sun, and Caitlin Pollock, "The New Solar System: China's Evolving Solar Industry and Its Implications for Competitive Solar Power in the United States and the World," Steyer-Taylor Center for Energy Policy and Finance, Stanford University, March 20, 2017, https://www-cdn.law.stanford.edu/wp-content/uploads/2017/03/2017-03-20-Stanford-China-Report.pdf.

Chapter 3

1. Vera Eckert, "European Power Grids Keep Lights on Through Solar Eclipse," *Reuters*, March 20, 2015, http://www.reuters.com/article/us-solar-eclipse-germany-idUSKBN0MG0S620150321.

2. Alex Perera and Colin McCormick, "Solar Eclipse in Europe Shows Grid Operators Can Be Successful with Renewables," World Resources Institute (WRI), March 31, 2015, http://www.wri.org/blog/2015/03/solar-eclipse-europe-shows-grid-operators-can-be-successful-renewables.

3. Eric Marx, "How Solar-Heavy Europe Avoided a Blackout During Total Eclipse," *Scientific American*, March 24, 2015, https://www.scientificamerican.com/article/how-solar-heavy-europe-avoided-a-blackout-during-total-eclipse.

4. Kerstine Appune and Sven Egenter, "Energiewende Passes Solar Eclipse Stress Test," *Clean Energy Wire*, June 27, 2016, https://www.cleanenergywire.org/news/energiewende-passes-solar-eclipse-stress-test.

5. Stefan Nicola, Weixin Zha, and Lorenzo Totaro, "Solar Age's First Eclipse Passes with Brief Surge in Power Price," *Bloomberg*, March 20, 2015, https://www.bloomberg.com/news/articles/2015-03-20/eclipse-tests-european-power-grid-flooded-by-solar-farms-i7hlfkm0.

6. Soren Amelang and Jakob Schelandt, "Germany's Electricity Grid Stable Amid Energy Transition," *Clean Energy Wire*, October 24, 2016, https://www.cleanenergywire.org/factsheets/germanys-electricity-grid-stable-amid-energy-transition.

7. Amy Gahran, "Germany's Course Correction on Solar Growth," *Greentech Media*, November 3, 2016, https://www.greentechmedia.com/articles/read/germanys-course-correction-on-solar-growth.

8. Fraunhofer ISE, "Recent Facts About Photovoltaics in Germany," Fraunhofer-Gesellschaft, 2017, https://www.ise.fraunhofer.de/en/publications/veroeffentlichungen-pdf-dateien-en/studien-und-konzeptpapiere/recent-facts-about-photovoltaics-in-germany.pdf.

9. Carmine Gallo, "Tesla's Elon Musk Lights Up Social Media with a TED Style Keynote," *Forbes*, May 4, 2015, http://www.forbes.com/sites/carminegallo/2015/05/04/teslas-elon-musk-lights-up-social-media-with-a-ted-style-keynote.

10. "Short-Term Energy Outlook," U.S. Energy Information Administration (EIA), 2017, https://www.eia.gov/outlooks/steo/query.

11. Jesse D. Jenkins and Samuel Thernstrom, "Deep Decarbonization of the Electric Power Sector: Insights from Recent Literature," Energy Innovation Reform Project (EIRP), March 2017, http://innovationreform.org/wp-content/uploads/2017/03/EIRP-Deep-Decarb-Lit-Review-Jenkins-Thernstrom-March-2017.pdf.

12. "Energy Technology Perspectives 2016—Towards Sustainable Urban Energy Systems," International Energy Agency (IEA), June 1, 2016, http://www.iea.org/etp/.

13. Mark Z. Jacobson and Mark A. Delucchi, "Providing All Global Energy with Wind, Water, and Solar Power, Part I: Technologies, Energy Resources, Quantities and Areas of Infrastructure, and Materials," *Energy Policy* 6, no. 3 (March 2011), doi: 10.1016/j.enpol.2010.11.040.

14. Peter J. Loftus et al., "A Critical Review of Global Decarbonization Scenarios: What Do They Tell Us About Feasibility?" *WIREs Climate Change* 6, no. 1 (November 5, 2014), doi: 10.1002/wcc.324.

15. Christopher T. M. Clack et al., "Evaluation of a Proposal for Reliable Low-Cost Grid Power with 100% Wind, Water, and Solar," *PNAS* 114, no. 26 (2017): 6722-6727, doi: 10.1073/pnas.1610381114.

16. International Energy Agency (IEA), "Energy Technology Perspectives 2017," 2017, http://www.iea.org/etp.

17. Diane Cardwell and Jonathan Soble, "Westinghouse Files for Bankruptcy, in Blow to Nuclear Power," *New York Times,* March 29, 2017, https://www.nytimes.com/2017/03/29/business/westinghouse-toshiba-nuclear-bankruptcy.html.

18. Ana Mileva, "Power System Balancing for Deep Decarbonization of the Electricity Sector," *Applied Energy* 162 (January 15, 2016): http://www.sciencedirect.com/science/article/pii/S0306261915014300.

19. Arnulf Grubler, "The Costs of the French Nuclear Scale-up: A Case of Negative Learning by Doing." *Energy Policy* 38, no. 9 (September 2010): http://www.sciencedirect.com/science/article/pii/S0301421510003526

20. Patrick Moriarty and Damon Honnery, "Can Renewable Energy Power the Future?" *Energy Policy* 93 (June 2016): 3–7, doi:10.1016/j.enpol.2016.02.051.

21. Patrick Moriarty and Damon Honnery, "What Is the Global Potential for Renewable Energy?" *Renewable and Sustainable Energy Reviews* 16, no. 1 (January 2012): 244–52, doi:10.1016/j.rser.2011.07.151.

22. Nathan Lewis and Daniel Nocera, "Powering the Planet: Chemical Challenges in Solar Energy Utilization." *Proceedings of the National Academy of Sciences* 103, no. 43 (October 24, 2006): 15729–15735, doi:10.1073/pnas.0603395103.

23. Ellen Thalman, "What German Households Pay for Power," *Clean Energy Wire,* December 21, 2016, https://www.cleanenergywire.org/factsheets/what-german-households-pay-power.

24. Michael Liebreich and Angus McCrone, "The Shift to 'Base-Cost' Renewables: 10 Predictions for 2017," *Bloomberg New Energy Finance,* January 19, 2017, https://about.bnef.com/blog/liebreich-shift-base-cost-renewables-10-predictions-2017/.https://about.bnef.com/blog/liebreich-shift-base-cost-renewables-10-predictions-2017/.

25. Christian Roselund, "BNEF: Global Solar Investment Fell 32% in 2016," *PV Magazine International,* January 12, 2017, https://www.pv-magazine.com/2017/01/12/bnef-global-solar-investment-fell-32-in-2016/.

26. Tom Randall, "World Energy Hits a Turning Point: Solar That's Cheaper Than Wind," *Bloomberg,* December 15, 2016, https://www.bloomberg.com/news/articles/2016-12-15/world-energy-hits-a-turning-point-solar-that-s-cheaper-than-wind.

27. Angus McCrone, "If Interest Rates Turn, Clean Energy Will Find It Tougher," *Bloomberg New Energy Finance*, January 27, 2017, https://about.bnef.com/blog/mccrone-interest-rates-turn-clean-energy-will-find-tougher/.

28. Ethan Zindler and Ken Locklin, "Mapping the Gap: The Road from Paris," *Bloomberg New Energy Finance*, January 27, 2017, https://www.ceres.org/resources/reports/mapping-the-gap-the-road-from-paris/.

29. Global Capital Finance, "The European Renewable Energy Investor Landscape," Clean Energy Pipeline, http://cleanenergypipeline.com/Resources/CE/ResearchReports/The%20European%20Renewable%20Energy%20Investor%20Landscape.pdf.

30. IRENA, "Financial Mechanisms and Investment Frameworks for Renewables in Developing Countries," IRENA, 2012, http://irena.org/Finance_RE_Developing_Countries.pdf.

31. Asian Development Bank (ADB), "ADB to Provide India $500 Million for Solar Rooftop Systems," 2016, https://www.adb.org/news/adb-provide-india-500-million-solar-rooftop-systems.

32. Vivek Sen, Kuldeep Sharma, and Gireesh Shrimali, "Reaching India's Renewable Energy Targets: The Role of Institutional Investors," Climate Policy Initiative (CPI), December 2016, https://climatepolicyinitiative.org/wp-content/uploads/2016/11/Reaching-Indias-Renewable-Energy-Targets-The-Role-of-Institutional-Investors.pdf.

33. Organization for Economic Co-operation and Development (OECD), "Progress Report on Approaches to Mobilising Institutional Investment For Green Infrastructure," September 2016, https://www.oecd.org/cgfi/resources/Progress_Report_on_Approaches_to_Mobilising_Institutional_Investment_for_Green_Infrastructure.pdf.

34. Mark Fulton and Reid Capalino, "Investing in the Clean Trillion: Closing the Clean Energy Investment Gap," Ceres, January 2014, https://www.ceres.org/resources/reports/investing-in-the-clean-trillion-closing-the-clean-energy-investment-gap.

35. Ilmi Granoff, J. Ryan Hogarth, and Alan Miller, "Nested Barriers to Low-Carbon Infrastructure Investment," *Nature Climate Change* 6, no. 12 (April 12, 2016): 1065–1071, doi:10.1038/nclimate3142.

36. Arijit Barman, "Abu Dhabi Sovereign Fund ADIA Eyes $200 Million Investment in Greenko," *The Economic Times*, May 25, 2016, http://economictimes.indiatimes.com/industry/energy/power/abu-dhabi-sovereign-fund-adia-eyes-200-million-investment-in-greenko/articleshow/52441639.cms.

37. The White House, Office of the Press Secretary, "Fact Sheet: Obama Administration Announces More Than $4 Billion in Private-Sector Commitments and Executive Actions to Scale up Investment in Clean Energy Innovation," National Archives and Records Administration, press release, June 16, 2015. https://obamawhitehouse

.archives.gov/the-press-office/2015/06/16/fact-sheet-obama-administration-announces-more-4-billion-private-sector.

38. Nathaniel J. Williams, Paulina Jaramillo, Jay Taneja, and Taha Selim Ustun, "Enabling Private Sector Investment in Microgrid-Based Rural Electrification in Developing Countries: A Review," *Renewable and Sustainable Energy Reviews* 52 (2015): 1268–281, doi:10.1016/j.rser.2015.07.153.

39. The White House. "Catalyzing Global Markets for Off-Grid Energy Access." (Washington DC: National Archives and Records Administration, 2016), https://obamawhitehouse.archives.gov/sites/default/files/docs/catalyzing_global_markets_for_off-grid_energy_access_final_cover.pdf.

40. Robert O'Brien, "Copper Price Fall Bad News for Chile But Not Disaster," *Reuters*, January 15, 2015, http://www.reuters.com/article/chile-copper-economy-idUSL6N0UU4WA20150115.

41. "Oil & Gas Security: Emergency Response of IEA Countries: Chile," International Energy Agency (IEA), 2012, 25.

42. Simon Currie, "Renewable Energy in Latin America: Chile," Norton Rose Fulbright, October 2016, http://www.nortonrosefulbright.com/knowledge/publications/134773/renewable-energy-in-latin-america-chile.

43. Shahriyar Nasirov and Carlos Silva, "Diversification of Chilean Energy Matrix: Recent Developments and Challenges," International Association for Energy Economics (IAEE), 2014, https://www.iaee.org/en/publications/newsletterdl.aspx?id=256.

44. Matt Craze, "Chile's Water Shortage Threatens Wines and Mines," *Bloomberg*, March 10, 2015, http://www.bloomberg.com/news/articles/2015-03-10/wines-to-mines-imperiled-as-chile-fights-california-like-drought/.

45. Ian Clover, "Chile: New 80-MW Merchant Solar Project Announced," *PV Magazine International*, January 12, 2015, https://www.pv-magazine.com/2015/01/12/chile-new-80-mw-merchant-solar-project-announced_100017736/.

46. Vanessa Dezem and Javiera Quiroga, "Chile Has So Much Solar Energy It's Giving It Away for Free," *Bloomberg*, June 01, 2016, https://www.bloomberg.com/news/articles/2016-06-01/chile-has-so-much-solar-energy-it-s-giving-it-away-for-free.

47. Vanessa Dezem, "Solar Sold in Chile at Lowest Ever, Half Price of Coal," *Bloomberg*, August 19, 2016, https://www.bloomberg.com/news/articles/2016-08-19/solar-sells-in-chile-for-cheapest-ever-at-half-the-price-of-coal.

48. Bentham Paulos, "How Wind and Solar Will Blow up Power Markets," *Greentech Media*, August 11, 2015, https://www.greentechmedia.com/articles/read/how-wind-and-solar-will-blow-up-power-markets.

49. Lion Hirth, "What Caused the Drop in European Electricity Prices?" USAEE Working Paper No. 16–282, November 23, 2016, https://ssrn.com/abstract=2874841

50. Soren Amelang and Julian Wettengal, "E.ON Shareholders Ratify Energy Giant's Split," Clean Energy Wire, June 9, 2016, https://www.cleanenergywire.org/factsheets/eon-shareholders-ratify-energy-giants-split.

51. Soren Amelang and Julian Wettengal, "RWE's Plans for New Renewable Subsidiary," Clean Energy Wire, June 5, 2016, https://www.cleanenergywire.org/factsheets/rwes-plans-new-renewable-subsidiary

52. Michael Kraus, "Almost a Reform: The New German Support Scheme for Renewable Electricity," Oxera, August 2014, http://www.oxera.com/Latest-Thinking/Agenda/2014/Almost-a-reform-the-new-German-support-scheme-for.aspx.

53. Varun Sivaram and Shayle Kann, "Solar Power Needs a More Ambitious Cost Target," *Nature Energy* 1, no. 4 (April 7, 2016): doi:10.1038/nenergy.2016.36.

54. Stefano Clò and Gaetano D'adamo, "The Dark Side of the Sun: How Solar Power Production Affects the Market Value of Solar and Gas Sources," *Energy Economics* 49 (May 2015): 523–530, doi:10.1016/j.eneco.2015.03.025.

55. Ivan Penn, "California Invested Heavily in Solar Power. Now There's so Much that Other States are Sometimes Paid to Take It," *Los Angeles Times,* June 22, 2017, http://www.latimes.com/projects/la-fi-electricity-solar/.

56. Peter Philips, "Environmental and Economic Benefits of Building Solar in California," Institute for Research on Labor and Employment at the University of California, Berkeley, November 10, 2014, http://laborcenter.berkeley.edu/pdf/2014/building-solar-ca14.pdf.

57. Intertek APTECH, "Power Plant Cycling Costs," National Renewable Energy Laboratory (NREL), 2012, AES 12047831–2-1, http://wind.nrel.gov/public/wwis/aptechfinalv2.pdf.

58. Lion Hirth, Falko Ueckerdt, and Ottmar Edenhofer, "Integration Costs Revisited—An Economic Framework for Wind and Solar Variability," *Renewable Energy* 74 (February 2015): 925–939, doi:10.1016/j.renene.2014.08.065.

59. Bentham Paulos, "Too Much of a Good Thing? An Illustrated Guide to Solar Curtailment on California's Grid," *Greentech Media,* April 3, 2017, https://www.greentechmedia.com/articles/read/An-Illustrated-Guide-to-Solar-Curtailment-in-California.

60. Sara Shapiro-Bengtsen, "Reducing Renewables Curtailment in China—An Air Quality Measure," Regulatory Assistance Project, April 5, 2017, http://www.raponline.org/blog/reducing-renewables-curtailment-china-air-quality-measure.

61. "Renewables Get Mature," *Nature Energy* 2, no. 2 (2017): 17017, doi:10.1038/nenergy.2017.17.

62. Paul Denholm, Kara Clark, and Matt O'Connell, "On the Path to SunShot: Emerging Issues and Challenges in Integrating High Levels of Solar into the Electrical Generation and Transmission System," NREL, 2016, NREL/TP-6A20–65800, http://www.nrel.gov/docs/fy16osti/65800.pdf.

63. Jan Von Appen, M. Braun, T. Stetz, K. Diwold, and D. Geibel, "Time in the Sun: The Challenge of High PV Penetration in the German Electric Grid," *IEEE Power and Energy Magazine* 11, no. 2 (March/April 2013): 55–64, doi:10.1109/mpe.2012.2234407.

64. Bryan Bollinger and Kenneth Gillingham, "Learning-by-Doing in Solar otovoltaic Installations," Yale University Working Paper, 2014, http://environment.yale.edu/gillingham/BollingerGillingham_SolarLBD.pdf.

65. Varun Sivaram and Shayle Kann, "Solar Power Needs a More Ambitious Cost Target," *Nature Energy* 1, no. 4 (April 7, 2016): doi:10.1038/nenergy.2016.36.

66. N.W. Miller, M. Shao, S. Pajic, and R. D'Aquila, "Western Wind and Solar Integration Study Phase 3—Frequency Response and Transient Stability," NREL, 2014, NREL/SR-5D00–62906, http://www.nrel.gov/docs/fy15osti/62906.pdf

67. International Renewable Energy Agency (IRENA), "Renewable Energy in the Water, Energy & Food Nexus," 2015, http://www.irena.org/DocumentDownloads/Publications/IRENA_Water_Energy_Food_Nexus_2015.pdf.

68. Paul Denholm and Robert Margolis, "Energy Storage Requirements for Achieving 50% Solar Photovoltaic Energy Penetration in California," National Renewable Energy Laboratory (NREL), 2016, NREL/TP-6A20–66595, http://www.nrel.gov/docs/fy16osti/66595.pdf.

69. U.S. Department of Energy (DOE), "Grid Energy Storage," December 2013, https://energy.gov/sites/prod/files/2014/09/f18/Grid%20Energy%20Storage%20December%202013.pdf.

70. Andrew D. Mills and Ryan H. Wiser, "Strategies to Mitigate Declines in the Economic Value of Wind and Solar at High Penetration in California," *Applied Energy* 147 (2015): 269–278, doi: 10.1016/j.apenergy.2015.03.014.

Chapter 4

1. Renewable Energy Policy Network for the 21st Century (REN21), "Renewables 2015 Global Status Report," http://www.ren21.net/wp-content/uploads/2015/07/REN12-GSR2015_Onlinebook_low1.pdf.

2. Christopher Martin, "SunEdison Emerging as Solar 'Supermajor' with $2.2 Billion Deal," *Bloomberg*, July 20, 2015, https://www.bloomberg.com/news/articles/2015-07-20/sunedison-agrees-to-acquire-vivint-solar-for-2-2-billion.

3. Antoine Gara, "SunEdison's Big Slide: When Financial Engineering Goes Wrong," *Forbes*, November 13, 2015, http://www.forbes.com/sites/antoinegara/2015/11/13/sunedisons-big-slide-when-financial-engineering-goes-wrong/.

4. Stephen Foley and Ed Crooks, "SunEdison: Death of a Solar Star," *Financial Times*, April 21, 2016, https://www.ft.com/content/04fca062-07a3-11e6-a70d-4e39ac32c284.

5. Angus McCrone and Michael Liebreich, "Yieldcos—Two Big Questions," *Bloomberg New Energy Finance*, July 30, 2015, https://about.bnef.com/blog/mccrone-liebreich-yieldcos-two-big-questions/.

6. Tom Hals, "TerraForm Global Sues SunEdison, Says Misappropriated $231 Million," *Reuters*, April 4, 2016, http://www.reuters.com/article/us-terraform-sunedison-lawsuit-idUSKCN0X11UC.

7. Lewis Milford, Devashree Saha, Mark Muro, Robert Sanders, and Toby Rittner, "Clean Energy Finance Through the Bond Market: A New Option for Progress," Brookings-Rockefeller, April 2014, https://www.cdfa.net/cdfa/cdfaweb.nsf/ord/brookings-cdfa-ceg-041614.html/$file/CleanEnergyFunds.pdf.

8. E. Cabell Massey, "Master Limited Partnerships: A Pipeline to Renewable Energy Development," University of Colorado Law School, April 11, 2016, http://lawreview.colorado.edu/wp-content/uploads/2016/01/12.-87.3-Massey_Final.pdf.

9. Preqin, "Global Infrastructure Report." 2017, https://www.preqin.com/item/2017-preqin-global-infrastructure-report/4/16507.

10. Antoine Gara, "Blackstone Unveils $40 Billion Infrastructure Mega Fund with Saudi Arabia as President Trump Visits," *Forbes*, May 20, 2017, https://www.forbes.com/sites/antoinegara/2017/05/20/blackstone-unveils-40-billion-infrastructure-mega-fund-with-saudi-arabia-as-trump-visits/.

11. Felix Mormann and Dan Reicher, "Smarter Finance for Cleaner Energy: Open up Master Limited Partnerships (MLPs) and Real Estate Investment Trusts (REITs) to Renewable Energy Investment," Brookings Institute, November 2012, https://www.brookings.edu/wp-content/uploads/2016/06/13-clean-energy-investment.pdf.

12. Ehren Goossens, "Market 'Saturated' by Yieldcos After 15 IPOs, Says NRG Yield CEO," *Bloomberg*, August 5, 2015, https://www.bloomberg.com/news/articles/2015-08-05/market-saturated-by-yieldcos-after-15-ipos-says-nrg-yield-ceo.

13. Ernst & Young, "The YieldCo Structure: Unlocking the Value in Power Generation Assets," Ernst & Young Global Limited, 2015, http://www.ey.com/Publication/vwLUAssets/ey-yieldco-brochure/$FILE/ey-yieldco-brochure.pdf.

14. Christopher Martin, "SunEdison Thirst for Yield Growth Drove $2.2 Billion Vivint Deal," *Bloomberg Technology*, July 21, 2015, https://www.bloomberg.com/news/articles/2015-07-21/sunedison-thirst-for-yield-growth-drove-2-2-billion-vivint-deal.

15. Tom Konrad, "The YieldCo Boom and Bust: The Consequences of Greed and a Return to Normalcy," *Greentech Media*, May 13, 2016, https://www.greentechmedia.com/articles/read/the-yieldco-boom-and-bust-the-consequences-of-greed.

16. John Dizard, "Yieldcos Have Caught Some Terrible Money Plague," *Financial Times*, September 11, 2015, https://www.ft.com/content/a1811362-5873-11e5-a28b-50226830d644.

17. Varun Sivaram, "Oil's Downward Spiral Is Spooking Renewable Energy Investors," *Fortune*, September 5, 2015, fortune.com/2015/09/05/oil-prices-renewable-energy-yieldcos.

18. Uday Varadarajan, David Nelson, Andrew Goggins, and Morgan Hervé-Mignucci, "Beyond YieldCos," Climate Policy Initiative (CPI), June, 2016, http://climatepolicyinitiative.org/wp-content/uploads/2016/06/Beyond-YieldCos-1.pdf.

19. Ronald Barusch, "Dealpolitik: Governance Was a Casualty of SunEdison's Financial Crisis," *The Wall Street Journal*, April 15, 2016, http://blogs.wsj.com/moneybeat/2016/04/15/dealpolitik-governance-was-a-casualty-of-sunedisons-financial-crisis.

20. "Financing India's Clean Energy Transition," Bloomberg New Energy Finance, November 1, 2016, https://www.bbhub.io/bnef/sites/4/2016/10/BNEF-Financing-Indias-clean-energy-transition.pdf.

21. Uday Varadarajan, David Nelson, Andrew Goggins, and Morgan Hervé-Mignucci, "Beyond YieldCos," Climate Policy Initiative, June 2016, https://climatepolicyinitiative.org/publication/beyond-yieldcos.

22. Richard Matsui, "Yieldcos, a Modern Solar Shakespearean Play," *PV Magazine*, May 16, 2017, https://pv-magazine-usa.com/2017/05/16/op-ed-yieldcos-a-modern-solar-shakespearean-play.

23. David C. Magagna, "Congress, Give Renewable Energy a Fair Fight: Passage of the Master Limited Partnerships Parity Act Would Give Renewable Energy the Financial Footing Needed to Independently Succeed," *Villanova Environmental Law Journal* 27 (2016): 149, http://digitalcommons.law.villanova.edu/elj/vol27/iss1/6.

24. Francis M. O'Sullivan and Charles H. Warren, "Solar Securitization: An Innovation in Renewable Energy Finance," MIT Energy Initiative Working Paper, July 2016, https://energy.mit.edu/wp-content/uploads/2016/07/MITEI-WP-2016-05.pdf.

25. Spriha Srivastava, "This Is the Next Subprime Fear Worrying Investors," *CNBC*, April 7, 2017, http://www.cnbc.com/2017/04/07/subprime-mortgage-autos-ubs-us.html.

26. Ann Carrns, "New Cars Are Too Expensive for the Typical Family, Study Finds," *The New York Times*, July 1, 2016, https://www.nytimes.com/2016/07/02/your-money/new-cars-are-too-expensive-for-the-typical-family-study-finds.html?_r=0.

27. Center for Sustainable Energy (CSE). "How Much Does a Typical Residential Solar Electric System Cost?" December 19, 2016, https://energycenter.org/solar/homeowners/cost.

28. Mike Munsell, "Direct Ownership of Solar Will Overtake Leasing in the US by 2017," *Greentech Media*, November 15, 2016, https://www.greentechmedia.com/articles/read/us-residential-solar-purchases-will-overtake-leasing-in-2017.

29. Drew Hyde and Paul Komor, "Distributed PV and Securitization: Made for Each Other?" *Electricity Journal* 27, no. 5 (2014): 63–70, doi:10.1016/j.tej.2014.05.002.

30. Pieter Gagnon, Robert Margolis, Jennifer Melius, Caleb Phillips, and Ryan Elmore, "Rooftop Solar Photovoltaic Technical Potential in the United States: A Detailed Assessment," National Renewable Energy Laboratory (NREL), 2016, http://www.nrel.gov/docs/fy16osti/65298.pdf.

31. Travis Lowder, Paul Schwabe, Ella Zhou, and Douglas J. Arent, "Historical and Current U.S. Strategies for Boosting Distributed Generation," National Renewable Energy Laboratory (NREL), 2015, http://www.nrel.gov/docs/fy16osti/64843.pdf.

32. Solar Energy Industry Association (SEIA), "Expanding Solar Deployment Opportunities in the C&I Sector," November 2016, http://www.seia.org/sites/default/files/resources/SEIA-CPACE_Expanding_Solar_Deployment_CI_Sector_April2017.pdf.

33. Sandeep Gupta, Jai Sharda, and Gireesh Shrimali, "The Drivers and Challenges of Third-Party Financing for Rooftop Solar Power in India," Climate Policy Initiative (CPI), September 2016, https://climatepolicyinitiative.org/wp-content/uploads/2016/09/The-Drivers-and-Challenges-of-Third-Party-Financing-for-Rooftop-Solar-Power-in-India.pdf.

34. Danielle Ola, "US Solar Market Maturity Means Securitisation on the Horizon," *PV-Tech*, September 22, 2016, http://www.pv-tech.org/news/us-solar-market-maturity-means-securitisation-on-the-horizon.

35. Frank Andorka, "Mosaic Secures Investor Support for Residential Loan Portfolio," *PV International*, February 10, 2017, https://www.pv-magazine.com/2017/02/10/mosaic-secures-investor-support-for-residential-loan-portfolio/.

36. O'Sullivan and Warren, "Solar Securitization: An Innovation in Renewable Energy Finance."

37. Labanya Prakash Jena, Vinit Atal, Dr. Gireesh Shrimali, and Vivek Sen. "Rooftop Solar Private Sector Financing Facility," India Innovation Lab for Green Finance, http://greenfinancelab.in/idea/rooftop-solar-private-sector-financing-facility.

38. Galen L. Barbose and Naïm R. Darghouth, "Tracking the Sun IX: The Installed Price of Residential and Non-Residential Photovoltaic Systems in the United States,"

Lawrence Berkeley National Laboratory, August 2016, https://emp.lbl.gov/publications /tracking-sun-ix-installed-price.

39. Jason Kaminsky, "Can Data Rescue Solar Stocks? Google Is Leading the Way," *Greentech Media*, March 9, 2016, https://www.greentechmedia.com/articles/read/Can -Data-Rescue-Solar-Stocks-Google-is-Leading-the-Way.

40. Ben Gallagher, "U.S. PV System Pricing H2 2016: System Pricing, Breakdowns, and Forecasts," GTM Research, November 2016, https://www.greentechmedia.com /research/report/us-solar-pv-system-pricing-h2-2016.

41. M. A. Cohen, P. A. Kauzmann, and D. S. Callaway, "Effects of Distributed PV Generation on California's Distribution System, Part 2: Economic Analysis," *Solar Energy* 128 (2016): 139–152, doi:10.1016/j.solener.2016.01.004.

42. Ignacio Pérez-Arriaga and Christopher Knittel, "Utility of the Future," MIT Energy Initiative Working Paper, 2016, https://energy.mit.edu/wp-content/uploads /2016/12/Utility-of-the-Future-Full-Report.pdf.

43. Michael Cragg, Richard Goldberg, Varoujan Khatchatrian, and Jehan DeFonseka, "Cleaning up Spark Spreads," The Brattle Group, March 2011, http://www.brattle .com/system/publications/pdfs/000/004/693/original/Cleaning_Up_Spark_Spreads _-_How_Plant_Owners_Can_Reduce_Risk_Through_Carbon_Markets_March_2011 .pdf?1378772120.

44. Richard Matsui, Jason Kaminsky, and Jared Blanton, "New Product: Solar Revenue Puts Project Finance," Chadbourne & Parke LLP, October 2016, https://www .chadbourne.com/new-product-solar-revenue-puts-project-finance-october-2016.

45. Travis Bradford, Peter Davidson, Lawrence Rodman, and David Sandalow, "Financing Solar and Wind Power: Insights from Oil and Gas," Columbia University Center for Global Energy Policy, 2017, http://energypolicy.columbia.edu/sites/default /files/energy/Financing%20Solar%20and%20Wind%20Power.pdf.

46. Mark Clifford, "Hong Kong Utility Executive on Paris Climate Talks: 'The World Doesn't Want Another Failure,'" *Forbes*, October 19, 2015, http://www.forbes.com /sites/mclifford/2015/10/12/hong-kong-utility-executive-on-paris-climate-talks-the -world-doesnt-want-another-failure.

47. CLP Holdings Limited, "Operating Information," 2014, https://www.clpgroup .com/en/investors-information/quick-facts/operating-information.

48. Travis Bradford, Peter Davidson, Lawrence Rodman, and David Sandalow. "Financing Solar and Wind Power: Insights from Oil and Gas," Columbia University Center on Global Energy Policy, March 2017, http://energypolicy.columbia.edu/sites /default/files/energy/Financing%20Solar%20and%20Wind%20Power.pdf.

49. Mike Munsell, "America's Community Solar Market Will Surpass 400MW in 2017," *Greentech Media*, February 6, 2017, https://www.greentechmedia.com/articles/read/us-community-solar-market-to-surpass-400-mw-in-2017.

50. Michael Wara, "Competition at the Grid Edge: Innovation and Antitrust Law in the Electricity Sector," *New York University Environmental Law Journal* 25, no. 2 (2016): https://ssrn.com/abstract=2765502.

51. Eric Wesoff, "Report: How Much Does a Solar PV System Cost in 2016?" *Greentech Media*, November 30, 2016, https://www.greentechmedia.com/articles/read/Report-How-much-does-a-solar-PV-system-cost-in-2016.

52. Can Sener and Vasilis Fthenakis, "Energy Policy and Financing Options to Achieve Solar Energy Grid Penetration Targets: Accounting for External Costs," *Renewable and Sustainable Energy Reviews* 32 (2014): 854–68, doi:10.1016/j.rser.2014.01.030.

53. "On Bill Energy Efficiency Repayment Plan," Environmental Defense Fund, 2011, http://blogs.edf.org/energyexchange/files/2011/09/On-Bill-Repayment-Summary.pdf.

54. Herman K. Trabish, "How Record Large-Scale Solar Growth Is Changing Utility IPPs," Utility Dive, July 21, 2016, http://www.utilitydive.com/news/how-record-large-scale-solar-growth-is-changing-utility-ipps/422726.

55. Tim Buckley and Simon Nicholas, "2016: Year in Review," Institute for Energy Economics and Financial Analysis (IEEFA), November 2016, http://ieefa.org/wp-content/uploads/2016/11/2016-Year-in-Review.pdf.

56. Tim Buckley and Simon Nicholas, "China's Global Renewable Energy Expansion," Institute for Energy Economics and Financial Analysis (IEEFA), January 2017, http://ieefa.org/wp-content/uploads/2017/01/Chinas-Global-Renewable-Energy-Expansion_January-2017.pdf.

57. Andrew Mulherkar, "Google, Amazon, and Apple Are Forging the Future of Corporate Energy Management," *Greentech Media*, July 8, 2016, https://www.greentechmedia.com/articles/read/What-Google-Amazon-and-Apples-Recent-Moves-Reveal-About-the-Future-of-Cor.

58. Julian Spector, "How MGM Prepared Itself to Leave Nevada's Biggest Utility," *Greentech Media*, September 16, 2016, https://www.greentechmedia.com/articles/read/How-MGM-Prepared-Itself-to-Leave-Nevadas-Biggest-Utility.

59. Julia Pyper, "Large Corporations Are Driving America's Renewable Energy Boom. And They're Just Getting Started," *Greentech Media*, January 10, 2017, https://www.greentechmedia.com/articles/read/Large-Corporations-Are-Driving-Americas-Renewable-Energy-Boom.

60. Aaron Bielenberg, Mike Kerlin, Jeremy Oppenheim, and Melissa Roberts. "Financing Change: How to Mobilize Private-Sector Financing for Sustainable Infrastructure," McKinsey & Co., January 2016, https://councilcommunity.files.wordpress.com/2016/03/financing_change_how_to_mobilize_private-sector_financing_for_sustainable-_infrastructure.pdf.

61. Christopher Kaminker and Fiona Stewart, "The Role of Institutional Investors in Financing Clean Energy," OECD Working Papers on Finance, Insurance and Private Pensions 23, August 2012, http://www.oecd.org/environment/WP_23_TheRoleOfInstitutionalInvestorsInFinancingCleanEnergy.pdf.

62. "Unlocking Renewable Energy Investment: The Role of Risk Mitigation and Structured Finance," International Renewable Energy Agency (IRENA), 2016, https://www.irena.org/DocumentDownloads/Publications/IRENA_Risk_Mitigation_and_Structured_Finance_2016.pdf.

63. Project Finance International (PFI), "The Innovative Seven Sisters," Thompson Reuters, 2015, http://www.pfie.com/the-innovative-seven-sisters/21177319.fullarticle.

64. "What Are Green Bonds?" World Bank Group (WBG), 2015, http://treasury.worldbank.org/cmd/pdf/What_are_Green_Bonds.pdf.

65. Climate Bonds Initiative, "Bonds and Climate Change the State of the Market in 2016," Hongkong and Shanghai Banking Corporation (HSBC) Limited, 2016, https://www.climatebonds.net/files/files/reports/cbi-hsbc-state-of-the-market-2016.pdf.

66. Swarnalakshmi Umamaheswaran and Seth Rajiv, "Financing Large-Scale Wind and Solar Projects—A Review of Emerging Experiences in the Indian Context," *Renewable and Sustainable Energy Reviews* 48 (2015): 166–177, doi:10.1016/j.rser.2015.02.054.

67. Arsalan Ali Farooquee and Gireesh Shrimali, "Reaching India's Renewable Energy Targets Cost-Effectively: A Foreign Exchange Hedging Facility," Climate Policy Initiative (CPI), June 2015, https://climatepolicyinitiative.org/wp-content/uploads/2015/06/Reaching-Indias-Renewable-Energy-Targets-Foreign-Exchange-Hedging-Facility_Technical-Paper.pdf.

Chapter 5

1. "Off-Grid Electric: Overview." Crunchbase, Inc. 2017, https://www.crunchbase.com/organization/off-grid-electric#/entity.

2. Varun Mehra, "Mobile Money: The Answer to Sustaining Revenue for Off-Grid Energy Service Providers?" The Energy Collective, November 20, 2015, http://www.theenergycollective.com/vmehra813/2286309/mobile-money-answer-sustaining-revenue-grid-energy-service-providers.

3. "Off-Grid and Mini-Grid: Q1 2017 Market Outlook," *Bloomberg New Energy Finance,* January 5, 2017, https://about.bnef.com/blog/off-grid-mini-grid-q1-2017-market-outlook/.

4. Saule Baurzhan and Glenn P. Jenkins, "Off-Grid Solar PV: Is It an Affordable or Appropriate Solution for Rural Electrification in Sub-Saharan African Countries?" *Renewable and Sustainable Energy Reviews* 60 (2016): 1405–1418, doi:10.1016/j.rser.2016.03.016.

5. Todd Moss and Benjamin Leo, "Maximizing Access to Energy: Estimates of Access and Generation for the Overseas Private Investment Corporation's Portfolio," Center for Global Development, January 2014, https://www.cgdev.org/publication/maximizing-access-energy-estimates-access-and-generation-overseas-private-investment.

6. Michael A. Levi, "Is U.S. Fossil Fuel Policy Keeping Millions Poor?" *Energy, Security, and Climate Blog, Council on Foreign Relations,* February 10, 2014, https://wwwhttps://www.cfr.org/blog/us-fossil-fuel-policy-keeping-millions-poor.

7. Mark Caine et al., "Our High Energy Planet," Breakthrough Institute, April 2014, http://thebreakthrough.org/images/pdfs/Our-High-Energy-Planet.pdf.

8. Morgan Bazilian and Roger Pielke, "Making Energy Access Meaningful," *Issues in Science and Technology* 29 (4): 74–78, http://sciencepolicy.colorado.edu/admin/publication_files/2013.22.pdf.

9. Ted Nordhaus, Shaiyra Devi, and Alex Trembath, "Debunking Microenergy: The Future Lies with Urbanization," *Foreign Affairs,* August 2016, https://www.foreignaffairs.com/articles/2016-08-30/debunking-microenergy.

10. Peter Alstone, Dimitry Gershenson, and Daniel M. Kammen, "Decentralized Energy Systems for Clean Electricity Access," *Nature Climate Change* 5, no. 4 (2015): 305–314, doi:10.1038/nclimate2512.

11. Sudeshna Ghosh Banerjee, Alejandro Moreno, Jonathan Sinton, Tanya Primiani, and Joonkyung Seong, "Regulatory Indicators for Sustainable Energy: A Global Scorecard for Policy Makers 2016," World Bank Group (WBG), 2016, http://documents.worldbank.org/curated/en/538181487106403375/pdf/112828-REVISED-PUBLIC-RISE-2016-Report.pdf.

12. Anton Eberhard, Katharine Gratwick, Elvira Morella, and Pedro Antmann, "Accelerating Investments in Power in Sub-Saharan Africa," *Nature Energy* 2 (2017): doi:10.1038/nenergy.2017.5, http://www.nature.com/articles/nenergy20175.

13. International Energy Agency (IEA), *Africa Energy Outlook,* 2014, https://www.iea.org/publications/freepublications/publication/WEO2014_AfricaEnergyOutlook.pdf.

14. Global Off-Grid Lighting Association (GOGLA), "Global Off-Grid Solar Market Report Semi-Annual Sales and Impact Data," October 2016, https://www.gogla.org

/sites/default/files/recource_docs/global_off-grid_solar_market_report_jan-june_2016_public.pdf.

15. PricewaterhouseCoopers (PwC), "Electricity Beyond the Grid," May 2016, https://www.pwc.com/gx/en/energy-utilities-mining/pdf/electricity-beyond-grid.pdf.

16. Bloomberg New Energy Finance (BNEF), Lighting Global, and Global Off-Grid Lighting Association, "Off-Grid Market Trends Report 2016," February 2016, http://www.energynet.co.uk/webfm_send/1690.

17. Shahriar Chowdhury, Shakila Aziz, Sebastian Groh, Hannes Kirchhoff, and Walter Leal Filho, "Off-Grid Rural Area Electrification Through Solar-Diesel Hybrid Minigrids in Bangladesh: Resource-Efficient Design Principles in Practice," *Journal of Cleaner Production* 95 (2015): 194–202, doi:10.1016/j.jclepro.2015.02.062.

18. Global Off-Grid Lighting Association (GOGLA), "Global Off-Grid Solar Market Report Semi-Annual Sales and Impact Data."

19. World Bank Group (WBG), "Solar Program Brings Electricity to Off-the-Grid Rural Areas in Bangladesh," October 12, 2016, http://www.worldbank.org/en/news/feature/2016/10/10/solar-program-brings-electricity-off-grid-rural-areas.

20. Shahidur R. Khandker et al., *Surge in Solar-Powered Homes: Experience in Off-Grid Rural Bangladesh* (Washington, DC: World Bank Group, 2014).

21. Several firms may have independently conceived the PAYG model, and it is difficult to determine which was first. For example, Robert Trezona, a British venture capitalist, recounted to me a 2010 board meeting for the East African start-up Azuri in which the founders presented the idea of using mobile payments to implement the PAYG model.

22. Stephan Faris, "The Solar Company Making a Profit on Poor Africans," *Bloomberg*, December 2, 2015, https://www.bloomberg.com/features/2015-mkopa-solar-in-africa/.

23. Sam Pothecary, "New Solar Frontiers: Unconnected Africa," *PV Magazine*, June 2016, https://www.pv-magazine.com/magazine-archive/new-solar-frontiers-unconnected-africa_100025029/.

24. Ijeoma Onyeji-Nwogu, Todd Moss, and Morgan Bazilian, "The Digital Transformation and Disruptive Technologies: Challenges and Solutions for the Electricity Sector in African Markets," Center for Global Development, May 30, 2017, https://www.cgdev.org/sites/default/files/challenges-and-solutions-electricity-sector-african-markets-final.pdf.

25. P. Sharath Chandra Rao, Jeffrey B. Miller, Young Doo Wang, and John B. Byrne, "Energy-Microfinance Intervention for Below-Poverty-Line Households in India," *Energy Policy* 37, no. 5 (2009): 1694–1712, doi:10.1016/j.enpol.2008.12.039.

26. Subhes C. Bhattacharyya, "Financing Energy Access and Off-Grid Electrification: A Review of Status, Options and Challenges," *Renewable and Sustainable Energy Reviews* 20 (2013): 462–472, doi:10.1016/j.rser.2012.12.008.

27. Justin Guay, "The World's First Securitization of Off-Grid Solar Assets," *Greentech Media*, December 17, 2015, https://www.greentechmedia.com/articles/read/the-worlds-first-securitization-of-off-grid-solar-assets.

28. Muthukumara Mani, *Assessing the Investment Climate for Climate Investments: A Comparative Framework for Clean Energy Investments in South Asia in a Global Context* (Washington, DC: World Bank, 2012).

29. James Crabtree, "India's Newly-Licensed Banks Carry Potential Seeds of Revolution," *Financial Times*, October 11, 2015, https://www.ft.com/content/fa50b6b2-6072-11e5-9846-de406ccb37f2.

30. Sevea Association, "Case Study Simpa," January 2013, http://www.seveaconsulting.com/wp-content/uploads/2016/02/Case_study_Simpa.pdf.

31. Paras Loomba, Sonal Asgotraa, and Robin Podmore, "DC Solar Micro-Grids—A Successful Technology for Rural Sustainable Development," *2016 IEEE PES PowerAfrica* (2016): doi:10.1109/powerafrica.2016.7556601.

32. Rohit Sen and Subhes C. Bhattacharyya, "Off-Grid Electricity Generation with Renewable Energy Technologies in India: An Application of HOMER," *Renewable Energy* 62 (2014): 388–398, doi:10.1016/j.renene.2013.07.028.

33. Ruud Kempener et al., *Off-Grid Renewable Energy Systems: Status and Methodological Issues* (Abu Dhabi: IRENA, 2015), http://www.irena.org/DocumentDownloads/Publications/IRENA_Off-grid_Renewable_Systems_WP_2015.pdf.

34. World Bank Group (WBG), "Scaling up Access to Electricity: Pay-as-You-Go Plans in Off-Grid Energy Services," 2015, http://documents.worldbank.org/curated/en/687851468320946678/pdf/937860REPF0BRI0ries00000LW150340OKR.pdf.

35. Kartikeya Singh, "Business Innovation and Diffusion of Off-Grid Solar Technologies in India," *Energy for Sustainable Development* 30 (2016): 1–13, doi:10.1016/j.esd.2015.10.011.

36. Neeraj Ramchandran, Rajesh Pai, and Amit Kumar Singh Parihar, "Feasibility Assessment of Anchor-Business-Community Model for Off-Grid Rural Electrification in India," *Renewable Energy* 97 (2016): 197–209, doi:10.1016/j.renene.2016.05.036.

37. "Solar Microgrid Firm Vies for Kenya's Last Mile Power Customers," *Reuters*, July 10, 2015, http://sustainability.thomsonreuters.com/2015/07/10/solar-microgrid-firm-vies-for-kenyas-last-mile-power-customers/.

38. Ashok Jhunjhunwala, "Innovative Direct-Current Micro-Grids to Solve India's Power Woes," *IEEE Spectrum: Technology, Engineering, and Science News*, January 31,

2017, http://spectrum.ieee.org/energy/renewables/innovative-direct-current-microgrids-to-solve-indias-power-woes.

39. Varun Mehra, "Optimal Sizing of Solar and Battery Assets in Decentralized Micro-Grids with Demand-Side Management," Master's thesis, Massachusetts Institute of Technology, Cambridge, MA, 2017.

40. Amol A. Phadke et al., "Powering a Home with Just 25 Watts of Solar PV. Super-Efficient Appliances Can Enable Expanded Off-Grid Energy Service Using Small Solar Power Systems," *Lawrence Berkeley National Laboratory* (2015): doi:10.2172/1229861.

41. Ashok Jhunjhunwala, Krishna Vasudevan, Lakshmi Narasamma, and Bhaskar Ramamurthi, "Technological and Deployment Challenges and User-Response to Uninterrupted DC (UDC) Deployment in Indian Homes," *IEEE* (2015): doi:10.1109/ICDCM.2015.7152006.

42. The Secretary General's Advisory Group on Energy and Climate Change (AGECC), "Energy for a Sustainable Future," United Nations, April 28, 2010, http://www.un.org/millenniumgoals/pdf/AGECCsummaryreport[1].pdf.

43. Michaël Aklin, Chao-Yo Cheng, Johannes Urpelainen, Karthik Ganesan, and Abhishek Jain, "Factors Affecting Household Satisfaction with Electricity Supply in Rural India," *Nature Energy* 1, no. 11 (2016): 16170, doi:10.1038/nenergy.2016.170.

44. Santosh M. Harish, Kaveri K. Iychettira, Shuba V. Raghavan, and Milind Kandlikar, "Adoption of Solar Home Lighting Systems in India: What Might We Learn from Karnataka?" *Energy Policy* 62 (2013): 697–706, doi:10.1016/j.enpol.2013.07.085.

45. Ashok Jhunjhunwala, "Innovative Direct-Current Micro-Grids to Solve India's Power Woes," *IEEE Spectrum: Technology, Engineering, and Science News*, January 31, 2017, http://spectrum.ieee.org/energy/renewables/innovative-direct-current-microgrids-to-solve-indias-power-woes.

46. Hannes Kirchhoff, Noara Kebir, Kirsten Neumann, Peter W. Heller, and Kai Strunz, "Developing Mutual Success Factors and Their Application to Swarm Electrification: Micro-Grids with 100% Renewable Energies in the Global South and Germany," *Journal of Cleaner Production* 128 (2016): 190–200, doi:10.1016/j.jclepro.2016.03.080.

47. Sebastian Groh and Mathias Koepke, "A System Complexity Approach to Swarm Electrification," University College London, 2015, http://discovery.ucl.ac.uk/1469412/1/283-290.pdf.

48. Sara Baidei, "'Swarm Electrification' in Bangladesh Lets Neighbours Swap Solar Electricity," *Motherboard*, November 29, 2016, https://motherboard.vice.com/en_us/article/mesolshare-rural-bangladesh-swarm-electrification-off-the-grid.

49. Bloomberg New Energy Finance (BNEF) "Off-Grid Market Trends Report 2016," *Bloomberg New Energy Finance and Lighting Global in cooperation with the Global Off-Grid Lighting Association,* February 2016, http://www.energynet.co.uk/webfm_send/1690.

50. Stephen D. Comello, Stefan J. Reichelstein, Anshuman Sahoo, and Tobias S. Schmidt, "Enabling Mini-Grid Development in Rural India," *World Development* 93 (2017): 94-107, doi: 10.1016/j.worlddev.2016.12.029.

51. Bernard Tenenbaum, Chris Greacen, Tilak Siyambalapitiya, and James Knuckles, *From the Bottom Up: How Small Power Producers and Mini-Grids Can Deliver Electrification and Renewable Energy in Africa* (Washington, DC: World Bank Group, 2014), https://openknowledge.worldbank.org/bitstream/handle/10986/16571/9781464800931.pdf?sequence=1&isAllowed=y.

52. Bloomberg New Energy Finance, "Q1 2017 Off-Grid and Mini-Grid Market Outlook," January 18, 2017, https://data.bloomberglp.com/bnef/sites/14/2017/01/BNEF-2017-01-05-Q1-2017-Off-grid-and-Mini-grid-Market-Outlook.pdf.

53. Dimitrios Mentis et al., "A GIS-Based Approach for Electrification Planning—A Case Study on Nigeria," *Energy for Sustainable Development* 29 (2015): 142–150, doi:10.1016/j.esd.2015.09.007.

54. Varun Sivaram, "India: The Global Warming Wild Card," *Scientific American* 316, May 2017, 48-53, doi: 10.1038/scientificamerican0517-48.

55. Subhes C. Bhattacharyya and Debajit Palit, "Mini-Grid Based Off-Grid Electrification to Enhance Electricity Access in Developing Countries: What Policies May Be Required?" *Energy Policy* 94 (2016): 166–178, doi:10.1016/j.enpol.2016.04.010.

56. X. Shi et al., "Assessment of Instruments in Facilitating Investment in Off-Grid Renewable Energy Projects," *Energy Policy* (2016), doi:10.1016/j.enpol.2016.02.001i.

Chapter 6

1. Henry Snaith, *Google Scholar Statistics,* https://scholar.google.com/citations?user=I2D3pUMAAAAJ&hl=en.

2. Thomson Reuters IP & Science, "Thomson Reuters Announces the World's Most Influential Scientific Minds," *PR Newswire,* January 13, 2016, http://www.prnewswire.com/news-releases/thomson-reuters-announces-the-worlds-most-influential-scientific-minds-300204299.html.

3. M. M. Lee, J. Teuscher, T. Miyasaka, T. N. Murakami, and H. J. Snaith, "Efficient Hybrid Solar Cells Based on Meso-Superstructured Organometal Halide Perovskites," *Science* 338, no. 6107 (2012): 643–647, doi:10.1126/science.1228604.

4. Juan-Pablo Correa-Baena et al., "The Rapid Evolution of Highly Efficient Perovskite Solar Cells," *Energy & Environmental Science* 10, no. 3 (2017): doi: 10.1039/c6ee03397k.

5. Sarah Kurtz et al., "Solar Research Not Finished," *Nature Photonics* 10, no. 3 (2016): 141–142, doi:10.1038/nphoton.2016.16.

6. Martin Green and Stephen Bremner, "Energy Conversion Approaches and Materials for High-Efficiency Photovoltaics," *Nature Materials* 16, no. 1 (2016): 23–34, doi: 10.1038/nmat4676.

7. Giles Eperon and David Ginger, "Perovskite Solar Cells: Different Facets of Performance," *Nature Energy* 1, no. 8 (2016): 16109, doi:10.1038/nenergy.2016.109.

8. Yaowen Li et al., "High-Efficiency Robust Perovskite Solar Cells on Ultrathin Flexible Substrates," *Nature Communications* 7 (2016): 10214, doi: 10.1038/ncomms10214.

9. Steve Albrecht and Bernd Rech, "Perovskite Solar Cells: On Top of Commercial Photovoltaics," *Nature Energy* 2, no. 1 (2017): 16196, doi:10.1038/nenergy.2016.196.

10. David Mcmeekin et al., "A Mixed-Cation Lead Mixed-Halide Perovskite Absorber for Tandem Solar Cells," *Science* 351, no. 6269 (2016): 151–155, doi:10.1126/science.aad5845.

11. Kevin Bush et al., "23.6%-efficient Monolithic Perovskite/Silicon Tandem Solar Cells with Improved Stability," *Nature Energy* 2 (2017): 17009, doi:10.1038/nenergy.2017.9.

12. Fan Fu et al., "High-Efficiency Inverted Semi-Transparent Planar Perovskite Solar Cells in Substrate Configuration," *Nature Energy* 2, no. 1 (2016): 16190, doi:10.1038/nenergy.2016.190.

13. Giles Eperon et al., "Perovskite-Perovskite Tandem Photovoltaics with Optimized Band Gaps," *Science* 354, no. 6314 (2016): 861–865, doi:10.1126/science.aaf9717.

14. Albrecht and Rech, "Perovskite Solar Cells: On Top of Commercial Photovoltaics."

15. Zhengshan Yu, Mehdi Leilaeioun, and Zachary Holman, "Selecting Tandem Partners for Silicon Solar Cells," *Nature Energy* 1, no. 11 (2016): 16137, doi:10.1038/nenergy.2016.137.

16. Kathryn Nave, "The Simple, Cheap Trick That Makes Solar Panels More Efficient," *Wired UK*, January 31, 2017, http://www.wired.co.uk/article/solar-panels-boosting-efficiency.

17. Donqin Bi et al., "Efficient Luminescent Solar Cells Based on Tailored Mixed-Cation Perovskites," *Science Advances* 2, no. 1 (2016): doi:10.1126/sciadv.1501170.

18. Michael Saliba, Wolfgang Tress, Antonio Abate, and Michael Grätzel, "Incorporation of Rubidium Cations into Perovskite Solar Cells Improves Photovoltaic Performance," *Science* 354, no. 6309 (2016): 206–209, doi:10.1126/science.aah5557.

19. Regan Wilks and Marcus Bär, "Perovskite Solar Cells: Danger from Within," *Nature Energy* 2, no. 1 (2017): 16204, doi:10.1038/nenergy.2016.204.

20. Wanyi Nie et al. "Light-Activated Photocurrent Degradation and Self-Healing in Perovskite Solar Cells," *Nature Communications* 7 (2016): 11574, doi:10.1038/ncomms11574.

21. Angèle Reinders, Pierre Verlinden, Wilfridus Sark, and Alexandre Freundlich, *Photovoltaic Solar Energy: From Fundamentals to Applications*, (Chichester, U.K.: Wiley, 2017).

22. Giulia Grancini et al., "One-Year Stable Perovskite Solar Cells by 2D/3D Interface Engineering." *Nature Communications* (2017), doi: 10.1038/ncomms15684.

23. Wilson Da Silva, "Trendy Solar Cells Hit New World Efficiency Record," UNSW Newsroom, 2016, http://newsroom.unsw.edu.au/news/science-tech/trendy-solar-cells-hit-new-world-efficiency-record.

24. Mengjin Yang et al., "Perovskite Ink with Wide Processing Window for Scalable High-Efficiency Solar Cells," *Nature Energy* 2 (2017): https://www.nature.com/articles/nenergy201738.

25. Xiong Li, Dongqi Bi, and Chenyi Yi, "A Vacuum Flash-Assisted Solution Process for High-Efficiency Large-Area Perovskite Solar Cells," *Science* 353, no. 6294 (2016): 58–62, doi: 10.1126/science.aaf8060.

26. Hairen Tan et al., "Efficient and Stable Solution-Processed Planar Perovskite Solar Cells via Contact Passivation," *Science* 355, no. 6326 (2017): 722–726, doi:10.1126/science.aai9081.

27. See Grid Edge Solar, a research program at the Massachusetts Institute of Technology (MIT): http://www.gridedgesolar.com.

28. Nam-Gyu Park, Michael Grätzel, Tsutomu Miyasaka, Kai Zhu, and Keith Emery, "Towards Stable and Commercially Available Perovskite Solar Cells," *Nature Energy* 1, no. 11 (2016): 16152, doi:10.1038/nenergy.2016.152.

29. Herman Trabish, "The Lowdown on the Safety of First Solar's CDTE Thin Film," *Greentech Media*, March 12, 2012, https://www.greentechmedia.com/articles/read/how-safe-is-first-solars-cdte-thin-film.

30. Nakita Noel et al., "Lead-Free Organic–Inorganic Tin Halide Perovskites for Photovoltaic Applications," *Energy & Environmental Science* 7, no. 9 (2014): 3061, doi: 10.1039/c4ee01076k.

31. K. P. Marshall, M. Walker, R. I. Walton, and R. A. Hatton, "Enhanced Stability and Efficiency in Hole-Transport-Layer-Free CsSnI3 Perovskite Photovoltaics," *Nature Energy* 1 (2016): 16178, doi:10.1038/nenergy.2016.178.

32. Prakash Singh and O. S. Kushwaha, "Progress Towards Efficiency of Polymer Solar Cells," *Advanced Materials Letters* 8, no. 1 (2016): 2–7, doi:10.5185/amlett.2017.7005.

33. Guglielmo Lanzani, Annamaria Petrozza, and Mario Caironi, "Organics Go Hybrid," *Nature Photonics* 11, no. 1 (2017): 20–22, doi:10.1038/nphoton.2016.260.

34. Miaomiao Li et al., "Solution-Processed Organic Tandem Solar Cells with Power Conversion Efficiencies >12%," *Nature Photonics* 11, no. 2 (2016): 85–90, doi:10.1038/nphoton.2016.240.

35. Sarah Holliday et al., "High-Efficiency and Air-Stable P3HT-Based Polymer Solar Cells with a New Non-Fullerene Acceptor," *Nature Communications* 7 (2016): 11585, doi: 10.1038/ncomms11585.

36. Jean-Luc Brédas, Edward Sargent, and Gregory Scholes, "Photovoltaic Concepts Inspired by Coherence Effects in Photosynthetic Systems," *Nature Materials* 16, no. 1 (2016): 35–44, doi: 10.1038/nmat4767.

37. Mingjian Yuan, Mengxia Liu, and Edward Sargent, "Colloidal Quantum Dot Solids for Solution-Processed Solar Cells," *Nature Energy* 1, no. 3 (2016): 16016, doi:10.1038/nenergy.2016.16.

38. Abhishek Swarnkar et al., "Quantum Dot-Induced Phase Stabilization of CsPbI3 Perovskite for High-Efficiency Photovoltaics," *Science* 354, no. 6308 (2016): 92–95, doi:10.1126/science.aag2700.

39. Hongbo Li, Kaifeng Wu, Jaehoon Lim, Hyung-Jun Song, and Victor Klimov, "Doctor-Blade Deposition of Quantum Dots onto Standard Window Glass for Low-Loss Large-Area Luminescent Solar Concentrators," *Nature Energy* 1 (2016): 16157, doi:10.1038/nenergy.2016.157.

40. Prashant Kamat, "Quantum Dot Solar Cells: The Next Big Thing in Photovoltaics," *Journal of Physical Chemistry Letters* 4, no. 6 (2013): 908–918, doi:10.1021/jz400052e.

41. Francois Lafond et al., "How Well Do Experience Curves Predict Technological Progress? A Method for Making Distributional Forecasts," *Journal of Technological Forecasting and Social Change*. In Press. 2017, https://arxiv.org/pdf/1703.05979.pdf.

42. Nancy M. Haegel et al., "Terawatt-Scale Photovoltaics: Trajectories and Challenges," *Science* 356, no. 6334 (April 14, 2017): doi: 10.1126/science.aal1288.

43. U.S. Department of Energy (DOE) Office of Energy Efficiency & Renewable Energy, "The SunShot Initiative's 2030 Goal: 3₵ per Kilowatt Hour for Solar Electricity," December 2016, https://energy.gov/sites/prod/files/2016/12/f34/SunShot%20 2030%20Fact%20Sheet-12_16.pdf.

44. Varun Sivaram and Shayle Kann, "Solar Power Needs a More Ambitious Cost Target," *Nature Energy* 1, no. 4 (April 7, 2016): doi:10.1038/nenergy.2016.36.

45. "The Future of Solar Energy," MIT Energy Initiative, 2015, https://energy.mit.edu/wp-content/uploads/2015/05/MITEI-The-Future-of-Solar-Energy.pdf.

46. Martin Green, "Commercial Progress and Challenges for Photovoltaics," *Nature Energy* 1, no. 1 (2016): 15015, doi:10.1038/nenergy.2015.15.

47. UN-Habitat, *Slum Almanac 2015–2016* (Nairobi, Kenya: UNON, Publishing Services Section, 2016).

48. Darren Lipomi and Zhenan Bao, "Stretchable, Elastic Materials and Devices for Solar Energy Conversion," *Energy & Environmental Science* 4, no. 9 (2011): 3314, doi: 10.1039/c1ee01881g.

49. Hoyeon Kim et al. "Empowering Semi-Transparent Solar Cells with Thermal-Mirror Functionality," *Advanced Energy Materials* 6, no.14 (2016), doi: 10.1002/aenm.201502466.

50. Moshe Schwartz, Katherine Blakeley, and Ronald O'Rourke, *Department of Defense Energy Initiatives: Background and Issues for Congress* (CRS R42558) (Washington, DC: Congressional Research Service, 2012), https://fas.org/sgp/crs/natsec/R42558.pdf

51. Daisuke Sato, Noboru Yamada, and Koji Tanaka, "Thermal Design of Photovoltaic/Microwave Conversion Hybrid Panel for Space Solar Power System," *IEEE Journal of Photovoltaics* 7, no. 1 (2017): 374–382, doi:10.1109/jphotov.2016.2629843.

52. Paul Marks, "Star Power," *New Scientist* 229, no. 3060 (2016): 38–41, doi: 10.1016/s0262-4079(16)30325-6.

53. Susumu Sasaki, "How Japan Plans to Build an Orbital Solar Farm," *IEEE Spectrum: Technology, Engineering, and Science News,* April 24, 2014, http://spectrum.ieee.org/green-tech/solar/how-japan-plans-to-build-an-orbital-solar-farm.

54. Jeffrey Ball, Dan Reicher, Xiaojing Sun, and Caitlin Pollock, *The New Solar System: China's Evolving Solar Industry and Its Implications for Competitive Solar Power in the United States and the World,* Report, Steyer-Taylor Center for Energy Policy and Finance, Stanford University, March 20, 2017.

55. Douglas M. Powell et al., "The Capital Intensity of Photovoltaics Manufacturing: Barrier to Scale and Opportunity for Innovation," *Energy and Environmental Science* 12 (2015): http://pubs.rsc.org/en/Content/ArticleLanding/2015/EE/C5EE01509J#!divAbstrat.

56. W. Brian Arthur, "Competing Technologies, Increasing Returns, and Lock-In by Historical Events," *The Economic Journal* 99, no. 394 (1989): 116-131, doi: 10.2307/2234208.

57. Robin Cowan, "Nuclear Power Reactors: A Study in Technological Lock-in," *Journal of Economic History* 50, no. 3 (1990): 541-567, http://www.jstor.org/stable/2122817?origin=JSTOR-pdf.

58. Varun Sivaram, "Unlocking Clean Energy," *Issues in Science and Technology* 33, no 2. (Winter 2017): http://issues.org/33-2/unlocking-clean-energy/.

59. David G. Victor and Kassia Yanosek, "The Crisis in Clean Energy: Stark Realities of the Renewables Craze," *Foreign Affairs*, July 2011, https://www.foreignaffairs.com/articles/2011-06-16/crisis-clean-energy.

60. Jonas Meckling et al., "Winning Coalitions for Climate Policy," *Science* 349 (2015), doi: 10.1126/science.aab1336.

Chapter 7

1. Kana Inagaki, "Toyota: Emission Control," *Financial Times*, https://www.ft.com/content/a7ad7876-d0ef-11e5-831d-09f7778e7377.

2. Drew Harwell, "Meet the Mirai: Why Toyota Wants to Make Your Next Car Run on Hydrogen," *Washington Post*, May 12, 2015, https://www.washingtonpost.com/business/economy/meet-the-mirai-why-toyota-wants-to-make-your-next-car-run-on-hydrogen/2015/05/12/0e85b0c0-f7ef-11e4-9030-b4732caefe81_story.html.

3. James Peltz, "Despite Tesla Frenzy, Electric Car Sales Are Far from Robust," *Los Angeles Times*, April 11, 2016, http://www.latimes.com/business/autos/la-fi-agenda-electric-cars-20160411-snap-htmlstory.html.

4. Tian Ying, "China Considers Dialing Back or Delaying Electric Car Quota," *Bloomberg*, March 5, 2017, https://www.bloomberg.com/news/articles/2017-03-05/china-considers-dialing-back-electric-car-quota-after-opposition.

5. Chisake Watanabe, "Japan Makes Big Push for Hydrogen Fuel Cells Scorned by Elon Musk as Impractical," *Japan Times*, http://www.japantimes.co.jp/news/2017/02/10/business/tech/japan-makes-big-push-for-hydrogen-fuel-cells-scorned-by-elon-musk-as-impractical.

6. "Toyota Fuel Cell Vehicle: Yoshikazu Tanaka Q&A," The Official Blog of Toyota GB, March 4, 2014, http://blog.toyota.co.uk/toyota-fuel-cell-vehicle-yoshikazu-tanaka-qa.

7. Akshay Singh, Evan Hirsh, Reid Wilk, and Rich Parkin, "2017 Automotive Trends," *PwC/Strategy&*, http://www.strategyand.pwc.com/trend/2017-automotive-industry-trends.

8. Aarian Marshall, "Solar Impulse Just Completed Its Momentous Flight Around the World," *Wired*, July 25, 2016, https://www.wired.com/2016/07/solar-impulse-just-completed-momentous-flight-around-world.

9. Nathan Lewis, "Research Opportunities to Advance Solar Energy Utilization," *Science* 351, no. 6271 (2016): doi:10.1126/science.aad1920.

10. U.S. Energy Information Administration (EIA), "International Energy Outlook 2016," Washington, DC, https://www.eia.gov/outlooks/ieo/pdf/0484(2016).pdf.

11. "Toyota Set to Sell Long-Range, Fast-Charging Electric Cars in 2022," *Reuters*, July 24, 2017, https://www.reuters.com/article/toyota-electric-cars-idUSL3N1KG03L.

12. E. W. Justi, *A Solar-Hydrogen Energy System*, (New York: Springer, 2011).

13. Matthew Shaner, Harry Atwater, Nathan Lewis, and Eric Mcfarland, "A Comparative Technoeconomic Analysis of Renewable Hydrogen Production Using Solar Energy," *Energy Environ. Sci.* 9, no. 7 (2016): 2354–2371, doi: 10.1039/c5ee02573g.

14. Sixto Giménez and Juan Bisquert, *Photoelectrochemical Solar Fuel Production: From Basic Principles to Advanced Devices* (Cham, Switzerland: Springer, 2016).

15. Shu Hu, Chengxiang Xiang, Sophia Haussener, Alan Berger, and Nathan Lewis, "An Analysis of the Optimal Band Gaps of Light Absorbers in Integrated Tandem Photoelectrochemical Water-Splitting Systems," *Energy & Environmental Science* 6, no. 10 (2013): 2984, doi:10.1039/c3ee40453f.

16. Adrian Cho, "Hubs Aim to Reinvent DOE Research Culture," *Science* 340, no. 6135 (2013): 914–918, doi:10.1126/science.340.6135.914.

17. Qimin Yan et al., "Solar Fuels Photoanode Materials Discovery by Integrating High-Throughput Theory and Experiment," *Proceedings of the National Academy of Sciences* 114, no. 12 (2017): 3040–3043, doi:10.1073/pnas.1619940114.

18. Juan Callejas, Carlos Read, Christopher Roske, Nathan Lewis, and Raymond Schaak, "Synthesis, Characterization, and Properties of Metal Phosphide Catalysts for the Hydrogen-Evolution Reaction," *Chemistry of Materials* 28, no. 17 (2016): 6017–6044, doi:10.1021/acs.chemmater.6b02148.

19. Fadl Saadi, Azhar Carim, and Jesus Velazquez, "Operando Synthesis of Macroporous Molybdenum Diselenide Films for Electrocatalysis of the Hydrogen-Evolution Reaction," *ACS Catalysis* 4, no. 9 (2014): 2866–2873, doi:10.1021/cs500412u.

20. S. Hu et al., "Amorphous TiO2 Coatings Stabilize Si, GaAs, and GaP Photoanodes for Efficient Water Oxidation," *Science* 344, no. 6187 (2014): 1005–1009, doi:10.1126/science.1251428.

21. Erik Verlage et al., "A Monolithically Integrated, Intrinsically Safe, 10% Efficient, Solar-Driven Water-Splitting System Based on Active, Stable, Earth-Abundant Electrocatalysts in Conjunction with Tandem III–V Light Absorbers Protected by Amorphous TiO2films," *Energy & Environmental Science* 8, no. 11 (2015): 3166–3172, doi:10.1039/c5ee01786f.

22. Shannon Bonke et al., "Renewable Fuels from Concentrated Solar Power: Towards Practical Artificial Photosynthesis," *Energy & Environmental Science* 8, no. 9 (2015): 2791–2796, doi: 10.1039/c5ee02214b.

23. Jingshan Luo et al., "Water Photolysis at 12.3% Efficiency via Perovskite Photovoltaics and Earth-Abundant Catalysts," *Science* 345, no. 6204 (2014): 1593–1596, doi:10.1126/science.1258307.

24. Thomas Hamann, "Perovskites Take Lead in Solar Hydrogen Race," *Science* 345, no. 6204 (2014): 1566–1567, doi:10.1126/science.1260051.

25. Stephen Hall, "Daniel Nocera: Maverick Inventor of the Artificial Leaf | Innovators," *National Geographic*, March 24, 2017, http://news.nationalgeographic.com/news/innovators/2014/05/140519-nocera-chemistry-artificial-leaf-solar-renewable-energy.

26. Steven Reece et al., "Wireless Solar Water Splitting Using Silicon-Based Semiconductors and Earth-Abundant Catalysts," *Science* 334, no. 6056 (2011): 645–648, doi:10.1126/science.1209816.

27. Hall, "Daniel Nocera: Maverick Inventor of the Artificial Leaf."

28. Bruce Parkinson, "Advantages of Solar Hydrogen Compared to Direct Carbon Dioxide Reduction for Solar Fuel Production," *ACS Energy Letters* 1 (2016), doi: 10.1021/acsenergylett.6b00377.

29. Harry L. Tuller, "Solar to Fuels Conversion Technologies," MIT Energy Institute, 2015, https://energy.mit.edu/wp-content/uploads/2015/03/MITEI-WP-2015-03.pdf.

30. Joseph Montoya et al., "Materials for Solar Fuels and Chemicals," *Nature Materials* 16, no. 1 (2016): 70–81, doi: 10.1038/nmat4778.

31. M. Schreier et al., "Efficient Photosynthesis of Carbon Monoxide from CO2 Using Perovskite Photovoltaics," *Nature Communications* 6, no. 7326 (2015), https://www.nature.com/articles/ncomms8326#methods.

32. Katherine Bourzac, "News Feature: Liquid Sunlight," *Proceedings of the National Academy of Sciences* 113, no. 17 (2016): 4545–4548, doi:10.1073/pnas.1604811113.

33. Eva Nichols et al., "Hybrid Bioinorganic Approach to Solar-to-Chemical Conversion," *Proceedings of the National Academy of Sciences* 112, no. 37 (2015): 11461–11466, doi:10.1073/pnas.1508075112.

34. Joseph Torella, Christopher Gagliardi, and Janice Chen, "Efficient Solar-to-Fuels Production from a Hybrid Microbial–Water-Splitting Catalyst System," *Proceedings of the National Academy of Sciences* 112, no. 8 (2015): 2337–2342, doi:10.1073/pnas.1424872112.

35. Chong Liu et al., "Water Splitting-Biosynthetic System with CO_2 Reduction Efficiencies Exceeding Photosynthesis," *Science* 352, no. 6290 (2016): 1210–1213, doi:10.1126/science.aaf5039.

36. David Biello, "Bionic Leaf Makes Fuel from Sunlight, Water, and Air," *Scientific American*, June 2, 2016, https://www.scientificamerican.com/article/bionic-leaf-makes-fuel-from-sunlight-water-and-air1/.

37. Chong Liu et al, "Ambient Nitrogen Reduction Cycle Using a Hybrid Inorganic–Biological System," *Proceedings of the National Academy of Sciences* 114, no.25 (2017), doi: 10.1073/pnas.1706371114.

38. George Dvorsky, "Solar Power Plant Can't Figure Out How to Stop Frying Birds," *Gizmodo*, September 2, 2016, http://gizmodo.com/solar-power-plant-can-t-figure-out-how-to-stop-frying-b-1786093431.

39. Cassandra Sweet, "Ivanpah Solar Plant May Be Forced to Shut Down," *Wall Street Journal*, March 16, 2016, https://www.wsj.com/articles/ivanpah-solar-plant-may-be-forced-to-shut-down-1458170858.

40. Sarah Zhang, "A Huge Solar Plant Caught on Fire, and That's the Least of Its Problems," *Wired*, May 23, 2016, https://www.wired.com/2016/05/huge-solar-plant-caught-fire-thats-least-problems/.

41. Renewable Energy Policy Network for the 21st Century (REN21), "Renewables 2016 Global Status Report," http://www.ren21.net/wp-content/uploads/2016/06/GSR_2016_Full_Report.pdf.

42. Lazard, "Lazard's Levelized Cost of Energy Analysis—Version 10.0." December 2016, https://www.lazard.com/media/438038/levelized-cost-of-energy-v100.pdf.

43. Raphael Minder, "Once a Darling, Spanish Solar Company Abengoa Faces Reckoning, *New York Times*, March 17, 2016, https://www.nytimes.com/2016/03/18/business/international/once-a-darling-spanish-solar-company-abengoa-faces-reckoning.html.

44. Joe Ryan, "NRG's Massive California Solar Plant Finally Making Enough Power," *Bloomberg*, February 1, 2017, https://www.bloomberg.com/news/articles/2017-02-01/nrg-s-massive-california-solar-plant-finally-making-enough-power.

45. "Spain's Abengoa Says Has Consents to Draw Down on Cash Injection," *Reuters*, February 28, 2017, http://www.reuters.com/finance/stocks/ABG.MC/key-developments/article/3537978.

46. "Concentrating Solar Power Market by Technology, Components, End-User, and Region—Global Forecast to 2021," Research and Markets, February 2017, http://www.researchandmarkets.com/research/52hhdp/concentrating.

47. Thomas Overton, "Crescent Dunes: 24 Hours on the Sun," *POWER Magazine*, October 13, 2016, http://www.powermag.com/crescent-dunes-24-hours-on-the-sun/?pagenum=1.

48. Robert Pietzcker, Daniel Stetter, Daniel Manger, and Gunnar Luderer, "Using the Sun to Decarbonize the Power Sector: The Economic Potential of Photovoltaics and Concentrating Solar Power," *Applied Energy* 135 (2014): 704–720, doi:10.1016/j.apenergy.2014.08.011.

49. Richard Schmalensee et al., *The Future of Solar Energy*, Working Paper, MIT Energy Initiative, 2015, https://energy.mit.edu/wp-content/uploads/2015/05/MITEI-The-Future-of-Solar-Energy.pdf.

50. Ming Liu et al., "Review on Concentrating Solar Power Plants and New Dvelopments in High-Temperature Thermal Energy Storage Technologies," *Renewable and Sustainable Energy Reviews* 53 (2016): 1411–1432, doi:10.1016/j.rser.2015.09.026.

51. Joshua Christian and Clifford Ho, "Design Requirements, Challenges, and Solutions for High-Temperature Falling Particle Receivers," In *AIP Conference Proceedings* 1734, no. 1, May 2016, doi:10.1063/1.4949060.

52. Mark Mehos, Craig Turchi, and Jennie Jorgenson, "Advancing Concentrating Solar Power Technology, Performance, and Dispatchability," National Renewable Energy Laboratory (NREL), May 2016, http://www.nrel.gov/docs/fy16osti/65688.pdf.

53. Manuel Blanco, *Advances in Concentrating Solar Thermal Research and Technology* (Amsterdam: Elsevier Science & Technology, 2016).

54. J. W. Schwede, T. Sarmiento, and V. K. Narasimhan, "Photon-Enhanced Thermionic Emission from Heterostructures with Low Interface Recombination," *Nature Communications* 4 (2013): 1576, doi: 10.1038/ncomms2577.

55. Gregory F. Nemet, Martina Kraus, and Vera Zipperer, "The Valley of Death, the Technology Pork Barrel, and Public Support for Large Demonstration Projects," *DIW Berlin*, 2016, https://www.diw.de/documents/publikationen/73/diw_01.c.540709.de/dp1601.pdf

Chapter 8

1. Schumpeter, "Sonic Boom," *The Economist*, April 1, 2017, http://www.economist.com/news/business/21719842-risk-one-japans-greatest-tech-tycoons-his-messianic-streak-masayoshi-son-goes?frsc=dg%7Cd.

2. Leo Lewis, Kana Inagaki, and Simon Mundy, "SoftBank: Waiting for the Next 'Big Idea,'" *Financial Times*, July 13, 2016, https://www.ft.com/content/213582f2-453e-11e6-9b66-0712b3873ae1.

3. John Boyd, "Trio of Nations Aims to Hook Asia Super Grid to Grids of the World," *IEEE Spectrum: Technology, Engineering, and Science News*, September 13, 2016, http://spectrum.ieee.org/energywise/energy/the-smarter-grid/trio-of-nations-aim-to-hook-asia-super-grid-to-grids-of-the-world.

4. John Fialka, "Clean Line, GE to Build $2.5B Wind Power Line," *E&E Climatewire*, November 2, 2016, https://www.eenews.net/climatewire/2016/11/02/stories/1060045154.

5. "Electricity Now Flows Across Continents, Courtesy of Direct Current," *The Economist*, January 14, 2017, http://www.economist.com/news/science-and-technology/21714325-transmitting-power-over-thousands-kilometres-requires-new-electricity.

6. Zhenya Liu, *Global Energy Interconnection* (San Diego: Elsevier Science Publishing, 2015).

7. John Fialka, "Renewable Energy: China's Breakneck Rise from Solar Dabbler to Dominator," *Environment & Energy Publishing*, December 19, 2016, http://www.eenews.net/climatewire/stories/1060047373/print.

8. John Fialka, "China has a 'Grand Vision for the Grid. Does Trump?" *Climate Wire*, December 21, 2016, https://www.eenews.net/climatewire/stories/1060047497.

9. Arthur Neslen, "Wind Power Generates 140% of Denmark's Electricity Demand," *The Guardian*, July 10, 2015, https://www.theguardian.com/environment/2015/jul/10/denmark-wind-windfarm-power-exceed-electricity-demand.

10. Alex Trembath, "A Look at Wind and Solar, Part 1: How Far We've Come," Breakthrough Institute, https://thebreakthrough.org/index.php/voices/energetics/wind-and-solar-how-far-weve-come.

11. International Energy Agency (IEA), "The Power of Transformation," 2014, https://www.iea.org/publications/freepublications/publication/The_power_of_Transformation.pdf.

12. International Energy Agency (IEA), "Large-Scale Electricity Interconnection," 2016, https://www.iea.org/publications/freepublications/publication/Interconnection.pdf.

13. O. Peake, "The History of High-Voltage Direct Current Transmission," Institution of Engineers Australia, 2010, http://ieeemilestones.ethw.org/images/d/d9/Ref3_Peake_2010_Australian_Journal_of_Multi-Disciplinary_Engineering.pdf.

14. Res. No. 013–187, *Adoption by Ordinance to Establish Design-Build Criteria of the Sylmar Filters Replacement Project*, Department of Water and Power of the City of Los Angeles, March 20, 2013, http://clkrep.lacity.org/onlinedocs/2013/13-0338_rpt_bwp_3-20-13.pdf.

15. John Shen, Gourab Sabui, Zhenyu Miao, and Zhikang Shuai, "Wide-Bandgap Solid-State Circuit Breakers for DC Power Systems: Device and Circuit Considerations," *IEEE Transactions on Electron Devices* 62, no. 2 (2015): 294–300, doi:10.1109/ted.2014.2384204.

16. Clark Gellings, "Let's Build a Global Power Grid," *IEEE Spectrum: Technology, Engineering, and Science News,* July 28, 2015, http://spectrum.ieee.org/energy/the-smarter-grid/lets-build-a-global-power-grid.

17. International Energy Agency (IEA), "World Energy Outlook 2014," 2014, https://www.iea.org/publications/freepublications/publication/WEO2014.pdf.

18. "Opinion Is Divided on China's Massive Infrastructure Projects," *The Economist,* January 12, 2017, http://www.economist.com/news/china/21714381-some-critics-may-be-wrong-opinion-divided-chinas-massive-infrastructure-projects.

19. Ying Li, Zofia Lukszo, and Margot Weijnen, "The Impact of Inter-Regional Transmission Grid Expansion on China's Power Sector Decarbonization," *Applied Energy* 183 (2016): 853–873, doi:10.1016/j.apenergy.2016.09.006.

20. Dmitrii Bogdanov and Christian Breyer, "North-East Asian Super Grid for 100% Renewable Energy Supply: Optimal Mix of Energy Technologies for Electricity, Gas, and Heat Supply Options," *Energy Conversion and Management* 112 (2016): 176–190, doi:10.1016/j.enconman.2016.01.019.

21. Ashish Gulagi, Dmitrii Bogdanov, Mahdi Fasihi, and Christian Breyer, "Can Australia Power the Energy-Hungry Asia with Renewable Energy?" *Sustainability* 9, no. 2 (2017): 233, doi:10.3390/su9020233.

22. Richard Martin, "Morocco's Massive Desert Solar Project Starts Up," *MIT Technology Review,* February 8, 2016, https://www.technologyreview.com/s/600751/moroccos-massive-desert-solar-project-starts-up.

23. Fraunhofer ISE, "Integration of Renewable Energy in Europe and Africa—Study on Supergrid Presents Scenarios and Technologies for a Renewable-Based Energy Supply," Fraunhofer-Gesellschaf news release, April 18, 2016, https://www.ise.fraunhofer.de/en/press-media/press-releases/2016/integration-von-erneuerbaren-energien-in-europa-und-afrika.html. .

24. Alexander E. Macdonald et al., "Future Cost-Competitive Electricity Systems and Their Impact on US CO_2 Emissions," *Nature Climate Change* 6 (2016): 52-531, www.nature.com/nclimate/journal/v6/n5/full/nclimate2921.html.

25. International Energy Agency (IEA), "Canada: Electricity and Heat for 2014," 2014, https://www.iea.org/statistics/statisticssearch/report/?country=CANADA=&product=electricityandheat.

26. Alejandro Chanona Robles, "Tracking the Progress of Mexico's Power Sector Reform," Wilson Center, April 2016, https://www.wilsoncenter.org/sites/default/files/tracking_progress_of_mexicos_power_sector_reform.pdf.

27. The White House, "Leaders' Statement on a North American Climate, Clean Energy, and Environment Partnership," press release, June 29, 2016, https://

obamawhitehouse.archives.gov/the-press-office/2016/06/29/leaders-statement-north-american-climate-clean-energy-and-environment.

28. New York City, "Chapter 6: Utilities," *A Stronger, More Resilient New York*, http://www.nyc.gov/html/sirr/downloads/pdf/final_report/Ch_6_Utilities_FINAL_singles.pdf.

29. Ning Lin, Kerry Emanuel, Michael Oppenheimer, and Erik Vanmarcke, "Physically Based Assessment of Hurricane Surge Threat Under Climate Change," *Nature Climate Change* 2, no. 6 (2012): 462–467, doi:10.1038/nclimate1389.

30. M. Finster, J. Philips, and K. Wallace, *Front-Resilience Perspectives: The Electrical Grid*, (Lemont, IL: U.S. Department of Energy (DOE), Argonne National Laboratory, 2016).

31. Peter Behr and Saqib Rahim, "Utilities: ConEd taps N.Y. Customers for 'Virtual' Power Plant Project," *E&E News Energy Wire*, http://www.eenews.net/energywire/stories/1060038694.

32. Gavin Bade, "ConEd Awards 22 MW of Demand Response Contracts in Brooklyn-Queens Project," *Utility Dive*, August 8, 2016, http://www.utilitydive.com/news/coned-awards-22-mw-of-demand-response-contracts-in-brooklyn-queens-project/424034.

33. New York State Public Utility Commission, "Order Adopting a Ratemaking and Utility Revenue Model Policy Framework," CASE 14-M-0101, May 19, 2016, http://documents.dps.ny.gov/public/Common/ViewDoc.aspx?DocRefId=%7BD6EC8F0B-6141-4A82-A857-B79CF0A71BF0%7D.

34. George Constable and Bob Somerville, *A Century of Innovation: Twenty Engineering Achievements That Transformed Our Lives* (Washington, DC: Joseph Henry Press, 2003).

35. California Public Utilities Commission, *California's Distributed Energy Resources Action Plan: Aligning Vision and Action*, September 29, 2016, http://www.cpuc.ca.gov/uploadedFiles/CPUC_Public_Website/Content/About_Us/Organization/Commissioners/Michael_J._Picker/2016-09-26%20DER%20Action%20Plan%20FINAL3.pdf.

36. Benjamin Mandel, "The Merits of an 'Integrated' Approach to Performance-Based Regulation," *Electricity Journal* 28, no. 4 (2015): 8–17, doi:10.1016/j.tej.2015.04.004.

37. Enrique Santacana, Gary Rackliffe, Le Tang, and Xiaoming Feng, "Getting Smart," *IEEE Power and Energy Magazine* 8, no. 2 (2010): 41–48, doi:10.1109/mpe.2009.935557.

38. Ryan Hanley, "A Pathway to the Distributed Grid," SolarCity White Paper, February 2016, http://www.solarcity.com/sites/default/files/SolarCity_Distributed_Grid-021016.pdf.

39. S. Abdi and K. Afshar, "Application of IPSO-Monte Carlo for Optimal Distributed Generation Allocation and Sizing," *International Journal of Electrical Power & Energy Systems* 44, no. 1 (2013): 786–797.

40. Stephen Lacey, "Microsoft Says 'Computational Demand Response' Could Lower Data Center Emissions 99%," *Greentech Media*, June 27, 2013, https://www.greentechmedia.com/articles/read/Microsoft-Says-Computational-Demand-Response-Could-Lower-Data-Center-Emis.

41. Hao Wang, Jianwei Huang, Xiaojun Lin, and Hamed Mohsenian-Rad, "Proactive Demand Response for Data Centers: A Win-Win Solution," *IEEE Transactions on Smart Grid* 7, no. 3 (2016): 1584–1596, doi:10.1109/tsg.2015.2501808.

42. Jamshid Aghaei and Mohammad-Iman Alizadeh, "Demand Response in Smart Electricity Grids Equipped with Renewable Energy Sources: A Review," *Renewable and Sustainable Energy Reviews* 18 (2013): 64–72, doi:10.1016/j.rser.2012.09.019.

43. Farshid Shariatzadeh, Paras Mandal, and Anurag Srivastava, "Demand Response for Sustainable Energy Systems: A Review, Application, and Implementation Strategy," *Renewable and Sustainable Energy Reviews* 45 (2015): 343–350, doi: 10.1016/j.rser.2015.01.062.

44. A. Bumpus and S. Comello,"Emerging Clean Energy Technology Investment Trends," *Nature Climate Change* 7 (2017), doi: 10.1038/nclimate3306.

45. Federal Trade Commission (FTC), *Internet of Things: Privacy & Security in a Connected World* (Washington, DC, November 2013, https://www.ftc.gov/system/files/documents/reports/federal-trade-commission-staff-report-november-2013-workshop-entitled-internet-things-privacy/150127iotrpt.pdf).

46. Jeff St. John, "US Smart Meter Deployments to Hit 70M in 2016, 90M in 2020," *Greentech Media*, October 26, 2016, https://www.greentechmedia.com/articles/read/US-Smart-Meter-Deployments-to-Hit-70M-in-2016-90M-in-2020.

47. Aghaei and Alizadeh, "Demand Response in Smart Electricity Grids Equipped with Renewable Energy Sources: A Review."

48. Christopher Findlay, "Strength in Numbers: Merging Small Generators as Virtual Power Plants," *Living Energy* 4 (2011), http://www.energy.siemens.com/us/pool/hq/energy-topics/publications/living-energy/pdf/issue-04/Living-Energy-4-Virtual-Power-Plants.pdf.

49. Matt Coleman, "'World's Largest Virtual Power Plant' Switched on in Adelaide," *ABC News*, March 15, 2017, http://www.abc.net.au/news/2017-03-16/virtual-power-plant/8358894.

50. Conor Kelly, John Ging, Aman Kansal, and Michael Walsh, "Balancing Power Systems with Datacenters Using a Virtual Interconnector," *IEEE Power and Energy Technology Systems Journal* 3, no. 2 (2016): 51–59, doi:10.1109/jpets.2016.2519611.

51. Massoud Amin, "Power of Microgrids," *IEEE Smart Grid* (2016): 48–53, http://smartgrid.ieee.org/images/files/pdf/power_of_microgrids.pdf.

52. Dushan Boroyevich, Igor Cvetkovic, Rolando Burgos, and Dong Dong, "Intergrid: A Future Electronic Energy Network?" *IEEE Journal of Emerging and Selected Topics in Power Electronics* 1, no. 3 (2013): 127–138, doi:10.1109/jestpe.2013.2276937.

53. Robert Hebner, "The Power Grid in 2030," *IEEE Spectrum*, April 2017, doi: 10.1109/MSPEC.2017.7880459.

54. Brian Patterson, *The ENERNET,* Emerge Alliance, October 26–27, 2015, http://www.emergealliance.org/portals/0/documents/events/lvdc/IEC_LVDC_India_2015_Enernet-_FINAL[1].pdf.

55. Hassan Farhangi, "The Path of the Smart Grid," *IEEE Power and Energy* Magazine 8, no. 1 (2010): 18–28, doi:10.1109/mpe.2009.934876.

Chapter 9

1. "Tesla Bid for SolarCity 'Shameful,'" *BBC News*, June 22, 2016, http://www.bbc.com/news/business-36602509.

2. Robert Ferris, "Too Early for Tesla to Merge with Solarcity? Elon Musk Says Deal 'May Even Be a Little Late,'" *CNBC*, November 4, 2016, http://www.cnbc.com/2016/11/04/tesla-solarcity-merger-may-even-be-a-little-late.html.

3. Elon Musk, "The Secret Tesla Motors Master Plan (Just between You and Me)," Tesla, Inc., June 28, 2012, https://www.tesla.com/blog/secret-tesla-motors-master-plan-just-between-you-and-me.

4. Timothy Lee, "The Secrets to Elon Musk's Success," *Vox*, April 10, 2017, http://www.vox.com/new-money/2017/4/10/15211542/elon-musk-success-secret.

5. Thomas Heath, "Tesla's 'Crazy' Climb to America's Most Valuable Car Company," *The Washington Post*, April 10, 2017, https://www.washingtonpost.com/business/economy/teslas-crazy-climb-to-americas-most-valuable-car-company/2017/04/10/de05b9ae-1dfd-11e7-be2a-3a1fb24d4671_story.html.

6. Peter Fairley, "2017 Is the Make-or-Break Year for Tesla's Gigafactory," *IEEE Spectrum: Technology, Engineering, and Science News,* December 30, 2016, http://spectrum.ieee.org/transportation/advanced-cars/2017-is-the-makeorbreak-year-for-teslas-gigafactory.

7. Jesse D. Jenkins and Samuel Thernstrom, "Deep Decarbonization of the Electric Power Sector: Insights from Recent Literature," Energy Innovation Reform Project (EIRP), March 2017, http://innovationreform.org/wp-content/uploads/2017/03/EIRP-Deep-Decarb-Lit-Review-Jenkins-Thernstrom-March-2017.pdf.

8. International Renewable Energy Agency (IRENA), *Energy Storage Technology Brief* (Abu Dhabi: IRENA, 2012), https://www.irena.org/DocumentDownloads/Publications/IRENA-ETSAP%20Tech%20Brief%20E18%20Electricity-Storage.pdf.

9. Xing Luo, Jihong Wang, Mark Dooner, and Jonathan Clarke, "Overview of Current Development in Electrical Energy Storage Technologies and the Application Potential in Power System Operation," *Applied Energy* 137 (2015): 511–536, doi:10.1016/j.apenergy.2014.09.081.

10. Jürgen Janek and Wolfgang Zeier, "A Solid Future for Battery Development," *Nature Energy* 1, no. 9 (2016): 16141, doi:10.1038/nenergy.2016.141.

11. "New Energy Outlook 2017," *Bloomberg New Energy Finance*, 2017, https://about.bnef.com/new-energy-outlook.

12. Xing Luo, Jihong Wang, Mark Dooner, and Jonathan Clarke, "Overview of Current Development in Electrical Energy Storage Technologies and the Application Potential in Power System Operation," *Applied Energy* 137 (2015): 511–536, doi: 10.1016/j.apenergy.2014.09.081.

13. "This Is Where Your Smartphone Battery Begins," *Washington Post*, September 30, 2016, https://www.washingtonpost.com/graphics/business/batteries/congo-cobalt-mining-for-lithium-ion-battery/.

14. Kaixiang Lin et al., "Alkaline Quinone Flow Battery," *Science* 349, no. 6255 (2015): 1529–1532, doi: 10.1126/science.aab3033.

15. Eric Wesoff, "Ambri Returns to the Energy Storage Hunt with Liquid Metal Battery Redesign," *Greentech Media*, December 15, 2016, https://www.greentechmedia.com/articles/read/Ambri-Returns-to-The-Energy-Storage-Hunt-With-Liquid-Metal-Battery-Redesign.

16. Varun Sivaram, "Ensuring Tesla Doesn't Crowd out the Batteries of the Future," *Forbes*, April 30, 2015, https://www.forbes.com/sites/thelabbench/2015/04/30/ensuring-tesla-doesnt-crowd-out-the-batteries-of-the-future/#43936cde4543.

17. Stephen Brick and Samuel Thernstrom, "Renewables and Decarbonization: Studies of California, Wisconsin and Germany," *The Electricity Journal* 29, no. 3 (2016): 6–12, doi: 10.1016/j.tej.2016.03.001.

18. Mathew Aneke and Meihong Wang, "Energy Storage Technologies and Real Life Applications – A State of the Art Review," *Applied Energy* 179 (2016): 350–377, doi: 10.1016/j.apenergy.2016.06.097.

19. Mark Jacobson, Mark Delucchi, Mary Cameron, and Bethany Frew, "Low-Cost Solution to the Grid Reliability Problem with 100% Penetration of Intermittent Wind, Water, and Solar for All Purposes," *Proceedings of the National Academy of Sciences* 112, no. 49 (2015): 15060–5065, doi: 10.1073/pnas.1510028112.

20. Varun Sivaram, "A Clean Energy Transition Needs More Technology Options," *The Aspen Institute*, June 19, 2017, https://www.aspeninstitute.org/blog-posts/clean-energy-transition-needs-technology-options/.

21. Christopher T. M. Clack et al., "Evaluation of a Proposal for Reliable Low-Cost Grid Power with 100% Wind, Water, and Solar," *PNAS* 114, no. 26 (2017): 6722-6727, doi: 10.1073/pnas.1610381114.

22. Eduardo Porter, "Fisticuffs Over the Route to a Clean-Energy Future," *New York Times*, June 20, 2017, https://www.nytimes.com/2017/06/20/business/energy-environment/renewable-energy-national-academy-matt-jacobson.html; Nathanael Johnson, "A Battle Royale has Broken Out between Clean Power Purists and Pragmatists," June 20, 2017, http://grist.org/briefly/a-battle-royale-has-broken-out-between-clean-power-purists-and-pragmatists/; Chris Mooney, "A Bitter Scientific Debate just Erupted over the Future of America's Power Grid," *The Washington Post*, June 19, 2017, https://www.washingtonpost.com/news/energy-environment/wp/2017/06/19/a-bitter-scientific-debate-just-erupted-over-the-future-of-the-u-s-electric-grid/?utm_term=.57ade3099d20; John Wenz and Jason Koebler, "The Clean Energy Debate is Fueling One of the Most Vitriolic Fights in Science Publishing," *Motherboard*, June 19, 2017, https://motherboard.vice.com/en_us/article/8x973b/the-clean-energy-debate-is-fueling-one-of-the-most-vitriolic-fights-in-science-publishing.

23. Volker Krey, Gunnar Luderer, Leon Clarke, and Elmar Kriegler, "Getting from Here to There – Energy Technology Transformation Pathways in the EMF27 Scenarios," *Climatic Change* 123, no. 3-4 (2014): 369–382, doi: 10.1007/s10584-013-0947-5.

24. Elmar Kriegler et al., "The Role of Technology for Achieving Climate Policy Objectives: Overview of the EMF 27 Study on Global Technology and Climate Policy Strategies," *Climatic Change* 123, no. 3-4 (2014): 353–367, doi: 10.1007/s10584-013-0953-7.

25. G. M. Morrison et al., "Comparison of Low-Carbon Pathways for California," *Climatic Change* 131, vol. 4 (2015): 545–557, doi: 10.1007/s10584-015-1403-5.

26. U.S. Energy Information Administration (EIA), "U.S. Energy-Related Carbon Dioxide Emissions in 2015 Are 12% Below Their 2005 Levels—Today in Energy," May 9, 2016, https://www.eia.gov/todayinenergy/detail.php?id=26152.

27. Jesse D. Jenkins and Samuel Thernstrom, "Deep Decarbonization of The Electric Power Sector: Insights from Recent Literature," Energy Innovation Reform Project (EIRP), March 2017, http://innovationreform.org/wp-content/uploads/2017/03/EIRP-Deep-Decarb-Lit-Review-Jenkins-Thernstrom-March-2017.pdf.

28. James H. Williams et al., *Pathways to Deep Decarbonization in the United States* (San Francisco: Energy and Environmental Economics, Inc., 2016), https://usddpp.org/downloads/2014-technical-report.pdf.

29. Gang He et al., "SWITCH-China: A Systems Approach to Decarbonizing China's Power System," *Environmental Science & Technology* 50, no. 11 (2016): 5467–5473, doi:10.1021/acs.est.6b01345.

30. M. M. Hand et al. *National Renewable Energy Laboratory. Renewable Electricity Futures Study (RE Study)*, National Renewable Energy Laboratory, 2012, http://www.nrel.gov/analysis/re_futures.

31. Brendan Pierpoint et al. "Flexibility the Path to Low-Carbon, Low-Cost Electricity Grids," Climate Policy Initiative, 2017, https://climatepolicyinitiative.org/wp-content/uploads/2017/04/CPI-Flexibility-the-path-to-low-carbon-low-cost-grids-April-2017.pdf.

32. O. Schmidt, A. Hawkes, A. Gambhir, and I. Staffell, "The Future Cost of Electrical Energy Storage Based on Experience Rates," *Nature Energy* 2 (2017), doi: 10.1038/nenergy.2017.110.

33. Arnulf Grubler, "The Costs of the French Nuclear Scale-Up: A Case of Negative Learning by Doing," *Energy Policy* 38, no. 9 (2010): 5174–5188, doi:10.1016/j.enpol.2010.05.003.

34. Ted Nordhaus, Jessica Lovering, and Michael Shellenberger, "How To Make Nuclear Cheap," The Breakthrough Institute, June 2014, https://thebreakthrough.org/images/pdfs/Breakthrough_Institute_How_to_Make_Nuclear_Cheap.pdf

35. Brad Plumer, "How Carbon Capture Could Become a Rare Bright Spot on Climate Policy in the Trump Era," *Vox*, April 12, 2017, http://www.vox.com/energy-and-environment/2017/4/12/15269628/carbon-capture-trump.

36. Paul Denholm and Robert Margolis, "Energy Storage Requirements for Achieving 50% Solar Photovoltaic Energy Penetration in California," National Renewable Laboratory (NREL), 2016, http://www.nrel.gov/docs/fy16osti/66595.pdf.

37. Ana Mileva, Josiah Johnston, James Nelson, and Daniel Kammen, "Power System Balancing for Deep Decarbonization of the Electricity Sector," *Applied Energy* 162 (2016): 1001–1009, doi:10.1016/j.apenergy.2015.10.180.

38. Whitney Herndon and John Larson, "Nukes in the Crosshairs Revisited: The Market and Emissions Impacts of Retirements," Rhodium Group, November 4, 2016, http://rhg.com/notes/nukes-in-the-crosshairs-revisited.

39. Patrick McGeehan, "New York State Aiding Nuclear Plants With Millions in Subsidies," *The New York Times*, August 1, 2016, https://www.nytimes.com/2016/08/02/nyregion/new-york-state-aiding-nuclear-plants-with-millions-in-subsidies.html.

40. Paul Joskow, "Capacity Payments in Imperfect Electricity Markets: Need and Design," *Utilities Policy* 16, no. 3 (2008): 159–170, doi:10.1016/j.jup.2007.10.003.

41. David Buchan and Malcolm Keay, "EU Energy Policy—4th Time Lucky?" Oxford Institute for Energy Studies, December 2016, https://www.oxfordenergy.org/wpcms/wp-content/uploads/2016/12/EU-energy-policy-4th-time-lucky.pdf.

42. C. K. Woo et al., "Merit-Order Effects of Renewable Energy and Price Divergence in California's Day-Ahead and Real-Time Electricity Markets," *Energy Policy* 92 (2016): 299–312, doi:10.1016/j.enpol.2016.02.023.

43. Andre Gensler et al., "Deep Learning for Solar Power Forecasting—An Approach Using AutoEncoder and LSTM Neural Networks," IEEE International Conference on Systems, Man, and Cybernetics, 2016, http://ieeexplore.ieee.org/document/7844673/.

44. E. Ela et al., "Wholesale Electricity Market Design with Increasing Levels of Renewable Generation: Incentivizing Flexibility in System Operations," *The Electricity Journal* 29, no. 4 (2016): 51–60, doi:10.1016/j.tej.2016.05.001.

45. Jenny Riesz and Michael Milligan, "Designing Electricity Markets for a High Penetration of Variable Renewables," *Wiley Interdisciplinary Reviews: Energy and Environment* 4, no. 3 (2014): 279–289, doi:10.1002/wene.137.

46. Michael Milligan et al., "Alternatives No More," *IEEE Power and Energy Magazine*, November/December 2015, 78-87, doi: 10.1109/MPE.2015.2462311.

47. M. Gottstein and S. A. Skillings, "Beyond Capacity Markets—Delivering Capability Resources to Europe's Decarbonised Power System," 9th International Conference on the European Energy Market, 2012, doi:10.1109/eem.2012.6254783.

48. "Using Renewables to Operate a Low-Carbon Grid," California Independent System Operator, 2017, http://www.caiso.com/Documents/UsingRenewablesToOperateLowCarbonGrid-FAQ.pdf.

49. Brian Penner, "Grid-Friendly Utility-Scale PV Plants," First Solar, 2013, https://www.caiso.com/Documents/FirstSolarPresentation_ReactivePowerRequirements_FinancialCompensation_WorkingGroup.pdf.

50. Malcolm Keay, "Electricity Markets Are Broken—Can They Be Fixed?" Oxford Institute for Energy Studies, December 2016, https://www.oxfordenergy.org/wpcms/wp-content/uploads/2016/02/Electricity-markets-are-broken-can-they-be-fixed-EL-17.pdf.

51. Michael Liebreich, "Six Design Principles for the Power Markets of the Future," *Bloomberg New Energy Finance*, 2017, https://data.bloomberglp.com/bnef/sites/14/2017/05/Liebreich-Six-Design-Principles-for-the-Power-Markets-of-the-Future.pdf.

52. Kevin Bullis, "Utilities Say Electric Cars Could Strain the Grid," *MIT Technology Review*, August 16, 2013, https://www.technologyreview.com/s/518066/could-electric-cars-threaten-the-grid/.

53. Jennifer MacDonald, "Electric Vehicles to Be 35% of Global New Car Sales by 2040," *Bloomberg New Energy Finance*, February 25, 2016, at https://about.bnef.com/blog/electric-vehicles-to-be-35-of-global-new-car-sales-by-2040/.

54. Kang Miao Tan, Vigna Ramachandaramurthy, and Jia Yang Yong, "Integration of Electric Vehicles in Smart Grid: A Review on Vehicle to Grid Technologies and Optimization Techniques," *Renewable and Sustainable Energy Reviews* 53 (2016): 720–732, doi:10.1016/j.rser.2015.09.012.

55. International Energy Agency (IEA), "Linking Heat and Electricity Systems," 2014, https://www.iea.org/publications/freepublications/publication/LinkingHeatandElectricitySystems.pdf.

56. Alessandro Pensini, Claus Rasmussen, and Willett Kempton, "Economic Analysis of Using Excess Renewable Electricity to Displace Heating Fuels," *Applied Energy* 131 (2014): 530–543, doi:10.1016/j.apenergy.2014.04.111.

57. "Smart Energy Systems for Coherent 100% Renewable Energy and Transport Solutions," *Applied Energy* 145 (May 2015): 139-154, doi: 10.1016/j.apenergy.2015.01.075.

58. White House, "United States Mid-Century Strategy for Deep Decarbonization," 2016, https://unfccc.int/files/focus/long-term_strategies/application/pdf/us_mid_century_strategy.pdf.

59. Glada Lahn, Paul Stevens, and Felix Preston, "Saving Oil and Gas in the Gulf," Chatham House, August 2013, https://www.chathamhouse.org/sites/files/chathamhouse/public/Research/Energy%2C%20Environment%20and%20Development/0813r_gulfoilandgas.pdf.

60. John H. Lienhard, Gregory P. Thie, David M.Warsinger, and Leonardo D. Banchik, *Low Carbon Desalination*, Report, Abdul Latif Jameel World Water and Food Security Lab, Massachusetts Institute of Technology, https://jwafs.mit.edu/sites/default/files/images/Report%20v6-final.2016nov28%20with%20citations%20formatted%20Exec.pdf.

61. Mai Mahmoud, "Water at the Nexus of Gulf Security and Growth Challenges," The Arab Gulf States Institute in Washington, 2016, http://www.agsiw.org/wp-content/uploads/2016/10/Mahmoud_Water_ONLINE-1.pdf.

62. Veera Gnaneswar Gude, "Energy Storage for Desalination Processes Powered by Renewable Energy and Waste Heat Sources," *Applied Energy* 137 (2015): 877–898, doi:10.1016/j.apenergy.2014.06.061.

63. Rabia Ferroukhi et al., "Renewable Energy in the Water, Energy and Food Nexus," International Renewable Energy Agency (IRENA), 2015, http://www.irena.org/DocumentDownloads/Publications/IRENA_Water_Energy_Food_Nexus_2015.pdf.

64. Varun Sivaram, "India: The Global Warming Wild Card," *Scientific American* 316, May 2017, 48–53, doi: 10.1038/scientificamerican0517-48.

Chapter 10

1. Clifton Yin, "Arun Majumdar Made ARPA-E an Energy Innovation Leader," *The Innovation Files,* May 14, 2012, http://www.innovationfiles.org/arun-majumdar-made-arpa-e-an-energy-innovation-leader.

2. Executive Office of the President, Office of Management and Budget, "America First: A Budget Blueprint to Make America Great Again," 2017, https://www.govinfo.gov/content/pkg/BUDGET-2018-BLUEPRINT/pdf/BUDGET-2018-BLUEPRINT.pdf.

3. U.S. Congress, Senate, Committee on Appropriations, *Energy and Water Development Appropriations (to Accompany S. 1609),* 115th Cong., 1st sess., 2017, S. Rep. 115-132, 91, https://www.appropriations.senate.gov/imo/media/doc/FY2018%20Energy%20and%20Water%20Development%20Appropriations%20Act%20-%20Report%20115-1321.pdf.

4. Bloomberg New Energy Finance (BNEF), "New Energy Outlook 2016," https://www.bloomberg.com/company/new-energy-outlook.

5. Vannevar Bush, "Science, the Endless Frontier," Report, U.S. Government Printing Office, 1945, https://www.nsf.gov/od/lpa/nsf50/vbush1945.htm#ch2.4.

6. Ibid.

7. Daniel Sarewitz, "Saving Science," *The New Atlantis* 49 (Spring/Summer 2016): 4–40.

8. J. J. Dooley, *U.S. Federal Investments in Energy R&D: 1961–2008*, PNNL-17952, U. S. Department of Energy (DOE), Office of Scientific and Technical Information, 2008, https://www.pnl.gov/main/publications/external/technical_reports/PNNL-17952.pdf.

9. Daniel M. Kammen and Gregory F. Netmet, "The Incredible Shrinking Energy R&D Budget," *The Access Almanac,* Spring 2007, 38-40, http://www.accessmagazine.org/wp-content/uploads/sites/7/2016/07/Access-30-06-Almanac-R-D-Budget.pdf.

10. Benjamin Gaddy, Varun Sivaram, Timothy Jones, and Libby Wayman, "Venture Capital and Cleantech: The Wrong Model for Energy Innovation," *Energy Policy* 102 (2017): 385–395, doi:10.1016/j.enpol.2016.12.035.

11. Jeff Brady, "After Solyndra Loss, U.S. Energy Loan Program Turning a Profit," *NPR,* November 13, 2014, http://www.npr.org/2014/11/13/363572151/after-solyndra-loss-u-s-energy-loan-program-turning-a-profit.

12. Charlie Wilson and Arnulf Grübler, *Energy Technology Innovation: Learning from Historical Successes and Failures* (New York: Cambridge University Press, 2014).

13. William Bonvillian and Charles Weiss, *Technological Innovation in Legacy Sectors* (New York: Oxford University Press, 2015).

14. Arnold Thackray, David Brock, and Rachel Jones, *Moore's Law: The Life of Gordon Moore, Silicon Valley's Quiet Revolutionary* (New York: Basic Books, 2015).

15. Venkatesh Narayanamurti and Toluwalogo Odumosu, *Cycles of Invention and Discovery: Rethinking the Endless Frontier* (Cambridge, MA: Harvard University Press, 2016).

16. Richard Schmalensee et al., "The Future of Solar Energy," working paper, MIT Energy Initiative, 2015, https://energy.mit.edu/wp-content/uploads/2015/05/MITEI-The-Future-of-Solar-Energy.pdf.

17. Jeffrey Ball, Dan Reicher, Xiaojing Sun, and Caitlin Pollock, *The New Solar System: China's Evolving Solar Industry and Its Implications for Competitive Solar Power in the United States and the World*, Report, Steyer-Taylor Center for Energy Policy and Finance, Stanford University, March 20, 2017, https://resources.solarbusinesshub.com/solar-industry-reports/item/the-new-solar-system-china-s-evolving-solar-industry.

18. American Energy Innovation Council, "The Power of Innovation," April 2017, http://americanenergyinnovation.org/wp-content/uploads/2017/04/AEIC-The-Power-Of-Innovation.pdf.

19. William Bonvillian, "The New Model Innovation Agencies: An Overview," *Science and Public Policy* 41, no. 4 (2013): 425–437, doi:10.1093/scipol/sct059.

20. Advanced Research Projects Agency—Energy (ARPA-E), "FOCUS Program Overview," https://arpa-e.energy.gov/?q=arpa-e-programs/focus.

21. A. P. Goldstein and V. Narayanamurti, "Simultaneous Pursuit of Discovery and Invention in the US Department of Energy," Working Draft, 2017, http://annagoldste.in/wp-content/uploads/2015/05/Basic-and-applied-research-at-ARPA-E-20170408.pdf.

22. National Academies of Sciences, Engineering, and Medicine, *An Assessment of ARPA-E*, (Washington, DC: The National Academies Press, 2017), doi: 10.17226/24778.

23. The White House, Office of the Press Secretary, "Fact Sheet: President's Budget Proposal to Advance Mission Innovation," Obama White House, news release, February 6, 2016.

24. Laura Diaz Anadon et al., "Transforming U.S. Energy Innovation," Report for Energy Technology Innovation Policy research group, Belfer Center for Science and International Affairs, Harvard Kennedy School, November 2011, http://www

.belfercenter.org/sites/default/files/legacy/files/uploads/energy-report-january-2012.pdf.

25. Laura Diaz Anadon, "Missions-Oriented RD&D Institutions in Energy: A Comparative Analysis of China, the United Kingdom, and the United States," *Research Policy* 41, vol. 10 (2012): 1742–1756, doi: 10.1016/j.respol.2012.02.015.

26. Ali Zaidi and Lynn Orr, "Advancing the Frontiers of Clean Energy Innovation," National Archives and Records Administration, https://obamawhitehouse.archives.gov/blog/2016/10/12/advancing-frontiers-clean-energy-innovation.

27. The White House, Office of the Press Secretary, "Fact Sheet: New Progress in a Resurgent American Manufacturing Sector," Obama White House, news release, October 6, 2016.

28. American Energy Innovation Council, "The Power of Innovation," April 2017, http://americanenergyinnovation.org/wp-content/uploads/2017/04/AEIC-The-Power-Of-Innovation.pdf.

29. Varun Sivaram, Teryn Norris, Colin McCormick, and David M. Hart, "Energy Innovation Policy: Priorities for the Trump Administration and Congress," Information Technology & Innovation Foundation, December 2016, http://www2.itif.org/2016-energy-innovation-policy.pdf.

30. David C. Mowery, "Federal Policy and the Development of Semiconductors, Computer Hardware, and Computer Software: A Policy Model for Climate-Change R&D?" in Rebecca M. Henderson and Richard G. Newell (eds.), *Accelerating Energy Innovation: Insights from Multiple Sectors* (Chicago: University of Chicago Press, 2011): 159–188.

31. John Alic, Daniel Sarewitz, Charles Weiss, and William Bonvillian, "A New Strategy for Energy Innovation," *Nature* 466, vol. 15 (2010): 316–317, http://cspo.org/legacy/library/100715F9KS_lib_SarewitzetalNatu.pdf.

32. H. R. Rep. and S. Rep. No. 115-JCX-3–17, Estimates of Federal Tax Expenditures for Fiscal Years 2016–2020, (2017), https://www.jct.gov/publications.html?func=startdown&id=4971.

33. David G. Victor and Kassia Yanosek, "The Crisis in Clean Energy Stark Realities of the Renewables Craze," *Foreign Affairs* (July/August 2011): 112–120, https://www.foreignaffairs.com/articles/2011-06-16/crisis-clean-energy.

34. Alex Trembath, Ted Nordhaus, Michael Shellenberger, and Jesse Jenkins, "Beyond Boom and Bust: Putting Clean Tech on a Path to Subsidy Independence," *The Breakthrough*, April 17, 2012, http://thebreakthrough.org/archive/beyond_boom_and_bust_report_ov.

35. Nichola Groom, "Prospect of Trump Tariff Casts Pall over U.S. Solar Industry," *Reuters*, July 25, 2017, http://www.reuters.com/article/us-usa-trade-solar-insight-idUSKBN1AA0BI.

36. Enrico Moretti, "Local Multipliers," *The American Economic Review* 100, no. 2 (May 2010): 272–337, http://www.aeaweb.org/articles.php?doi=10.1257/aer.100.2.1

37. Gilbert Metcalf, "The Impact of Removing Tax Preferences for U.S. Oil and Gas Production," Discussion paper, Council on Foreign Relations, August 2016, http://www.cfr.org/energy-policy/impact-removing-tax-preferences-us-oil-gas-production/p38150.

38. Rob Nikolewski, "PG&E Files Plan to Shut Down Diablo Canyon Nuclear Power Plant," *Los Angeles Times*, August 11, 2016, http://www.latimes.com/business/la-fi-nuclear-power-pacific-gas-20160811-snap-story.html.

39. Daniel Shea and Kristy Hartman, "State Options to Keep Nuclear in the Energy Mix," Report, National Conference of State Legislatures, January 2017, http://www.ncsl.org/Portals/1/Documents/energy/StateOptions_NuclearPower_f05_WEB.pdf.

40. Felix Mormann, Dan Reicher, and Victor Hanna, "A Tale of Three Markets: Comparing the Renewable Energy Experiences of California, Texas, and Germany," *Stanford Environmental Law Journal* 45, vol. 1 (2016), 55–99.

41. Dan Reicher, "Setting the Climate Agenda for the Next President Toward a More Effective Federal Clean Energy Toolkit," Discussion paper, In *New U.S. Leadership, Next Steps on Climate Change,* Steyer-Taylor Center for Energy Policy and Finance, Stanford University, Stanford University Press, 2016, 166-182, http://docplayer.net/49114393-New-u-s-leadership-next-steps-on-climate-change.html.

42. Felix Mormann and Dan Reicher, "Smarter Finance for Cleaner Energy: Open Up Master Limited Partnerships (MLPs) and Real Estate Investment Trusts (REITs) to Renewable Energy Investment," Renewing the Economy series, The Brookings Institution, November 13, 2012, https://www.brookings.edu/research/invest-but-reform-smarter-finance-for-cleaner-energy-open-up-master-limited-partnerships-mlps-and-real-estate-investment-trusts-to-renewable-energy-investment-reits.

43. Joseph Aldy and Robert Stavins, "The Promise and Problems of Pricing Carbon: Theories and Experience," *Journal of Environment and Development*, Special Issue, October 27, 2011, https://research.hks.harvard.edu/publications/getFile.aspx?Id=734.

44. James A. Baker, III et al., "The Conservative Case for Carbon Dividends," Climate Leadership Council, February 2017, https://www.clcouncil.org/media/TheConservativeCaseforCarbonDividends.pdf.

45. Matt Hourihan and Robert D. Atkinson, "Inducing Innovation: What a Carbon Price Can and Can't Do," Information Technology and Innovation Foundation, March 2011, http://www.itif.org/files/2011-inducing-innovation.pdf.

46. Daron Acemoglu et al., "The Environment and Directed Technical Change," *American Economic Review* 102 (2012): 131-166, https://www.aeaweb.org/articles?id=10.1257/aer.102.1.131.

47. Varun Sivaram and Sagatom Saha, "The Trouble with Ceding Climate Leadership to China," *Foreign Affairs*, December 20, 2016, https://www.foreignaffairs.com/articles/united-states/2016-12-20/trouble-ceding-climate-leadership-china.

48. Daniel L. Sanchez and Varun Sivaram, "Saving Innovative Climate and Energy Research: Four Recommendations for Mission Innovation," *Energy Research and Social Science* 29 (2017), doi: 10.1016/j.erss.2017.05.022.

49. Colin McCormick and David Sandalow, *Solar Together: A Proposal*, Report, SIPA Center on Global Energy Policy, Columbia University, 2016, http://energypolicy.columbia.edu/sites/default/files/energy/Center%20On%20Global%20Energy%20Policy_Solar%20Together_April%202016.pdf.

50. Jeffrey Ball, Dan Reicher, Xiaojing Sun, and Caitlin Pollock, "The New Solar System: China's Evolving Solar Industry and Its Implications for Competitive Solar Power in the United States and the World," Report, Steyer-Taylor Center for Energy Policy and Finance, Stanford University, March 20, 2017, https://resources.solarbusinesshub.com/solar-industry-reports/item/the-new-solar-system-china-s-evolving-solar-industry.

51. Nathan Associates, Inc, "Beyond Borders: The Global Semiconductor Value Chain," Semiconductor Industry Association, May 2016, https://www.semiconductors.org/clientuploads/Trade%20and%20IP/SIA%20-%20Beyond%20Borders%20Report%20-%20FINAL%20May%206.pdf.

Figure Credits

Chapter 1

1.1 Varun Sivaram, Gireesh Shrimali, and Dan Reicher, "Reach for the Sun: How India's Audacious Solar Ambitions Could Make or Break Its Climate Commitments," Stanford Steyer-Taylor Center for Energy Policy and Finance, December 8, 2015, https://law.stanford.edu/reach-for-the-sun-how-indias-audacious-solar-ambitions-could-make-or-break-its-climate-commitments.

Chapter 2

2.1 National Renewable Energy Laboratory (NREL), "Best Research-Cell Efficiencies," 2017, http://www.nrel.gov/pv/assets/images/efficiency_chart.jpg.

2.6 Eric Wesoff and Stephen Lacey, "Solar Costs Are Hitting Jaw-Dropping Lows in Every Region of the World," *Greentech Media*, June 27, 2017, https://www.greentechmedia.com/articles/read/solar-costs-are-hitting-jaw-dropping-lows-in-every-region-of-the-world.

2.7 Benjamin Attia, Manan Parikh, and Tom Heggarty, "Global Solar Demand Monitor: Q2 2017," *Greentech Media*, July, 2017, https://www.greentechmedia.com/research/report/global-solar-demand-monitor-q2-2017.

2.8 Bloomberg New Energy Finance (BNEF), "New Energy Outlook 2017," June 2017, https://www.bloomberg.com/company/new-energy-outlook.

Chapter 3

3.1 "Energy Technology Perspectives 2017—Catalysing Energy Technology Transformations," International Energy Agency (IEA), June 6, 2017, http://www.iea.org/etp.

3.2 Figure reprinted with permission from Varun Sivaram and Shayle Kann, "Solar Power Needs a More Ambitious Cost Target," Nature Energy 1, no. 4 (April 7,

2016): doi:10.1038/nenergy.2016.36. Data from: Richard Schmalensee et al., "The Future of Solar Energy," working paper, MIT Energy Initiative, 2015, https://energy.mit.edu/wp-content/uploads/2015/05/MITEI-The-Future-of-Solar-Energy.pdf; Lion Hirth, "Market Value of Solar Power: Is Photovoltaics Cost Competitive?" *Institution of Engineering and Technology Renewable Power Generation* 9, no. 1 (2014): 37-45, doi:10.1049/iet-rpg.2014.0101; and Andrew Mill and Ryan Wiser, "Changes in the Economic Value of Variable Generation at High Penetration Levels: A Pilot Case Study of California," Lawrence Berkeley National Lab, 2012, LBNL-5445E, https://emp.lbl.gov/sites/all/files/lbnl-5445e.pdf.

3.3 Panel (a) adapted from J. P. Hansen, P. A. Narbel, and D. L. Aksnes, "Limits to Growth in the Renewable Energy Sector," *Renewable and Sustainable Energy Reviews* 70 (2016): doi:10.1016/j.rser.2016.11.257; Panel (b) generated from data in BP, "BP Statistical Review of World Energy 2017," June 2017, https://www.bp.com/content/dam/bp/en/corporate/pdf/energy-economics/statistical-review-2017/bp-statistical-review-of-world-energy-2017-full-report.pdf.

3.5 Figure reprinted with permission from Varun Sivaram and Shayle Kann, "Solar Power Needs a More Ambitious Cost Target," *Nature Energy* 1, no. 4 (April 7, 2016): doi:10.1038/nenergy.2016.36. Data from GTM Research, "PV Cost Database 2016," 2016, https://www.greentechmedia.com/research/publications/category/solar.

Chapter 4

4.2 Varun Sivaram, "Solar's Paradoxical 2015 in Three Charts," *Energy, Security, and Climate Blog*, Council on Foreign Relations, January 14, 2016, https://www.cfr.org/blog/solar-powers-paradoxical-2015-three-charts.

4.4 Ethan Zindler and Ken Locklin, "Mapping the Gap: The Road from Paris," Bloomberg New Energy Finance, January 27, 2016, https://www.ceres.org/resources/reports/mapping-the-gap-the-road-from-paris.

Chapter 5

5.3 Bloomberg New Energy Finance (BNEF), Lighting Global, and Global Off-Grid Lighting Association, "Off-Grid Market Trends Report 2016," February 2016, http://www.energynet.co.uk/webfm_send/1690.

5.4 Figure reprinted from International Energy Agency (IEA), World Energy Outlook 2014, November 12, 2014, http://www.worldenergyoutlook.org/weo2014. Figure originally published in Mentis et al., "A GIS-Based Approach for Electrification Planning—A Case Study on Nigeria," *Energy for Sustainable Development*, no. 29 (2015): 142–150. doi:10.1016/j.esd.2015.09.007.

Chapter 6

6.2 Varun Sivaram, Samuel Stranks, and Henry J. Snaith, "Perovskite Solar Cells Could Beat the Efficiency of Silicon," *Scientific American*, July 2015, https://www.scientificamerican.com/article/perovskite-solar-cells-could-beat-the-efficiency-of-silicon.

6.3 Steve Albrecht and Bernd Rech, "Perovskite Solar Cells: On Top of Commercial Photovoltaics," *Nature Energy*, no. 2 (2017), https://www.nature.com/articles/nenergy2016196.

6.4 U.S. Department of Energy (DOE) Office of Energy Efficiency & Renewable Energy, "The SunShot Initiative's 2030 Goal: 3₵ per Kilowatt Hour for Solar Electricity," December 2016, https://energy.gov/sites/prod/files/2016/12/f34/SunShot%202030%20Fact%20Sheet-12_16.pdf.

Chapter 7

7.2 "Solar Fuels and Artificial Photosynthesis: Science and Innovation to Change Our Future Energy Options," Royal Society of Chemistry, June 2012, http://www.rsc.org/globalassets/04-campaigning-outreach/policy/research-policy/global-challenges/solar-fuels-2012.pdf.

7.4 "On the Path to Sunshot," U.S. Department of Energy, 2016, http://www.nrel.gov/docs/fy16osti/65688.pdf.

Chapter 8

8.1 Clark Gellings, "Let's Build a Global Power Grid," *IEEE Spectrum: Technology, Engineering, and Science News*, July 28, 2015, http://spectrum.ieee.org/energy/the-smarter-grid/lets-build-a-global-power-grid.

Chapter 9

9.2 Energy Information Administration (EIA), "Electricity Storage Technologies Can Be Used for Energy Management and Power Quality," December 14, 2011, https://www.eia.gov/todayinenergy/detail.php?id=4310.

9.3 Jesse D. Jenkins and Samuel Thernstrom, "Deep Decarbonization of The Electric Power Sector: Insights From Recent Literature," Energy Innovation Reform Project (EIRP), March 2017, http://innovationreform.org/wp-content/uploads/2017/03/EIRP-Deep-Decarb-Lit-Review-Jenkins-Thernstrom-March-2017.pdf.

9.4 Jesse Jenkins, Nestor Sepulveda, Patrick Brown, Shayle Kann, and Varun Sivaram, "Effect of Solar and Storage Costs on Economically Optimal Solar PV Penetration," Working Paper, 2018.

Chapter 10

10.1 Mission Innovation, "Baseline and Doubling Plans," http://mission-innovation.net/our-work/baseline-and-doubling-plans.

10.2 Richard Schmalensee et al., "The Future of Solar Energy," MIT Energy Initiative, 2015, https://energy.mit.edu/wp-content/uploads/2015/05/MITEI-The-Future-of-Solar-Energy.pdf.

10.3 Benjamin Gaddy, Varun Sivaram, Timothy Jones, and Libby Wayman, "Venture Capital and Cleantech: The Wrong Model for Energy Innovation," *Energy Policy* 102 (2017): 385–395, doi:10.1016/j.enpol.2016.12.035.

Index

Boxes, figures, and glossary entries are designated by *b, f,* and *g,* respectively.